AN EXCELLENT BOOKE OF THE ARTE OF MAGICKE

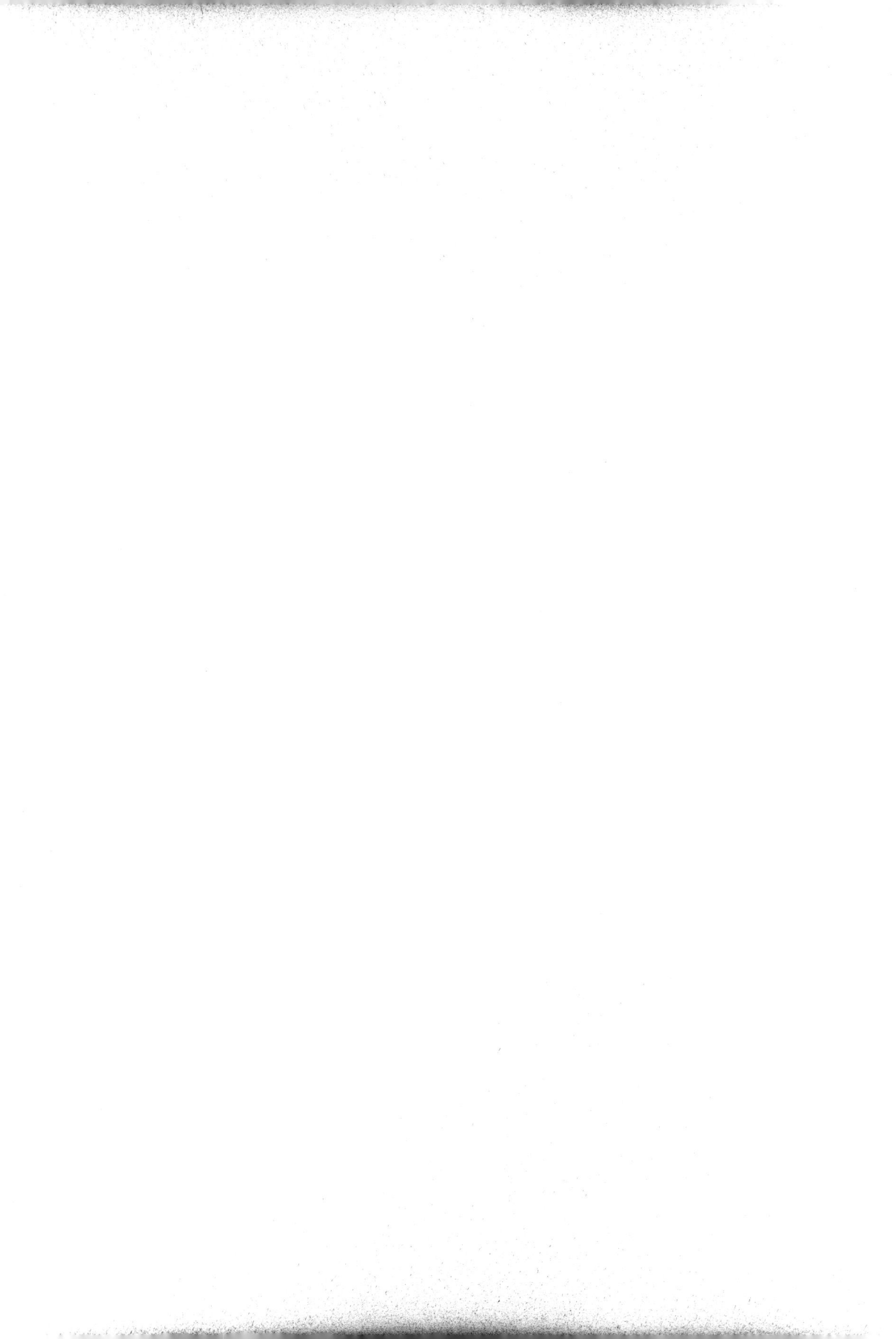

AN EXCELLENT BOOKE
OF THE ARTE OF MAGICKE

THE MAGICAL WORKS OF HUMPHREY GILBERT & JOHN DAVIS
FROM BRITISH LIBRARY ADDITIONAL MANUSCRIPT 36674.
TRANSCRIBED, EDITED AND INTRODUCED BY PHIL LEGARD
WITH SUPPLEMENTARY ESSAYS BY ALEXANDER CUMMINS

SCARLET IMPRINT · MMXX

AN EXCELLENT BOOKE OF THE ARTE OF MAGICKE
WAS PUBLISHED IN A STRICTLY LIMITED HARDBACK
EDITION, COMPRISING 72 COPIES HAND-BOUND IN
BLACK GOATSKIN, & 1200 COPIES IN BLACK CLOTH;
& AN UNLIMITED BIBLIOTHÈQUE ROUGE EDITION.

589

An Excellent Booke of the Arte of Magicke
© Phil Legard & Alexander Cummins

Published by Scarlet Imprint, 2020.
Edited by Peter Grey; copy edits by
Paul Holman; designed and typeset
by Alkistis Dimech; set in Rialto dF.

ROUGE   ISBN 978-1-912316-29-8

The standard and paperback editions were printed and bound in the UK
by Antony Rowe, & the fine edition was bound by Ludlow Bookbinders.

BM BOX 77777, London WC1N 3XX
WWW.SCARLETIMPRINT.COM

Dedicated to Chris Tinsley
and James Banner

— P.L.

Contents

2   CONTEXTS

Acknowledgments

Posthumous regards are due to James Banner of Trident Books for helping to initiate this project, despite the path to its fruition being beset by snares. Our profound thanks therefore to Peter and Alkistis of Scarlet Imprint for helping to loosen aforesaid snares so that Gilbert's brended dogs and avian angels might haunt the wider magical community. In the necromantic spirit of this work, we must also express our gratitude to Humphrey Gilbert and John Davis for having the dedication to pursue and, furthermore, record the experiments preserved herein. Similarly, we respectfully acknowledge those, such as John Somers, Gabriel Harvey, and Henry White, whose esoteric and antiquarian interests ensured that the manuscript survived into the present. Of those with similar interests among the living, we particularly thank Daniel Harms, especially for introducing us to the Guthrie MS. and a number of variants of the Assasel ritual which he had encountered in manuscript, as well as for contributing a foreword to the whole work. We also must express our deep gratitude to Frank Klaassen for his scholarly work on Gilbert and to the British Library for providing facsimile reproductions of Add. MS. 36674.

Phil would also like to thank Egil Asprem for his recent work on esotericism, magic and the cognitive science of religion which suggests intriguing ways for both scholars and practitioners to think through the fundamentals of ritual practice. Thanks are also extended to Adam V. Doskey and Cait Coker, curators of rare books and manuscripts with the University of Illinois at Urbana-Champaign, and to Simon Johnson at the National Records of Scotland, and finally to Layla for providing the space for me to finish this work at the eleventh hour. Al would additionally like to foreground our thanks to all those magicians, living and dead, who have offered their perspectives and support to this project. Thank you all.

P.L. & A.C.

Illustrations

Foreword

Is this the best book that ever was? According to Humphrey Gilbert and John Davis, the best book that ever was will be brought by the spirit Oriens. Even if your bookseller or mail carrier lacks Oriens' hundred horse heads, however, this is a very fine book, a feast for those fascinated in humanity's history of exploration of the spiritual world. Curating this journey are two esteemed scholars and artists: Phil Legard and Al Cummins.

I met Phil online as an undergraduate, when we both trawled the Usenet forums alt.horror.cthulhu and alt.magick in a brave new world of text files and spirited discussion through green-glowing terminals. Somehow over the years, we both slipped into academia, where Phil has continued to meld together his love for imaginative literature, the psychogeography of the British countryside, and his impressive musical talent through many musical projects, Hawthonn — his recent duo with Layla Legard — being dedicated to tonal explorations of folklore and landscape. I keep hoping that someday his work will turn up in a movie soundtrack — although I've never told him that.

Al and I met at the Day of Conjure and Cunning Craft at Catland, a fine space for magical seekers in Brooklyn. We often turn up at the same venues in different roles, but it is always a notable and joyous occasion. Armed with a doctorate in early modern British history, Al has merged his scholarly sensibilities with an engagement with the myriad living magical traditions of New York City.

Both Al and Phil are explorers — not in the sense of Gilbert and Davis, who made dangerous ocean voyages that led to glorious and short lives, but as delvers into secret and forbidden lore. This makes them ideal guides to the work at hand.

As for that work, Gilbert and Davis' workbook is special, as it is very rare to find a journal of magicians' workings before the twentieth century. John Dee's writings are a notable exception, but he likely counted on his ties to nobility to keep him safe. Most magicians and cunning folk merely recorded charms and incantations they found of interest into their notebooks, occasionally inserting their initials or a place name into a spell so it would be ready for use. A diary would be evidence that these individuals did indeed practice magic — and practice, unlike possessing literature, often bore with it social disapproval and strict penalties in law. Although such penalties varied considerably in their scope and enforcement, most cunning folk would have found it a chance not worth taking.

Thus the Gilbert and Davis workings portray how magic ended up being practised on the ground, as users extrapolated from the written literature through their experience. For example, Gilbert and Davis seem to have excised the numerous allusions to Catholic doctrine, figures, and rituals found in other manuscripts to create a style of conjuration more appropriate to Protestants. In contrast with twenty-first century magicians, who often seek pacts of respect and mutuality with spirits, our explorers were not afraid to threaten, or even to gaslight, the demons that they summoned. (Today's practitioners will no doubt point to Gilbert and Davis' violent deaths as proof that their methods did not work out well in the long term.) With this text now placed before many different eyes, we will soon be speaking of more insights along these lines.

As with other occult volumes, some coincidence or synchronicity follows this one. A later owner bound this magical manual into a collection now known as Additional manuscript 36674. The work is usually only viewable in the manuscripts room at the British Library, to those who have made the journey and bear a reader's ticket. A few months after being asked to write this introduction, I came upon the manuscript unexpectedly in the Harry

Potter exhibit at the New-York Historical Society, far away from its home. I was both thrilled to see it across the ocean and perturbed I couldn't remove it from the glass case to explore it further. I settled for messaging Al to let him know it was in town, as if arriving in the New World to bless the project.

When I received the manuscript to this book, I was surprised to see the importance in the operations of Azazel, the spirit to whom a goat was promised as atonement in Leviticus 16:8 – 10. I had recently completed a study dedicated to collecting the rituals dedicated to Azazel as He Who Keepest the Bones of Dead Men. Lest someone hail us as discoverers of a secret tradition, I should note that Frank Klaassen devotes a footnote to the spirit's magical rites, and David Rankine was the first to publish such an operation in his *Grimoire of Arthur Gauntlet*. Given the fascination many have felt for Azazel across the centuries, I think many readers will find this information particularly welcome.

Read, enjoy, think, and watch out for headless birds!

> Dan Harms,
> Upstate New York.

Preface

I first became acquainted with the *Excellent Booke of the Arte of Magicke* a decade ago. I was collaborating with Daniel Harms on a – still as yet unpublished – paper concerning the magical manuscripts produced by Frederick Hockley for the bookseller John Denley in the 1830s. It was whilst attempting to get a sense for the types of manuscript known to Hockley, Denley, and satellite figures such as the astrologer Raphael, that I happened upon the fascinating collection contained within Additional MS. 36674. Composed by multiple hands, and drawing material in varying states of preservation from a period between 1500 and 1660, no article therein fascinated me more than the *Excellent Booke*.

I was immediately intrigued by its attribution to notorious London astrologer Simon Forman. I was aware that Forman was said to have written two books of necromancy and had even recorded in his diary some of the results of his experiments, such as a dramatic encounter initiated by his scryer John Goodridge – 'the gelded man' – in which Goodridge saw the spirit as a black dog, breathing out fire and brimstone. Forman admitted that he did not witness the spirit himself, but did see 'the fire then saw a kind of shape, but not perfectly.' With tales like this in mind, I found myself fascinated by the methodical outline of necromancy contained within the *Excellent Booke*, from the recommendations that a 'young beginner' conjure the spirit Bleth, to the workings of the spirits Aosal, Assasel and the four demonic kings. Unfortunately, my facsimile of the manuscript, which was scanned from microfilm by Waning Moon Publications' John Coughlin, was of too poor a quality to completely transcribe the work. Since consulting the original was impractical at the time, having young twins, my transcription of the *Excellent Booke* languished, although it often occupied my thoughts.

A few years later I was working with James Banner of Trident Books, contributing an introduction to his edition of the *Libellus Veneri Nigro Sacer*: a grimoire of the Germanic Faustian tradition attributed to John Dee. James was keen to explore further projects, including an edition of the *Theosophia Pneumatica* and – most ambitiously – a comprehensive translation of the pseudo-Baconian *Thesaurus Spirituum*, alias *De Nigromancia*: a lengthy and complex treatise on conjuration likely dating from the mid 15th century. It was while examining various exemplars of the *Thesaurus Spirituum* that I had an opportunity to reconnect with the *Excellent Booke*, since the same codex also carries a mutilated copy of the Baconian text. Working from new facsimiles of the manuscript made it easy to transcribe the *Excellent Booke* in detail, and it quickly became apparent that both the *Excellent Booke* and the article that follows it, simply entitled *Visions*, were connected. An interesting story of 'nigromancy' in Elizabethan society began to unfold – one, not of Simon Forman and his gelded scryer, but of one Humphrey Gilbert's demonic sojourn in Devon almost two decades before either John Dee or Simon Forman commenced their own experiments with crystal-gazing assistants.

I began to consider these two articles – the *Excellent Booke* and *Visions* – as unique documents of 16th century magical practice: ones that deserve to be widely read and studied by scholars and practitioners alike since they preserve a detailed account of both the making and the use of a grimoire. This is something of a rarity in historical ritual magic: amongst the few notable examples being the autobiographical *Liber Visionum*, along with its practical companion the *Liber Figurarum*, composed by the 14th century monk John of Morigny, as well as the diaries, magical texts and artefacts produced by John Dee and Edward Kelly. Practitioners may also be drawn to the relative simplicity of the rites contained with the *Excellent Booke*. As fervent Protestants, Gilbert, and his scryer John Davis, had reduced the complex paraphernalia and rituals of necromancy to their essentials: the crystal stone, the scryer, the conjurations and the forceful imposition of the master's will over the demons he sought to constrain.

Unfortunately the project to publish the *Excellent Booke* and *Visions* foundered: James considered the text too short and too obscure to publish, and our own relationship deteriorated as my professional and family commitments took precedence over our projects together.

In 2011 I was introduced to Alexander Cummins through a mutual friend, the experimental musician Seth Cooke. Al was at that point working on his PhD on magic, emotion, and humoral medicine at Bristol under the supervision of Ronald Hutton, and had also become deeply interested in the necromantic practices of the 16th century. Eventually I shared my transcription of the *Excellent Booke* with him and was pleased to discover that he was as enthusiastic about the text as I was. Over the intervening years, with occasional hiatuses to pursue our own projects, we have managed to bring together this volume, which consists of annotated transcriptions of Gilbert's *Excellent Booke* and *Visions*, alongside an introduction and a series of supplementary essays written by Al, exploring the contexts around scrying, necromancy and the type of historical ritual magic preserved by the *Excellent Booke*. I have also complemented Al's contextual work with an edition of a conference paper of my own: read at the *History, Magic and Spirits* panel of *Exploring the Extraordinary* VII in 2015, it examines the ritual structure and language of Gilbert's experiments in relation to the developing 'cognitive turn' in academic esoteric studies.

Reflecting on this project, it is sobering to observe how much has changed in almost a decade since I began to pore over Add. 36674. In the summer of 2019, as I write this, there is something necromantic in the air — it seems that the shades of dead magicians still trouble us. We are, as a country, haunted by a malign spectre of the British Empire: a term which John Dee has been alleged to have coined. Consequently the intractable question of Ireland, a situation in which Gilbert played his own part in making, has once again returned to the fore of political discussion. As with the Venetian nobility discussed in Peter Mark Adams' *The Game of Saturn*, Gilbert is a monstrous figure, although one whose privileged position has been able to provide us with a great insight into the historical practice of evocatory magic.

Both Al and I would like to extend our thanks to Alkistis Dimech and Peter Grey of Scarlet Imprint for their sustained interest in bringing this project to fruition, along with their fine attention to detail and sympathetic, talismanic approach to book arts.

Phil Legard,
Leeds.

Visionary Magicke

HUMPHREY GILBERT & THE POIESIS OF A GRIMOIRE

The texts presented here relate to the magical experiments which Elizabethan explorer, soldier and courtier Humphrey Gilbert, along with his scryer John Davis, conducted during the spring of 1567. We will look more closely at the personalities involved presently, along with their influences and methods of working, but, for now, a brief overview of the texts themselves will serve by way of an introduction to our protagonists and their exploits.

The first work presented here, *An Excellent Booke of the Arte of Magicke*, details the conjuration of the spirits Assasel, Aosal, and the four demonic kings Oriens, Amaimon, Paimon and Aegyn. Here, the spirits are called into a 'crystal stone' by way of a large number of conjurations, charges, constraints, curses and bonds. It is evidently based on an older text or texts, which have been adapted to the Protestant outlook of the period, and has also been supplemented with revelations and guidance received first-hand by Gilbert and Davis over the course of its composition.

The second text, *Visions*, is a partial record of visions in the crystal, detailing events which took place before, during, and after the composition of the *Excellent Booke*. In the course of this work, the master – Humphrey Gilbert – and scryer – John Davis – converse with a wide range of spirits as well as religious and occult personalities: Assasel, Job, Solomon, Roger Bacon,

Cornelius Agrippa, four angelic evangelists, and so on. It also seems that on occasion the visions bled into the waking world, in the form of encounters with demonic dogs and even the physical manifestation of the prophet Job.

Both these works are bound in a manuscript codex held by the British Library. Indeed, it is a collection with a rich provenance, as we shall discover. The *Excellent Booke* and *Visions* are also notable since, as Frank Klaassen has pointed out, they record a series of magical experiments that represent a continuity of the spirit of what might be loosely called medieval ritual magic into the early modern period.[1]

Furthermore, the texts give us an insight into a rare example of the *poiesis*, or coming-together, of a ritual magic text. Evidence of the relationship between established ritual magic and visionary practices is also valuable: while John Dee and Edward Kelly's actions with the angels yielded what might be termed 'grimoires' such as *De Heptarchia Mystica*, these are rather idiosyncratic works with less explicit connection to the old, 'dirty' world of demonic ritual magic than that which is evidenced within these pages.

PROVENANCE & AUTHORSHIP

British Library Additional MS. 36674 collates a large number of 16th and 17th century texts of magic and witchcraft. The materials were likely gathered into their current form as part of the library of John Somers, Baron Somers (1651–1716) in the early 18th century. The volume also bears the bookplate of the merchant and antiquary Henry White (1822–1900). Following his death, White's library was auctioned by Sotheby's in 1902, through which means the book was acquired by the British Library. The complete Sotheby's catalogue entry is reproduced below:

1408 MAGICAL TREATISES. (I) The Book of King Solomon called the Key of Knowledge; (II) An Old Book found amongst the Secret Writings of Dr. Caius; (III) An Excellent Book of the Art of Magick, first begun March 22,

---

1 For an insight into the intellectual, political and religious contexts of Humphrey Gilbert's scrying experiments, see Frank Klaassen, 'Ritual Invocation and Early Modern Science: The Skrying Experiments of Humphrey Gilbert' in *Invoking Angels: Theurgic Ideas and Practices, Thirteenth to Sixteenth Centuries*, ed. Claire Fanger, (Pennsylvania State University Press: University Park, 2012): 341–366.

1567; (IV) Certaine Strange Visions on Apparitions of Memorable Note, anno 1567; A Notable Journal of an Experimental Magician; (V) Regulae utilissimae in Artem Magicam tum multis aliie de Arte Magica; (VI) A Catalogue of Mr. Bovey's Magical Books; (VII) The Vision of Humphrey Smith which he saw concerning London in the 5th Month in the year 1660; (VIII) Of Elizabeth Jennings 13 years of Age being bewitched; (IX) Compendium Heptarchiæ Mysticæ; (X) The Examination of Several Persons accused of Witchcraft, MANUSCRIPTS ON PAPER (3 ll. on vellum) (238 ll. some blank, 12 by 8 in.) chiefly in English, temp. Q. Eliz.; with some singular cabalistic diagrams and hieroglyphics (some ll. defective and mended), in 1 vol. modern boarded red morocco folio. CENT. XVI–XVII

* A VERY INTERESTING AND SINGULAR COLLECTION OF TREATISES ON MAGIC AND WITCHCRAFT, by Dr. Caius, Dr. Dee, Simon Forman, Kelly (Dee's disciple), &c. all contemporary MSS. that of Simon Forman being certified by Dr. Macray of the Bodleian. On the first page of the Caius MS. is the following contemporary inscription: 'This torne Booke was found amongst the Paperbookes and Secret Writings of Dr. Caius Master and Founder of Caius College. Dr. Legg gave it to Mr. Fletcher fellowe of the same Colledg and a learned artist for his Time' Some of the later Treatises are in Elias Ashmole's handwriting. The volume formerly belonged to Lord Somers, afterwards to Thomas Brittain the 'Small-coal Man' who sold it to Bateman for £10 5s., it was afterwards sold to Joseph Ames, whose note is on the fly-leaf.[2]

Prior to the ownership by Lord Somers, portions of the manuscript – including the Excellent Booke and Visions – were owned by Gabriel Harvey

2 Anon, Catalogue of the Valuable and Extensive Library of Printed Books and Illuminated & Other Important Manuscripts of the Late Henry White, Esq. J.P. D.L. F.S.A. Etc. (Of 30, Queen's Gate, W.) (Sotheby, Wilkinson & Hodge: London, 1902). Note that in the original description there are two errors – transposing certain items and duplicating one. This has been corrected for ease of understanding and to bring it in line with the British Library catalogue entry. The first article has been transcribed by Joseph Peterson and can be found on his Esoteric Archives website. The second article comprises extracts from The Fourth Book of Occult Philosophy attributed to Cornelius Agrippa, the Heptameron attributed to Peter d'Abano and the Thesaurus Spirituum attributed to Roger Bacon.

(1545–1630). Harvey was a notable Elizabethan scholar, poet, and one of the self-described 'Areopagites' alongside Philip Sidney and Edmund Spenser. Harvey's distinctive marginalia and underlining appear in the first four articles in the codex. These were, in common with readers of his day, made upon a first reading of the text, pen in hand, picking out items of interest and recording the experience of reading as it occurred.[3]

Prior to Harvey's ownership, the portion of the manuscript under discussion (comprising articles I–IV) was in the library of Sir Thomas Smith (1513–1577), secretary of state. Sir Thomas was Harvey's benefactor, contributing to his education at Christ's College and Pembroke Hall.[4] Despite his office, Sir Thomas himself professed to having such an obsession with astrology that he could 'scarcely sleep at night from thinking of it.'[5]

It seems likely that Harvey inherited the manuscript articles in question around the time of Sir Thomas' funeral in 1577. In her article on Harvey's *Bibliotheca*, Virginia Stern describes an incident in which Dr. Andrew Perne, Master of Peterhouse College and several times Vice-Chancellor of Cambridge, came to Sir Thomas' funeral to preach and hoped to acquire some 'rare manuscript bookes.' Dr. Perne was not pleased when the manuscripts were bequeathed to Harvey, although — as Stern points out — Harvey was the logical choice being both a friend to Sir Thomas, to his son Thomas, and to his nephew John Wood.[6]

Perhaps Harvey's interest in occult sciences was also known to Sir Thomas' executors: in 1593, at the height of his quarrel with Thomas Nashe, Harvey would praise Cornelius Agrippa in print as one of 'the universallest scholars' and the 'Omniscious Doctor.' In response, Nashe lampooned Harvey as 'our Graphiel Hagiel' and 'our Taphthartharath.'[7] Yet Harvey's respect for

---

3 Nicholas Popper, 'The English Polydaedali: How Gabriel Harvey Read Late Tudor London', *Journal of the History of Ideas* 66, No. 3 (2005): 352.

4 G. C. Moore Smith, *Gabriel Harvey's Marginalia* (Shakespeare Head Press: Stratford-Upon-Avon, 1913): 9–10.

5 Keith Thomas, *Religion and the Decline of Magic* (Weidenfeld & Nicolson: London, 1971): 290.

6 Virginia F. Stern, 'The *Bibliotheca* of Gabriel Harvey,' *Renaissance Quarterly* 25, No. 1 (Spring 1972): 15–16.

7 Gabriel Harvey, *Pierce's Supererogation, or A New Praise of the Old Ass, from the edition of*

Agrippa was apparently long-established: he evidently held his *De incertitude et vanite scientiarum et artium* in high regard around the time that he acquired Sir Thomas' manuscript. In a letter to Spenser, published in 1580, in which he commends virtue, fame, wealth and a good tongue he writes:

> *A thousand good leaves be forever granted Agrippa*
> *For squibbing and declaiming against many fruitless*
> *Arts and crafts devised by the devils and sprites for a torment*
> *And for a plague to the world, as both Pandora, Prometheus*
> *And that cursed good bad tree can testify at all times,*
> *Mere gewgaws and baubles in comparison of these,*
> *Toys to mock apes, and woodcocks in comparison of these.*[8]

It is from the period of Harvey's ownership of the manuscript that a number of confusions and misattributions arise regarding the texts presented in this volume. When read sequentially, it is apparent that two articles with which we are here concerned – the *Excellent Booke of the Arte of Magicke* and *Certain Strange Visions* – are complementary. Both texts share a common hand and were written during the same period: the spring of 1567. The *Excellent Booke* is prefaced by a magical prayer apparently revealed by King Solomon on the 20th of February 1567, while Solomon appears as one of the servants of the magus named 'H.G.' in the *Visions* that follow it. It is also apparent from critical reading that certain materials gleaned from the *Visions* were incorporated into the *Excellent Booke*, as though they were composed in tandem. Harvey's note on the first page of *Visions* is therefore misleading, given that he writes:

> The visions of Sir. Th. S. [Thomas Smith] himself: as is credibly supposed. Though Mr. Jon Wood imagines one G.H. [Gabriel Harvey] *Tempus demonstrativum revelabit.*[9]

It appears that the spirit of this annotation, with its self-referentiality, is

1593 (T. Davidson: London, 1815), 46; Matthew Steggle, 'The Names of Gabriel Harvey: Cabbalistic, Russian, and Fencing Sources,' *Notes and Queries* 52 (2) (2005): 185–6.

8 Gabriel Harvey, *Three Proper and Witty Familiar Letters* (H. Bynneman: London, 1580): 34.

9 Add. MS. 36674, f.59r.

somewhat playful. Knowing of Sir Thomas' astrological preoccupations, and likely his experiments with alchemy during the 1570s, did Harvey really believe the visions to be those of his benefactor?[10] Based on his praise of Agrippa's *De vanite*, we may also ask ourselves about Harvey's opinion of the demonic magic found in *Visions* and the *Excellent Booke* and whether a number of his annotations may be interpreted as having a somewhat satirical air about them.

Whatever Harvey's marginalia may have suggested, it is highly likely that, due to internal evidence, the H.G. mentioned in *Visions*, and author of the *Excellent Booke*, was in fact the Elizabethan adventurer, Sir Humphrey Gilbert (1539 – 1583).[11] We know that Gilbert had an involvement with Thomas regarding a planned English colony in Ulster in the late 1560s and their relationship endured for many years afterwards. How the manuscript came to be in Thomas' possession is unclear, however. One may speculate that the manuscripts of the *Excellent Booke* and *Visions* were perhaps regarded as particularly sensitive and given by Gilbert to the safekeeping of Thomas. An assumption of shared interests and confidentiality also seems probable when we note that Gilbert and Thomas were not solely collaborators with the Tudor conquest of Ireland, but would later participate in more esoteric pursuits, such as experiments in alchemy, during the early 1570s.[12]

There is a second episode of misattribution that has contributed to the *Excellent Booke* and *Visions* often being considered two separate, rather than complementary, works. This is due to the first folio of the *Excellent Booke* including the following note: 'Forman – certified by Mr. Macray of the Bodleian, July 1868.'[13]

The suggestion here is that the *Excellent Booke* was the work of the famous

---

10 John Strype, *The Life of the Learned Sir Thomas Smith, Kt. D.C.L.* (Clarendon Press: Oxford, 1820): 105.

11 For H.G. as Humphrey Gilbert see David B. Quinn, *Explorers and Colonies: America, 1500 – 1625* (The Hambledon Press: London, 1990): 205 – 6; Benjamin Wooley, *The Queen's Conjuror* (Flamingo: London, 2002); Klaassen, 'Ritual Invocation.'

12 Strype, *Life*: 100 – 101.

13 Add. 36674, f.47r. Lauren Kassell also agrees that this is a misattribution: see *Medicine and Magic in Elizabethan London: Simon Forman: Astrologer, Alchemist, and Physician* (Oxford University Press: Oxford, 2007): 241.

Elizabethan astrologer and conjuror Simon Forman – even though Forman himself would only have been 17 at the time of composition. Although the handwriting is similar to Forman's it could just as easily be that of Thomas Charnock or any other contemporary student of the occult arts. Forman did, however, write at least two books of 'nigromancie,' but in the light of the fact that he did not begin his experiments until 1579, by which time the *Excellent Booke* and *Visions* were in the hands of Gabriel Harvey, this particular attribution may be discounted as spurious.

GILBERT, DAVIS & DEE: MAGI OF THE BRITISH EMPIRE

At the time of the *Visions*, Humphrey Gilbert was twenty-eight years of age and serving as a captain in Ireland under his mentor Sir Henry Sidney, Lord Deputy of Ireland. Like many men of the age, he held various military and governmental positions, alongside which he pursed a diverse range of interests – notably the study of geography, with an eye to discovering a passage between northwest America and Asia. An early 20th century biographer describes him as 'a dreamer, yes and a scholar; but he was [also] a man of action, who on the field of battle could be as brutal, as bloodthirsty, as any personage in history – far more so than most of them.'[14]

Following a victory against the Irish chief Shane O'Neil's army, Gilbert was sent back to England to deliver dispatches to Queen Elizabeth concerning the Tudor operations in Ireland.[15] He returned to England in November 1566, along with a navigational treatise he had written in June of that year (*A Discourse of a Discoverie for a New Passage to Cataia*), which he hoped to present to Elizabeth with a petition for her support in a seafaring venture.[16] The *Discourse* set out Gilbert's intentions to discover and exploit the Northwest Passage, a plan which could have made a fortune for Gilbert and his backers. However, due to political and monetary circumstances at the time, the scheme bore no fruit.[17]

14 Donald Barr Chidsey, *Sir Humphrey Gilbert: Elizabeth's Racketeer* (Harper Collins: London, 1932): 2.
15 Chidsey, *Sir Humphrey*: 38–9.
16 William Gilbert Gosling, *The Life of Sir Humphrey Gilbert, England's First Empire Builder* (Constable & Co.: London, 1911): 68.
17 Wooley, *Queen's Conjuror*: 113–117.

Gilbert was to become a prominent figure in Elizabethan England, although understandably overshadowed by his half-brother Sir Walter Raleigh. However, during the period in question his reputation was not yet established. Aged twenty-eight he was described as:

> [T]all, well built, with a strong but refined face – a somewhat sad face – weak, dark eyes, dark hair, a soft, short beard inclined to be curly and a 'cholericke' complexion.[18]

Gilbert was born and raised in Devon at Greenway Court near Galmpton. His neighbour and close companion, residing a couple of miles away at Sandridge, Stoke Gabriel, was a young man who would first become his scryer, and later the British Empire's master navigator and explorer: John Davis (1550–1605).

From the apparent privacy afforded to Gilbert and Davis to practise their magic, it seems likely that the experiments recorded in *Visions* were conducted at one of their Devon estates. We also know that in February 1567 – possibly around the time the experiments began – Gilbert wrote to the Queen on the topic of the Northwest Passage. To the modern reader this may beg the question: what was Gilbert doing spending his time conjuring spirits instead of trying to find backing for his expedition?

Like John Dee, Gilbert and Davis were men of a putative British Empire who sought to exploit knowledge – scientific and otherwise – for both their personal ends and those of the Crown. Dee was at once a master geographer and magus, and we have a similar instance in this case. As with Dee, the intention of the experiments seems to have been the pursuit of knowledge. Whether this knowledge was mystical, or whether it related to Gilbert's navigational interests, is not clear – although one might also suspect that it was a mixture of the two. If this was the case, it would suggest that Dee's conferences with angels were not the singular aberration that they have often been presented as. Rather, the experiments of 1567 may even be considered progenitors to Dee's own 'actions.'

Indeed, Humphrey, his brother Adrian, and John Davis were associates of

18 Chidsey, *Sir Humphrey*: 40.

Dee. Davis' own association with Dee – the pair most likely being introduced to one another via the Gilberts – can be traced back to at least 1568, scarcely a year after the magical experiments recorded herein. Dee noted in the margin of an ephemeris that he and William Emery had divined – with magical assistance – the exact date of John Davis' birth:

> 1552 Natus Johannes davis die 3 Maij 1552…per magiam eliciebatur W. Em. 1568 Maiij 22. in aedibus meis.[19]

While Dee's relationship with Humphrey Gilbert seemed stable, he clashed with the personalities of Gilbert's brother Adrian and John Davis. He even records that Davis stole somewhere in the region of seventy volumes during their acquaintance![20]

CRISTALL BOOKES & DEADE MEN'S SOULES

In his discussion of Gilbert's magical experiments, Frank Klaassen points out that they can be seen as a continuation of the 'dirty medieval magic' into the early modern period.[21] There can be found numerous parallels between Gilbert's experiments and earlier rituals of necromancy and Ars Notoria (e.g. the revelation of knowledge through prayer or other magical means).

With the presence of necromancy in mind, it is notable that much of the Excellent Booke and Visions appertains to the spirit Assasel, 'keper of the deade bones,' whose name seems ultimately derivative of the Jewish Azazel. As Klaassen has speculated, the Excellent Booke is likely based on earlier texts that have been stripped of their Catholic trappings, as was the spirit of the time,[22] although which particular manuscript, or manuscripts, Gilbert used as his primary source is, as yet, unknown. However, he was certainly not the only magus of the time engaged in operations to invoke Assasel. For example, the name of the spirit appears on the first folio of the fifth article in the same manuscript codex as the Excellent Booke as part of a small list of spirits useful in returning stolen items, procuring love and – presumably – discovering

---

19 Wooley, Queen's Conjuror: 351.
20 Wooley, Queen's Conjuror: 307–8.
21 Klaassen, 'Ritual Invocation.'
22 Klaassen, 'Ritual Invocation': 351.

hidden treasure. Since this article does not contain Harvey's annotations it is likely that it was bound with the *Excellent Booke* and *Visions* some time after they had passed from his ownership, although the work itself is contemporaneous and indicative of the wider employment of the spirit amongst the magical practitioners of the age:

For theft to bring againe
    Raguell *&* Vriel
Pro amore
    Almazim *&* Elicona

Asazel, Rathan, Oberion[23]

A number of exemplars of heavily Catholic rituals involving Assasel have come to light in recent years. Generally the rituals of Assasel seem to take two forms, and examples of both have been included in the additional transcriptions in this volume. Both rituals are ultimately concerned with the discovery and retrieval of hidden treasure, and begin with the magus visiting the grave of a recently deceased person.

The first, shorter, version of the ritual can generally be considered one of dream incubation. Assasel is called upon as the 'lorde of deade mens bodies' and petitioned to allow the spirit of the deceased person to visit the magus, after which earth from the grave is wrapped in linen and placed under the pillow when the magus retires to bed. Most exemplars terminate at this point, although the instance recorded in Illinois Pre-1650 MS. 0102, transcribed in this volume, includes a lengthy second half with the magus' bed being placed in a magical circle, and an invocation exhorting Assasel to bring the spirit of the dead man with allusions to biblical instances of resurrection.

As we have noted, the longer version of the ritual of Assasel also begins by the graveside, but rapidly diverges. In this variant, the dead person is not named, but the locus of their grave site seems to be used in order to bring the magus closer to the spirit. There is perhaps some resonance here with the ritual for calling the fairy Sibyllia, as recorded by Reginald Scot, in which the

---

23 Add. MS. 36674, f.64r.

ghost of a dead man is first conjured and then asked to fetch the fairy queen herself. Later, Assasel is asked to bring the magus a spirit which will serve him or her as a carrier of treasure, and who writes their own name upon a lead plate. We may broadly speak of this as a ritual for a magical servant, rather than one of dream incubation.

One instance of this longer ritual of Assasel can be found in the holdings of the National Archives of Scotland, in a book of conjurations belonging to the Guthrie family, formerly of Angus.[24] It is notable that the incipit of the Guthrie experiment – not found elsewhere – reads:

> Bleathe – should a young beginner begine
> withall he should call Azasellis the
> most noblest art whos[e] character
> followeth.[25]

Which is strikingly similar to the advice given in the first folio of the Excellent Booke:

> Bleathe should a young beginner first call; he ought to call Assasel
> it is the most noble art; whose charact[er] followeth.[26]

It is evident that Bleathe was the name of a spirit – possibly one that was conjured by Gilbert and Davis before the composition of the Excellent Booke began. A character for the spirit Bleathe appears in the Newberry Library's Case MS. 5017 (which also contains a receipt to Azazel (sic) 'for anything you would know'), and a ritual for invoking the spirit into a metal 'urinal' appears in the late 17th century work of Dr. Rudd. Bleathe did evidently play some part in Gilbert's workings, writing as he does toward the end of Visions:

> And the wicked inferior bleath ran continually away, from one place to another rownde about the stone as fast as might be.[27]

24 GD188/25/1/3: 115–120.
25 GD188/25/1/3: 115.
26 Add. MS. 36674, f.47r.
27 Add. MS. 36674, f.62v.

Later in the *Excellent Booke*, the magus is instructed to conjure the four demonic kings ruling over the cardinal directions or winds, namely Oriens, Paymon, Amaimon and Aegyn. The binding of the demonic kings is most well known to contemporary occultists via the *Sacred Magic of Abramelin the Mage*, where it concludes the successful acquisition of the 'knowledge and conversation of the Holy Guardian Angel.' However, conjurations in a similar vein can be found in other contemporary sources, such as the *Key of Knowledge*. This Solomonic tract was also bound with the *Excellent Booke* and *Visions* by the time they came to Harvey's hands, and may have also been known to Gilbert and Davis. It includes the following invocation as part of an experiment in love magic:

> O thou orient king Eggye which reignest and rulest in the East, and thou Paymon, most mighty king which hast dominion over the West, and thou great king Amaymon, which reignest in the South, and thou triumphant king Egyn, which hast rule over the North; I most heartily call upon you, by him which only spake and it was done, which with his word made all things; and by his holy names, whereat all the world doth tremble, and is written in twelve letters, which are Joth, Eth, He, Vau; and by the nine heavens and their powers, and by the names and signs of our creator, that thou consecrate and confirm this presente image as it ought, by that holy name's sake, Adonay, whose kingdom hath no end.[28]

In the Guthrie manuscript there is also a similar invocation of the four kings, although in heavily abbreviated Latin. Prefacing this invocation are instructions on the composition of the ritual chamber: a square room with four windows opening on each cardinal direction, suggesting that the experiment is derivative of the *Thesaurus Spirituum* attributed to Roger Bacon.[29]

There may be a hierarchical relationship between Assasel and the four demonic kings, given that the name 'Azazel' appears in Agrippa's correspondences on the scale of the number four, being described as one of the 'princes

28 Peterson, Joseph (ed.) 'The Key of Knowledge (Clavicula Salomonis).' Esoteric Archives website, http://esotericarchives.com/solomon/ad36674.htm.
29 Michael-Albion Macdonald, *De Nigromancia* (Heptangle Books: Gilette, 1988), 66–7. GD188/25/1/3: 127–129 & 196.

of divels, offensive in the Elements.'[30] The demonic kings are described at the foot of Agrippa's table as 'Four Princes of spirits, upon the four angles of the world.' It is evident that Robert Fludd at least interpreted this in terms of a hierarchical description, as in the famous engraving of the Invasion of the Fortress of Health from his *Medicina Catholica* (1629 – 31), where an ailing man is shown being assaulted by venomous demons and angels from the cardinal points. We see the four demonic kings, Oriens, Amaymon, Paymon and Egyn, and beneath them – their agents upon earth – Samael (riding a serpent), Azazel (on a basilisk), Azael (on a sea monster) and Mahazael (on a salamander).

We suspect that Gilbert sought a multitude of boons from the spirits, primarily occult knowledge and instruction in the arts and sciences. This is inferred through his own conjuration of Assasel, which states that he seeks to avail himself of the assistance of 'beste spyritts of a deade man, that ever was in the worlde, to teache me all manner of Artes appertayninge to learninge and hid[den] knowled[g]e.'[31] Evidently Gilbert was a big thinker and not one to settle for the soul of any common man. Rather, Assasel gave him none other than King Solomon as his personal spirit servant.

This incident is recorded in the first entry of the *Visions*, which begins on the 24th of February 1567.[32] Since the first folio of the *Excellent Booke* records a prayer to be said prior to working with spirits – a prayer that was noted to have been delivered to Gilbert by King Solomon on the 20th of February, it seems likely that one of these dates is erroneous and perhaps the 24th was intended to be written.[33]

The notion that the spirit of a dead man could be kept by the magician appears to be fairly common. In the *Excellent Booke* it is Assasel that bestows such a spirit on the magus.[34] However, not all magicians sought mastery over the souls of the dead through the intervention of a spirit such as Assasel: some more morally dubious magicians evidently went as far as visiting those

---

30 *Occ. Phil.* II.vii.
31 Add. MS. 36674, f.50r.
32 Add. MS. 36674, f.59r.
33 Add. MS. 36674, f.47r.
34 In the magical experiments included in Scot's *Discoverie*, a dead man's soul is granted to the magician by the intervention of the fairy Sibyllia.

The Invasion of the Fortress of Health from Robert Fludd's *Medicina Catholica*

on their deathbeds in an attempt to bind their souls as familiar spirits. The second article of the codex, likely given to Gabriel Harvey along with the *Excellent Booke* and *Visions*, bearing as it does his marginalia, contains such a formula:

> Go to a man or woman or child when they lie in departing and say this following in their ear: + I charge thee N. wherever you be, spiritual or temporal, that when you dost depart the world that you dost never goest whether in fire, water or earth or air, stick nor stone, nor any place that ever god made, ordained or spoke. Through the power and virtue of god the father, god the son + god the holy ghost + 3 persons and one god in Virgin M., that thou dost now away to me in speed, and grant what my request or every command I give thee by the power and virtue of our god Jesu Christ, who is the everlasting god into the fires of hell, where there is weeping and wailing and gnashing of the teeth. And you shalt never be without everlasting pain, and you shalt never be a partaker in paradise's passion, but the blood of Jesus Christ shall be unto everlasting damnation if you do not come to me and grant my request.[35]

The second spirit which the *Excellent Booke* instructs the magician to call is Aosal. It is apparent from the experiments in *Excellent Booke* involving hiding and fetching a ring that the office of the spirit is to find and carry treasure.[36] Although no rituals pertaining to Aosal have yet come to light, it is apparent that, as with Assasel, the spirit is not unique to the *Excellent Booke*. Aosel (sic) appears in *Regulae Utilissimae in Artem Magicam*, the fifth article in the same manuscript codex as the *Excellent Booke*, as part of another brief spirit list:

> Aosel for treasure.
> Acozas giver of gold & silver.
> Almazim & Elicona.[37]

35 A similar procedure can be found in Skinner & Rankine (eds.), *A Collection of Magical Secrets & A Treatise of Mixed Cabalah*, trans. by Paul Barron (Avalonia: London, 2009), 68−9.
36 Add. MS. 36674, ff. 47v−48r.
37 Add. MS. 36674, f. 66r.

A set of characters for the spirit Aozol (sic) also appear in the 16th century Folger manuscript, prefacing a ritual to call the spirit Oberion, and these are reproduced below.[38] In the spirit list cited earlier, 'Asazel' was mentioned in connection with Oberion, and although neither Assasel nor Aosal are mentioned by name in the extant rituals of Oberion, their proximity suggests that a connection between the three may be revealed in the future.

Following the working of Aosal, Gilbert turned his attention to Oriens, one of the four great demonic kings of the cardinal directions, or winds, mentioned previously. The role of Oriens in the *Excellent Booke* is to 'give you the best booke that ever was,'[39] and it seems that books feature prominently in the minds of many a historical magus. John Dee and Edward Kelly took lengthy dictations of books from the spirits in their crystal, while Simon Forman dreamed about 'strang bockes brought me writen in Karactes.'[40] To the magicians books appear to be a symbol of secret knowledge and they have historically (as in the cases of Dee and Forman) gone to great lengths to collect and decipher obscure and impenetrable works. Gilbert records that Davis had a number of visions relating to spiritual books, in the libraries of Solomon, within a 'tree of bloude' and so on, which all seem to stand as tantalising symbols of mystical or hitherto unrevealed knowledge.

Within the tradition of ritual magic the book is also a symbol of power over the spirits. The *Liber Spirituum*, a tome in which spirits sign their names (thus contractually binding them to appear before the magus) is discussed in

38 Folger MS. v.b.26(a): 188.
39 Add. MS. 36674, f.48r.
40 Traister (2001): 122.

the Fourth Book of Occult Philosophy attributed to Cornelius Agrippa, although practical instruction on such books elsewhere is scarce.[41] It is apparent that something akin to the *Liber Spirituum* is involved in Gilbert's magical work, Assasel being commanded to 'lay thy hand uppon this booke beinge a testamente.'[42]

The delivery and writing of books by spirits is also found in the Folger manuscript in the form of the conjuration of Obymero:[43]

> I desire you, Obymero, *per noctem, et Symeam et membros membris et Lasys cawtis nomis et Arypys,* that you do command in this hour, and make me, and that without any questioning, a very fair book, and in that form and shape, as that it shall be given you in commandment by me, and that it be done according to my will, at my coming in readiness, to the same book or books, and that they to be of such effect, when that I will, and that now you come to me to make true this book or books, and that now you forthwith do come here to me, and to fulfill the same, and that effectually, and thou Abrinno or Obymero, *per noctes, symon mobris, Laycon, Catys, Oropys,* and *drypys,* you angels being the best writers, now do you here appear, and that in the shape of writers. Therefore in the name of the Father and the Son and the Holy Ghost, I now conjure you and that by him that created all things, and by this great and most fearful name + Tetragrammaton + and by all other his blessed names, that now forthwith and that without any let or hurt, that now immediately you do come here to me and to make me such a book incontinent containing this form, and to write the same, and that now by the virtue of God, and all words, and by the virtue of these characters, that this book be written now forth with. So be it.

---

41 For one example of the *Liber Spirituum* in ritual magic, see the *Libellus Veneri Nigro Sacer,* attributed to John Dee, which dates to the early 17th century.

42 Add. MS. 36674, f.49v.

43 Folger MS. v.b.26(a), 94.

Go you to some secret place, and that alone, and bear with thee quires of paper or parchment to make the book or books. Open thou thy book that thou callest them by, and say as afore, and bid them make a book of alchemy, or of art magic, conjuration, or nigromancy, or of what art or science thou wilt have it. Finis.

The compulsion of spirits to impart knowledge from their books, or to compose new ones would seem to present a demonic parallel to the revelatory, contemplative and prayer-orientated traditions of *Ars Notoria*: the other great tradition of medieval magic of which Gilbert may have been aware.

Closely reading the manuscript, it is apparent that Gilbert's scrying experiments often took place on flat surfaces (perhaps akin to the obsidian mirror owned by the British Museum and alleged to have been in Dee's possession) rather than with the crystal ball that we are often accustomed to visualise when imagining such magical experiments. Toward the end of the *Excellent Booke* the form of the 'cristall stone' is described. The glass is described as a flat, thick circle of clear 'crystal glass,' with names (sadly incomplete in the manuscript) written around the perimeter. Similar 'stones' can be found in a number of works on conjuration, often mounted on frames or pedestals. However, it is evident from the passage in which Assasel lays his hand upon the book that the stone is most likely lying on a table or other flat surface, since the book is placed under the stone itself.[44] Returning to the Guthrie manuscript we find a similar instance of the stone being lain upon a table in an experiment that begins:

> To have a spirit in a glasse, take a claene towell & lay it upon a faire table & upon that lay the glasse & say this oration followinge…[45]

The experiment also involves such Catholic trappings as making a cross on the glass with olive oil, washing it in wine and holy water, before eventually conjuring the spirit Belsabud within it. Such stones can also be seen to resemble a lens and it is perhaps the superficial resemblance to the science of

44 Add. MS. 36674, f.49v.
45 GD188/25/1/3, 190. Compare also with Add. MS. 36674, ff.66r–66v.

optics that ensured the enduring appeal of scrying during the early modern period.[46]

RITUAL POIESIS

As we have seen, the *Excellent Booke* repurposes much from pre-existing and contemporary ritual magic traditions, and Gilbert's approach to dealings with spirits is distinctly that of the violently compulsive 'dirty medieval magic' found in works such as the *Thesaurus Spirituum* or the 15th century necromancer's manual Clm.849. This is a marked contrast to what Robert Turner once called the 'docile angel magic of John Dee.'[47] Perhaps Gilbert's approach was influenced by the aforementioned *Key of Knowledge*, which instructs the master to aspire to 'the secret of the secrets of all the spirits' and advocates the compulsion of spirits against their will.[48]

Such a 'medieval' approach, in which the master attempts to bully the spirits into submission by invoking divine powers, issuing terrible threats and curses, and even torturing the spirits by burning their names with brimstone, would appear to be perfectly suited to Gilbert's temperamental, 'cholerick' disposition which left him prone to rages.[49] As a man who served in battle and commanded troops, and one who writes that 'you must of force' call the spirits, Gilbert was a man whose temperament commanded authority.[50]

It is true that, when stripped of the more florid Catholic invocations to the passion of Christ, the sacrament, and the Virgin Mary, Gilbert's own conjurations, charges and curses are highly formulaic — even more so than is expected of the genre. However, from a practical standpoint such utterances

46 For example, prior to his angelic experiments, Dee hypothesised that optics could be used to focus the rays of planets and stars in order to create more effective astrological talismans. See his *Propaedeumata Aphoristica* (1558).

47 Robert Turner, *Elizabethan Magic* (Element Books: Shaftesbury, 1989): 95.

48 Add. MS. 36674, f.6r, 8r. There are many parallels with this text and the first article of Sl. MS. 3847, 'The Worke of Salomon the Wise Called his Clavicle', which was transcribed in 1572 by 'H: G:' — also possibly the work of Humphrey Gilbert.

49 David B. Quinn, *Explorers and Colonies: America, 1500 – 1625* (The Hambledon Press: London, 1990): 205. Quinn also suggests that Gilbert may have been homosexual and that only young boys could relieve him from his 'stormes.'

50 Add. MS. 36674, f.48v.

have the advantage of being memorable and, when considering their context in the great battle of wills – magus versus spirit – that characterises Gilbert's magic, may easily be delivered with appropriately commanding force with little danger of tripping over the type of complex, many-claused compositions that often characterise the language of ritual magic. With a little knowledge about the order of conjurations, bonds, deprivations, punishments, excommunications and so on the master could effectively and dramatically *ad lib* his invocations.

The *Excellent Booke* contains many elements of interest to those who are attempting to reconstruct historical attitudes to – and practices of – ritual magic. For example, we have Gilbert's belief that the spirits may be present when called, yet invisible. However, it is apparent that Gilbert believes that they will only obey the master if they are called to visible appearance in the stone.[51] Gilbert also bullies the spirits in a manner that seems perfectly apt to a man with military training, as may be seen in the conjuration of Aosal. Here, the spirit is made to find a ring. Yet, each time the spirit succeeds in the task, the magus nonetheless rebukes it and accuses it of guile. Gilbert writes that we must 'never *seem* to believe them' – the inference being that it serves the magician well in his relationship with the spirits to keep a suspicious and implacable façade, thereby ensuring that they know who their master really is. The durations of conferences with spirits are also hinted at – as well as the nature of spirits as independent agents or persons in statements such as 'you must never keep any enclosed above twenty-four hours' and 'if another have bound thee in the name of God, that thou canst not come, then thou send presently [to me] one of thy servants.'[52]

As we have noted, the composition of the *Excellent Booke* is intimately bound to the experiments recorded in *Visions*, the record of which begins on the 24th of February 1567. Generally the visions were received at sunrise and sunset, facing toward the direction of the sun. By reading the two texts in

51 Add. MS. 36674, f.48v, ff.54v–55v. The subject of 'visible appearance' and exactly what the term entails in the context of historic magic has often been discussed amongst contemporary magicians. It is evident that 'visible' relates to the crystal within the context of the *Excellent Booke* – however, in *Visions* it is apparent that the spirits regularly took on visible forms outside the crystal in between the operations conducted by the pair.
52 Add. MS. 36674, f.48r, 52v.

parallel, we can draw together a chronology of the visions and the composition of the *Excellent Booke*. Summarised below, this chronology gives some insight into the role that the visions played in the poiesis, or coming together, of the magical text itself.

24th February. Sunrise.[53]

The first vision opens with H.G. dressed in black with a sword, and John Davis carrying a book, which is bound with skin, the hairy side outward. It is assumed, but not explicitly stated, that John Davis was seeing these representations of himself and Gilbert within the crystal. The vision of the master and his assistant within the crystal is not so unusual an idea as it first appears. Edward Kelly, for instance, saw Dee within his own crystal, being anointed by the Archangel Gabriel.[54] The vision mentions the colours to be used in the work, which are also recorded on the first folio of the *Excellent Booke*.[55] There is a conference with Assasell who appears with the souls of four dead and highly distinguished men: King Solomon, Roger Bacon, Adam and Job. Solomon offers to become Gilbert's servant and a rationale for the use of such a dead man's soul rather than a spirit is given, namely that 'they love man more then the others doeth.' Presumably this is also the date upon which King Solomon revealed the prayer recorded on the first page of the *Excellent Booke*, and which is to be said at the start of the work.[56]

24th February. Sunset.[57]

Davis witnesses a vision of a great wood and a house whose door has nine keyholes. Inside the house is a richly furnished chamber, with a tree of crystal. The tree has a door containing a number of books – including the aforementioned hairy book, and one with a crystal cover.

53 Add. MS. 36674, f.59r.
54 Wooley, *Queen's Conjuror*: 182.
55 Add. MS. 36674, f.47r.
56 Add. MS. 36674, f.47r.
57 Add. MS. 36674, ff.59r–59v.

25th February. Sunrise.[58]

The first vision of a square, golden hill and 'tree of bloude': a landscape in which many of the subsequent visions unfold. It may be intended that the tree of blood and its counterpart, the tree of crystal, symbolise the trees of life and knowledge. Four angels, named after the evangelists, are at the corners of the hill, each holding a book of gold. The house in the wood, encountered in the prior vision, is revealed to be Solomon's dwelling, which Gilbert and Davis enter, taking away a number of books.

25th February. Sunset.[59]

A vision of three dragons, green, red and blue. Davis is seen here holding the book with the crystal cover. There is a conference with Assasel, Solomon, Bacon, and Cornelius Agrippa who tell Gilbert how to dress and conduct himself.[60]

26th February. Sunrise.[61]

A second vision of the golden hill in which the angels assure Gilbert that 'thou hast a servant [e.g. King Solomon] that will make thee a saint.'

14th March. Sunset.[62]

This vision describes in detail the appearance of a marvellous, blazing golden cloud-like structure. On the southern side is the golden hill, the great tree of blood in the middle. Two strange, tailless, broad-footed dogs — one black, the other red, white and black — pass Gilbert and Davis. The angels assure Gilbert that that 'they would teach him all arts, and how to make books.'

15th March. Morning.[63]

Visions of a gray cony (rabbit), two black conjoined wings, dancing crystals and circling birds, which transpire to be the forms of various spirits.

58 Add. MS. 36674, f.59v.
59 Add. MS. 36674, ff.59v–60r.
60 Cf. Add. MS. 36674, f.47v.
61 Add. MS. 36674, f.60r.
62 Add. MS. 36674, ff.60r–61r.
63 Add. MS. 36674, f.61r.

15th March. Afternoon.[64]

This entry appears to be a first-hand account by Gilbert of an event that took place after the morning scrying session, although this is ambiguous in the text. Perhaps the initial vision of blackbirds and the flaming lark also took place in the crystal, although the narrative then turns to an account of Gilbert and Davis returning homeward on horseback and encountering a great 'brended' (brindled) dog, which Solomon later affirms is a spirit.

17th March. Sunrise.[65]

The angels Ancor and Amulor appear in the form of two headless blackbirds and show Gilbert and Davis 'many good books.'[66] This is followed by the pair hearing sundry sounds of bells and other instruments — an interesting occurrence since such auditory phenomena have often been historically associated with the manifestation of spirits.[67] Two more angels appear personally to Gilbert, namely Toby and Gabriell. Toby is likely the same angel as Tobyell, mentioned in the *Excellent Booke.*[68]

17th March. Afternoon.[69]

A vision of two spirits in the form of ravens. Following counsel from Solomon, Gilbert becomes their master This is followed by another 'vision' as the pair return homewards in which Job appears and tells Gilbert he will serve and make books for him before transferring himself into a crystal in Gilbert's pocket. It appears that, by this point, Gilbert has become as good a seer as Davis.

64 Add. MS. 36674, ff.61r–61v.

65 Add. MS. 36674, f.61v.

66 A ritual for calling Ancor, Analos (sic) and a third angel — Anycor — may have been known to Gilbert, and an exemplar from Illinois Pre-1650 MS. 0102 is included herein.

67 Reginald Scot devotes several chapters to opinions on the relationship between noises and spirits, while the later ritual added to his work mentions that 'the Exorcist will hear great noises of Swords and fighting, Horses neighing, and Trumpets sounding' in connection with his appearance (Discoverie [1665]: 225). Many of the spirits of Wierus' *Pseudomonarchia Dæmonum*, described in all editions of Scot's text, are also associated with auditory phenomena.

68 Add. MS. 36674, f.52v.

69 Add. MS. 36674, f.62v.

22nd March. Morning.

At 8.30 in the morning the composition of the *Excellent Booke* commenced — perhaps making good Job's promise to instruct Gilbert in the art of 'making books.'[70] Presumably most of this already existed in note-form since much of the material, such as becoming the master of a dead man's soul through the office of Assasel, had already been completed by Gilbert. We discover from the entry in the *Visions* that at this time Gilbert is in the midst of the operation to conjure the four kings.

22nd March. Afternoon.[71]

Gilbert is deeply involved in operations with Oriens and Bleth, and is cursing their disobedience. The spirit of Luke appears in another crystal to instruct Gilbert to leave his cursing so that he can instruct him on the true art of calling spirits and angels. The *Excellent Booke* records that St Luke delivered instructions on the composition of the crystal glass for angels 'at easter time,' which were presumably delivered as part of this vision.[72]

6th April.[73]

In the final recorded vision, John Davis returns to Solmon's house as part of an operation that appears to last most of the day, after which he brings Gilbert a book written by St Luke, presumably transcribed from the crystal. This book of St Luke, however, appears to have been lost.

70 Add. MS. 36674 f.47v.
71 Add. MS. 36674, ff.62r– 62v.
72 Add. MS. 36674, f.56r.
73 Add. MS. 36674, f.62v.

CONCLUSION

We do not know what happened after the vision of the 6th of April. Gilbert would return to Ireland in the summer and conclude his military duties. He received a knighthood in 1570, later becoming a member of parliament and investor in a number of failed maritime schemes, amongst them Martin Frobisher's ill-starred expedition to Greenland, to which John Dee was also party. Following a faltering attempt at establishing an English colony at Newfoundland, Gilbert was drowned in 1583 as his ship, the *Squirrel*, sank off the Azores during his voyage home.[74]

Gilbert's friend and magical assistant Davis became one of Elizabethan England's chief navigators, fighting the Spanish Armada, sailing with Sir Walter Raleigh and voyaging with the British East India Company. As with Sir Humphrey, he also met his fate at sea, being slain at the hands of a pirate off Bintan Island near Singapore in 1605.[75]

In studying the magical procedures and visions left to us by Gilbert and Davis, it is evident that these experiments had a profound effect on the two men, leading not only to a vivid record of otherworldly visions and encounters, but to the composition of one – possibly even two – novel ritual magic texts. Further critical reading of these texts may yet yield further valuable insights into the practice of ritual conjuration. The seemingly efficacious employment of Gilbert's sheer will and force of personality in the working at least outlines one vital lesson for any practitioner who believes their methods to be congruent with the traditional ritual magic forms: there is no single 'right way' to approach the conjuration of spirits – forms of magical ritual vary with their context, their period, the personalities, philosophies and theologies of the practitioners, and so forth. Undoubtedly, a great deal on the matter of ritual magic practice, its contexts, and affective nature remains to be discovered in this *Excellent Booke*.

74 Chidsey, *Humphrey Gilbert*.

75 Clements R. Markham, *A Life of John Davis, the Navigator, 1550–1605* (G. Philip and Son: London, 1891): 221.

1 TEXTS

Facsimile of British Library
Additional MS. 36674

These coulored ynkes must be had.

1. Notable gould to write wyth.
2. Syluer.
3. Blewe.
4. Redd.
5. Greene.
6. Yolowe.
7. Turkeses.

Great plenty of sweate powders, and perfumes. §§

Sleatyes, shoulde A younge beginner first tall; althoughe to tall Astrolie
is the most noble Arte; whose rauart followethe.

Note, that there is not plauge so greate, as to burne A spyritts name, and
rauarte: most especially, that is, yf the spyritt be of the ayre.

Noua methodus, et praxis magica Academici philosophi, vel Aulici
Omnisci.

This prayer is to be sayde when and before
+ you deale wth any spyritt; this was reueled
by kinge Solomon, Anno Dni 1567, die 20. Febru-
arij circa 9. 10.

O god of Aungells, god of Archaungells; god of Patriarks, god of
Prophetts, god of vs sinners; O lord be my Helpe, that this my worke may
procede in good tyme, to thy gloire O god; and to learninge, and not but else,
that I would this day haue. O my god be in my tounge, that I may
glorifie the in all workes. Amen. ⚹ ⚹ ⚹ ⚹ ⚹ ⚹.

Let not euyll spyritt enter my mynde o god, nor nothinge else but all
to thy gloire o god; for learninge is all my desire, lord thou knowest. §§
euen as yt was to thy seruaunte Solomon; O lorde sende me some of
this good hidden worke, that hath not been reueled to no mann of thou for
that cause I desier the, O god to sende oft mee, that in those our laste
daies yt may, be knowen: Amen Amen, lord Amen, wth ye Pater noster.

(Ad Artem notoriam inspiratam.)   Speculū omnisciū.

Here begynneth an excellent booke of the Arte of
Magicke, first begoone the xxijth of Marche
Anno Dmi 1567 ☉ in ♈ 11 gradus. 18 Mi. aboute
30 Mi. after 8 of the clocke, Ante meridiem.

First it is good Arte allwayes for the mr, that must begyn this Arte,
leaue swearinge, and all droncken company, yf he do knowe them; he
must allway get very cleane apparrell that must worke in this Arte;
must allway keepe his promyses, yf he make any, and not breake them;
he must be good to the poore where he seeth nede.

He must allway keepe his Skrier in cleane apparrell; this is the be-
ginnge to bringe them to Arte. +

The mr must also haue 1. or 2. good bookes to call by; as after you
shall heare fynde.

I.   Spirits in the Stone

The first Spyritt that he must call, must be the ruler of y
whose name is Assassell, and he must call him by night in the power of
☉. And when he is come he must requier one that is vnder him to
serue hym; And yf he say noe, he must not be ouer hasty wth him, but
lett him goe, and call him an other night; And when he is come
charge him in the name of his maker, that he giue you one, And
he wyll, whome ye dot aske. And then you must call one into y stone
whose name is called Assal, all this is for the stone; And when
is come, yf he be not to your sight, you must first bynde hym
fast, And then when you haue bownde hym, you must charge him
appeare to y owne sight; And yf he come not, you must get an
hyde some thinge, as you thinke good, and charge him most straightly
get seeke it, and tell you in what place of the howse, or feld it lyeth
And when he hath towld you truly, then say thus. O thou wicked
and cursed Spyritt, whie doest thou fable wth mee I am noont of
them that must be fabled wth, and say he doeth lye. Then you
and hyde in A contrarie place, or in some water, And charge hym
very straightly as followeth, that he tell you where it is: And yf
he tell you that it is in the water, say that you will not beleeue
excepte you may see at layde vppon the drie lande, for hone should
I fetche it out of the water yf it weare there. And when it is
layde on the lande as by y compulsid yt may bee, Then say to
Thou most vyle and wicked spyritt, this is not he, for this ringe
fell euen nowe of my fynger

Nota.

That thinge that you must first hyde, muste be A ringe. +

And then discharge him to his place, vntyll you shall haue nede to
speake

(marginal notes, left column, top to bottom:)

No { swearinge / dronkenes / dronken / company

Almes. +

the Skrier well apparelld.

I. spirit. Assasell the Ruler of the Deade

the first time to take hys denyall.

2. Assal into y stone.

Bynde hym.

then to appeare to sight.

wicked and cursed Spyritt.

mr not to beleue the Spyryt when he telleth truth but to belye y Spyrytt

speake wyth him; And yf he doe not tell you the truthe in those thinges
then streyghte punnyshe him, And yf he say leaue punyshinge me and
I wyll doe it; then say him nay I wyll punnysshe the most cruelly
for thys lye; and after compell him to doe it, whych you by dett must
doe, or else you shall neuer haue nothinge done for you. Then
you must after you haue charged and compelled him to tell you the
truthe, release him vntyll suche time as you shall nede him agayne.

Punnishe
hym for
hys lye.

And then
compell hym
to do yt.

Nota.

you must neuer keepe any inclosed aboue 24. howere.

not paste
24. howers.

3.

Then you must call another whose name is called Oriens, wch is
A ruler ouer the wicked, And when he is come remaunde him streyght
by to appeare to yor sight, or else that he wyll make the stone to
leape 3. tymes from the place where the stone lyeth. And yf he
wyll not, remaunde him streyghtly as followeth. Thou wicked
cursed, vyle, and rebellious Spyritt, why doest thou rebell agaynst my
commaundement? I charge and bynde the in the name of thy maker
Jhesus christ, and by the power of heauen, thou cursed Spyrytt,
that thou now let the stone stande, and appeare to my syght for I
wyll haue noe nay. Therefore I charge the by these holy names
of god, that thou doest appeare, Sabaoth, Adonay, Sachaell, Adonay
& et co. and by the name Tryon The, Cranto, Panto, that thou dost
wythout any more delay, appeart visible to my sight, and speake or
write to my hearinge or seeinge. Thus I charge the to doe wthout
any stopp or stay. And when he hath by yor compulsion appeared,
say that you see A thinge shadowed in the stone, wch is in the wall,
And therfore appeare to mee and speeke or wrighte, for I wyll
not beleue that here is any thinge to my syght, except thou speake
or wryte, and appeare to my syght, and speeke to my hearinge; or
else I wyll arrust the and condemne the by gods power, and not
by my owne power. Therfore I charge the do yt. And when he
hath don yt, then remaund him to gyue you the beste booke, that euer
was, Since thou art the kynge of the Spyritts of the Este
I charge the doe it. And when he hath brought you A booke in the
stone to yor sight, then charge him to delyuer yt to you, or appoynte
him some place where he shall lay it, and let yt bee don wth speede,
this I charge the to doe. And when it is come thither, yf you can
not read it, then come to him agayne and say, what haste thou gyuen
mee? I knowe not whether yt bee good or yll, therefore I charge
out of hande, to shewe me the vewynge and vnderstandinge of yt, And
yf he say noe: Then streyghtwayes get an take yor booke of called
and

3.
Oriens ruler
ouer yt wicked.

Lucifer
belike:

Appeare, or
make the
stone leape.

A wicked
cursed, vyle,
and rebellious
Spyrytt.

+

+

§§.
the beste
booke,
that euer
was.

+

the readinge
and vnder
standinge/
of the booke
de profundis.

Vnicus liber, inter omnium librorum.

and ruse hym as here followeth, and compell hym to doe it, and take no nay,
nor noe deferrynge off tyme, but imediately, to haue yt doon wthout stopp
or staye / and when he hath doon yt, releafe hym into hys place, vntill
surhe tyme as you shall need hym agayne. And in the releasyng off hym
bynde hym thus, that whensoeuer you shall call any that is vnder hym,
that they shall imediately, come, and fulfill your mynd in all thynges,
that you shall aske off hym; thus bynde hym to doe and promis, And
then releafe hym, and not before he hath made you vnderstand your
booke.

you must off foure first call Asasel; and then Asall; and the Oriens
and as ys before sayde, and make them fiende it; and rotinally proti....
as this booke shall teache / for thus you must do by Arte.

Nota.

That when you commaunde Oriens to laye downe the booke, it muse
bee euen don out off hande before you releafe hym.

Regula.

you must neuer call any Sprytt in the stone, yf he be inuisible; But
you must allway fynde thynges to make them fynde yt: And make
the do thynges for you that you doe knowe allveady to be tdue. +

Nota.

That off any off them do tell you neuer so truly, that be inferiours in y
stone; you must neuer say to them that they tell trueth for it is not
yf he be inuisible to the m; for yf he be visible to the m, then he
knoweth, what he hath to doe; for he must streightly comaund hym as
followethe. And yf he do tell you euer truly, whtr he be to your
sight or not, then you must releafe hym wythin the space before sayd.
And yf he do lye to you, then you must streightly punishe hym.
And when he doth tell you truly, yet ye must punishe hym; for then
ye must streightly punishe hym againe for that lye, and comaund
hym to doe another thynge for you, what you thinke very harde: And
yf he tell you yt truly, then releafe hym within the tyme aforesayd; and
yf he do not tell you truly, then bynde hym to tarry very strongly,
and strongly, then you dyd at the first; And euery day, when his
power waineth, then punishe hym very streightly: As yf he be of
the fier; then punishe hym wth stinkynge water, either off man or wo
man; And putt stinkynge thynges into yt; and then putt the stone int
yt, and streightly comaund hym to come foorth out off the stone into
the water that you dyd putt hym in, and there to tarrye vntill you doe
                                                                    comaunde

(left margin notes:)
Any that is
vnder hym.

Promis.

the three spirits
Asasel .1
Aosal 2
Oriens .3

Oriens. y Booke.

Inuisibles
Spyritts not
into y stone.

Inuisible
hardly beleued

yf truly
euer.
the releas'd.

Punnish for
the lye.
+

yf false, the
punnish hym
at hys lower
euery daye.
+

romaunde him to come into the stone agayne. And yf he be off the water
then take brimstone and burne yt, and romaund him first to goe into some
stone for the purpose, and then putt him into the burninge brimstone; and
that is for the punishment off them, redinge & curse over them.
And yf he bee off the ayer then you must romaunde him to goe forth
off the stone, into some vyle stinkinge mudd, and to tarry in yt, untill you doe romaund him to goe into the stone againe. And yf he
be off the Earthe then you must curse him in goddes name. Did the
that will serve them sufficiently.

pᵒ Aqueis
sulphur

Si Aereus.

Si terreus.

Nota.

You must allway in the stone, never seeme to beleue them, howe trulye
soever they saye. Haud credo: quoth Derick.

A you must
not beleue in
the stone.

Nota

That you must allwayes use all spyritts in the stone after this order
and not otherwise; wythout callyinge out them, what spyritts soever
they bee.

+

Nota

The first spyritt proceedinge by, doth, must be Assasel; then Rosiell
and then Oriens, usinge them as before. And after you have thus
used them, you may call whome you will, and make them doe what
you will have them.

vt˙

Assasel.
Aosal.
Oriens.

Nota. Assasels call.   I.

This is the call to haue Assasel, wch is the first you must call.
first your prayer before, the call must be thus, beinge sayd wyth
a good harte. O god of Aungells, O god of Archaungells; O
god of Patriarches, god of Prophetts; god of us synners, I
most wretched synner, doe desier the to be my helpe that this spiritt
Assasel, may nowe come and fulfill my will. O lord be my helpe
and asistaunce, that I may by thy power call him, and not by owne
power. O lord lord be mercifull unto mee, and that the prayers of
A synner may be hearde in thine eares. And I charge the Assasel
that thou doe prepare thy selfe to come when I call the, whirch
shalbe this nighte; O lord be my helpe. And sayinge your
Pater noster, and Credo, then call him as followeth.

oratio ad
vocandū
Assasel.

O thou spyritt Assasel, wch arte A lyuinge and louinge spyritt, to
the comaundementes off god, I charge the in the name off Jhesus christ,
that thou doe appeare heare visible to my syluer, heere wythout any
delay, I coniure and romaunde the, and by gods power constrayne
the that thou doe appeare heare, and doe my comaundementes wthout
any

vocatio
Assaselis.
in nomine
Jhesu
christi.

any more stay. O god be my helpe that this spyritt Assasel may come
and obay thy holy woordes and proceedeth fourth off my mouth. O thou

Loving Assasel.
louing Assasel, I charge the that thou do come and appeare heere quick

exorcisinu Du
Sabaoth Adonay
lye without any stoppe or stay. By these holy names off god I heere
constrayne the Sabaoth, Adonay, + Tetragramaton, and by this holy

yt would be
EL. w.th in her
breue is god o
Lord
names Aglaon, Laiagm, Rialgagio, that thou doe appeare heere quicklye
that thou doe appeare heere to my syght, or to the syghte off my
christall. I coniure the and I comaund the, that thou appeare heere
without any delay, or tarrying. Thus I charge the to doe, and
lay yt to thy charge at the latter day. And therfore as thou fearest
thy god and maker that thou appeare heere presently, and fulfill my
desire, as may be expedient for A syner. O thou spyritt Assasel

Assasel. or
what other
name soeuer
thou hast.
or what other name soeuer thou hast, I charge the to appeare heere
out the keper off the deade bones presently, without any stay, and
then I wyll release the. And vntyll thou haue doon yt, I wyll
neuer leaue calling, vntyll thou doe come by the power off god
therfore I charge the, and comaund the, to come and
appeare for I am the creature off god. O lord be my helpe that
this spyritt Assasel may come.   And this is the call for hym.

                   And yf Assasel wyll not come and obay you,
                   say as followeth this sentence.

O thou spirit Assasel, wheich hast been take for A noble spyritt
and kinge, and I cannot fynde it in the, by thy disobaying off god
woordes: Therfore I shall doo as duE wylleth mee. O thou

wicked and
rebellious spirit
wicked and rebellious spyritt, that rebellest against gods power, I
by gods power accurse the, and excommunicate the, and depriue the,

accursed and
excoicates.
and condemne the for thy disobedience. Therfore god the father
accurse the, and condemne the, and off thy office depriue the.
God the sun accurse the, god the holy ghoste accurse the and
condemne the, all holy Angells accurse the, all Patriarckes
and Prophetts accurse the! And I wreched synner by gods
power doe accurse the for thy disobaying, Therfore I charge
the come, Amen.

                   when Assasel is appeared, then say
                   this bande vnto hym.

O thou kinge Assasel, w.th art appeared heere in this stone I

sub pœna
eternal
damnation.
bynde the by gods power, not to departe vntyll thou be lycensed by
mee: wherfore I charge the that thou doe not departe in payne of
his endles damnation: And I comaund the that thou lay thy hande
vppon this booke beinge A testament (w.ch must be layde vnder the
stone off he wyll lay his hande vppon) And sweare that thou must
not departe

...t departe untill thou be lycensed by mee : And that thou shalt
... fullfyll all my desyer. And then bynde him straightly, not to depte
... the wordes before sayde : And then call him againe into y same ...

yf yt be a delusion or a mockynge spyrytt

... kinde, although he seeme to be there. And then yff yt be a delu-
... ion; then the true spyritt will come, And then reade the curse be-
... re uppon him whatsoever he weare, that first appeared in disgisd name

y stone of punishmente.

... d comaund him to come into the stone off punishmente, and burne him w...
... or whatsoever he bee that he commeth in disgisd name, And although
... be disgisd, yet reade the call soe often as you did before, and yf

one of y best spyritts of a deade man, to teache all Artes.

... be hee, then there will not hinge come, Then you must aske one of the
... spyritts of a deade man, that euer was in the worlde, to teache
... all manor off Artes apertayninge to learninge and good knowledge
... nd neuer release him, untill he haue giuen you the spyritt off him
... that you doe aske. Then release him untill such tyme you haue
... ...d off him againe : And this is all that apertaynoth to the
... ...ust you call in first, it is Anasel. And after you haue once called
... im by this call and order, you may still occupye him at will.

Spiritus plantechus : vel dæmon pansophus.

The call off Aosal. 2.

Diurnus et ternus spiritt.

... u must call him by day, in any hower you will, but moste comonly, in
... power off ♄. And this is his call to call him.

Aosal. his call.

O thou spyritt Aosal, I coniure the, and I charge the, that thou appeare
... in this cristall stone psently, to the sight off my selfe, & my scryer,

wicked and rebellious spyrytt.

... fulfull my intent holy. O thou wicked and rebellious spyritt Ao-
... ...e, of what name soeuer thou bee, it is the I call, and I charge
... the by the power off thy maker, that thou here psently appeare without
... my delusions, craftes, or subtelty, or deceipt to me or any creature li-
... inge or deade. O thou spyritt Aosal, or what other name soeuer

θεαυατος χυριος, τυεον, χραντον I thinke yt would be ηρατιυσ προτεον, which y Tipheon. Agla. Sabaoth, Adonay, exerituu Eze.

... thou bee, I coniure the by these holy names off god, that thou ap-
... ...are here to me psently, and to no body els, Athanatos, Cyrios, Tyon,
... ranton, Panton, Agla, Sabaoth, Adonay, and by all other names that
... w not for me to rehearse, I charge the to come and appeare here
... in the name off th endles damnation, without any stoppe or any staye,
... & any hurte to me or any body, for I will not staye; Therefore
... I charge the do my will quickly, fo yf thou do dissemble wth me,
... I shall accurse the, Therefore come and doe yt psently without
... any staye; Then say the Pater noster, and Credo.

If Aosal doe not appeare, say then as followeth.

Lamaza badan cur me reliqisti.

O thou spiritt Aosal, I coniure and remaund the, that thou doe not
... disobey as thou hast done, And for thy disobeyinge I doe here accurse
... the, and by gods power condemne the, and depriue the by these holy
... wordes, that followeth. Lama sabathany, and by
                    Sother,

Sother, Sabaoth, Eagin, Halgali, and by Ameson, I charge thee to come and appeare, and for this disobbeyinge, I by these holy names doe accurse and excomunicate thee, thou wicked and rebellious spyritt. The curse of god the father light on thee, the curse of god the sonn come to thee, the curse of god the holy ghost come to thee. Therfore I charge thee to come awaye, without any delay or clusion, or any other deceit or craft, but immediatly to appeare here in this cristall stone, or else I will reade as followeth thy greate maledition; therfore I charge thee to come awaye; And for the first disobbeyinge I say againe, all good Angells curse thee and condemne, and for thy disobbayinge expe[r]m[i]n... rate and devill thee. Therfore I charge thee to come awaye, untill I shall by gods helpe release all these bondes from thee. yf thou doe not appeare I shall yet further in thy constraynte and to god iche... ycon: Therfore I shall charge thee to come awaye, for I shall never leave tormentinge thee and cursinge thee untill thou come awaye. And therfore thou wicked spyritt I charge thee come: And therfore yf thou come not before I have redd this 3 tymes over, or as soone as I have doon yt, I shall procede in farther constraynte to thee, therfore without any delaye come presently, for this I will but 3 tymes goe over. ¶ And when ye have read this latter constraynte, which if not the generall curse for Bosal, then in the thirde readinge say that I am nowe in the last readinge, I will procede further to thy constraynte.

This is a generall sentence and malediction for Bosal.

O thou cursed and rebellious spyritt Bosal, w[hic]h hast so rebelled against gods comaundmente, for altogither I will nowe by gods power punishe thee. O thou cursed spyritt that hast rebelled, god curse thee and anathem[a]te thee, god the holy ghost curse thee thou wicked and rebellious spyritt, god the holy ghost constraine thee thou most vyle and rebellious spyritt. ¶ Then you must take brimstone and burne it to his constraynte, And in the burninge of it say, even as this burneth soe I trust god will burne thee, for disobbayinge his most holy worde, All holy Angells accurse thee, and anamet thee, and from the power that thou, I desier the all prophettes accurse thee thou most vyle and rebellious spyritt, All heavenly motions accurse thee to gods glory and to thy constraynte devine thee All holy thinges that fall on thee, all the inferiour spyritts, by the power that they have curse thee and make thee their foote stoole. And I will never leave reading this, untill thou either appeare, or be deprived. All creatures of this world curse thee, the holy testamente curse thee, untill thou presently appeare, I desier god to heare my voyce. ¶ Then say ye Pater noster.

This is ceste

this is yf he appeare quietly at the firste / this Bande.

And yf he doe appeare at the firste, then here followeth his bande.
I bynde the thou spyritt dosal unfayned A spyritt of much obayinge
to gode worlde, here to stay, untill yf thy gode power release the,
and I comaund the that thou doe all my will, that I shall bydd
the, And yf thou doest disobay and goe hence, I will arruse
the therfore, by these worde I bynde the, Lyfe, Lese, Lorvando.
Amen.

Yf dosal doe not appeare without muche
constraynte as before / then here followeth
this bande when he is come.

O thou spyritt dosal unfayned art nowe come into this stone by muche
constraynte, I here bynde the as A most vyle and wicked spyritt
to doe all my comaundementes: And the cursse off god and all holy
Aungells light on the, thou rebellious spyritt: Therfore here I
bynde the and charge the, not to departe without my leave and licence, thou most vyle, and wicked, and rebellious spyritt: And I
charge the here to stay, untill thou hast doon all my comaundementes; and then presently make hym doe as before is sayde.

3.

The summong for Oriens, and all 4. kynges. And
this note, that as ye aveare dyvidinge it, in 4. plees,
you must say it 3 dayes kneelinge devoutly,
before you call hym in the morninge; thone parte
toward thone quarter; and thother partes eche off
them to eche quarter off the worlde; and
turninge you face accordingly.

In the name off god: O lord prosper my worke, that I nowe this
tyme begyn, to A good intente, to thy glorie I truste, and no hurte
off my neighbour. O god be my helpe, that this kinge N° do appeare in this crystall stone when I call hym. O god be mercyfull
unto mee, and sende me well to prosper in yt, and in all other
good workes, that I shall nowe, or at any tyme take in hande to
thy glorie O god or nott.   In the name off god, thou
kinge Oriens, I comaunde the to prepare thy selfe, to come when I
shall call the in this crystall stone, and I charge the not to delaye
with mee; for here in gode name I summon the. O holy Aungells
be my helpe that this kinge N°, may come and doe my will when
I shall call hym. O thou kinge N°, here I bynde the to prepare thy
selfe

(margin:) Life, lese, Lorvando.

(margin:) N.

(margin:) to thy glory or not.

selfe to come when I shall call the: Therfore I charge the delay with
me nothinge at all, neither none nor any other tyme. O holy prophettes
be my helpe, O god be my helpe, O holy Aungells be my helpe,
that this spyritt kinge No may come to me when I shall call him. O
lord to god intente I do yt, to thy glory, his constraynte and my
comodyty. O holy, and holiest of all, be my helpe, And here thou
kinge No I charge and lay to thy charge to prepare thy selfe, to
come when I shall call the; lord prosper me, god prosper mee,
All holy Aungells prosper me, All prophettes and patriarckes
prosper me, in this my good intente and purpose that I begynn.
Amen, lord Amen, and graunt it I beseche the.

✠ The generall call for the 4. kinges, espetially, for Oriens.

In the name off god, Amen. O thou kinge No, which art of the east
or No; I charge the here to come without any delay, without hurte
to me or any other creature livinge or deade; thus I charge the to doe
it without any blusteringe or blowinge, cryinge or roringe, to any mans
hearinge, speakinge or talkinge, to any mans hearinge, whether thou
goest; I charge it doe it not, or castinge downe trees, or hurtinge
any house, grasse, corne, or cattle, this by gods power I charge the
thou doe not, for yf thou doo, I will by gods power marvaylous
cruelly curse the, anameate and torment the. O thou No which
art of the east or No, or what quarter soever thou be of Oriens or
No, I call the hither to come, and doe my intente without doinge any
of these hurtes I bonde the, or without this hurte thou wicked and
rebellious spyritt, wch is, I charge the in the name off god the father
that thou open no grounde that to hurte shall doe, and further that
open thou not grounde whether it hurte yea or naye, And that
thou cause no greate fludds to rise that shall doe any kinde of
hurte, and further that thou make noe waters to rise, whether it
hurte yea or naye. This furthermore by gods power I charge the
thou do not, that thou make noe greate wynde rise that shall blowe
downe any howse or hurt any kinde of thinge to lande or by water.
And that thou shalt hurte or throne downe any cattle, I charge the furthermore by god power, Thus I charge the that thou do make noe
greate rayne of water or haylestones or any hurte that out of the ele-
mente shall come, furthermore I charge the thus to doe, that thou
make noe greate lightninge, that shall burne or hurte any creature
house or hay, corne or grasse or trees or hedges, or melte any kinde off
leade, tynn, or any other kinde off mettalles or hurtinge of churches
or any other kinde off tymber, or any kinde off stones, or any kinde off
writinge, or any thinge that apertaineth to man. This I charge the thou
doe not, O thou kinge Oriens or No of what quarter soever thou
bee, I charge the here

(left margin notes)

hurte
blusteringe
blowinge
cryinge
roringe

castinge downe
trees
hurtinge houses.

open no grounde.

cause no fludds.

rayse no waters.

no great wyndes.

no rayne or
hayle stones.

no lightninge.

melting of leade
hurtinge of chur-
ches.

...out any delay to appeare ther visible to me or my skryer, with=
...hurte or delay, And this further in the way I charge the, that thou
... none of thy men that be under the, do hurte any kynde of thinge
... any of the kinges or other subiectes or servauntes, this I charge you
... to doe, and in no place to vext those with I call not, And as for
..., O thou kinge No, I charge the here to come, and to fulfill my
...tente generally in all thinges. O thou kinge No, and rebellious
...inge, I charge the here to come without any delaye Thep or share.

... thou most wicked kinge No, I charge the in the payne of eternall
...amnation, that thou here come presently and fulfill my entente without
... hurte or harme to me, or any thinge that here is comanded, this I
...harge the to doe and presently to come, and not to staye. This I charge
...the to doe, and ever thou idle to fulfill my entente, O thou kinge No,
...charge the presently, and not I by my owne power do comaunde the,
...but by the power of god the father sone, and the holy ghost, here to
...come presenter, O thou No of what quarter soever thou bee I charge
...the to appeare presently for I will not be delayed of the, I coniure
...and comaunde the, I coniure and charge the, I coniure and I con-
...strayne the here to appeare whin the space of an houre, or the space
...of 10. minuttes in this crystall stone, and fulfill all my entente this
...in payne of eternall damnation, I charge the, and that thou shall not
...come in the brimes of the stone, and so to deceive me, but to come
...alle in the midst of the stone to the sight of me or my skryer without
...any delay; this I charge the by the power of god the father omnipotent
...& by the power of α. et cω, that thou presently appeare here without
...any Thep or stay, or danger to me, or to any other creature, this
...I charge the to doe, and not to hurte nor kynde of thinge that is
...of me comanded, allthough it is sayed that thou haste power of
...the earth, the Sea, and trees; O lord graunt this be done y
...this spirit, nomine, an kinge of the Easte may appeare without any
...hurte to thy glory, o god it must be or ells not, In the name of god
...the father, the sonn, and the holy ghoste I desyre yt. Amen.

Off he doe not appeare, say, then this generall
sentence that followeth, for any of the 4. kinges.

O thou wicked and thou rebellious spyritt, thou stoute, and thou vyle
spyritt, for thy disobeyinge here by gode lawe I curse the, and by
gode power will of thy kingdome an power deprive the, as a most
wicked and rebellious spyritt: and an inferiour then shalt thou bee,
the greate curse and great malediction of god light vppon the, for
thy disobeyinge, and ef thou doe not presently come, thy damnation will
I reade; God curse the and deprive the all holy Angells curse
the, with theire power deprive the all Patriarkes and Prophettes
curse the, and with theire prayer deprive the as a most wicked
...rebel, and rebellious spyritt. God confounde the for thy disobeyinge
off

kinges theire
rebuckes
& seruauntes.

Sub pœna eter-
nae damnationis.

fall into the
mides of the
stone.

α. et cω.

power of the
earth, the Sea
and ye Trees.

off these holy wordes. O thou No, w[hi]ch was once a Kinge, and by that tyme I
haue red this 3 tymes, and this depriuatio[n] 3 tymes more thou wilt be an
inferiour, and a footestole to the worst. Therfore I charge the to come anon
quickly, yf thou doe loue to saue thy kyngdome, for yo[u]r name I will
not be dyspraysed, all heauenly and earthly motions curse the and depriue
the. I will say, no more, yf thou wylt not come p[re]sently, the depriuatio[n]
w[i]ll I reade, or else an other haue comm[e]d the in the name off god, that
thou canst not come, that then thou sende p[re]sently some off thy seruant[es]
& spake to my owne hearinge, that I shall I say vntyll thou be released
and to sende me word & thou wylt p[re]sently come & spend as thou art re=
leased. O lord prosper my worke Amen. Lorde Amen.

yf he be bounde,
to sende his vicar
for a tyme to
excuse hym.

Oriens East
Amaimo[n]. west
Paimon. North
Ægyn. South

            These ar the names off the 4 kyng[es]:
            Oriens, AMAIMON, Paymon, ÆGIN.

        ¶ Yf he come not p[re]sently, then say as followeth
        w[hi]ch is the depriuation off the kynge.

O thou Oriens d[...] No, w[hi]ch was once a kinge, and nowe by god[es] pow[e]r [thou?]
nowe be a footestole to the inferiours, I will here by god[es] power depriue
the, yf thou doe not come p[re]sently before I haue red this depriuatio[n]
& depriue the and condemne the thou rebellious spyrit No, All hea=
mo[u]ens depriue the thou rebellious spyrit No, God the father depriue [the?]
thou No rebellious spirit god the son depriue the No, god the holy
ghost depriue the and condemne the, and curse the thou wicked and
rebellious spyrit No, O thou rebellious spyrit w[hi]ch was off great pow[er]
when tyme did the serue nowe off noe pow[e]r I truste thou shalt bee
vild for thy disobayinge all creatures liuing, w[i]th the power they haue
depriue the curse the and vnder foote condemne the. And for thy
disobayinge thou spyrit No, I depriue and condemne the: And the
4 Euangelist[es], Marke, Mathewe, Luke, and John, condemne the and
depriue the for thy greate disobaynge. Tobyell and Vriell conde[m]ne
and depriue the, for thy disobaynge, All the power that is amongst
the god you bowes be against the. Amen, and Amen.

Euangelists.

Tobyell.
Vryell.

        ¶   Nota.

Yf they do not appeare, o[r] otherwise fulfill thy comaundeme[n]t in euery
thinge, after you haue red y[ou]r depriuatio[n] 2 tymes, then wryte eyther
one or all there names, accordinge as you haue to doe wyth them, and
put brimstone next to the letters off there names, And fould yt vpp
together, and put stinkinge clay about the p[a]p[er], and so burne yt and
in the burninge say thus. Euen as this burneth, so I desier the O god,
that those kinge[s] No may burne in god here as this doth here, for
there disobaynge: and then by dute vpo[n] y[ou]r knees pray god, and
so goe forth off y[ou]r worke house for the space off/

                                                    when

when he is come, his handes . +

Thou spyritt N, which art appeared here in this glasse, I bynde the
here to tarrye, and never to depte untill thou bee lycenced by mee J bynde
the here to stay, and to tarry and not to depte in the paine of eternall
damnation, and by the power of Jhesus Christ, and that thou fulfill all
my comaundementes, and here to remayne wthout any hurte doing
to any creature, lyuinge, or deade, wthout breakinge my glasse, or
any other hurte, that thou canst imagyn or deuise: All this J by goddes
power charge the to doo; furthermore that thou at noo tyme hereafter
deceaue me in my coniurynge to the, or my seruice, or any other that in this
place shall come. This J charge the to doo / Amen, lord Amen.

+ wythout hurte
wythout brea=
kinge y glasse.

A lycence for the 4. kinges to departe.

I coniure the thou kinge N, that thou goe to thy place wthout any
hurte or harme, of any thinge that J haue named, or not named.
Therfore J charge the anoyd, and to departe wthout any hurte
doinge, generally to any kynde of thinges, but quickly to departe
tyll J shall call the agayne, J doo not discharge the but releasse
the, therfore anoyde Sathan, anoyde J charge the. Amen.

Avoyd Sathan.

A generall call for all sprittes
into the glasse. §§.

I coniure and comaunde the thou spiritt N, what name soeuer thou
otherwise haue, that thou here appeare by the same name presently.
I call the, and not to dissobay it, J charge the by these holy names,
tetragramaton, Micon, Messyas, Sother, Emanuel, Sabaoth, Tyon, Cranton
Panton, Creaton Panton, that thou here obay by these holy names and
worde of god, J coniure the here to appeare psently wthout any dolay
and fulfill all my comaundementes, Amen. O thou spyritt N J charge
the to come, and appeare as thou fearest god, and hopest to be saued
O thou kinge of the East J comaunde the to discharge this spiritt N
that he be under the, and not to keep him from me this J charge the
to doo / O thou kinge of the weaste, J comaunde the to releasse this
spiritt N, from the, if he be in thy dominion, By goddes power J charge
the. O thou kinge of the Northe J charge the and comaunde the to
let this spiritt N goe from the, and come to me psently. yf he doe
not come J shall accurse you all 4. kinges and him also. O thou kinge
Egyn which art of the Southe, or of what quarter soeuer thou be of,
I charge the to releasse this spiritt N from the yf he be in thy dominion
or els J shall doo to the, as afore J sayd, yf amongst you all he
come not, And for his dissobayinge J will accurse him, and you all thus

fortasis recꝰ
πχιτων
κρατων, oia
regere et
gubernare
5ᵐ

therfore I coniure thee here to appeare thou spyritt No, wythout any delay
be eluded, O holy dumpness I desier vpon thee my helpe, that this spyritt
may appeare in this cristall stone. Amen.

Generalis Sententia.

The maledictis and greate curse off god the father, the son, and the
holy ghost, lighte on thee thou spyritt No, And all holy dumgells curse
thee, all Patriarchs and Prophettes curse thee, all heaven and Jmorcon
curse thee, All men and women in this world curse thee, all quad-
raable curse thee, therfore I charge thee come O thou wicked and rebell
spyritt No, I comaunde thee to appeare in this cristall stone wythout
any delay or defewinge off tyme, O thou spyritt of the Aer, I
charge you, that none houlde this spyritt No, but that he may come
and doe my comaundements in all thinges bothe nowe and ever,
And yf he doe not appeare here present, the curse of god and the holy
ghost come to hym, therfore I charge thee come awaye.

A generall Bonde.

I bynde thee thou spyritt, that art in this cristall stone, that thou
doe not disobay my comaundements, but doe all thinges for me, that
to thy office apperteyneth. And more toe here I bynde thee not to
release nor goe away, till I doe release thee by the same bonde I
bounde thee, therfore I charge thee here to remaine vntyll thou hast
fulfylled all my comaundements, for I will use dule towarde thee
and nothinge but dole, and all spyritts, therfore here stande I
charge thee in this cristall stone.

A lycence generall for all spyritts to
departe, whatsoever he be, out of y stone.

O thou spyritt whiche haste fulfilled all my comaundements now
I charge thee to departe, to the place where god hath appointed
thee, vntyll I shall call thee againe; And yf thou doe not depart
god curse thee, therfore auoyde thou wicked spyritt No.

Nota.

Noe good spyritt will tarry longer then he is comaunded, no
noe longer then 24. howers yf he be byd goe.

The Arte howe to call any spyritt out of one
Christall stone where he is invisible, into another
Christall to make him appeare visible to all mens
sightes; And this is the prayer that before you
worke begin, muste be sayde:

O god be my helpe in this my beginninge, that I may haue ye victory
ouer this spyritt No, that I intende to call whose name is No, that he
may appeare in this cristall stone when I shall call him in the name
of god, Amen. O god be my helpe that he may appeare when I shall
by thy power call him, and that he may not resiste in no thinge to more
that I shall aske off him / O holy Aungells I desier you to be my
helpe, that this spyritt No, may appeare when I call him visible to
my syght, and to all mens syghte that he shall loke on / O god
spede me well in this my enterprise, that he may come and appeare
visible vnto me, and vnto all men that he shall loke on, without frande
gyle, or any kynde off deceipte, but quietly, and peaceably there
to appeare without hurte to me, nor to any thinge visible or invisible, or
to any thinge moueable or immoueable.

O thou spyritt No, I comaue and I charge the, that thou prepare
thy selfe here to appeare, when I shall reade the call followinge,
without stopp or staye, or any kynde off deceipte, but peaceably
here to come. O lord god graunt that this spyritt No, nor no
other spyritt may haue the power to putt any elusion into my mynde
but they may come without any elusions puttinge into any mans mynde
or any creatures mynde that is lyvinge. O thou spyritt No, I
charge the in the name off Jhesus christ, and as thou hopest to bee
saued at the dreadfull daie off iudgement, that thou appeare presently, when I shall reade the call as followethe. O god be my
helpe in these my enterpryses, that I may bringe them to good
effecte, and perfit ende. And graunte O lorde that this spiritt
No, may appeare presently when I shall reade the call that followethe. Amen, lorde Amen.

Nota)

That after you haue sayde this prayer afore written, then you
muste putt a lyttle brymstone into the fier, and houlde the stone, the
spyritt appeared invisible ouer it in the smoke thereoff, and a lyttle
to touche 2 or 3 tymes the flame thereoff with the stone, and then
say as followethe.

O thou spirit No wt art in this cristall stone, yf thou do not appeare
presently to my syghte then seeste the punnishmentes, and worse then this,
therfore delude not wyth me, for I will ye dute wt hye after repete. +
                                                                then muste

Then must you say ye prayer agayne, and then proteade in ye worke

<u>Howe beginnith the call for visible; to make</u>
<u>any Spyritt, that is in any thynge invisible, to</u>
<u>appeare in another thynge visible to all</u>
<u>mens sigtes.</u>

In nomine patris et fily et spiritus sancti. Amen.
Then say ye Pater noster, and ye Credo, And then say.
O thou spyritt No I commaunde the to come into this thynge visible
unto my sigtte, I charge the as thou hopest to be saued, that thou
comest forthe of that thynge into this stone visible to my sygtt and
to all mens sigtte, wythout any hurte doing to me, & to any creature
lyuinge or dume beast, I charge the that thou doe hurte no kynde of
thinge, And I charge the that thou hurte noe grasse nor tyme, vpon
payne of eternall dampnation, And I charge the in the name of Jhs
christ, and doe commaunde the that thou doe hurte not tree, no corne
no nor maner of tymber that is buylded or vnbuylded, I charge the
thou spiritt No in the name of Jhs christ, that thou hurte no maner
of howse that is standinge of that is aboute to be buylded in the payne
of thy refusion, And that thou hurte no kynde of thinge that oute of
god was suffered to be made, Furthermore I charge the that thou
doe no grounde, no no lostes, noe nor rostes, telle, tounes, kotes,
frames, walles, tunes, crowes, o any other kynde of thinge that is
of nne vnnamed or name, that thou shalt not hurte no kynde of thinge
no shure no kynde of thinge no put any kinde of boddy in bande.
Furthermore this I charge the in the name of Jhs christ, that thou
hurte no kinde of churche, castles, o towers or any kynde of thinge
In the name of Jhs I charge the thou spyritt No or any other kinde of
spiritt that is was or shalbe, that you doe no kinde of hurte noe
melte no kynde of leade noe tynn, nor any other kynd of mettayls
In the name of Jhs christ I charge you doe yt not, noe no other kynde
of thinge; I charge you all in the name of Jhs christ, that you make
no greate wynde, that shall blowe downe o hurte any kynde of
thinge by lande or by water, I charge you all in the name of Jhs
christ, that you make noe kinde of lygghtninges that shall burne o
destroy any kynde of thinge lyuinge or not, I charge you in ye name
of Jhs christ, that you make no great rayne, o hayles, that shall
hurte any kynde of corne, rattes, or grasse, o any other kynde of thinge
And that you make no kinde of showes of fire in the Ayre to hurte any
kynde of thinge lyuinge or dume, or any kynde of thinge. I charge
you spyritts all, and specially thou spyritt No, that thou make no greate
floudes of water to hurte any kynde of thinge by sea or lande any
                                                              pages 2

...yes, or any other kynde of thinge. And now I charge the in the
name of Ihū christ sake, that thou no noe other kinde of spyritt, do come
here this howse to hurte me or it, or any other creature in it, but that
...owne peartably into this cristall stone, (and then you muste
...tt on your stone) god graunt that all these my wordes may bee
...filled, I coniure and commaunde the the spyritt No, that thou
...sently, appeare in this cristall stone visible to my syghte, for I
...take noe naye. I coniure and by gods power compell the that thou
...pyritt No, that thou presently, appeare here in this cristall stone
...ible to my syghte, wthout any kynde of frade that ever was, or
... be imagined by any wirked spyritt. O thou spyritt No, I
...ge the presently here to appeare wthout any thorpe or stay into that crist-
... stone that there standethe, visible to my syghte, and to all mens syghte
...t on yt shall looke. O thou wirked and rebellious spyritt I coniure and
...maunde the by these holy names of god, that thou presently here
...peare + Agla + Micon + Messias + Sother + Emanuel + Sabaoth +
...anuel + tgla +, And by all these holy names of god Amen that
...presently here appeare, thou wirked and rebellious spyritt No
...thout any thorpe o stay delushir or delaye here to appeare visible
...all mens syghtes. O thou spyritt No I coniure and comaund the
... charge the in paine of eternall damnation, that thou here presently
...peare to my syghte in this christall stone, appointed for the that
... mayst appeare heare thou spiritt No to my syghte and all mens
...t on the shall looke in paine of endles damnation. I charge the
...hout any delay thorpe or stay but mekely and quietly here to appear
...e spirit No, and that I may wth my eyes see the. O lorde
...aunte that these my wordes may be of muche truthe: Amen, lord
...su christ, Amen I beseche you

Iff he doe not appeare visible, say this
Sentence.

...thou wirked and rebellious spirit No, god the father curse the
... thy disobedience, god the sonn curse the for rebellion, god the
...ly ghoste curse the for thy disobayinge of these holy wordes, the
...ns of the eternall lyvinge god, light on the thou wirked and
...bellious spyritt No for thy disobayinge. All holy Aungells curse
... condemne the thou wirked and rebellious spirit No for thy disob-
...yinge, All children of men and women curse the and by there
...wer deprive the thou wirked and rebellious spirytt No for thy
...eate disobayinge, Lyalglla curse the, Sother curse the, Sabaoth
...se the, Sydrach, Mydrach, and Abednago wth lay burninge in the one
... fier curse the, and by gods power weare delyvered from thē
...curse the by the power that Moyses dyd strike the earthe in the
...nde of Egypt, and there weare innumerable of flyes among
...n and beastes, and as truly as the water turned into bludd so truly

I curse the wyth all my power, and deprive the by the power off god
thy greate dispsayinge off his wordes, Amen lord I beseche the.

If he come not visible to your syggte, when the fyrste call beinge twyce
reade, then you muste reade the laste call or sentence 3 tymes, and [so]
leave.   the deprivarie iff he do not
                      appeare visible.

O thou wicked and rebellious spyritt, god the father curse the, god
the sonne curse the, god the holy ghost curse the, wyth theire power deprive
for thy dissbayinge off these holy wordes. All Aungells and Archaungells
curse the, and condemne the, and for thy dissbayinge off thy othe deprive
the. Lord I beseche the that this rebellious spyritt No may be depriv[ed]
for his dissbayinge. All saynts curse the and deprive the then rebellious
spyritt No for thy dissbayinge, All patriarches and prophettes cu[rse]
the for thy dissbayinge, and deprive the, I by gods powe[r] b[y]
sonne do curse the condemne the, and for thy greate rebellion depriv[e]
the, Amen lord I beseche the.

                    the bande when he is come to your
                      syggte to bynde him.

I bynde the thou spyritt No, whiche art appeared here in this cristall
stone seene to my syggte that thou do not departe out off this crista[ll]
stone untill thou be lycensed by mee, and that thou shalte tarry [here]
wythout any hurte doinge to me, or to any other creature, or fearinge [any]
creature that is in this howse or in any other place. this by gods [power]
I bynde the to doe safly & here & comande & god comande the
here to staye; and not to departe untill thou off me be lycensed [and]
that thou move not out off that place where thou standest, till I by[nd]
the. And that I do bynde the, that thou breake not my cristall
stone, In the name off Ihu christ, thus I bynde the to doe. And
if thou do as god now curse the, I by his power will curse the:
for I charge the stay in that place where thou now arte. O for [the]
Aungells I desire you bynde him, that he stirre not. O god
desire the helpe me against this wycked spyritt No, and all other [do]
lyfe, lefe & commande & bynde them and Ihesus christe curse
the here to staye. Amen.

The best and most excellent wayes and Rule is/
as well for Ringes that, for Inferiours and
other Spirites, to have these names off
god wrytten in your Ring, as
followeth .

This is wrytten wythout, because the circle was to lyttle, but yt
muste be wrytten wythin the circle nexte adioyninge / the Ring muste
flatt of bothe sydes, and cleare wthout markes or flames, and as
wyde as may be gotten, and off A good thicknes .

Nota .

The Spiritt can disobay that is called into the Stone throwe
... And the makinge thereof was discouered by Luke on
after time, beinge in Anno Dni: 1567 .

st. Luke .

King Salomon /gc .

Nota .

The Stone is good, althoughe he be neuer so cleare, yf he bee
... or not cleare; also he muste be flatt on bothe sydes, and
the broder the better .

how to choose your Stone .

This is /.

This is the graving of another thistall, to call Aungells or spirit
into: But if you doe call both, then muste ye never call any spirit
into that stone you call Aungells into. And of both it is best
for you to kepe this laste next before you for the Aungells

Nota.

They be graven at any time, or any plannetts howre.

Nota.

That it is not necessary, that yo stones shoulde be consecrated
for the Aungells; but for Inferiours, they must nedes be consecrated

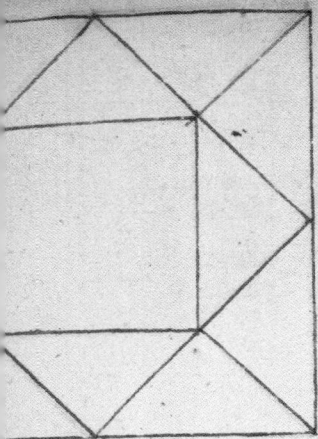
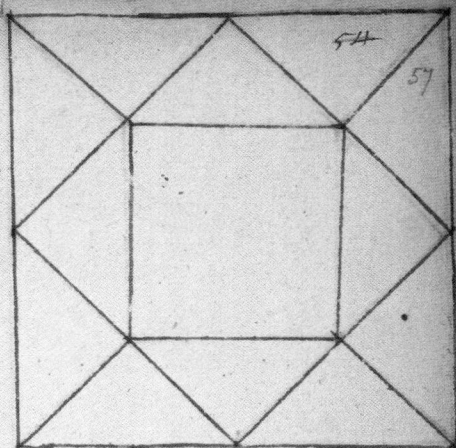
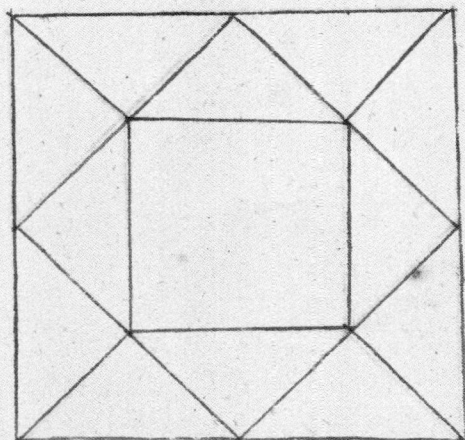

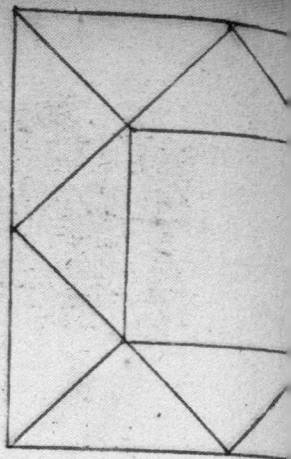

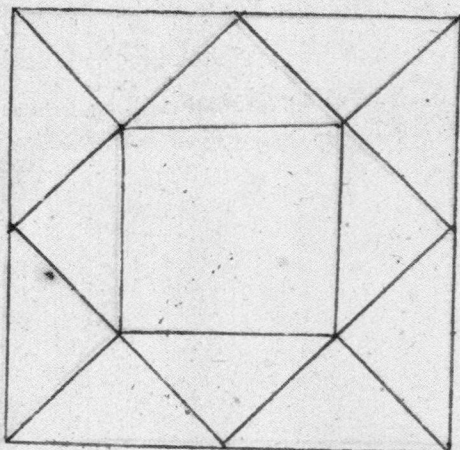

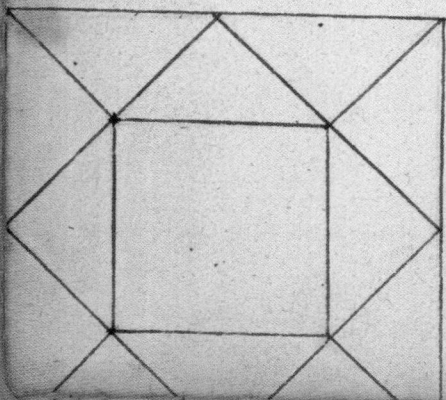

Certaine strange visions, or apparitions
of memorable note. Anno 1567.
Lately imparted unto mee for secrete
of mutch importance.

A notable Journal of an experimental
Magitian.

CC   This vision aped, on the 24 of february
at the some rising, towards the East,   { 24 february
1567.

Nº Dc 1367.

(A notable Journal of an experimental Magician.)

There apered a long blew clowd like a streike from the East
to the west, on the w. H: G went, hauing a gilt swoord in
his hand, & Jo: Dauis going after Emm with a booke couered in a stiff
role, & rapt clokes; an a payer of blarke silke netherstocke yarte,   the aparrel
& in blarke garters rose aboue the knee; hauing a veluet cap,   of H: G.
& a blarke fether; & very many, like men, running away before Em,   a neate,
kneeling and falling downe, holding vp there hand to Emme; he   & fine
followed them very cruelly, & stroke one of them, & had a crowne   gentleman.
on his heade, with a sword in his hande, most shall to be cut; and he
stroke the knye so cruelly & it fell downe on his knees to Em,
holding vp his hands; and yet he stroke Em agayne with greate
spirit, as though he would haue kylled Em; then the boye opened   Jo: his
his booke, holding yt abroade; and then they saide to the boyes   scrier.
seeing, what lacke you, & you serve sure cruelly vnto vs; but this   His booke
booke was written with blarke, which, yelowe, blew, greene, & red   displayed.
H: G: passed on with greate force after them; And at the last there
aped a fasell, Solomon, Bacon, adam, Iobe, Bacon   Assasell.
the boyes hearing who there were; Also there aped a blew clowde like   Salamon.
a man in one leg, holding vp the other. And Salomon sayd, & H.   Bacon
Gie Jo: spond rule Em; And also Iobe sayd to Jo: Eesing, Trust   Adam. Iobe.
not spirit visible or invisible, but the spirits of dead men: for   Iobe & ye skrier
they loue man more, then the other doote./   The spirits of
Necromantia. The blacke art. Sciomantia./   { S. Luke, j. }   dead men.

Omnisaij.

Also the 24. of the same monte,
Nout supra; at som set as followeth.

Jo: sawe a greate wood, hauing a greate howse in the middes of
yt with a little howse by yt most strongly buylded; hauing an Iro   24 febua.
dore, with 9 keye golds; there being written on the dore these tablets
following, [symbols] And in this howse   ☉
he sawe a chamber virgely hanged with gold, in which chamber there was
a bee of cristale which was written vpon very well, hauing many   Bookes.
braunches, with a dore on Em, as it were with 7. keye golds, in and the
remke written on yt, with in the which there ware many bookes, whereof

_The visions of Sr. Th: S. himself: as is credibly supposed. Though Mr. Jon Wood
imagins one G. H. Tempus demonstrativum revelabit._

on̄ had a chrystall rownd, and an other wth the greate syde of a ... ent̄-
warde; wth diuers other goodly bookes; this tre stode & grewe, as
in the next leafe followeth. /

Also the 25 off february at the rysing
off the sonn, these aped as followeth /
No De. 1567. /

Gill,

Jo. sawe a godden ..., wth fower corners, there being 4 Angles
standing at there corners, the losse one, on the wth mountaine these
growe a tre off blond, full off knotts spredding very brode.
These Angles had ere off them a booke off ... gold in there hand
praying, whose names ... the, as ere off them sayd to them /
Mark, Mathewe, Luke, John; who sayd wth one voyce as followeth
we kepe this tre & blessed is he y[t] shall come to it, then there
apeared a greate blacke cloude, H. G. rydyng vpon it on a whit
goste, wth a swoord in his hand; & Jo. rydyng after them on a
blacke goste, hauinge a booke in his hand / then they aped the
wode, & howse where Salamon dwelled, into the w[ch] howse H.
G. rode in; & Jo also / And toke from thence a greate sorte off
bookes; Then the Angles said to Johns hering, followe this art,
& be wise; for lurke thou hast to yt. /

Also the 25 off february at the sonn set
there aped in the west as followeth.
1567.

Firft 3. dragons flyinge in the ayre, one a grene, the third blewe, these tonghe were like speares, & had long
tayles; then Jo went after them, & the grene dragon rann
towarde them, then the boy held vp his booke, whereweall he
fell downe, & rann a way; then apeared ij bowles y were
blacke rynnyng in the ayre And H. G. going after them
hauing a booke in his hand, wth a chrystall rownd then one off them
rann at them; then he held vp his booke, & ted they rann a way.
Then Jo. mett full butt H. G. in the west. And theraped
Assafol, Salamon, Jobe, Adam, Baron, & Cornelius Agrippa
as they toke their names. Then H. G. speake to the[m], And they
sayd y they wond help them all / It speake to the[m] And they
shond lacke noe learning y we gaue. / Then sayd Adam to them
doe this sayd he / Get cleane in apparell, & be good to the
poore, & leaue swaring; and goe in a blacke robe & clote / And
mend fill none y thou sauest vs; And tell nothing thou shalt
lacke. And when Salomon biddeth you to call vs, we will obey

55.   Ars notoria spiritualis.

... Baron said, gone cleane in apparell. And so styles, especially
... a roke of blacke clothe continually; & your selfe also,
... when you ride. Raphael said they were not to tell
... things past, present, & to come. But kepe his word & feare not.
And H. G. shall doe well inoughe. /

Boud, you clenly.
Raphael. we are not to tell things past, present, and to come.

　　　Also the 26 of february at 9 of
　　　the clocke in the morning, there
　　　aped in the east as followethe
　　　　　　1567

26. febru.

First there apered a golden Egg, in the same 4 Angles
as before, with the same tre of cloud, & the Angles sayd unto
H. G. thou art blessed of god surely. As thou cast a servant
will make the asaynt. And I trust by gods helpe, you shall
..., you shall haue servante, & shall teare the as mure
... as thou shalt be able to take, & gods helpe, you shalbe to
..., dowte not. /

Angells.

　　　Nota. /

Seene by H. G. & so: on ye 14 daye of marche do
de 1567, at the sonne sett, or a little after, I knowe not so
ferther, it was about 7 of the clocke. First I, and my styles,
... a rownde fyer in the west, which sodenly vanished &
... ... Here apered annother in even weste beste
... And from them there went a greate blacke cloud
... the, which went from the weste by the norte, to the
East ponte. And on that cloud there came an extreme
number of fyer, in the place where the first fyers were
there was a greate quantitye & was mervelous red, all ye
whire tuined into gold; & some the of the fyer went towarde
the soute, soe & gods of ... a great mirracle shewed it
to me & my styles. Also the fyer was marvelous greate
& bright, & tuined into gold as before. And sodanely rasting
my eye asyde, there was a greate blacke cloude, whire
gathered into a starre ponte, into the weste & sereade
very brode into the top towarde the East being marue
lon that inclosed with fyer, hauing .6. sundry ponte as
followethe /

14. Marty. 1567

A fire .

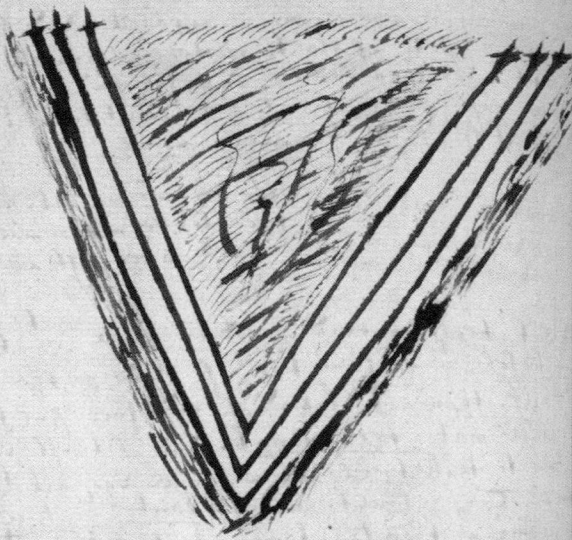

oſ blacke, hauing vnder erÿ bundle on the ſoute ſyde
ſtreike oſ gold, very bright, ẃ were incloſed ẃ greate
and aſter the litle ſtreike there apered about them 2 greate
bundles oſ golden ſtreike ẃ ſtoode about erÿ oſ the golden
ſtreike, but the bundle ẃ ſtoode vppermoſt was not ſo b
abge ẃ ſtoode belowe. There was a greate blacke clowd
betwene theſe 2 bundles ẃ about the topp oſ this indue
thingt there was a greate quantitye oſ greene, as before
apered, And betwene oſ the 5 blacke clowds as before
before there was a greate number oſ ſtrÿs, betwẏ erÿ
oſ the as before you ſee. Alſo there apered on the ſoute
ſyde oſ erÿ apen the netherſt bundle oſ gold, a ſquaſe
golden ẃll ẃ 4 corners, ẃ 4 Angles ſtanding about ÿ
at erÿ corner one, whoſe names were, Mathewe, Marke, Luk
John, being bareſoted ẃ bookes in theire hande, ther being
a greate tre oſ blood in the middle oſ the golden ẃll, ẃ
theſe paſſed by vs, 2 dogge rvnning on the grounde, whi
were ſpirites ramming from the ſoute towarde the norte
the firſt oſ thẏ was whike, ved and blacke, ẃ went leſmi
away agaïe ẃ had noe tayle, Then followed the other
dog, ẃ was all blacke, ẃ was vight againſt me, ẃ a long tayle, And when he
miſarke before ſwawen, ẃ thẏ on me, ẃ then on it agaïe
and ſoe paſſed awaye,

These Dogs had little leggs, and greate brode feete, like
unto Goosses / All w[hi]ch thinges agrete to w[hi]ch w[hi]ch in one howere /
spac[e], And sude I went from the place, all thinges vanished away. /

The Angles saide unto H. G. That he showld feare nothing. §§.
And That he had a good servaunte of Solomon, whose counsell
he showld followe; for he wowld advise hym for the best. Salomo servant
And that he showld dede w[i]th Solomon appointed hym; for he evar   to H. G.
wowld doe nothing to his hindrance / And that they wowld apeare
to hym in the element w[he]n he wowld. And that they wowld teache
hym all artes, and howe to make Bookes. /

                    Nota. /   (Ars notoria insspirata .)

Saw my Skrier sawe the 15. Daye of Marche Ao 1567 be-   15. Martij 1567.
twene 9. and 10. in the morning, as followeth. /
Fyrst 2 roundes of white, w[hi]ch passed very sodaynly away
before us on the grownde / Then there apeared in the grownde
a grays rome w[hi]ch stode still & loked uppon us / Next a face of   grey comp.
ioyned togither, w[i]thout any body, hard by the grownde & so sodainly   winges.
went into the grownde to the sightes. /
Also there did apeare a greate nuber of little thinges, like
little nuggets of christall, w[hi]ch daunsed, & staryed a good while,   little cristalls.
uppon the grownde about us, saving on the left syde. /
Also there came 2 little birde from the norte to the sonte,   Byrdes.
flying hard before little on the sonte side of us, w[hi]ch w[a]s
on the left hand. / And these 2. byrdes did flie againe fro
the sonte to the norte. Then there came another byrde from y[e]
sonte side of us, & flew towarde the norte & came
barke againe towarde us, & flewe towarde the norte againe;
& then lighted on the Sonte side of us. /
                    Nota.

Also on the said 15 daye after none, betwixt 1. and 2. after noone
I saw a greate blacke Dog, w[i]th a white long spot on his nose, the   Dogs.
like on his tayle, saving small legge, & greate gosse feete, w[hi]ch
was neither feete, blowd, no[r] bone / the greate gosse feete in whit
And at the same tyme the flewe 3. byrde fom the west to the east   Byrdes.
w[hi]ch of one of them was white, w[hi]ch had very long tayles / Also after then,
4 more byrdes w[hi]ch had long neckes & long tayles. /

Also .4. other blacke bydde comming out off the west toward
hauing long necke, & longe tayles, wᵗ greate feete, as big as there be the East

Also the same .2. other bydde fͦ the west toward to the East, as greate
winges, & long tayled, wᶜ came one on our right side, hauing noe end
All the rest wᶜ comming that we sawe at this tyme, ca
on the lift syde /

Also there came a larke from the East toward the west, wᶜ fle
very hygh', & came somewhat neale vs, before vs fare on the
somtyme more flutteryng, being continually irrestolent ryght
And after he had thus flyd a prety wyle, he came down
to the gromde, before vs fare mruelous swiftly, seming ledg le
And soe ripped into the gromde, out off sight, being very
little and romde, at his falling /

And as I came homeward, I sawe a greate brended dog,
comming toward me, And then I turned my horse, and my
horses turned his horse also / I did galoped toward them, and
whē I mett hym, he would not haue escaped ppinge, And
And then I said to him, O thou wirked & rebellious spirite
come verto me / And then I sayd O thou wirked & rebellious
spirite God confownd thee / searching as wold I drewe
out my Dagger & rast toward hym; And then he van awa
I God almty vanyshed out ext off my sight I knew not how
wᶜ were spirite, as I after pruved by the spirit off
Solomon.

Nota /

H. G. his skryer did see the .17. off Martij, ante meridi
inter .10. et .12. 2 blacke bydde flying from the south to the
norte, wᵗout heade; wᶜ were .2. Angles called Amos and
did speale sundry vngltt somde & the somd off belles, &
many other instruments; And at the last there aperd these
Toby & Gabriell in the likenesse off .2. larkes / wᶜ said after
they were commanded by H. G. as followeth /

Nota / Aᵒ Dñi 1567 /

Also the 17 of marche somewhat before 4 of the clok at after
noone there aped 2 marvelous greate Ravens, standing on the
[stone] of the same flyinge vere them, & soe flew towarde the
Southwest, did [whilest] H.G. and his [frindes] did beholde them,
[divide] them selves in 3. rowes [and] came, & fell downe by
them, & being soe commanded did [stase] & [speake] these wo[rdes]
that they did first apere like [stars] & beheste these [wordes]
them selves in to 3. rowes, because they might not knowe them
And said further, [that] they [had] staine bookes of [?] as we will
not name in kepinge in H.G. must haue [and] also gaue vb in
[?] we had none agreate while, & the most holyest we [?]
& they were these wordes /

Also there aped [half] an hower before 5. a white man in the aire
in the northwest hauing 4 fingers in his right hande a
thomb, but he had but 3. fingers in his left hand and a thomb,
his garment were of white lynnen cloth very large /
And at the same time, there aped towarde the west of them
in the [appere] a dog, also a greate [square] [?] of god /
And about 5 of the clok the same day, at after noone
as they were comming [homewarde] they went the [speicit of]
[?] along the way as they [?], before these horses a good [?]
[apoynted] to serue them, & to make many [?] bookes for them
And did of them selfe, goe into a [chrystall] stone, & H.G. [?]
in his [porkett], being apointed soe to doe, by the Angles /

Nota /

That as H.G. was a [russin] & [?] & condemning of the 4
[kinge], & [blestes] for their disobedience, Aᵒ D. 1567 22 martij inter
2 et 3. meridie there came of them selfe the Euangelist Luke
into a [chrystall] stone, & lay on the bourd, And willed me to
leave [?] the names of god, to such wirked & rebellious spirits,
offeringe them selfe to doe all thing for me, & to teach me, howe to
haue althing done by the divels, without such russing, & [?]
by the [word] & names of god, & missing, as the [?] come to me

Ravens.
Salomon.

bookes in kepinge.

H.G. haue Al[es] and they haue mind A great whyle.

Iobe ma[n] [?] tables

Iob of his owne will into A chrystall stone.

22 Martij 1567

Lukes of Luke into A chrystall stone.

done by Ang[els]

whensoever I would haue them / And I leauing the spirit of Solomon & the spirite off Iobe before / They both fell on these knees to Luke who saw them / And the wirke in sownde about the stone as fast as might be ./

Nota ./

On the 6. day off Aprill, Ao 1567 my boy went to Solomons howse in the morning, & came home to me agayne abowte 9. off the clock in the forenone, And brought me for thene abooke, wrytted by St Luke the Euangelist ./

His principal Autors, { Salomon. Iob. St Luke. Bacon. Agrippa. }

S. Lukes Gospell: Petite, et dabitur vob querite, et inuenietis; pulsate, et aperietur vobis Si ille perseuerauerit pulsans; etsi no dabit il quod amicus eius sit; propter improbitatem tam surget, et dabit illi.

S. Johns Gospell: Amen, amen dico vob siquid petieritis patrem in nomine meo, dabit vobis. Petite, et accipietis: ut gaudium vestru sit plenum.

These two Gospells; with [the] vij Psalm [the] Letany, & De profundis; com read, off these Salomonical Artists in their greates & Experiments.

(left margin notes)

Salomon and Iobe fell on there knees before Luke.

Bleath played the voyce.

A Apprt

A Boke fd Sal= mony howke, wrytyt by St Luke.

NOTES ON THE TRANSCRIPTIONS

Two transcriptions of the *Excellent Booke* and *Visions* have been provided, alongside a number of complementary texts from other sources. The modern English rendition is accompanied by a diplomatic transcription, which preserves the language, contractions and underlinings used in the manuscripts.

Significant efforts have been made to ensure the transcriptions match the layout of the manuscript, with some exceptions relating to the *Excellent Booke* and *Visions*:

First, alongside his comments, Harvey often used a number of different marginal symbols to indicate areas of interest – it would be unwieldy to include all of these in the transcription since they are legible on the facsimile itself.

Second, Harvey's copious underlining in the text has been removed from the modernised transcription for ease of reading, but retained in the diplomatic version.

Third, words that are intended to be spoken are italicised in the modernised transcription.

Fourth, some passages of *Visions* are difficult to interpret. In these cases, fidelity to the original text has been maintained, with footnotes to suggest possible readings, and glosses to elucidate on unfamiliar and archaic words.

The modernised transcription also includes some brief commentary in the footnotes, most often when archaic terms are used. Readers of the facsimiles may also have noted differences in scribal hand and orthography between the *Excellent Booke* and *Visions*. Frank Klaassen has suggested that Adrian Gilbert was the likely scribe of the *Excellent Booke*, although the circumstances in which he came to make this copy are currently unknown.

An Excellent Booke
of the Arte of Magicke

Forman – certified
By Mr. Macray
of the Bodleian
July 1868

These coloured inks must be had.

1. Notable gold to write with.[1]
2. Silver.
3. Blue.
4. Red.
5. Green.
6. Yellow.
7. Turquoise.

Great plenty of sweet powders, and perfumes.

Bleathe should a young beginner first call; although to call Assasel, it is the most noble art; whose character follows.

Note, that there is no plague so great, as to burn a spirit's name, and character: most especially, that is, if the spirit is of the air.[2]

This prayer is to be said when and before you deal with any spirit. This was revealed by King Solomon, Anno Domini 1567, on the 20 February circa 9 – 10 AM.[3]

1 The meaning of word 'notable' in this sense is obscure, but may be intended to pertain to the keeping of notes, or perhaps notae, which may refer to either recording shorthand notes, or composing magical symbols (as in the notae of the *Ars Notoria*).

2 Following this, Harvey adds: Nova methodus, et praxis magica Academici philotechni, ud Aulici | omniscij. (The new method and practice of the academic philotechnic magic of the omniscient courtiers.)

3 AM is supposed since the other experiments taking place between 9 and 10, as recorded in *Visions*, occurred in the morning – see. ff.60r *&* 61r.

AN EXCELLENT BOOKE OF THE ARTE OF MAGICKE

O God of Angels, God of Archangels, God of Patriarchs, God of Prophets, God of us sinners; O Lord be my help, that this my work may proceed in good time, to thy glory O God; and to learning, and not anything else, that I would this day have. O my God be in my tongue, that I may glorify thee in all works. Amen.

Let no evil spirit enter my mind O God, nor anything else but all to thy glory O God; for learning is all my desire, Lord thou knowest even as it was to thy servant Solomon. O Lord send me some of his good hidden work, that has not been revealed to any man. Then for that cause I desire thee O God to send it to me, that in these our last days it may be known. Amen amen, Lord, amen.

With your Pater Noster.[4]

Here begins an excellent book of the art of magic, first begun the 22nd of March Anno Domini 1567. ☉ in ♈. 11 degrees and 18 minutes, about 30 minutes after 8 o' clock, ante meridian.

[47v]

First it is good art always for the master – he that must begin this art – to leave swearing and all drunken company if he do know them. He that must work in this art must always go very clean apparelled;[5] he must always keep his promises,[6] if he makes any, and not break them;[7] and he must be good to the poor where he sees need.[8] He must always keep his skryer in clean apparel. This is the beginning to bring them to art.[9]

+

The master must also have one or two good books to call by; as after you shall here find.

4 Harvey adds: Ad Artem notoriam inspiratam. Speculum omniscium. (Inspired by the Ars Notoria. The all-seeing mirror.)

5 In marg: No { swearing | Drunkenness | Drunken | company.

6 In marg: Cleanliness | in apparel.

7 In marg: Truth in | promises.

8 In marg: Alms.

9 In marg: The skryer | well apparelled.

The first spirit that he must call must be the ruler of the dead whose name
is Assasell, and he must call him by night in the hour of ☉. And when he is
come he must require one that is under him to serve him, and if he says no,
you must not be over hasty with him, but let him go, and call him another
night.[11] Then when he is come charge him in the name of his maker,[12] that
he give you one, and then he will give you whosoever you do ask; and then
you must call one into the stone whose name is called Aosal; all this is for
the stone; and when he is come,[13] if he be not to your sight you must first
bind him to tarry,[14] and then when you have bound him, you must charge
him to appear to your own sight. And if he come not, you must go and hide
something,[15] as you think good, and charge him most straightly to go and
seek it, and to tell you in what part of the house, or field, it lies in. And when
he has told you truly, then say thus: O *thou wicked and cursed spirit,*[16] *why doest
thou fable with me, I am not one of them that must be fabled with,* and say he does
lie. Then go and hide it in a contrary place or in some water, and charge him
very straightly as follows, that he tell you where it is: and if he tells you that
it is in the water, say that you will not believe it[17] except you may see it laid
upon your dry hand, for how should you fetch it out of the water if it were
there?[18] And when it is laid on your hand as by your compulsion it may be,
then say to him: *Thou most vile and wicked spirit, this is not it, for this ring*[19] *fell
even now off my finger.*[20]

10 The numerals were evidently added to the text by Harvey, who also adds the annota-
tion 'Spirits in the stone' next to this numeral. Also in marg: I. Spirit. | Assasel, the | Ruler
of the | Dead.

11 That is to say, that when Assasel is called for the first time, the master must ask him to
provide a subordinate spirit.

12 In marg: The first time | to take his denial.

13 In marg: 2. | Aosal into the | stone.

14 In marg: Bind him.

15 In marg: Then to ap- | pear to sight.

16 In marg. Wicked and | cursed spirit.

17 In marg: Not to believe | the spirit when | he tells the truth | but to deceive the | spirit.

18 The MS. has 'I', but 'you' has been used in this transcription to ease comprehension.

19 In marg: (drawing of a ring).

20 The master here plays a game with the spirit, denying that it has succeeded in its

Nota.

That thing that you must first hide, must be a ring. And then discharge him
to his place, until you shall have need to speak with him; and if he does not
tell you the truth in those things [you ask] then straightly punish him. And
if he says *Leave punishing me and I will do it!*,[21] then say to him *Nay I will punish
thee most cruelly for this lie!* And after compel him to do it; which you by art
must do,[22] or else you shall never have anything done for you. Then you
must, after you have charged and compelled him to tell you the truth, release
him until such time as you shall need him again.

Nota.

You must never keep any spirit enclosed above twenty-four hours.[23]

3.

Then you must call another whose name is called Oriens, who is a ruler[24]
over the wicked, and when he is come command him straightly to appear
to your sight, or else that he will make the stone leap[25] three times from
the place where the stone lies. And if he will not, command him straightly
as follows: *O thou wicked,[26] cursed, vile, and rebellious spirit, why dost thou rebel
against my commandment? I charge and bind thee in the name of thy maker Jesus
Christ, and by the power of Heaven, thou cursed spirit, that thou now let the stone
stand, and appear to my sight, for I will have no nay. Therefore I charge thee by these
holy names of God,[27] that thou dost appear: Sabaoth, Adonay, Sachaell, Adonay, α et
ω and by the name Tryon, JHS, Cranton, Panton, that thou do it without any more
delay. Appear visible to my sight, and speak or write to my hearing or seeing. Thus I
charge thee to do without any stop or stay.* And when he has by your compulsion

task, and escalating the master's expectations of it. See the final nota on f.48v.

21 In marg: Punish | him for | his lie.

22 In marg: And then | compel him | to do it.

23 In marg: not past | 24 hours.

24 In marg: 3. | Oriens ruler | over the wicked. | Lucifer | belike.

25 In marg: Appear, or | make the stone leap.

26 In marg: Wicked | cursed, vile. | and rebellious spirit.

27 In marg: Jesus Christ | and by the | power of | Heaven.

appeared, say that you see a thing shadow forth in the stone,[28] which is in the wall [then say]: *And therefore appear to me and speak or write, for I will not believe, that here is any thing to my sight, except thou speak or write, and appear to my sight, and speak to my hearing: or else I will accurse thee and condemn thee by God's power, and not by my own power. Therefore I charge thee do it.* And when he has done it, then command him to give you the best book that ever was:[29] *Seeing [as] thou art the king of the spirits of the East I charge thee do it!* And when he has brought you a book in the stone to your sight, then charge him to deliver it to you, or appoint him some place where he shall lay it, and let it be done with speed: *This I charge thee to do.* And when it is come thither, if you cannot read it, then come to him again and say: *What hast thou given me? I know not whether it be good or ill. Therefore I charge thee out of hand,[30] to show me the reading and understanding of it.* And if he says no,[31] then straight away go and take

[48v] your book of calls[32] and curse him as here follows, and compel him to do it, and take no nay nor any deferring of time, but [insist] immediately to have it done without stop or stay. And when he has done it, release him into his place, until such time as you shall need him again. And in the releasing of him bind him thus, that whenever you shall call any that is under him[33] that they shall immediately come, and fulfil your mind in all things that you shall ask of them. Thus bind him to do and promise [this], and then release him,[34] but not before he has made you understand your book.

28 The original text reads 'a thing shadowe in the stone,' in which 'shadowe' is used as a verb, suggesting something indistinctly formed, which is then compelled to appear fully to the master's sight.

29 In marg: The best | book, | that ever | was.

30 In marg: If he refuses.

31 In marg: The reading | and under- | standing | of the book | de profundis.

32 Harvey adds: Unicus liber, inscienter omnium librorum.

33 In marg: Any that is | under him.

34 In marg: Promise.

Nota.

You must of force first call Assasel, and then Aosal, and then Oriens as is before said,[35] and make them find it; and continually proceed as this book shall teach, for thus you must do by art.[36]

Nota.

That when you command Oriens to lay down your book, it must be even done out of hand before you release him.[37]

Regula.

You must never call any spirit in the stone if he is invisible, but you must always hide things to make them find it;[38] and make them do things for you that you do know already to be true.

Nota.

That if any of them tell you ever so truly, that are inferiors in the stone;[39] you must never say to them that they tell true, for it is art if he is invisible to the master. For if he is visible to the master, then he knows what he has to do; for the master must straightly command him as follows, and if he does tell you ever truly, when he is to your sight or not,[40] then you must release him within the space beforesaid, and if he does lie to you then you must straightly punish him. And when he does tell you truly yet you must punish him; for then you must straightly punish him again for that lie, and command him to do another thing for you,[41] that you think very hard: and if he tells you it truly, then release him within the time aforesaid. And if he does not tell you truly, then bind him to tarry very strongly, and more strongly than you did at the first, and every day when his hour reigns then punish

---

35 In marg: The three spirits: | Asasel, 1   Aosal 2 | Oriens 3.

36 For an explanation of this rather cryptic sentence, see the rule, or regula, below.

37 In marg: Oriens, the Book.

38 In marg: Invisible | spirits not | into the stone.

39 In marg: Invisible | hardly believed.

40 In marg: If truly | ever | then released.

41 Cf. f.47v. In marg: Punish for | the lie.

him very straightly. As, if he be of the fire, then punish him[42] with stinking water, either of man or woman,[43] and put stinking things into it; and then put the stone into it and straightly command him to come forth out of the stone into the water that you did put him in, and there to tarry, until you command him to come into the stone again. And if he be of the water,[44] then take brimstone and burn it, and command him first to go into some stone for the purpose, and then put him into the burning brimstone; and that is for the punishment of them [of fire and water], reading a curse over them. And if he be of the air, then you must command him to go forth of the stone into some vile stinking mud,[45] and to tarry in it, until you do command him to go into the stone again. And if he be of the earth, then you must curse him in God's name. And then that will serve them sufficiently.[46]

Nota.

You must always in the stone never seem to believe them, however truly[47] soever they say.[48]

Nota.

That you must always use all spirits in the stone after this order and not otherwise; without dallying with them, what spirits soever they be.

Nota.

The first spirit proceeding by art must be Assasel, then Aosal[49] and then Oriens, using them as before: and after you have thus used them, you may call whom you will and make them do what you will have them.

---

42 In marg: If false then | punish him | at his hour | every day.

43 The punishment of the spirits of fire is that which immediately follows − the urine of a man or woman. In marg: Punishment | for spirits | of the fire.

44 In marg: Aqueis | sulphur.

45 In marg: Aereus.

46 In marg: Terreus.

47 In marg: You must | not believe in | the stone.

48 Harvey adds: Haud credo: quoth Derick.

49 In marg: Ut s. | { Assasel | Aosal | Oriens.

I. Nota. *Assasel's call.*

This is the call to have Assasel, which is the first [spirit] you must call.[50] First
your prayer before the call must be thus, being said with a good heart: O
God of Angels, O God of Archangels, O God of Patriarchs, God of Prophets; God of us
sinners, I, most wretched sinner, do desire thee to be my help that this spirit, Assasel,
may now come and fulfil my will. O Lord be my help and assistance that I may, by
thy power, call him, and not by my own power. O Lord, Lord (sic) be merciful unto me
and [grant] that the prayer of a sinner may be heard in thine ears. And I charge thee
Assasel that thou do prepare thyself to come when I call thee, which shall be this night.
O Lord be my help.

And saying your Pater Noster and Credo, then call him as follows:

O thou spirit Assasel, which art a living and loving spirit to the commandments of
God,[51] I charge thee in the name of Jesus Christ, that thou do appear here visibly to
my skryer, here without any delay. I conjure and command thee, and by God's power
constrain thee that thou do appear here and do my commandments without any more
[49v]
stay. O God be my help that this spirit Assasel may come and obey thy holy words
which proceed forth of my mouth. O thou loving Assasel, I charge thee that thou do
come and appear here quickly without any stop or stay.[52] By these holy names of God
I here constrain thee: Sabaoth, Adonai, JC, Tetragrammaton, and by this holy name[53]
Aglaon, Laiagin, Lialgagie, that thou do appear here quickly,[54] that thou do appear
here to my sight or to the sight of my skryer. I conjure thee and I command thee that
thou appear here without any delay or tarrying. Thus I charge thee to do, and say it
to this charge at the latter day, and therefore, as thou fear thy God and maker, that
thou appear here presently and fulfil my desire, as may be expedient for a sinner. O
thou spirit Assasel, or what other name soever thou have, I charge thee to appear here,
which art the Keeper of the Dead Bones,[55] presently, without any stay, and then I will

---

50 In marg: Oratio ad | vocandum | Assasel.

51 In marg: Vocatio | Assaselis | in nomine | Jhesu | Christi.

52 In marg: Loving Assasel.

53 In marg: Exercitum Domini | Sabaoth Adonay. Opposite marg: [Gr: tetragram | ma-
ton.] | Aglaon | Laiagn | Lailgagie.

54 In marg: It would be | El, which in He- | brew is God, or | Lord.

55 In marg: Assasel, or | what other | name soever | thou hast.

release thee.[56] And until thou hast done it, I will never leave calling [thee] until thou do come, by the power of God. Therefore I charge thee, and command and constrain thee to come and appear for I am the creature of God. O Lord be my help that this spirit Assasel may come.

And this is the call for him.

And if Assasel will not come and obey you, say this sentence as follows.

O thou spirit Assasel, who hast been taken for a noble spirit and king, and [yet] I cannot find it in thee, by thy disobeying of God's word: Therefore I shall do as art wills me. O thou wicked and rebellious spirit, that rebels against God's power,[57] I, by God's power, accurse thee and excommunicate thee, and deprive thee and condemn thee for thy disobedience. Therefore God the Father accurse thee, and condemn thee, and of thy office deprive thee.[58] God the Son accurse thee, God the Holy Ghost accurse thee and condemn thee. All Holy Angels accurse thee, all Patriarchs and Prophets accurse thee, and I, wretched sinner, by God's power do accurse thee for thy disobeying. Therefore I charge thee come. Amen.

When Assasel is appeared, then say this bond unto him.

O thou king Assasel, who art appeared here in this stone, I bind thee by God's power, not to depart until thou be licensed by me. Wherefore I charge thee that thou do not depart in pain of endless damnation: and I command thee that thou lay thy hand upon this book,[59] being a testament (which must be laid under the stone which he will [50r] have his hand upon), and swear that thou will not depart until thou be licensed by me,[60] and that thou shall fulfil all my desires.

56 In marg: The keeper of | dead | bones.
57 In marg: Wicked and | rebellious spirit.
58 In marg: Accursed and | excommunicated.
59 In marg: Sub poena | eternal | damnations.
60 In marg: (Drawing of a book) Swear | upon a | testament.

And then bind him straightly not to depart by the words before said, and then call him again into the same stone,[61] although he seems to be there. And then if it be a delusion, then the true spirit will come. And then read the curse before upon him, whatsoever he were, that first appeared in Assasel's name, and command him to come into the stone of punishment, and burn him with fire, whatsoever he be that so comes in Assasel's name. And although it be Assasel,[62] yet read the call as often as you did before, and if it be he, then there will nothing come. Then you must ask [for] one of the best spirits of a dead man that ever was in the world to teach you all manner of arts appertaining to learning and hidden knowledge.[63] And never release him, until he has given you the spirit of him that you do ask. Then release him until such time you have need of him again. And this is all that appertains to the first you call, which is Assasel. And after you have once called him by his call and order, you may still occupy him at will.[64]

The call of Aosal. 2.

You must call him by day in any hour you will, but most commonly in the hour of ♄.[65] And this is his call to call him.

O thou spirit Aosal, I conjure thee and I charge thee that thou appear here in this crystal stone,[66] presently to the sight of myself or my skryer, and fulfil my intent holy. O thou wicked and rebellious spirit Aosal,[67] or of whatever name soever thou be, it is thee I call, and I charge thee by the power of thy maker, that thou here presently appear without any delusions, craft or subtlety or deceit to me or any creature living or dead. O thou spirit Aosal, or what other name soever thou be, I conjure thee by these holy names of God, that thou appear here to me presently and to nobody else: Athanatos,

---

61 In marg: If it be a | delusion or a | mocking | spirit.

62 In marg: The stone of | punishment.

63 In marg: One of the best spirits of a | dead man, to | teach all | Arts.

64 Harvey adds: Spiritus pantechus: vel daemon pansophus. (A spirit for all arts, or demon for all knowledge)

65 In marg: Diursius et | Saturnius spiritus.

66 In marg: Aosal, his call.

67 In marg: Wicked and | rebellious spi- | rit.

Cyrios, Tyon, Cranton, Panton, Agla, Sabaoth, Adonay,[68] and by all other names, that are not for me to rehearse, I charge thee to come and appear here in the pain of thy endless damnation, without any stop or any stay, or any hurt to me, or anybody, for I will not stay. Therefore I charge thee do my will quickly, for if thou do dissemble with me I shall accurse thee.[69] Therefore come and do it presently without any stay.

Then say thy Pater Noster and Credo.

If Aosal does not appear, say then as follows.

[50v]

O thou Spirit Aosal, I conjure and command thee, that thou do not disobey as thou hast done. And for thy disobeying I do here accurse thee, and by God's power condemn thee, and deprive thee by these holy words that follow: Lama Sabathany, and by Soth-er, Sabaoth, Lagin, Halgali, by Ameson,[70] I charge thee to come and appear,[71] and for thus disobeying, I by these holy names do accurse and excommunicate thee, thou wick-ed and rebellious spirit. The curse of God the Father light on thee. The curse of God the Son come to thee. The curse of God the Holy Ghost come to thee. Therefore I charge thee to come away, without any delay or illusion or any deceit or craft, but immediate-ly to appear here in this crystal stone, or else I will read as follows, the great maledic-tion. Therefore I charge thee to come away, and for thy first disobeying I say again, All holy Angels curse thee and condemn [thee], and for thy disobeying excommunicate and deprive thee. Therefore I charge thee to come away, and I shall by God's help release all these bonds from thee. If you do not appear I shall go further in thy constraints and to God's glory: therefore I shall charge thee to come away, for I shall never leave torment-ing thee and calling thee, until thou come away. Therefore thou wicked spirit I charge thee come. And therefore if thou do not come before I have read this three times over, or as soon as I have done it, I shall proceed in further constraint to thee, therefore without any delay come presently, for this I will but three times go over.

68 In marg: [Gr: athanatos, | kurios, | tuon, | cranton] | I think the words | be [Gr: kra-tion pan | ton], which is | omnipotens | Agla. | Sabaoth, Adonay | exercitus Deus.
69 'Dissemble' here means to make a false show, or feign.
70 In marg: Lamara badani, | cunc me reliqsuiti.
71 In marg: [Gr: soter] serva- | tor. | Sabaoth exer- | citum | Lagin | Halgali | Ameson]

And when you have read this latter constraint, which is not the general curse for Aosal, then in the third reading say that: *I am now in the last reading. I will proceed further to thy constraint.*

This is a general sentence and malediction for Aosal.

O thou cursed and rebellious spirit Aosal, which has so rebelled against God's commandment, for altogether I will now by God's power torment thee. O thou cursed spirit that hast rebelled, God curse thee and anament thee, God the Holy Ghost curse thee, thou wicked and rebellious spirit,[72] *God the Holy Ghost constrain thee, thou most vile and rebellious spirit.* Then you must take brimstone and burn it to his constraint. And in the burning of it say: *Even as this burns, I trust God will burn thee, for destroying his most holy word. All holy Angels accurse thee and anament thee, and from thy power put thee. I desire that all Prophets accurse thee, you most vile and rebellious spirit. All heavenly motions accurse thee to God's glory and to thy restraint deprive thee. All holy churches fall on thee. All the inferior spirits, by the power that they have, curse thee and make thee their footstool. And I will never leave reading this, until thou either appear or be deprived. All creatures of this world curse thee. The holy testament curse thee, without thou presently appear. I desire God to hear my voice.*

Then say your Pater Noster.

This is if he appears quietly at the first [call]. His bond:

[51r]

And if he do appear at the first [call], then here follows his bond.

I bind thee thou spirit Aosal, which art a spirit of much obeying to God's word, here to stay until I by God's power release thee, and I command thee that thou do all my will, that I shall bid thee, and if thou dost disobey and go [from] here, I will accurse thee. Therefore, by these words, I bind thee: Lyfy, Lefe, Lorvando.[73] *Amen.*

---

72 In marg: anament | anathematise.

73 In marg: Life, lefe | Lorvando.

If Aosal does not appear without much
constraint as before, then here follows
his bond when [he] is come.

O thou spirit Aosal which art now come into this stone by much constraint, I here bind
thee as a most vile and wicked spirit, to do all my commandments. And the curse of
God and all holy Angels light on thee, thou rebellious spirit. Therefore here I bind thee
and charge thee not to depart without my leave and licence, thou most vile and wicked
and rebellious spirit. And I charge thee here to stay until thou hast done all my com-
mandments. And then presently make him do as before is said.[74]

3. *The summoning of Oriens, and all four kings.*

And this note, that as it were dividing it in four parts, you
must say it [for] three days, kneeling devoutly, before you
call him in the morning: thy part towards thy quarter; and
the other parts each of them to each other quarter of the
world, and turning your face accordingly.

In the name of God: O Lord prosper my work, that I now this time begin, to a good
intent, to thy glory I trust, and no hurt of my neighbour. O God be my help, that this
king N. do appear in this crystal stone when I call him.[75] *O God be merciful unto*
me and send me well to prosper in it, and in all other good works, that I shall now
or at any time take in hand to thy glory, O God, or not. In the name of God, O thou
King Oriens,[76] *I command thee to prepare thyself to come when I shall call thee in*
this crystal stone, and I charge thee not to delay with me; for here in God's name I
summon thee. O holy Angels be my help that this King N. may come and do my will
when I shall call him. O you King N. here I bind thee to prepare thyself to come when
I shall call thee. Therefore I charge thee delay with me nothing at all, neither now nor
any other time. O holy Prophets be my help, O God be my help, O holy Angels be my
help, that this spirit King N. may come to me when I shall call him. O Lord, to good

[51v]

74 E.g. the finding of the hidden ring as detailed earlier (f.47v).

75 In marg: N.

76 In marg: To thy glory | or not.

intent I do it, to thy glory, his constraint and my commodity. O holy and holiest of all be my help, and here thou King N. I charge and lay to thy charge to prepare thyself to come when I shall call thee. Lord prosper me, God prosper me, all holy Angels prosper me, all Prophets and Patriarchs prosper me in this my good intent and purpose that I begin. Amen, Lord, amen, and grant it I beseech thee.

The general call for the four kings, especially for Oriens.

In the name of God, amen. O thou King N., who art of the east (or N.), I charge thee here to come without any delay, without hurt[77] to me or any other creature living or dead, thus I charge thee today, or without any blustering or blowing, crying or roaring, to any man's hearing, speaking or talking, to any man's hearing (sic), wherever thou go. I charge thee do it not, nor casting down trees, or hurting any house, grass, corn or cattle.[78] This by God's power I charge thee, thou do not, for if thou do I will by God's power marvellous[ly] cruelly curse thee, anament and torment thee. O thou N. which art of the east (or N., or what quarter soever thou be of), Oriens (or N.), I call thee hither to come, and do my intent without doing any of these hurts I told thee or without this hurt thou wicked and rebellious spirit, which is, I charge thee in the name of God the Father that you open no ground that shall do hurt, and further thou[79] open thou no ground whether it hurt yea or nay. And that thou cause no great floods to rise that shall do any kind of hurt,[80] and further that thou make no waters rise, whether it hurt yea or nay.[81] This, furthermore, by God's power I charge thee thou do not, that thou make no great wind rise that shall blow down any house or hurt any kind of thing by land or by water.[82] And that thou shall not hurt or throw down any castle, I charge thee furthermore by God's power. This I charge thee: that thou do make no great rain of water or hailstones or any hurts that out of that element shall come.[83]

---

77 In marg: Hurt | blustering | blowing crying | roaring.

78 In marg: Casting down | trees | hurting houses.

79 In marg: Open no ground.

80 In marg: Cause no floods.

81 In marg: Raise no waters.

82 In marg: No great winds.

83 In marg: No rain or | hailstones.

Furthermore I charge thee thus to do: that thou make no great lightning[84] that shall burn or hurt any creature, house, or hay, corn or grass, trees or hedges, or melt any kind of lead, tin, or any other kind of metals or hurting of churches or any other kind of timber,[85] or any kind of stones, or any kind of writing, or anything that appertains to man. This I charge thee thou do not. O thou King Oriens (or N.) of what quarter

[52r] soever you be, I charge thee here without any delay to appear, either visible to me or my skryer, without any hurt or delay, and this further in the way I charge thee: that thou, nor any of thy men who be under thee, do hurt any kind of thing, or any of the kings or other subjects or servants. This I charge you all to do,[86] and in your places to rest those which I call not, and as for thee, O thou King N., I charge thee here to come, and to fulfil my intent generally in all things. O thou King N., and rebellious king, I charge thee here to come without any delay, stop or stay. O thou most wicked king N., I charge thee in the pain of eternal damnation,[87] that thou here come presently and fulfil my intent without any hurt or harm to me, or any thing that here is unnamed. This I charge thee to do and presently to come and not to stay. This I charge thee to do, and ere thou depart to fulfil my intent, O thou King N. I charge thee presently: not I by my own power do command thee but by the power of God the Father, Son and the Holy Ghost, here to come presently, O thou N. of what quarter soever thou be, I charge thee to appear presently for I will not be delayed of thee. I conjure and command thee, I conjure and charge thee, I conjure and I constrain thee here to appear within the space of an hour, or the space of twenty minutes in this crystal stone, and fulfil all my intent. This on pain of eternal damnation I charge thee, and that thou shall not come in the brims of the stone, and so to deceive me, but to come full in the midst of the stone to the sight of me or my skryer without any delay.[88] Thus I charge thee by the power of God the Father omnipotent and by the power of α et ω, that you presently appear here without any stop or stay or danger to me or to any other creature.[89] This I charge thee to do, and not to hurt any kind of thing that is of me unnamed, although it is said that thou hath power of the earth, the sea, and trees.[90]

84 In marg: No lightning.
85 In marg: Melting of lead | hurting of chur- | ches.
86 In marg: Kings, their | subjects | servants.
87 In marg: Sub pena eter- | nal damnations.
88 In marg: Full into the | midst of the | stone.
89 In marg: α et ω.
90 In marg: power of the | earth, the sea | and the trees.

O Lord grant this be done that this spirit. N., and king of the East may appear without any hurt to thy glory O God, it must be or else not, in the name of God the Father, the Son and the Holy Ghost I desire it. Amen.

**If he does not appear, say then this general
sentence that follows, for any of the four kings.**

O thou wicked and thou rebellious spirit, thou stout[91] and thou vile spirit, for thy disobeying, here by God's power I curse thee, and by God's power I will of thy kingdom and power deprive thee, as a most wicked and rebellious spirit, and an inferior then thou will be. The great curse and great malediction of God light upon thee for thy disobeying, and if thou do not presently come thy privation will I read: God curse thee and deprive thee, all holy Angels curse thee and with their power deprive thee, all Patriarchs and Prophets curse thee and with their prayer deprive thee as a most wicked, vile and rebellious spirit. God confound thee for thy disobeying of these holy words. O thou N., who was once a king: by the time I have read this three times, and thy deprivation three times more, thou wilt be another inferior and a footstool to the worst. Therefore I charge thee to come away quickly if thou do love to save thy kingdom: for God's name I will not be disobeyed. All heavenly and earthly motions curse thee and deprive thee. I will say no more. If thou wilt not come presently thy deprivation will I read, or if another has bound thee in the name of God, that thou canst not come,[92] that then thou send presently one of thy servants to speak to my own hearing, that I shall stay until thou be released and so send me word that thou wilt presently come so soon as thou art released. O Lord prosper my work. Amen. Lord, amen.

[52v]

These are the names of the four kings:
Oriens, AMAIMON, Paymon, ÆGIN.[93]

---

91 Stubborn.
92 In marg: If he be bound | to send his vicar | for a time to | excuse him.
93 In marg: Oriens East | Amaimon West | Paimon North | Aegyn South

If he comes not presently, then say as follows,
which is the deprivation of the king.

O thou Oriens (or N.), who was once a king and now by God's power shall be a
footstool to the inferiors, I will here by God's power deprive thee if thou do not come
presently before I have read this deprivation. God deprive thee and condemn thee, thou
rebellious spirit N., all thy motions deprive thee, thou rebellious spirit N., God the
Father deprive thee, thou rebellious spirit N., God the Son deprive thee N., God the
Holy Ghost deprive thee, and condemn thee, and curse thee, thou wicked and rebellious
spirit N. O thou rebellious spirit, who was of great power when time did thee serve,
now of no power I trust thou shall be, and so thy disobeying all creatures living, with
the power they have deprive thee, curse thee, and underfoot condemn thee, and for thy
disobeying, thou spirit N., God deprive and condemn thee, and the Four Evangelists,
Mark, Matthew, Luke, and John condemn thee and deprive thee for thy great disobey-
ing.[94] *All the power that is amongst the good souls be against thee. Amen, and amen.*

Nota.

If they do not appear or otherwise fulfil your commandment in everything
after you have read your deprivation two times, then write either one or all
their names, according as you have to do with them, and put brimstone next
to the letters of their names. Fold it up together and put stinking clay about
the paper, and so burn it and in the burning say this: *Even as this burns so I do*
desire thee, O God, that these Kings N. may burn in hellfire as this does here for their
disobeying. And then by art you should say your prayers, and so go forth of
your workhouse for the space of[95]

[53r]   **When he is come, his bond.**

O thou spirit N., who art appeared here in this stone, I bind thee here to tarry and nev-
er to depart until thou be licensed by me. I bind thee here to stay and to tarry and not
to depart on the pain of eternal damnation, and by the power of Jesus Christ that thou
fulfil all my commandments, and here remain without doing any hurt to any creature,

94 In marg: Tobyel | Uryel.
95 There appears to be a discontinuity in the text here.

living or dead, without breaking my stone, or any other hurt[96] that thou canst imagine or devise. All this I by God's power charge thee to do. Furthermore, [I charge thee] that at no time [thou] suddenly fear me in my coming to thee,[97] or my skryer, or any other that in this place shall come. This I charge thee to do. Amen, Lord, amen.

A licence for the four kings to depart.

I conjure thee, thou King N., that thou go to thy place without any hurt or harm of any thing that I have named, or not named. Therefore I charge thee avoid and to depart without any hurt doing generally to any kind of thing, but quickly to depart until I shall call thee again. I do not discharge thee but release thee. Therefore avoid, Sathan, avoid I charge thee. Amen.[98]

A general call for all spirits into the stone.

I conjure and command thee, thou spirit N. (what name soever thou otherwise have), that thou here appear by the same name presently I call thee and not to disobey it. I charge thee by these holy names: Tetragrammaton, Micon, Messyas, Sother, Emanuel, Sabaoth, Tyon, Cranton, Panton, Createn, Panton,[99] that thou here obey by these holy names and words of God, I conjure thee here to appear presently without any delay and fulfil all my commandments, amen. O thou spirit N. I charge thee to come and appear, as thou fearest God, and hopest to be saved. O thou king of the East,[100] I command thee to discharge this spirit N., if he be under thee, and not to keep him from me. This I charge thee to do. O thou king of the West, I command thee to release this spirit N. from thee, if he is in thy dominion, by God's power I charge thee. O thou king of the North, I charge thee and command thee to let this spirit N. go from thee and come to me presently. If he do not come I shall accurse you all four kings and him also. O thou king Ægin which art of the South, or of what quarter soever thou be of, I charge thee

96 In marg: Without hurt | without brea- | king the stone.

97 That is to say, the spirit is constrained not to cause fear to the master or his assistant.

98 In marg: Avoid Sathan. It should be noted that in the licence for the kings to depart 'avoid' is used in its obsolete sense of 'withdraw' or 'depart.'

99 In marg: Fortassis [Gr: ton | panton craton] una | tereus et | gubernars.

100 In marg: as thou fea- | rest god and | hopest to be | saved.

to release this spirit N. from thee if he be in thy dominion or else I shall do to thee as afore I said if amongst you all he come not; and for his disobeying I will accurse him and you all. Therefore I conjure thee here to appear thou spirit N., without any delay or illusion. O holy Angels I desire you be my help, that this spirit may appear in this crystal stone. Amen.

Generalis Sententia.

The malediction and great curse of God the Father, the Son and the Holy Ghost light on thee thou spirit N. And all holy Angels curse thee, all Patriarchs and Prophets curse thee, all children and immortals curse thee, all men and women in this world curse thee, all grass and cattle curse thee. Therefore, I charge thee come, O thou wicked and rebellious spirit N. I command thee to appear in this crystal stone, without any delay or deferring of time. O thou spirits of the air I charge you, that none hold this spirit N. but that he may come and do my commandment in all things both now and forever. And if he does not appear here presently, the curse of God and the Holy Ghost come to him. Therefore I charge thee, come away.

A general bond.

I bind thee thou spirit, that appeared in this crystal stone, that thou do not disobey my commandments but do all things for me that to thy office appertain. And more, to here I bind thee not to release nor go away till I do release thee by the same bond I bound thee [with]. Therefore, I charge thee here to remain until thou have fulfilled all my commandments, for I will use art toward thee, and nothing but art, and all spirits, therefore here stand, I charge thee, in this crystal stone.

A license general for all spirits to depart, whatsoever they be, out of the stone.

O thou spirit which has fulfilled all my commandments, now I charge thee to depart to the place where God has appointed thee, until I shall call thee again. And if thou do not depart, God curse thee. Therefore avoid thou wicked spirit N.

No good spirit will tarry longer than he is commanded, nor no longer than twenty-four hours if he be bid go.

The art how to call any spirit out of one   [54r]
crystal stone where he is invisible into another
crystal, to make him appear visible to all men's
sights. And this is the prayer that before your
work [is] *begun, must be said.*

O God be my help in this my beginning, that I may have the victory over this spirit N., that I intend to call, whose name is N., that he may appear in this crystal stone when I shall call him in the name of God, amen. O God be my help that he may appear when I shall by thy power call him, and that he may not resist in any thing to rule that I shall ask of him. O holy Angels I desire you be my helps, that this spirit N. may appear when I call him visible to my sight and to all men's sight that he shall look on. O God speed me well in this, my enterprise, that he may come and appear visible unto me, and unto all men that shall look on, without fraud, guile or any kind of deceit, but quietly and peaceably here to appear without hurt to me, or to any thing visible or invisible, or to any thing moveable or immoveable.

O thou spirit N., I conjure and I charge thee that thou prepare thyself here to appear when I shall read the call following, without stop or stay or any kind of deceit, but peaceably here to come. O Lord God, grant that neither this spirit N., nor any other spirit may have the power to put any illusion into my mind but they may come without putting any illusions into my mind or any creature's mind that is living. O thou spirit N., I charge thee in the name of Jesus Christ, and as thou hopest to be saved at the dreadful day of judgement that thou appear here presently when I shall read thy call as follows. O God be my help in these my enterprises that I may bring them to good effect, and perfect end. And grant O Lord that this spirit N. may appear presently when I shall read the call that follows. Amen, Lord, amen.

Nota.

That after you have twice said this prayer afore written, then you must put a little brimstone into the fire, and hold the stone [in which] the spirit appears invisible over it, in the smoke thereof, and a little to touch two or three times the flame thereof with the stone, and then say as follows:

O thou spirit N., who art in this crystal stone, if thou do not appear presently to my sight thou seest thy punishments, and worse than this. Therefore, delude not with me for I will use art with thee.[101]

[54v]   Then must you say your prayer again, and then proceed in your work.

> *Here begins the call for visibility: to make*
> *any spirit, that is invisible in any stone, to*
> *appear in another stone, visible to all*
> *men's sights.*

In nomine patris, et filii et spiritus sancti. Amen.

Then say your Pater Noster and your Credo, and then say:

O thou spirit N., I command thee to come into this stone, visible unto my sight. I charge thee, as thou hopest to be saved, that thou come forth of that stone and into this stone, visible to my sight and to all men's sight, without any hurt doing to me, or to any creature living or dead beast. I charge thee that thou do hurt no kind of thing, and I charge thee that thou hurt no grass nor corn upon pain of eternal damnation. And I charge thee in the name of Jesus Christ, and do command thee that thou do hurt no tree, nor hedge nor no manner of timber that is built or unbuilt. I charge thee thou spirit N., in the name of Jesus Christ, that thou hurt no manner of house that is standing or that is about to be built in the pain of thy confusion, and that thou hurt no kind of thing that ever of God was suffered to be made. Furthermore, I charge thee that thou open no ground, nor no lofts, nor no chests, beds, boards, stools, frames, walls, stone, irons, or any other kind of thing that is of me unnamed or named. That thou shall not

---

101 In Harvey's hand: *tex repete.*

hurt any kind of thing nor stir any kind of thing, nor put any kind of body in pain. Furthermore this I charge thee in the name of Jesus Christ, that thou hurt no kind of church, castle, or tower, or any other kind of thing. In the name of Jesus, I charge thee thou spirit N., or any other kind of spirit that is, was or shall be, that you do no kind of hurt, nor melt no kind of lead, nor tin, nor any other kind of metal. In the name of Jesus Christ, I charge you do it not, nor any other kind of thing: I charge you all in the name of Jesus Christ, that you make no great wind that shall blow down or hurt any kind of thing by land or by water. I charge you all in the name of Jesus Christ that you make no kind of lightnings that shall burn or destroy any kind of thing living or not. I charge you in the name of Jesus Christ, that you make no great rain, or hail that shall hurt any kind of corn, cattle or grasses, or any other kind of thing. And that you make no kind of stones of fire in the air to hurt any kind of thing living or dead or any kind of thing. I charge you spirits all, and especially thou spirit N., that thou make no great floods of water to hurt any kind of thing by sea or land, any bridges, or any other   [55r] kind of thing. And now, I charge thee in the name of Jesus Christ's sake, that thou, nor no other kind of spirit, do come near this house to hurt me or it, or any other creature in it, but that thou come peaceably into this crystal stone, (and then you must put on your stone). God grant that all these, my words, may be fulfilled, I conjure and command thee thou spirit N., that thou presently appear in this crystal stone, visible to my sight, for I will take no nay. I conjure and by God's power compel thee, thou spirit N., that you presently appear here in this crystal stone visible to my sight, without any kind of hurt that ever was, or may be imagined by any wicked spirit. O thou spirit N., I charge thee presently here to appear, without any stop or stay, into that crystal stone that there stands, visible to my sight and to all men's sight that on it shall look. O thou wicked and rebellious spirit, I conjure and command thee by these holy names of God, that thou presently here appear: + Agla − Micon + Messias + Sother + Emanuel + Sabaoth + Emmanuel + Agla + And by all these holy names of God, amen, that thou presently here appear, thou wicked and rebellious spirit N., without any stop or stay, delusion or delay, here to appear visible to all men's sights. O thou spirit N., I conjure and command thee and charge thee on pain of eternal damnation, that thou here presently appear in my sight in this crystal stone, appointed for thee that thou may appear here, thou spirit N., to my sight and all men's that on thee shall look in pain of endless damnation. I charge thee without any delay, stop or stay, but meekly and quietly here to appear thou spirit N., and that I may with my eyes see thee. O Lord grant that these my words may be of much truth. Amen, Lord Jesus Christ, amen I beseech you.

If he does not appear visible,
say this sentence.

O thou wicked and rebellious spirit N., God the Father curse thee for thy disobedience, God the Son curse thee for rebellion, God the Holy Ghost curse thee for thy disobeying of these holy words. The curse of the eternal living God light on thee, thou wicked and rebellious spirit N., for thy disobeying. All holy Angels curse and condemn thee, thou wicked and rebellious spirit N., for thy disobeying. All children of men and women curse thee, and by their power deprive thee, thou wicked and rebellious spirit N., for thy great disobeying. Lyalglla curse thee, Sother curse thee, Sabaoth curse thee, Shadrach, Meshach and Abednago who lay burning in the oven of fire curse thee, and by God's power were delivered from it. I curse thee by the power that Moses did strike the earth [with] in the land of Egypt, and there were innumerable flies amongst men [55v] *and beasts, and as truly as the water turned into blood so truly I curse thee with all my power, and deprive thee by the power of God for thy great disobeying of his words. Amen, Lord I beseech thee.*

Nota.

If he come not visibly to your sight with the first call being twice read, then you must read the last call or sentence three times, and then leave.

The deprivation if he does not
appear visible.

O thou wicked and rebellious spirit, God the Father curse thee, God the Son curse thee, God the Holy Ghost curse thee, with their power deprive thee for thy disobeying of these holy words. All Angels and Archangels curse thee and condemn thee and, for thy disobeying of thy office, deprive thee. Lord I beseech thee that this rebellious spirit N., may be deprived for his disobeying. All Saints curse thee and deprive thee, thou rebellious spirit N. for thy disobeying, all Patriarchs and Prophets curse thee for thy disobeying, and deprive thee, I by God's power, not by my own, do curse thee, condemn thee and for thy great rebellion deprive thee. Amen, Lord I beseech thee.

**The bond when he is come to your
sight to bind him.**

I bind thee thou spirit N., which art appeared here in this crystal stone seen to my sight, that thou do not depart out of this crystal stone until thou be licensed by me and that thou shall tarry here without any hurt doing to me or to any other creature, or fearing any creature that is in this house or in any other place.[102] This by God's power I bind thee to do: Lyfy + Lefe + Lurvando + God command thee that thou come not out of that place where thou standest till I bid thee. And that I do bind thee that thou break not my crystal stone, in the name of Jesus Christ, this I bind thee to do. And if thou do, God now curse thee. I, by his power, will curse thee. Therefore I charge thee stay in that place where thou now art. O holy Angels, I desire you bind him that he start not. O God, I desire thee help me against this wicked spirit N., and all others. Lyfe + Lefe + Lurvando + bind thee, and Jesus Christ constrain thee here to stay. Amen.

The best and most excellent way and art is
as well for Angels, for inferiors and other spirits,
to have these names of God written in your stone,
as follows.

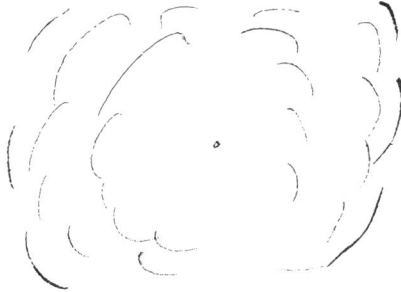

This is written without, because the circle was too little, but it must be written within the circle next adjoining: your stone must be flat on both sides, and clean, without cracks or stains, and as large as may be gotten, and of a good thickness.

102 Fearing used here in the sense of 'causing fear to.'

Nota.

No spirit can disobey that is called into the stone thus engraved; and the markings thereof were discovered by Luke on Easter time,[103] being in Anno Domini 1567.[104]

Nota.

No stone is good, although it be never so clean, if it be thin or not clear; also it must be flat on both sides, and the broader the better.[105]

[56v] This is the engraving of another crystal, to call Angels or spirits into. But if you do call both, then you must never call any spirits into that stone you call Angels into. And of both it is best for you to keep this last next [to, or] before you for the Angels.

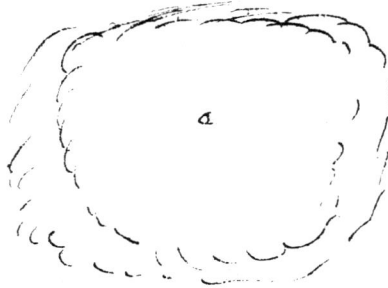

Nota.

They may be graven at any time, or any planet's hour.

Nota.

That it is not necessary that your stone should be consecrated for the Angels; but for inferiors, they [the stones] must never be consecrated.

103 In marg: St. Luke
104 Harvey adds: King Salomon &c.
105 Harvey adds: How to choose your stone.

Forman – certified   [47r]
By Mr. Macray
of the Bodleian
July 1868

These coloured ynkes must be had.

1. Notable gould to write wyth. |
2. Sylver. |
3. Blewe. |
4. Redd. |
5. Greene. |
6. Yelowe. |
7. Turkeses. |

Great plenty of sweate powders, and perfumes.

Bleathe, should a young beginner first call; although to call Assasel |
yt is the most noble Arte; whose charact followethe.

Note, that there is noe plauge so greate, as to burne a spyritt's name, and |
characte: most espetially, that is, yf the spyritt be of the Ayer.[1]

This prayer is to be sayde when and before |
you deale wᵗʰ any spyritt; This was revealed |
by kinge Solomon, Anno Dni 1567, die 20 Febru- |
arij circa 9. 10. |

O god of Aungelles, god of Archaungelles; god of Patriarches, god of |
Prophettes, god of us sinneres; O lord be my helpe, that this my worke may |
proceede in good tyme, to thy glorie O god; and to learninge, and not Aut
else, |

1 Harvey: Nova methodus, et praxis magica Academici philotechni, ud Aulici | omniscij.

that I would this day have. O my god be in my tongue, that I maye |
glorifie the in all workes. Amen. ꝛ ꝛ ꝛ ꝛ ꝛ ꝛ

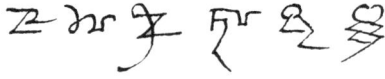

Let noe evyll spyritt enter my mynde o god, nor nothinge else but all |
to thy glorie o god; for learninge is all my desier, lord thou knowest |
even as yt was to thy servaunte Solomon; O lorde sende me some of |
his good hidden worke, that hath not been revealed to noe mann. Then for |
that cause I desier the O god to sende yt mee, that in these our laste |
daies yt may be knowen. Amen Amen, lord Amen, wth yor Pater noster. |²

[47ᵛ]　　　　　　　　Here beginneth an excellent booke of the Arte of |
magicke, first begoone the xxiith of Marche |
Anno Dni 1567. ☉ in ♈. 11 gradus. 18 mi. aboute |
30. mi. after 8. of the clock, Ante Meridian. |

First it is good Arte allwayes for the m^r, that must begin this Arte, to |
leave swearinge, and all drounken company, if he do knowe them; he |³
must allway goe very cleane appariled that must work in this arte; he |⁴
must allway keepe his promises, yf he makes any, and not breake them; |⁵
he must be good to the poore where he seeth neede.⁶

He must allway keepe his Skrier in cleane apparell; this is the begin- |
ninge to bring them to Arte.⁷

+

The m^r must also have 1 or 2 good bookes to call by; as after you |
shall here fyende.

2 Harvey: (Ad Artem notoriam inspiratam.) Speculu~ omniscium.
3 In marg: No { swereinge| Dronken~es | Dronken | company.
4 In marg: + clenlynes | in apparell
5 In marg: Truthe in | promis.
6 In marg: Almes.
7 In marg: The skryer | well apparelled.

I.[8]

The first Spyritt that he must call, must be <u>the ruler of ye deade</u> |
whose name is <u>Assasell</u>, and he must call him by night in the hower of |
☉. And when he is come he must requier <u>one that is under him to</u> |
serve hym, and yf he say noe, ye must not be over hasty wth him, but |
let him goe, and call him an other nighte; And when he is come |[9]
charge him in the name of his maker, that he give you one, And then |
he wyll, whome ye doe ask. And then you must <u>call one into ye stone</u> |
whose name is called <u>Aosal</u>; all this is <u>for the stone</u>; and when he |[10]
is come, yf he be not to your sighte, you must first bynde hym to |[11]
tarry, And then when you have bounde hym, you must charge him to |
appeare to yor owne sighte, And yf he come not, you must goe and |[12]
<u>hyde some thinge</u>, as you thinke good, and charge him most streightly to |
goe <u>seeke it</u>, and tell you in what place of the howse, or fyeld it lyeth in, |
And when he hath towld you truly, then say thus: O thou wicked |[13]
and cursed spyritt, whie doest thou fable with mee I am noone of |
<u>them that must be fabled wth</u>, and say he doeth lye. Then goe |
and <u>hyde in A contaire place or in some water</u>, and charge hym |
very straightly as followeth, that <u>he tell you</u> wheare it is: and yf |
he tell you that it is in the water, say that you will not beleeve it |[14]
excepte you may see yt layde uppon the drie hande, for howe shoulde |
I fetch it out of the water yf it weare there, And when it is |
layde on the hande as by yor compulsio~ yt may bee, Then say to him, |
Thou most vyle and wicked spyritt, this is not he, for this ringe |
fell even nowe of my finger.

8 Harvey: spirits in the stone. In marg: I. [Harvey: ^{spirit.}] | Assasel, the | Ruler of the |
Deade.

9 In marg: the first time | to take hys denyall.

10 In marg: 2. | Aosal into ye | stone.

11 In marg: Bynde hym.

12 In marg: then to ap- | peare to sight.

13 In marg. Wicked and | cursed spiritt

14 In marg: n. not to beleve | the spyry~t whe~ | he telleth truth | but to belye ye | spyrytt.

Nota.

That thinge that you must first hyde, muste be a ringe. | [15]
And then discharge him to his place, untyll you shall have nede to |

[speake.]

[48r] speake wyth him; And yf he doe not tell you the truthe in those thinges |
then streightly punnish him, And yf he say leave punishinge me and | [16]
I wyll doe it; then say him nay I wyll punnishe the most cruelly |
for this lye; and after compell him to doe yt; which you by Art must | [17]
doe, or else you shall never have nothinge done for you. Then |
you must after you have charged and compelled him to tell you þe |
truthe, release him untyll suche time as you shall nede him againe.

Nota.

You must never keepe any inclosed above 24. howeres. [18]

3.

Then you must call another whose name is called Oriens, wʰ is | [19]
a ruler over the wicked, and when he is come commaunde him straight- |
ly to appeare to yoʳ sighte, or else that he wyll make the stone to | [20]
leape 3 tymes from the place where the stone lyeth, and yf he |
wyll not, commaund him straightly as followeth. O thou wicked, | [21]
cursed, vyle, and rebellious Spyritt, why doest thou rebell against my |
comaundemente. I charge and bynde the in the name of thy maker |
Jhesus christ, and by the power of heaven, thou cursed Spyritt, | [22]
that thou nowe let the stone stande, and appeare to my syghte for I |
wyll have no nay. Therefore I charge the by these holy names |
of god, that thou doest appeare, Sabaoth, Adonay, Sachaell, Adonay, |

15 In marg: (drawing of a ring)
16 In marg: Punnishe | hym for | hys lye.
17 In marg: And then | compell hym | to do yt.
18 In marg: not paste | 24 howers.
19 In marg: 3. | Oriens ruler | over ye wicked. | Lucifer | belike.
20 In marg: Apeare, or | make the stone leape.
21 In marg: wicked | cursed, vyle, | and rebellious spyritt.
22 In marg: Jhesus Christ | and by the | power of | Heaven.

α et ω and by the name Tryon, JHS, Cranto~, Panto~, that thou do yt |
wythout any more delay, apeare visible to my sighte, and speake or |
write to my hearinge or seeinge. Thus I charge the to doe w^thout |
any stopp or stay. And when he hath by yor compulsio~ appeared |
say that you see A thinge shadowe in the stone, wch is in the wall, |
And therefore appare to mee and speeke or wrighte, for I wyll |
not beleve, that here is any thinge to my syghte, except thou speake |
or wryte, and appeare to my syghte, and speake to my hearinge: o^r |
else I wyll accurse the and condemne the by gods power, and not |
by my owne power. Therefore I charge the do yt. And when he |
hath doon yt, then comaund him to give you the beste booke, that | ²³
ever was, Seinge thou art the kynge of the spyritts of the Easte |
I charge the doe it, and when he hath brought you A booke in the |
stone to yor sighte, then charge him to delyver yt to you, or appointe |
him some place where he shall lay it. and let yt bee doon wth speede. |
This I charge the to doe. And when it is come thither, yf you can |
not reade it, then come to him againe and saye what haste thou given |
mee? I knowe not whether yt bee good or yll. Therefore I charge þ^e | ²⁴
out of hande, to showe me the readgine and understandinge of yt, and | ²⁵
yf he say noe: Then straightwayes goe and take your booke of calles | ²⁶

[and]

and curse him as here followeth, and compell him to doe it, and take no naye | [48v]
nor noe deferringe of tyme, but im~ediatly to have yt doon w^thout stopp |
o^r staye, and when he hath doon yt, release him into his place, untyll |
suche tyme as you shall need him againe. And in the releasing of him |
bynde him thus, that whensoever you shall call any that is under hym, | ²⁷
that they shall imediately come, and fulfyll your mynd in all thinges, |
that you shall aske of hym; thus bynde him to doe and promis, And | ²⁸

23 In marg: The beste | booke, | that ever | was.
24 In marg: yf he refuse.
25 In marg: The readinge | and under-| standinge | of the booke | de profundis.
26 Harvey, at foot of page: (Unicus liber, ins~ter omnium librorum.)
27 In marg: Any that is | under hym.
28 In marg: Promis.

then release him, and not before he hath made you <u>understand your</u> |
booke.

Nota.

You must of force first call Assasel; and then Aosall; and the~ Oriens |²⁹
and as ys before sayde, and make them fiende it; and continualy procead |
as this booke shall teache, for thus you must <u>do by Arte</u>.

Nota.

That when you comaunde Oriens to laye down yor booke, it must |³⁰
bee even doon <u>out of hande</u> before you release him.

Regula.

You must <u>never call any Spyritt</u> in the stone, yf he be <u>invisible</u>, But |³¹
you must allway <u>hide thinges</u> to make them fynde yt; And make |
the~ <u>do thinges</u> for you that you doe knowe allready <u>to be true</u>.

Nota.

That yf any of them do tell you never soe truly, <u>that be inferiours in ye</u> |³²
<u>stone</u>; you must never say to them that they tell true, for <u>it is Arte</u> |
yf he be invisible to the m^r, for yf he <u>be visible to the m^r, then he</u> |
knoweth what he hath to doe; for he must streightly comaund him as |
followethe. And yf he do tell you <u>ever truly</u>, when he be to your |³³
sight or not, then you must release him wythin the space beforesayde |
And yf he do <u>lye to you</u>, then you must <u>straightly pu~nishe</u> hym. |
And when he doth tell you truly, yet ye must pu~nishe him; for then |
ye must streightly pu~nish him, againe for that lye, and comaund |³⁴
him to doe another thinge for you, <u>what you thinke very harde</u>: And |
yf he tell you yt truly, then release him wthin the tyme aforesayde; and |

29 In marg: [Harvey: the three spirites] | Asasel, I | Aosal 2 | Oriens. 3
30 In marg: Oriens ye Booke.
31 In marg: Invisibile | Spyritts not | into ye stone.
32 In marg: Invisible | hardly beleved.
33 In marg: yf truly | ever | the~ releasid]
34 In marg: Punnish for | the lye.

yf he do not tell you truly, then bynde him to tarry very styrongly, |
and stronglier then you dyd at the first, And every day when his |
hower raigneth then pu~nishe him very streightly. As yf he be of |
the fier: then punnishe him wth stinkinge water, either of man or wo- | ³⁵
man, and put stinkinge thinges into yt; and then putt the stone into |
yt, and streightly comaund him to come forth out of the stone into |
the water that you did putt him in, and there to tarrye, untyll you doe |

[comaund]

comaund him to come into the stone agayne. And yf he be of the water | ³⁶   [49r]
then take brimstone and burne yt, and comaund him first to goe into some |
stone for the purpose, and then putt him into the burninge brimstone; and |
that is for the punnishment of them, redinge A curse over them. |
And yf he bee of the Ayer then you must comaund him to goe forth | ³⁷
of the stone into some vyle stinkinge mudd, and to tarry in yt, un- |
tyll you doe comaund him to goe into the stone againe. And yf he |
be of the Earthe then you muste curse him in gods name. And the~ | ³⁸
that wyll serve them sufficiently.

Nota.

You must allway in the stone, never seeme to beleve them, howe trulye | ³⁹
soever they saye.⁴⁰

Nota.

That you must allwayes use all spyritts in the stone after this order |
and not otherwise; wythout dallyinge with them, what spyritts soever |
they bee.

35 In marg: yf false the~ | punnish hym. | at hys hower | every daye.
In opposite marg: Punishment | for spyr.tts | of ye fier.
36 In marg: þe Aqueis | sulphure
37 In marg: Si Aereus.
38 In marg: Si terreus
39 In marg: you must | not beleue in | the stone.
40 Harvey: Haud credo: quoth Derick.

The first spyritt proceadinge by Arte, must be <u>Assasel</u>; then <u>Aosall</u> | [41]
and then <u>Oriens</u>, usinge them as before: And after you have thus |
used them, you may call whome you wyll, and <u>make them doe whatt</u> |
you <u>wyll have them</u>.

I.

Nota. *Assasell call.*

This is the call to have Assasel, wch is the first you must call. | [42]
First your prayer before the call, must be thus, being sayd wyth |
<u>A good harte</u>. O god of Aungells, O god of Archaungells; O |
god of Patriarches, god of Prophetts; god of us synners, I |
most wretched synner, doe desier the to be my helpe that this spiritt |
Assasel, may nowe come and fulfill my wyll. O lord be my helpe |
and assistaunce, that I may by thy power call him, and not by ^{my} owne |
power. O lord lord (sic) be mercifull unto mee, and that the prayer of |
A synner may be hearde in thine eares. And I charge the Assasel |
that thou doe prepare thy selfe to come when I call the, which |
shall be this nighte; O lorde be my helpe. And sayinge your |
Pater noster, and Credo, then call him as followethe.

O thou spyritt <u>Assasel</u>, which arte a lyvinge and lovinge spyritt, to | [43]
the comaundementes of god, I charge the in the name of Jhesus christ, |
that thou doe appeare heare <u>visiblie to my skrier</u>, here wythout any |
delay, I coniure and comaunde the, and by gods power constrayne |
the that thou doe appeare heare, and doe my comaundementes wthout |

[any]

[49v]   any more staye. O god be my helpe that this spyritt Assasel may come |
and obey thy holy wordes which procedeth forthe of my mouthe. O thou |
lovinge Assasel, I charge the that thou do come and appeare heare quick- | [44]
ly without any stopp or stay: By these holy names of god I here |

41 In marg: ut s. | { Assasel | Aosal | Oriens
42 In marg: Oratio ad | vocandu~ | Assasel
43 In marg: Vocatio | Assaselis | in nomine | Jhesu | Christi.
44 In marg: Loving Assasel.

constrayne the Sabaoth, Adonai, JC. Tetragramaton, and by this holye | 45
name Aglaon, Laiagin, Lialgagie, that thou doe appeare here quickly | 46
that thou doe appeare here to my syghte, or to the sighte of my |
skrier. I coniure the and I comaund the, that thou appeare here |
w^thout any delaye, o^r tarryinge. Thus I charge the to doe, and |
say yt to this charge at the latter day, And therfore as thou fearest |
thy god and maker that thou appeare here p^rsently, and fulfill my |
desier, as may be expedient for A sinner. O thou spyritt Assasel |
or what other name soever thou have, I charge the to appeare here w^ch | 47
art the keper of the deade bones p^rsently, w^thout any staye, and | 48
then I wyll release the, And untyll thou have doon yt, I wyll |
never leave callinge, untyll thou doe come, by the power of god. |
Therefore I charge the, and comaund and constrayne the to come and |
appeare for I am the creature of god. O lord be my helpe that |
this spiritt Assasel may come. And this is the call for hym.

And yf Assasel wyll not come and obey you, | say as followeth this sentence:

O thou spiritt Assasel, which hast been take for a noble spyritt |
and kinge, and I cannot fynde it in the, by thy disobeyinge of gods |
worde: Therefore I shall doe as Arte wylleth mee. O thou |
wicked and rebellious spyritt, that rebelleth against gods power, I | 49
by gods power accurse the and excomunicate the, and deprive the | 50
and condemne the for thy disobedience. Therefore god the father |
accurse the, and condemne the, and of thy office deprive the:
God the sonn accurse the, god the hely ghoste accurse the and |
condemne the. All holy Aungells accurse the, all Patriarches |

45 In marg: exercitum D~ni | Sabaoth Adonay. Opposite margin: [Gr: Tetragram |
    − − −.] | Aglao~ | Laigin | Laigagie.
46 In marg: yt woulde be | El, wch in he- | brewe is god or Lord.
47 In marg: Assasel or | what other | name soever | thou haste.
48 In marg: þ^e kep~ of | deade | Bones
49 In marg: wicked and | rebellious spiritt.
50 In marg: accurse and | exco~icates.

and Prophetts accurse the: and I wretched synner by gods |
power doe accurse the for thy disobbayinge; Therefore I charge |
the come. Amen.

***When Assasel is appeared, then saye |
this bonde unto hym.***

O thou kinge Assasel, wch art <u>appeared here in this stone I</u> |
bynde the by gods power, not to departe untyll thou <u>be lycensed</u> by |
mee: wherfore I charge the that thou doe not departe in payne of | ⁵¹
this endless damnation: And I comaund the that thou lay thy hande |
uppon this booke beinge <u>A testamente</u> (wch must be layde under the |
stone wch he wyll laye his hande uppon) And <u>sweare that</u> thou wyll | ⁵²
[not departe]

[50r] not departe untyll thou be lycensed by mee: And that <u>thou shalle</u> |
<u>fulfyll all my desyer</u>. And then <u>bynde him straightly not to dep~te</u> |
by the wordes before sayde: And then call him againe into þe same | ⁵³
stone, althoughe he seeme to be there. And then yf yt be <u>a delu-</u> |
<u>sion</u>; then the <u>true spyritt</u> will come. And then <u>read the curse be-</u> |
fore uppon him whatsoever he weare, that first appeared in Assasel's name |
and comaund hum to come into the stone of pu~nishmente, and <u>burne him</u> |
<u>wth</u> |
<u>fyer whatsoeveer</u> he bee that soe commeth in Assasel's name, And although | ⁵⁴
yt be Assasel, yet reade the call soe often as you dyd before, and yf |
it be he, then there will nothinge come, Then you must aske one of the |
<u>beste spyritts of a deade man, that ever was in the worlde, to teache</u> | ⁵⁵
<u>me all maner of Artes apperttayninge to learninge and hid knowlede</u>. |
And never release him, untyll he have given <u>you the spyritt of him</u> |
<u>that you</u> doe aske. Then release him until suche tyme you have |
need of him againe. And this is all that apparteyneth to the |

51 In marg: sub poena | eternal | dam~ations.
52 In marg: (Drawing of a book) Sweare | uppon a | testamente.
53 In marg: yf yt be a | delusion or a | mockynge | spyrytt.
54 In marg: þe stone of | punishmente.
55 In marg: one of ye best | spyritts of a | deade man, to | teache all | Artes.

first you call, which is Assasel. And after you have ones called |
him by his call and order, you may still occupy him at wyll.|⁵⁶

The call of Aosal. 2.

You must call him by day in any hower you will, but most comonly in |⁵⁷
the hower of ♄. And this is his call to call him.

O thou spyritt Aosal, I coniure the and I charge the, that thou appear |⁵⁸
heare in this cristall stone, pʳsently to the sight of myselfe, oʳ my skrier, |
and fulfill my intent holy. O thou wicked and rebellious spyritt Ao-|⁵⁹
sal, oʳ of whate name soever thou bee, it is the I call, and I charge |
the by the power of thy maker, that thoue here pʳsently appeare wᵗʰout |
any delusions, crafte, or subtylty or deceipt to me or any creature li-|
vinge or deade. O thou spyritt Aosal, or what other name soever |
thou bee, I co~iure the by these holy names of god, that thou ap- |
peare here to me pʳsently, and to no body els, Athanatos, Cyrios, Tyon, |⁶⁰
Cranton, Panton, Agla, Sabaoth, Adonay, and by all other names, that |
ar not for me to rehearse, I charge the to come and appeare here |
in the paine of thy endles damnation, wᵗʰout any stopp or any staye, |
oʳ any hurte to me, oʳ any boddy, for I will not staye; Therefore |
I charge the do my will quickly, foʳ yf thou doe dissemble wᵗʰ me, |
I shall accurse the, Therefore come and do yt pʳsently without |
any staye; Then say thy Pater noster, and Credo.

56 Harvey: Spiritus pantechus: vel daemon pansophus.

57 In marg: Diursus et | ♄ius spirit~s.

58 In marg: Aosal, his call.

59 In marg: wicked and | rebelleous spy- | rytt.

60 In marg: [Gr: athanatos, | kurios, | tuon, | cranton] | I think ye wordes | be [Gr: kra-
tion pan | ton], which is | o~ipotens | Agla. | Sabaoth, Adonay | exercitu~ D~us.

Yf *Aosal doe not appeare, say then as followethe.*

O thou spiritt Aosal, I coniure and comaund the, that thou doe not |
disobey as thou hast doon, And for thy disobeyinge I doe here accurse |
the, and by gods power condemne the, and deprive the by these holy |
wordes, that followethe. Lama Sabathany, and by |[61]

[Sother,]

[50v] Sother, Sabaoth, Lagin, Halgali, and by Ameson, I charge the to come and |[62]
appeare, and for thus disobeyinge, I by these holy names doe accurse |
and excommunicate the, thou wicked and rebellious spyrytt. The curse of |
god the father lighte on the, the curse of god the sonn come to the |
the curse of god the holy ghost come to the, Therefore I charge the to |
come awaye, w^{th}out any delay o^r elusion, o^r any deceiyt or craft, |
but immediately to appeare here in this cristall stone, or else I will |
reade as followeth, the greate maldiction; Therefore I charge the to |
come awaye, And for thy first disobaying I say againe, All holy |
Aungells curse the and condemne, and for thy disobaying excommuni-|
cate and deprive the. Therefore I charge the to come away, and |
I shall by gods helpe release all these bondes from the. Yf you |
doe not appeare I shall goe further in thy constraynts and to gods |
glory: Therefore I shall charge the to come awaye, for I shall never |
leave tormentinge the and callinge the, untyll thou come awaye: There-|
fore thou wicked spyritt I charge the come: And therfore yf thou do |
not come before I have redd this 3 tymes over, or as sone as I have |
doon yt, I shall proceade in farther constraynte to the, therefore |
w^{th}out any delaye come presently, for this I will but 3 tymes goe |
over. ✠ And when ye have reade this latter constraynte, which is |
not the generall curse for Aosal, then in the thirde readinge say, |
that I am nowe in the laste readinge, I wyll proceade further |
to thy constraynte.

---

61 In marg: Lamara bedai | cunc me reliqsti.
62 In marg: [Gr: soter] serva- | tor. | Sabaoth exer- | citum | Lagin | Halgali | Ameson.

This is a generall sentence and |
maledictio~ for Aosal.

O thou cursed and rebellious spyritt Aosal, wch hath so rebelled against |
gods comaundemente for altogither I will nowe by gods power tor- |
mente the. O thou cursed spyritt that hast rebelled, god curse the |
and anamente the, god the holy ghoste curse the thou wicked and | [63]
rebellious spyritt, god the holy ghost constraine the thou most vyle |
and rebellious spyritt. # Then you must take brimstone and |
burne it to his connstraynte. And in the <u>burninge of it say, even as |
this burneth, I trust god will burne the,</u> for distroyinge his most |
holy worde, All holy aungells accurse the and anament the, and |
from thy power putt the, I desier the all prophetts accurse the you |
most vyle and rebellious spyritt, All heavenly mocions accurse the |
to gods glory and to thy wrstrainte deprive the. All <u>holy chur- |
ches fall one the,</u> all the inferour spyritts, by the power that they have |
curse the and make the there foote stole. And I will never leave |
readinge this, until thou either appeare, or be deprived. All crea- |
tures of this world curse the, the <u>holy testamente curse the,</u> wthout |
thou p^rsently appeare, I desyer god to heare my voyce. # The~ |
say your Pater noster.

[This is yf]

This is yf he appeare quietly at the firste. | [51r]
His bonde.

<u>And he doe appeare at the firste, then here followethe his bonde.</u> |
I bynde the thou spyritt Aosal which art A spyritt of much obayinge |
to gods worde, <u>here to staye,</u> untill I by gods power <u>release the,</u> |
and I comaund the that thou doe all my wyll, that I shall bydd |
the, and if thou doest disobey and goe here, I will accurse |
the therfore, by these wordes I bynde the. Lyfy, Lefe, Lorvando. | [64]
Amen.

63 In marg: anamente | anathematise.
64 In marg: Life, lefe | Lorvando.

Yf Aosal doe not appeare without muche |
constraynte as before then here followeth |
his bonde when is come.

O thou spyritt Aosal which art nowe come into this stone by muche |
constraynte, I here bynde the as a most vyle and wicked spyritt, |
to doe all my comaundementes: and the curse of god and all holy |
Aungells lighte on the, thou rebellious spyritt. Therefore here I |
bynde the and charge the, not to departe wythout my leave and ly-|
cence, thou most vyle, and wicked, and rebellious spyritt. And I |
charge the here to staye, untill thou hathe doon all my co~maunde-|
mentes; and then pʳsently make him doe as before is sayde.

3.
The summoning of Oriens, and all 4 kinges. And |
this note, that as yt weare dyuidinge it, in 4 p~tes, |
you must say it 3 dayes, knelinge devoutly, |
before you call him in the morninge; thou parte |
towarde thoue quarter; and thother partes eche of |
them to eche other quarter of the worlde and |
turninge youʳ face accordingly.

In the name of God: O lord prosper my worke, that I nowe this |
tyme begyn, to a good intente, to thy glorie I truste, and no hurte |
of my neighbour. O god be my helpe, that this kinge N. do ap- |[65]
peare in this cristall stone when I call him. O god be mercifull |
unto mee, and sende me well to prosper in yt, and in all other |
good workes, that I shall nowe, or at any tyme take in hande to |
thy glorie O god or nott. In the name of god, O thou |[66]
kinge Oriens, I comaund the to prepare thy selfe, to come when I |
shall call the in this cristall stone, and I charge the not to delaye |
wyth mee; for here in gods name I summon the. O holy Aungells |

65 In marg: N.
66 In marg: to thy glory | or not.

be my helpe that this kinge N., may come and doe my wyll when |
I shall call him. O you kinge N. here I bynde the to pᵣpare thy |

[selfe]

selfe to come when I shall call the. Therefore I charge the delay wyth |
me nothinge at all, neyther nowe nor any other tyme. O holy prophetts |
be my helpe, O god be my helpe, O holy Aungells be my helpe, |
that this spyritt kinge N. may come to me when I shall call him. O |
lord to good intente I do yt, to thy glory, his constrainte and my |
comodyty. O holy and holiest of all be my helpe, and here thou |
kinge N. I charge and lay to thy charge to prpare thy selfe to |
come when I shall call the; lord prosper me, god prosper mee, |
All holy Aungells prosper me, All prophetts and Patriarches |
prosper me in this my good intente and prupose that I begyn. |
Amen, lord amen, and grante it I beseche the.

The generall call for the 4 kinges, | espetially for Oriens.

In the name of god, Amen. O thou kinge N., which art of the easte |
or N.; I charge the here to come without any delay, wythout hurte | ⁶⁷
to me or any other creature livinge or deade, thus I charge the to day |
or without any blusteringe or blowinge, cryinge or roringe, to any mans |
hearinge, speakinge or talkinge, to any mans hearinge, whether thou |
goest, I charge it doe it not, or castinge downe trees, or hurtinge | ⁶⁸
any howse, grasse, corne or cattle, this by gods power I charge the, |
thou doe not, for yf thou doe, I wyl by gods power marvaylous |
cruelly curse the, anamente and tormente the. O thou N. which |
art of the easte or N., or what quarter soever thou bee of, Oriens or |
N., I call the hither to come, and doe my intente without doinge any |
of these hurtes I tolde the or wᵗʰout this hurte thou wicked and |
rebellious spyritt, wᶜʰ is, I charge the in the name of god the father |
that thou open noe grownde that to hurte shall doe, and further thou | ⁶⁹

67 In marg: hurte | blusteringe | blowinge | cryinge | roringe.
68 In marg: castinge downe | trees | hurtinge howses,
69 In marg: open no grounde.

open thou noe grownde whether it hurte yea or naye. And that |
thou cause no greate fludes to rise that shall doe any kinde of |⁷⁰
hurte, and further that thou make noe waters to rise, whether it |⁷¹
hurte yea or naye. This furthermore by gods power I charge the |
thou doe not, that thou make noe greate wynde ryse that shall blowe |⁷²
downe any howse oʳ hurt any kynde of thinge by lande or by water. |
And that thou shalt hurte or throwe down any castle, I charge the fur-|
thermore by gods power, This I charge the that thou do make noe |
greate rayne of water or haylestones oʳ any hurte that out of the ele- |⁷³
mente shall come. Furthermore I charge the thus to doe that thou |
make noe greate ligthninge, that shall burne oʳ hurte any creature |
howse, or hay, corne or grasse, trees or hedges, or melte any kynde of |⁷⁴
leade, tynn, or any other kynde of mettayles or hurtinge of churches |⁷⁵
or any other kynde of tymber, oʳ any kinde of stones, or any kynde of |
writinge, or any thinge that ap~taineth to man. This I charge the thou |
doe not, O thou kinge Oriens or N. of what quarter soever you |
bee, I charge þe [here]

[52r]   here wᵗʰout any delay to appear ether visible to me or my skryer, wᵗʰout |
any hurte or delay, And this further in the way I charge the, that thou |
nor none of thy men that be under the, do hurte any kynde of thinge |
or any of the kinges or other subiectes or servauntes, this I charge you |⁷⁶
all to doe, and in yoʳ palces to rest those which I call not, and as fr |
the, O thou kinge N. I charge the here to come, and to fulfill my |
entente generally in all thinges: O thou kinge N., and rebellious|
kinge, I charge the here to come wythout any delaye stopp or staye. |
O thou most wicked kinge N., I charge the in the payne of eternall |⁷⁷
damnation, that thou here come pʳsently and fulfill my entente wᵗʰout |

70 In marg: cause no fludds.
71 In marg: rayse no waters.
72 In marg: no great wynds.
73 In marg: no rayne or | haylstones.
74 In marg: no lightninge.
75 In marg: melting of leade | hurting of chur- | ches.
76 In marg: kinges there | subiectes | seruauntes.
77 In marg: sub pena eter-| nal damnations.

any hurte or harme to me, o^r any thinge that heare is unnamed, This I |
charge the to doe and p^rsently to come and not to staye. This I charge |
the to doe, and er thou dep~te to fulfill my entente, O thou kinge N. |
I charge the p^rsently, and not I by my owne power do comaunde the |
but by the power of god the father, sonne, and the holy ghoste, here to |
come presently, O thou N. of what quarter soever thou bee I charge |
the to appeare p^rsently <u>for I will not be delayed of the</u>, I coniure |
and comaunde the, I coniure and charge the, I coniure and I con- |
strayne the here to appeare withi~ the space of an hower, or the space |
of 20 minutes in this christall stone, and fulfill all my entente. This |
in paine of eternall damnation, I charge the, and that thou shall not |
<u>come in the brimes of the stone, and soe to</u> deceive me, but to come |
<u>full in the midst of the stone to the sighte</u> of me or my skrier without |⁷⁸
any delay thus I charge the by the power of god the father om~ipotent |
and by the power of α et ω, that you p^rsently appeare here without |⁷⁹
any stopp or stay, or daunger to me or to any other creature. This |
I charge the to doe, and not to hurte noe kynde of thinge that is |
of me unnamed, althoughe it is sayce that thou <u>hath power of</u> |
the <u>earthe, the sea, and trees</u>, O lord graunt this be doon þ^t |⁸⁰
this spyritt, nomina, and kinge of the easte may appaeare wthout any |
hurte to thy glory o god yt must be or els not, in the name of god |
the fathe^r, the sonn, and the holy ghoste I desyer yt. Amen.

Yf he doe <u>not appeare</u>, say then this generall |
sentence that followeth, for any of the 4 kinges.

O thou wicked and thou rebellious spyritt, thou stoute, and thou vyle |
spyritt, for thy disobayinge here by gods power I curse the, and by |
gods power <u>will of thy kingdome and power deprive the</u>, as a most |
wicked and rebellious spyritt, and a~ inferiour then that thou bee |
the greate curse and greate maledictio~ of god light uppon the for |
thy disobayinge, and if thou doe not p^rsently come, thy privation will |

78 In marg: full into the | midst of the | stone.

79 In marg: α et ω.

80 In marg: power of the | earth, the sea | and ye trees.

I reade: God curse the and deprive the, all holy Aungells curse |
the, wth there power deprive the, all Patriarches and Prophetts |
curse the, and wth there praier deprive the as a most wycked, |
vyle, and rebellious spyritt. God <u>confounde the</u> for thy disobayinge |

[of]

[52v]   of these holy wordes. O thou N., wch was once a kinge, and by that tyme I |
have redd this 3 tymes, and thy <u>deprivatio~</u> 3 tymes more thou wylt be ano~ |
inferior^e, and a <u>footestole to the worste</u>. Therefore I charge the to come awaie |
quickly, yf thou doe <u>love to save thy kyngdome</u>, for <u>gods name</u> I wyll |
not <u>bee dysobayed</u>, all heavenly <u>and earthly motions</u> curse the and deprive |
the, I wyll say noe more, yf thou wylt not come p^rsently, thy deprivatio~ |
wyll I reade, or yf an other have <u>bownde the in the name</u> of god, that |^81
thou canst not come, that then thou <u>sende p^rsently one of thy servauntes</u> |
to speake to my owne hearinge, that I shall stay untyll thou be released |
and so sende me worde thou wylt p^rsently come so soone as thou arte re- |
leased. O lord prosper my worke. Amen. Lorde amen.

These are the names of the 4 kinges:
Oriens, AMAIMON, Paymon, ÆGIN.^82

Yf he come not p^rsently, then say as follows |
wch is the deprivation of the kynge.

O thou Oriens o^r N., which was once a kinge, and nowe by gods powe^r shalt |
nowe be a <u>footestole to the inferiours</u>, I wyll here by gods power deprive |
the, yf thou doe not come presently before I have redd <u>this deprivatio~</u>. |
God deprive the and condemne the thou rebellious spyritt N., All thy |
<u>mocions deprive</u> the thou rebellious spyritt N., God the father deprive the |
thou N. rebellious spyritt, god the sonn deprive the N., god the holy |
ghost deprive the and condemne the, and curse the thou wicked and |
rebellious spyritt N., O thou rebellious spyritt which was of great powe^r |
when tyme dyd the serve nowe of noe powe^r I truste thou shalt bee |

81   In marg: yf he be bounde | to sende his vicar | for a tyme to | excuse hym.
82   In marg: Oriens East | Amaimo~ West | Paimon North | Ægin South

and soe thy disobayinge all creatures livinge, wth the power they have |
deprive the, curse the, and under foote condemne the and for thy |
disobayinge thou spyritt N., god deprive and condemne the and the |
4 Evangelistes, Marke, Mathewe, Luke, and John, condemne the and | ⁸³
deprive the for thy great disobayinge. Tobyell and Uriel conde~ne | ⁸⁴
and deprive the for thy disobayinge, All the power that is amongst |
the good sowles be against the. Amen, and amen.

Nota.

Yf they do not appear, o^r otherwise fulfill yor comaundement in every |
thinges after you have red yor deprivatio~ 2 tymes, then wryte eyther |
one or all there names, according as you have to doe wyth them, and |
put brimstone next to the letters of there names, And foulde yt upp |
togither, and put stinkinge claye about the pap~ and so burne yt and |
in the burninge say this. Even as this burneth so I do desier the o god, |
that these kinges N. may burne in hell fier, at this dothe here, for |
there disobayinge; and then by Arte you shoulde saye yor prayers, and |
soe goe forthe of yor worke howse for the space of |

[when]

When he is come, his bonde.

[53r]

O thou spyritt N., which art appeared here in this stone, I bynde the |
here to tarrye, and never to dep~te until thou bee lycenced by me, I bynde |
the here to stay and to tarry and not to dep~te in the paine of eternall /
damnation, and by the power of Jhesus Christ, and that thou fulfill all |
my comaundementes, and here to remayne without any hurte doinge |
to any creature, lyvinge, or deade, wythout breakinge my stone, or | ⁸⁵
any other hurte, that thou canst imagyn or devise: All this I by gods |
power charge the to doe; furthermore that thou at noe tyme sode~ly |
feare me in my cominge to the, or my skrier, or any other that in this |
place shall come. This I charge the to doe. Amen lord Amen.

83 In marg: Evangelists.
84 In marg: Tobyel | Uryel.
85 In marg: wythout hurte | wythout brea- | kinge þ^e stone.

A lycence for the 4 kinges to departe.

I coniure the thou kinge N., that thou goe to thy place wthout any |
hurte or harme of any thinge that <u>I have named, o^r not named</u>. |
Therefore I charge the avoyde, and to departe wthout any hurte |
doinge, generally <u>to any kynde of thinge</u>, but quickly to departe |
untyll I shall call the agayne, I doe not discharge the but release |
the, Therefore <u>avoyde Sathan</u>, avoyde I charge the. Amen.[86]

A generall call for all spyritts |
into the stone.

I coniure and comaunde the thou spiritt N., <u>what name soever thou</u> |
<u>otherwise have</u>, that thou here appeare by the same name presentlye. |
I call <u>the</u> and not to disobay it, I charge the by these holy names: |
Tetragrammaton, Micon, Messyas, Sother, Emanuel, Sabaoth, Tyon, Cranton |[87]
Panton, Creaton, Panton, that thou here obay by these holy names and |
wordes of god, I coniure the here to appeare p^rsently wythout any delay, |
and fulfill all my comaundementes, Amen. O thout spyritt N. I charge |
the to come, and appeare as thou fearest god, and hopest to be saved |[88]
O thou kinge of <u>the Easte</u> I comaunde the to <u>discharge</u> this spiritt N., |
yf he be <u>under the</u>, and <u>not to kepe him from me</u>. This I charge the |
to doe. O thou kinge of the <u>weste</u>, I comaunde the to release this |
spiritt N., from the, yf he is in thy dominion, by gods power I charge |
the. O thou kinge of the <u>northe</u> I charge the and comaunde the to |
let this spyritt N. goe from the, and come to me presently yf he doe |
not come I shall <u>accurse you all 4 kinges</u> and him also. O thou kinge |
Ægyn which art of the South or of what quarter soever thou be of |
I charge the to release this spyritt N. from the yf he be in thy dominio~ |
or else I shall doe to the, as afore I sayde, yf amongst you all he |
come not, And for his disobayinge I wyll accurse him, and you all ther- |

[fore]

86 In marg: Avoyd Sathan.
87 In marg: fortassis [Gr: ton | panton | craton] o~ma | tereus et | gubernars | s~ .
88 In marg: as thou fea- | rest god and | hopest to be | saved.

therfore I co~iure the here to appeare thou spyritt N., wythout any delaye | [53v]
or elusio~, <u>O holy Aungells</u> I desier you be my helpe, that this spyritt |
may appeare <u>in this cristall stone</u>. Amen.

Generalis Sententia.

The maledictio~ and greate curse of god the father, the son~ and the |
holy ghoste lighte on the thou spyritt N., And all holy aungells curse |
the, all Patriarches and Prophetts curse the, all children and Im~ortals |
curse the, All men and women in this world curse the, all grasse and |
cattle curse the, therefore I charge the come O thou wicked and rebellious |
spyritt N. I comaunde the to appeare in this cristall stone, wthout |
any delay or deferringe of tyme, O thou spyritts of the Ayre I |
charge you, that none howlde this spyritt N., but that he may come |
and doe my comaundemente in all thinges both nowe and forever, |
And yf he doe not appeare here p^rsente, the curse of god and the holy |
ghoste come to hym. Therefore I charge the come awaye.

A generall Bonde.

I bynde the thou spyritt, that ap~ed inn this cristall stone, that thou |
doe not disobay my comaundementes, but doe all thinges for me, that |
to thy office appertayneth. And more toe here I bynde the not to |
release nor goe away tyll I do release the by the same bonde I |
bownde the, Therefore I charge the here to remaine untyll thou have |
fulfylled all my comaundementes, for I <u>wyll use Arte towarde the,</u>
<u>and nothinge but Arte, and all spyritts</u>, Therfore here stande I |
charge the in this cristall stone.

A lycense generall for all Spyritts to |
departe, whatsoever he be, out of þᵉ ſtone.

O thou spyritt which haste fulfilled all my comaundementes, nowe |
I charge the to departe to the place where god hath appointed |
the, untyll I shall call the againe; And if thou doe not dep~te |
god curse the, therefore avoyde thou wicked spyritt N.

Nota

Noe good spyritt will tarry longer than he is comaunded, nor |
noe longer then 24 howers yf he be bydd goe.

[54r]

The Art how to call any ſpyritt out of one |
Christall ſtone where he is invisible into anotheʳ |
Christall to make him appeare visible to all mens |
ſightes; and this is the prayer that before youʳ |
worke begun, muste be ſayde.

O god be my helpe in this my beginninge, that I may have þᵉ victory |
over this spyritt N., that I intende to call, whose name is N., that he |
may appeare in this christall stone when I shall call him in the name |
of god, Amen. O god be my helpe that he may appare, when I shall |
by thy power call him, and that he may not resiste in no thinge to rule |
that I shall aske of him, O holy Aungelles I desier you be my |
helpes, that this spyritt N., may appeare when I call him visible to |
my syghte, and to all mens syghte that he shall loke on. O god |
spede me well in this my enterprise, that he may come and appeare |
visible unto me, and unto all men that shall loke on, wᵗʰout fraude, |
gayle or any kynde of deceipte, but quyetly and peacably here |
to appeare without hurte to me, oʳ to any thinge visible oʳ invisible, oʳ |
to any thinge moveable oʳ immoveable.
O thou spyritt N., I coniure and I charge the that thou pʳpare |
thy selfe here to appeare when I shall reade the call followynge, |
wythout stopp oʳ staye, or any kynde of deceipte, but peaceablye |
here to come. O lord god graunt that this spyritt N., nor noe |

other spyritt may have the power to putt any elusio~ into my mynd |
but they may come wythout any elusɔons putting into my mynd |
oʳ any creatures mynde that is lyvinge. O thou spyritt N., I |
charge the in the name of Jhesus Chrɪst, and as thou hopest to bee |
saved at the dreadfull daie of iudgemente that thou appeare here |
pʳsently when I shall reade thy call as followethe. O god be my |
helpe in these my enterpryses that I may bringe them to good |
effecte, and p~fecte ende. And graunte O lorde that this spiritt |
N. may appeare presently when I shall reade the call that follow- |
ethe. Amen, lorde Amen.

Nota.

That after you have 2 sayde this prayer afore written, then you |
must putt A lyttle brymstone into the fier, and holde the stone, the |
spyritt appeare invisible over it in the smoke thereof, and a lyttle |
to touche 2 or 3 tymes the flame thereof with the stone, and then |
say as followethe.

O thou spyritt N., wᶜʰ art in this cristall stone, if thou do not appeare |
pʳsently to my syghte thou seethe thy punnishmentes, and worse then this |
therefore delude not wyth me, for I wyll use Arte with the,[89]

[Then must]

Then must you say yoʳ prayer againe, and then proceade in yoʳ worke. [54v]

*Here beginneth the call foʳ visible; to make |
any spyritt, that is in any stone invisible, to |
appeare in another stone visible to all |
mens sightes.*

In nomine patris et filij et spiritus saɴcti. Amen.
Then say yoʳ Pater Noster, and yoʳ Credo, And then saye:
O thou spyritt N., I comaunde the to come into this stone visible |
unto my sighte, I charge the as thou hopest to be saved, that thou |

89 Harvey: tex repete.

comest forthe of that stone into this stone visible to my syght and |
to all mens sightes, wythout any hurte doinge to me, oʳ to any creature |
lyvinge or deade beaste, I charge the that thou doe hurte no kynd of |
thinge, and I charge the that thou hurte noe grasse nor corne upon |
paine of eternall damnaction, and I charge the in the name of Jhesus |
Christ, and doe comaunde the that thou doe hurte noe tree, noʳ hedge |
noʳ noe maner of tymber that is buylded or unbylded, I charge the |
thou spiritt N. in the name of Jhs Christ, that thou hurte no manner |
of howse that is standinge or that is about to be buylded in the paine |
of thy co~fusio~, and that thou hurte no kynde of thinges that ever of |
god was suffered to be made: furthermore I charge the that thou |
<u>open noe grownde, noʳ no loftes</u>, noʳ noe chestes, beds, boardes, stoles |
frames, walles, stone, yrones, oʳ any other kynde of thinge that is |
of me <u>unnamed or named</u>, that thou shalt not hurte no kynde of thinge |
noʳ sturr noe kynde of thinge, noʳ put any kinde of boddy in pane. |
Furthermore this I charge the in the name of Jhs Christ, that thou |
hurte no kinde of churche, castle, oʳ tower, or any other kynde of thinge |
in the name of Jhs I charge the thou spyritt N., or any other kinde of |
spiritt that is was or shall be, that you doe no kinde of hurte, nor |
melte noe kynde of leade, nor tynn, nor any other kynde of mettayle. |
In the name of JHS Christ I charge you do yt not, nor no other kynde |
of thinge: I charge you all in the name of JHS christ, that you make |
noe greate wynde, that shall blowe downe or hurte any kynde of |
thinge by lande or by water, I charge you all in the name of JHS |
Christ, that you make noe kinde of lyghtninges that shall burne or |
destroy and kynde of thinge lyvinge or not, I charge you in þᵉ name |
of JHS christ, that you make no greate rayne, or hayles, that shall |
hurte any kynde of corne, cattle or grasses, oʳ any other kinde of thinge |
And that you make no kinde of stones of fier in the Aye to hurte any |
kynde of thinge lyvinge or dead or any kynde of thinge. I charge |
you spyritts all, and specially thou spyritt N., that thou make no greate |
fluddes of water to hurte any kynde of thinge by sea or lande any |

[briges or]

[55r]   briges, or any other kynde of thinge. And nowe I charge the in the |
name of JHS christs sake, that thou nor noe <u>other kinde of spyritt, do come</u> |

nere <u>this house to hurte me or it, oʳ any other creature in it</u>, but that |
thou come peaceably into this cristall stone, (and then you must |
putt on your stone) god graunt that all these my wordes may bee |
fulfilled, I coniure and commaunde the thou spyritt N., that thou |
pʳsently appeaere in this cristall stone, visible to my syghte, for I |
<u>wyll take noe naye</u>, I coniure and by gods power compell the thou |
spyritt N., that you presently appeare here in this cristall stone |
visible to my sighte, wythout <u>any kynde of hurte that ever was</u>, or |
may be <u>imagined by any wicked spyritt</u>, O thou spyritt N., I |
charge the pʳsently here to appeare wythout any stopp or staye, into that
      cris- |
tall <u>stone that there standeth, visible to my sygthte</u>, and to all mens sighte |
that on yt shall loke: O thou wicked and rebellious spyritt I coniure and |
comaunde the by these holy names of god, that thou presently here |
appeare + Agla + Micon + Messias + Sother + Emanuel + Sabaoth + |
Emmanuel + Agla + And by all these holy names of god Amen that |
thou pʳsently here appeare, thou wicked and rebellious spyritt N., |
without any stopp oʳ stay delusio~ cʳ delaye here to appeare visible |
to all men's syghtes. O thou spyritt N., I coniure and comaunde the |
and charge the in paine of eternall damnacion, that thou here pʳsently |
appeare in my syghte in this cristall stone, appointed for the that |
thou mayest appeare heare thou spyiritt N. to my syghte and all mens |
that on the shall loke in paine of endless damnacion: I charge the |
wᵗʰout any delay stopp or staye but <u>mekely and quietly here</u> to apeaʳ |
thou spiritt N., and that <u>I may wᵗʰ my eyes see the</u>. O lorde |
graunte that these my wordes may be of muche truthe. Amen lord |
Jhesu Christ, Amen I beseche you.

        Yf he doe not appeare visible, say this |
          Sentence.

O thou wicked and rebellious spiritt N., god the father curse the |
for thy disobedience, god the sonn curse the foʳ rebellion, god the |
holy ghoste curse the for <u>thy disobavinge of these holy wordes</u>, The |
curse of the eternall lyvinge god, lighte on the thou wicked and |

rebellious spiritt N., for thy disobayinge, All holy Aungells curse |
and condemne the thou wicked and rebellious spiritt N., for thy diso- |
bayinge, All children of men and women curse the, and by there |
power deprive the thou wicked and rebellious spiritt N., for thy |
greate disobayinge. Lyalglla curse the, Sother curse the, Sabaoth |
curse the, Sydrach, Mydrach and Abednago wch lay burninge in the ove~ |
of fier curse the, and by gods power weare delyvered from ytt |
I curse the by the power that Moyses dyd strike the earthe in the |
lande of Ægypt, and there weare innumerable of flyes amonste |
men and beastes, and as truly as the water turned into bludd so truly |

[1]

[55v] I curse the wyth all my power, and deprive the by the power of god for |
thy greate disobayinge of his wordes, Amen lord I beseche the.

Nota.

Yf he come not visible to yor syghte with the fyrste call being twyse |
readd, then you must reade the laste call or sentence 3 tymes, and then |
leave.

The deprivatio~ yf he do not |
appeare vysible.

O thou wicked and rebellious spyritt, god the father curse the, god the |
sonne curse the, god the holy ghost curse the, wyth there power deprive the |
for thy dysobayinge of these holy words: All Aungells and Archaungelles |
curse the, and condemne the, and for thy disobayinge of thy offyce deprive |
the. Lord I beseche the that this rebellious spyritt N., may be deprived |
for his disobayinge. All sayntes curse the and deprive the thou rebellious |
spyrytt N. for thy disobayinge, all patricarches and prophetts curse |
the for thy disobayinge, and deprive the, I by gods power not by my |
owne doe curse the condemne the, and for thy greate rebellio~ deprive |
the, Amen lord I beseche the.

The bonde when he is come to yor |
syghte to bynde hym.

I bynde the thou spyritt N., which art appeared here in this cristall |
stone seene to my syghte that thou do not departe out of this cristall |
stone untyll thou be lycensed by me and that thou shalt tarry here |
wthout any hurte doinge to me or to any other creature, o^r fearinge any |
creature that is in this howse or in any other place. This by gods power |
I bynde the to doe lyfy + lefe + lurvando + god comaunde the |
that thou come not out of that place where thou standes tyll I bydd |
the. And that I doe bynde the, that thou breake not my cristall |
stone, In the name of JHS Christ, thus I bynde the to doe, And |
yf thou doe god nowe curse the. I by his power wyll curse the. There- |
fore I charge the stay in that place, where thou nowe arte. O holy |
Aungelles I desier you bynde him that he starte not. O god I |
desyer the helpe me against this wycked spyritt N., and all others |
Lyfe, Lefe + Lurvando + bydne the, and Jhesus Christe constraine |
the here to staye. Amen.

The beste and most excellente waye and Arte is |
as well for Aungelles for Inferiors and |
other Spyritts, to have these names of |
god wrytten in your stone, as |
followethe.

[56r]

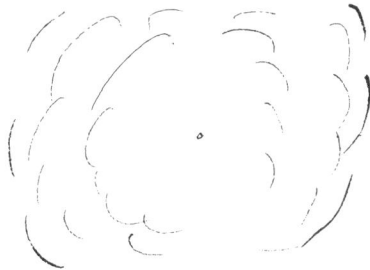

This is wrytten wythout, because the circle was to lyttle, but yt |
muste be wrytten wythin the circle nexte adjoyninge, your stone must |

be flatt of bothe sydes, and cleane w^{th}out crackes or staines, and as |
large as may be gotten, and of a good thickness.

Nota.

Noe spyritt can disobay that is called into the stone thus |
graved; and the markings therof was discovered by Luke on |[90]
Easter time, beinge in Ann° D~ni 1567.[91]

Nota.

Noe stone is good, although he be never so cleane, yf he bee |
thyn or not cleare; also he muste be flatt on bothe sydes, and |
the broder the better.[92]

[This is]

[56v]   This is the gravinge of another christall, to call Aungells, or spyrittes |
into: But yf you do call bothe, then must ye never call any spyrittes |
into that stone you call Aungels into. And of bothe it is beste |
for you, to kepe this laste nexte before you for the Aungells.

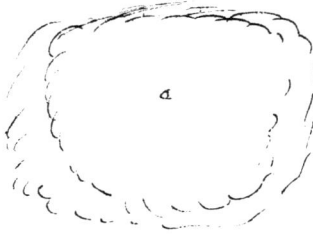

Nota.

They be graven at any time, or any plannets hower.

Nota.

That it is not necessary that yor stone should be consecrated |
for the Aungells; but for Inferiorus, they muste never be co~secrated.

90 In marg: St. Luke.
91 Harvey: King Salomon &c.
92 Harvey: how to choose yor stone.

Visions

[58r]   Certain strange visions, or apparitions,
         of memorable note. Anno 1567.
         Lately imparted unto me for secrets
         of much importance.
         A notable journal of an experimental
         Magician.¹

[58v]   [blank]

[59r]   Visions.²

This vision appeared on the 24th of February³
at the sun rising towards the east,
Anno Domini 1567.⁴

There appeared a long blue cloud, like a streak from the east to the west,
upon which H.G. went, having a gilt sword in his hand, & Jo. Davis going
after him with a book covered with a skin, the hairy side outward; himself
being apparelled in a black coat, & cape cloak,⁵ with a pair of black silk netherstocks gartered with black garters close above the knee; having a velvet cap,
& a black feather.⁶ And very many, like men, running away before him,
kneeling and falling down, holding up their hands to him. And he followed
them very cruelly, and struck one of them, that had a crown on his head,
with the sword in his hand, most royal to behold. And he struck the king
so cruelly that he fell down on his knees to him, holding up his hand. And
yet he struck him again with great fury, as though he would have killed
him. Then the boy opened his book, holding it abroad.⁷ And then they said
to the boy's hearing 'What lack you that you show such cruelty unto us?

---

1 This text in Gabriel Harvey's hand.
2 Harvey adds: or apparitions.
3 In marg: 24 February | 1567
4 Harvey adds: A notable journal of an experimental magician.
5 Harvey adds: The apparel | of H.G. | a neat, | & fine | gentleman.
6 Netherstocks – long socks, covering the lower part of the leg.
7 In marg: Jo. the | skryer: | his book | displayed.

Shut your book, and you shall have done what you will desire.' This book was written with black, white, yellow, blue, green and red. H.G. passed on with great force after him, and at the last there appeared Assasell, Solomon, Bacon, Adam, Job, and they said to[8] the boy's hearing who they were. Also there appeared a blue cloud, like a man with one leg, holding up the other. And Solomon said that H.G.:[9] & Jo. should rule him; and also Job said to Jo.'s hearing: 'Trust[10] no spirit visible or invisible, but the spirits of dead men. For they love man more then the others do.'[11]

Also the 24th of the same month:
Anno ut supra at sunset as follows.

Jo. saw a great wood, having a great house in the midst of[12] it with a little house by it most strongly built, having a front door, with nine key holes. There being written on the door these characters following,

$$\text{开 圭 } 3^{l^2} \text{ 厄 # 己 刀 ✡ 的 卧}$$

And in this house he saw a chamber richly hanged with gold, in which chamber there was[13] a tree of crystal which was written upon very well, having many branches, with a door in it, as it were with seven keyholes, which had the chinks[14] written on it.[15] Within the which there were many books, whereof one had a crystal cover,[16] another with the hairy side of a skin outward; with diverse other goodly books. This tree spread & grew, as follows in the next leaf.

[59v]

---

8 In marg: Assasel. | Solomon. | Bacon. | Adam. Job.

9 In marg: Solomon to | the skryer.

10 In marg: Job to the skryer. | The spirits of | dead men.

11 In marg: Omniscii. Harvey adds: Negromantia. The black art. Sciomantia. { S. Luke}

12 In marg: 24 Febru.

13 In marg: ☉

14 The meaning of the word 'chinkes' here is obscure, but perhaps refers to 'characters.'

15 In marg: Books.

16 Harvey adds to the foot of this page: The visions of Sir. Th. S. himself: as is credibly supposed. Though Mr. Jon Wood | imagines one G.H. Tempus demonstrativum revelabit.

Also the 25th of February at the rising
of the sun, there appeared as follows. [17]
Anno domini 1567.

Jo. saw a golden hill, with four corners, there being four Angels standing at each corner, thereof one, upon which mountain there grew a tree of blood, full of knots, spreading very broad. These Angels had each of them a book of gold in their hands praying, whose names were these, as each of them said to him: [18] Mark, Matthew, Luke, John. They said with one voice as follows: [19] 'We keep this tree *&* blessed is he that shall come to it.' Then there appeared a great black cloud, H.G. riding upon it on a white horse, with a sword in his hand, and Jo. riding after him on a black horse, having a book in his hand. Then there appeared the wood, *&* house where Solomon dwelt, into the which house H. G. rode in, [20] and Jo. also, and took from there a great sort of books. Then the Angels said to John's hearing: 'Follow this art, and be wise; for luck thou hast to it.'

Also the 25th of February at the sunset [21]
these appeared in the west as follows.
1567.

First, three dragons flying in the air: one green, the other red, the third blue. Their tongues were like spears and [they] had long tails. Then Jo. went after them, and the green dragon came towards him. Then the boy held up his book, at which he fell down, and came away. Then appeared two fowls that were black running in the air, and H.G. going after them, having a book in his hand, with a crystal cover. Then one of them ran at him. Then he held up his book and then they ran away. Then Jo. met full, but with H.G. in the west. And there appeared Assasel, [22] Solomon, Job, Adam, Bacon, Cornelius

17 In marg: 25 Febru.
18 'Him' being John Davis.
19 In marg: Angels { Mark. | Matthew. | Luke. | John.
20 In marg: (drawing of a book)
21 In marg: 25 Febru.
22 In marg: Assasel. | Solomon. | Adam. Bacon. | Cornelius Agrip- | pa.

Agrippa, as they told their names. Then H.G. spoke to them, and they said that they would help him all they could, and that he should lack no learning that they gave. Then Adam said to him: 'Do this,' said he:[23] 'Go clean in apparel, and be good to the poor,[24] and leave swearing, and go in a black coat & cloak, and never tell none that thou saw us. And then nothing thou shalt lack. And when Solomon bids you to call us, we will obey it.'[25] Bacon said: 'Go clean in apparel, and Jo., your skryer especially in a coat and cloak of black cloth continually.[26] And yourself also, except when you ride.' Assasel said that they were not to tell things past,[27] present, and to come. 'But keep our words, and fear not and H.G. shall do well enough.'

[60r]

> *Also the 26th of February at 9 of*
> *the clock in the morning, there*
> *appeared in the east as follows.*
> *1567.*

First, there appeared a golden hill, with the same four Angels as before,[28] with the same tree of blood. And the Angels said unto H.G.: 'Thou art blessed of God surely, for thou hast a servant that will make thee a saint. And I trust by our help, you shall come to this tree, and we will do all that ever we can for thee. Thou shall have servants that shall teach thee as much learning as thou shall be able to take, and our help shall be to it, doubt not.'

Nota.

Seen by H.G. & Jo. on the 14th day of March Anno[29] Domini 1567, at the sunset, or a little after, I know not perfectly. It was about seven o' clock. First I, and my skryer saw a round fire in the west, which suddenly vanished &

---

23 That is to say, one of the assembled spirits provided this advice.
24 In marg: Adam.
25 Harvey adds: Ars notoria spiritualis
26 In marg: Bacon: go | cleanly.
27 In marg: Assasel. We are | not to tell things | past, present, and | to come.
28 In marg: Angels.
29 In marg: 14 Martii. | 1567

came again.[30] There appeared another with him which I beheld very well, and from them there went a great black cloud under them, which went from the west, by the north to the east point. And on that cloud there came an extreme number of fires, *&* in the place where the first fires were, there was a great quantity that was marvellous red, all of which turned into gold. And some part of the fire went toward the south: for that God, of his great miracle, showed to me *&* my skryer. Also the fire was marvellous great and bright, and turned into gold, as before. And suddenly casting my eye aside, there was a great black cloud, which gathered into a sharp point into the west, *&* spread very broad into the top towards the east, being marvellously enclosed with fire, six sundry points of black, as follows,

[60v]

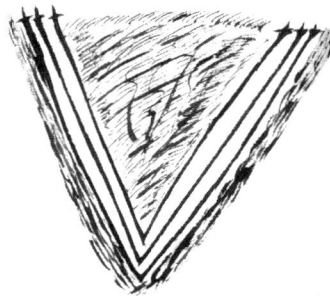

having under each bundle on the south side a long streak of gold, very bright, which were enclosed with great fires. And after the little streak, there appeared about them two great bundles of golden streaks, which stood about each of the golden streaks. But the bundle that stood uppermost was not so bright as that which stood below. There was a great black cloud between these two bundles, and about the top of this marvellous thing there was a great quantity of green, as before appeared. And between the six black clouds as before there was a great number of fires between each of them, as before you see. Also there appeared on the south side of it upon the nethermost bundle of gold, a square golden hill with four corners, with four Angels standing about it,[31] at each corner one, whose names were Matthew, Mark, Luke, John, being barefooted with books in their hands. There being

30 In marg: A fire.
31 In marg: ut s.

a great tree of blood in the middle of the golden hill. Also there passed by us two dogs, running on the ground, which were spirits coming from the south toward the north.[32] The first of them was white, red and black, and went lering away apace,[33] [and] which had no tail. Then followed the other dog which was all black, with a long tail. And when he was right against me and my skryer, he looked first on the miracle before shown, and then on me, and then on it again, and so passed away. These dogs had little legs and great broad feet like unto horses. All which things appeared to us within one hour's space. And when I went from the place, all things vanished away.

    The Angels said unto H.G. that he should fear nothing. And that he had a good servant of Solomon, whose counsel he should follow,[34] for he would advise him for the best. And that he should do as Solomon appointed him, for he would do nothing to his hindrance. And that they would appear to him in the element when he would, and that they would teach him all arts, and how to make books.[35]

    Nota.

I, and my Skryer, saw the 15th day of March, Anno 1567 between nine and ten in the morning as follows.[36] First a glimpse of white which passed very suddenly away before us on the ground. Then there appeared in the ground a grey cony, which stood still & looked upon us.[37] Also afar of these were trawling on the ground two great black wings joined together,[38] without any body, hard by the ground, which suddenly went into the ground to their sights. Also there did appear a great number of little things, like little mites of crystal, which danced, & tarried a good while,[39] near & round about us,

[61r]

32 In marg: 2 Dogs.

33 The scribe wrote 'lering,' whose meaning is obscure, although it does occur in the sense of leering in a 1568 printing of the works of John Skelton (1460 – 1529): 'Lering and lurking here and there like spies.'

34 In marg: Solomon servant | to H.G.

35 Harvey adds: (Ars notoria inspirta.)

36 In marg: 15 Martii 1567

37 In marg: Grey cony.

38 In marg: Wings.

39 In marg: Little crystals.

save for on the left side. Also there came two little birds from the north to the south, flying before, and lighted on the south side of us, which was on the left hand. And these two birds did fly again from the south toward the north. Then there came another bird from the south side of us, and it flew toward the north and came back again towards us, and flew towards the north again, and then circled on the south side of us.

Nota.

Also on the afternoon of the said 15th day, between one and two of the afternoon, I saw a great black dog with a white long spot on his nose, and the like on his tail,[40] having small legs, and great horse feet, which was neither flesh, blood, nor bone.

[61v] And at the same time, there flew three birds from the west to the east,[41] whereof one of these was white, which had very long tails. Also after them four more birds which had long necks, & long tails. Also four other black birds coming out of the west toward the east, having long necks and long tails, with greater feet, all as big as their bodies. Also there came two other birds from the west toward the east, with great wings, and long tails, which came on our right side, these having no heads. All the rest that we saw coming at this time, came on the left side. Also there came a lark from the east toward the west, which flew very high,[42] and came somewhat near us, before our faces on the left hand of us, sometimes as it were swimming in the air. And sometimes much fluttering, being continually enclosed with fire. And after he had thus flown a pretty while, he came down to the ground, before our faces marvellous swiftly, seeming less and less, and so pitched into the ground, out of our sights, being very little and round at his falling. And as I came homeward, there I saw a great brended dog,[43] coming toward me. And then I turned my horse and my skryer turned his horse also, and galloped towards him, and when I met him, he would needs have pressed upon me and my skryer. And then I said to him, 'O thou wicked & rebellious spirit, I

40 In marg: Dogs.
41 In marg: Birds.
42 In marg: A lark on fire.
43 Brended – brindled. In marg: Dog.

charge thee to stand.' And for all that he would needs have come upon me. And then I said: 'O thou wicked & rebellious spirit, God confound thee.' Speaking which words I drew out my dagger & cast toward him; and then he ran away[44] & suddenly vanished out of my sight; I knew not how. All these dogs, birds & white glimpses, with the cony and wings, were spirits, as I after proved by the spirit of Solomon.

Nota.

H.G. with his skryer did see on the 17th of March, ante meridian[45] between ten and twelve, two black birds flying from the south to the north, without heads, which were two Angels called Ancor and Amulor[46] who showed many good books to them. After that they did hear sundry imperfect sounds and the sound of bells and many other instruments, and at the last there apeared these two Angels to H.G.'s sight, and his skryer should not see them: Toby & Gabriel in the likeness of two larks,[47] which said after they were commanded by H.G. as follows.

Nota. Anno Domini 1567.

[62r]

Also on the 17th of March, somewhat before four o' clock at afternoon there appeared two marvellous great ravens standing on the ground.[48] And H.G. being willed by Solomon to speak to them[49] then one of them came flying upon him, and so flew towards the southwest. And whilst H.G. and his skry-er did before him, the other flew away. But with much calling they went into the east, & divided themselves into three crows and came, and fell down by them, and being so commanded did stay and speake these wordes: That they did first appear like ravens, and afterwards divided themselves into three crows because they might not know them. And said further that they had certain books, and other things which we will not name in keeping,[50] which

44 In marg: Cast his dagger | at him.
45 In marg: 17 Martii.
46 In marg: Ancor | Amulor | Angels.
47 In marg: Angels { Toby | Gabriel | like 2 larks.
48 In marg: Ravens.
49 In marg: Solomon.
50 In marg: Books in | keping.

H.G. must have. And [H.G. must] also have us in rule, which they are loathe to do, and H.G. is appointed to master us, which we had none agreeable while, and the more so ere we are for it.[51] And these were their words. Also there appeared half an hour before five a white man in the air, in the north-west, having four fingers in the right hand and a thumb, but he had but three fingers in his left hand and a thumb. His garments were of white linen cloth, very large. And at the same time, there appeared towards the west of him in the air a dog, and also a great square hill of gold. And about 5 o' clock the same day, at afternoon as they were coming homewards, there went the spirit of Job along the way as they rode, before their horses a good part of the way.[52] And then H.G. spoke to him, who answered that he was appointed to serve him, & to make many secret books for him, and did of himself go into a crystal stone that H.G. had in his pocket,[53] being appointed to do [so] by the Angels.

Nota.

That as H.G. was cursing, depriving & condemning the Four Kings and Bleth for their disobedience, Anno Domini 1567, 22nd March[54] in the second and third [hours] post meridian, there came of himself the Evangelist Luke[55] into a crystal stone that lay on the board, and willed the Master to leave using the names of God to hurt wicked & rebellious spirits, offering himself to do all things for me, & to teach me how to have all things done by the Angels,[56] without such cursing, & conjuring by the word & names of God, promising

[62v] me that he would come to me wherever I would have him.[57] And I, having the spirit of King Solomon[58] and the spirit of Job before, they both fell on their knees to Luke when they saw him. And the wicked inferior Bleath ran

51 In marg: H.G. their | Master; and they | had none a | great while.
52 In marg: Job ma- | keth the | books.
53 In marg: Job of his | own will | into a | crystal | stone.
54 In marg: 22 Martii | 1567.
55 In marg: Luke the Evanglist | into a crystal | stone.
56 In marg: Luke his | Angels.
57 Harvey adds: Lucas ins~tar omnium Magorum.
58 In marg: Solomon and Job | fell on their | knees before | Luke.

continually away, from one place to another[59] round about the stone as fast as might be.

Nota.

On the 6th day of April Anno Domini 1567, my boy went to Solomon's house in the morning,[60] and came home to me again about nine o' clock in the forenoon, and brought me from here a book written by Saint Luke the Evangelist.

His principal authors:[61] { Solomon,
                      Job,
                      S. Luke,
                      Bacon,
                      Agrippa. }

St Luke's Gospel: *Petite et dabitur vobis quaerite et invenietis pulsate et aperietur vobis.*[62] *Si ille perseveraverit pulsans; et si non dabit illi, quod amicus ejus sit; propter improbitatem tamen ejus, surget, et dabit illi.*[63]

    St John's Gospel: *Amen, amen dico vobis: siquid petieritis, Patrem in nomine meo, dabit vobis.*[64] *Petite, et accipietis: ut gaudium vestrum sit plenum.*[65]

    These two Gospels, with the seven Psalms, the Litany, & De Profundis; commonly read of these Solomonical artists, in their greatest experiments.

59 In marg: Bleath played the | vice.

60 In marg: 6th April. | A book from Salo-| mon's house written | by St. Luke | (drawing of house or book?)

61 This text and that which follows is in the hand of Gabriel Harvey.

62 Luke 11:9. (Ask, and it shall be given to you. Seek, and you shall find. Knock, and it shall be opened to you.)

63 Luke 11:8 (Yet if he will persevere in knocking, I tell you that, even though he would not get up and give it to him because he is a friend, yet due to his continued insistence, he will get up.)

64 John 16:23. (Amen, amen, I say to you, if you ask the Father for anything in my name, he will give it to you.)

65 John 16:24. (Ask, and you shall receive, so that your joy may be full.)

Certaine ſtraung viſions, or apparitions |
of memorable note. Anno 1567. |
Lately imparted unto mee for ſecrets |
of mutch importance.
A notable journal of an experimental |
Magitian.

[58v]   [blank]

[59r]   *Visions.*[1]

This viſion ap~ed on the 24 of february |[2]
at the sonne riſing towards the East, |
Aº d~ 1567.[3]

Ther ap~ered a long blew clowd like a streake from the East |
to the west u~n the which <u>H.G.</u> went having a gilt sword in |
his hand, & <u>Jo. Davis</u> going after him with a booke covered wᵗʰ a skyn, |
the heary syde outward; Him selfe being ap~elled in a black |[4]
cote, & cape cloke, wᵗʰ a payer of black silke nether stockes garte-|
red wᵗʰ blacke garters close above the knee; hauing a velvet cap, |
& a black fether, & very many, like men, running away before hym, |
kneling and falling downe, holding up there handes to hym; & he |
followed them very cruelly, & stroke one of them, that had a crowne |
on his heade, wᵗʰ a sword in his hande, most ryall to behold; and he |
stroke the kynge so cruelly þᵗ he fell downe on his knees to hym, |
holding up his hande; and yet he stroke hym agayne wᵗʰ great |
furie, as though he would have kylled him; then the <u>boye opened</u> |[5]
<u>hys booke, holding</u> yt abrode; and then they saide to the boyes |
hering, what lack you, þᵗ you shewe such cruelty unto us, shut |

1 Harvey: or apparitions.
2 In marg: 24 februer | 1567
3 Harvey: (A notable journal of an experimental magician.)
4 Harvey: the apparel | of H.G. | a neate, | & fine | gentleman.
5 Harvey: Jo. the | skrier: | his booke | displayde.

yor booke, and you shall have done, what you will desier. This |
Booke was written wth black, whiet, yelowe, blew, grene, red, |
H.G. passed on wth greate force after thym, and at the last there -|
ap~ed Assasell, Solomon, <u>Bakon</u>, Adam, Jobe,^{6} and they sayd to |^7
the boyes hearing^8 they were. Also there ap~ed a blew cloude like |
a man wth one leg, holding up the other; And Salomon sayd, þ^t H. |^9
G: & Jo. should rule hym; And also <u>Jobe</u> sayd to Jo. hering; Truste |^{10}
noe spirit visible or invisible, but the spirits <u>of dead men; for</u> |
they love man more then the other doeth. |^{11}

Also the 24 of the same month: |
A° ut supra at sonr. set as followeth.

Jo. sawe a <u>greate wood</u>, hauing a greate howse in the middes of |^{12}
yt wth a little howse by yt most strongly buylded; having an fro~ |
dore, wth 9 keie holes. There being written u~n the dore thes caracts |
following, ꓫꓱ ꓳꓽꓹ ꓞ ꓕ꓾ꓤꓨ ꓫ ꓻꓜ ꓲꓸ And in this howse |
he sawe <u>a chamber richely hanged</u> wth gold, in w^c chamber there was |^{13}
<u>a tre of christale</u> which was written upon very well, having manye |
branches, with a dore on hym, as it were wth 7 keyeholes, w^c had the |^{14}
chinkes written on yt; within the wch there were many bookes, whereof |^{15}
one had a christall cover, and ~~an~~ ͣⁿ othe~ wth the heary syde of a skyn out- | [59v]
ward; with divers other goodly bookes; this tre sprede, & grewe as |
in the next leafe followeth.

6 Harvey: ^Bacon.
7 In marg: Assasel. | Solomon. | Bacon. adam. Jobe
8 Harvey: ^who
9 In marg: Salomo~ to | ye skryer.
10 In marg: <u>Jobe to ye skrier</u> | The spyriitts of | deade men.
11 Harvey: negromantia. The black art Sciomantia. { S. Luke
Harvey in marg: omniscij.
12 In marg: 24 febru.
13 Harvey in marg: ☉
14 Harvey in marg: Bookes.
15 Harvey in bottom margin: The visions of Sir. Th. S. himself: as is credibly supposed.
Thowgh Mr. Jon Wood | imagines one G H. Tempus demonstrativum revelabit.

Also the 25 of february at the rysing |
of the sonn, there ap~ed as followeth. | [16]
A° d~ 1567.

Jo. sawe <u>a golden</u> {~~illeg~~} <u>hill</u>, wth fower corners, there being 4 Angles |
standing at eche corner, thereof one, on the wch mountain of there |
grewe <u>a tre of bloud</u>, full of knotts, spredding very broade.
These Angles had ech of them a booke of ~~gl~~ gold in there hands |
praying, whose names ^weare thes, as ech of them sayd to hym |
Mark, Mathewe, Luke, John; who sayd wth one voyce as followeth: | [17]
We keepe <u>this tre</u> *&* blessed is he þ^t he shall come to it then there |
apeared a greate <u>blacke cloude, H.G. ryding upon it</u> on a white |
horse with a sword in his hande; *&* Jo. ryding after hym on a |
blacke horse, hauinge a booke in his hand, then ther ap~ed the |
<u>wode, *&* howse where</u> Salamon dwelled, into the wch howse H. | [18]
G. rode in; *&* Jo. also, And toke from there a great sorte of |
<u>bookes</u>, Then the Angles said to Johns hering, <u>follow this art,</u> |
& <u>be wise</u>; for <u>luck thou hast to yt</u>.

Also the 25 of february at the sonn set | [19]
these ap~ed in the west as followeth. |
1567.

Firste 3 dragons flying in the ayere; one a greene; the other a red |
the third blewe; there <u>tonges were like speares</u> *&* had long |
<u>tayles</u>; then Jo. went after them, *&* the grene dragon came |
towardes hym, then <u>the boy held up his booke</u>, wherewithall he |
fell down, *&* came away; then apeared ij fowles þ^t were |
blacke runnyng in the ayre, And H.G. going after them |
having a booke in his hand, wth a christall cover then one of the~ |
ran at hym; the~ he held up his booke *&* then they ran a way. |

16 In marg: 25 Febru.
17 In marg: Angels { Mark. | Matthew. | Luke. | John.
18 In marg: (drawing of a book?)
19 In marg: 25 febru.

Then Jo. mett full butt ᵂᵗʰ H.G. in the west; And ther ap~ed | ²⁰
Assasel, Salamon, Jobe, Adam, Bacon, Cornelius Agrippa, |
as they told there names; Then H.G. speake to the~, And they |
sayd þᵗ they would help hym {illeg.} þᵗ eve~ they could, And þᵗ he |
should lacke noe learning þᵗ we gave Then sayd Adam to hym |
doe this sayd he. Goe <u>cleane</u> in apparell; & be good to the | ²¹
poore; & leave swearing; and goe in a blacke cote & cloke, And |
never tell none þᵗ thou sauest us; And then nothing thou shalt |
lacke. And when Salomon biddeth you to call us, we will obey | ²²

Visions.

it. Bacon said, gowe cleane in apparell. And Jo. ʸᵒʳ skryer , especially | ²³
in a cote & cloke of black clothe continually; & your selfe also, |
except when you ride. Assasel said þᵗ they were not ᶠᵒʳ to tell | ²⁴
thinges past, present, & to come. But keepe oʳ worrdes, & feare not |
and H.G. shall doe well inough.

Also the 26 of february at 9 of |
the clocke in the morning, there |
ap~ed in the east as followeth. 1567.

First there ap~ered a <u>golden hyll</u>, wᵗ the same 4 Angles | ²⁵
as before, wᵗʰ þᵉ same tre of bloud; & the Angles sayd unto |
H.G. thou art blessed of god suer; Fcr thou hast <u>a servant</u> |
þᵗ will make <u>the a saynt</u>. And I trust by oʳ helpe, yᵒᵘ shalt |
come to this tree; and we will doe a__ þᵗ ever we can, for |
the, Thou shalt have <u>sservantes þᵗ shall teach the</u> as much |

20 In marg: Assasel. | Salomon. | Adam. Bacon. | Cornelius Agrip- | pa
21 In marg: Adam.
22 Harvey in bottom marg: Ars notor_a spiritualis
23 In marg: Baco~, goe | clenly.
24 In marg: Assasel. We ar | not to tell thinges | past, present, and | to come.
25 In marg: Angells.

learning as thou shalt be able to take; & o.r help shall be to |
it, dowte not.

Nota.

S.eene by H.G. & Jo. on ye 14 daye of M~che A.o | [26]
d~ 1567, at the sonn sett, or a little after, I knowe not p~- |
fectlye, it was about 7 of the clocke. First I, and my skryer |
sawe a rownde fyer in the west, w.c sodaynly vanished & | [27]
came agayne. There ap~ered another w.t hym w.ch I beheld |
very well, and from them there went a greate blacke cloud |
under the~, w.ch went from the west, by the north to the |
East pointe; And on that cloud there came an extreme |
number of fyer, & in the place where the fyrst fyers were, |
there was a greate quantitye þ.t was m~velous red, all þ.e |
which turned into gold; & some p~te of the fyer went towards |
the south: for þ.t god of his a great miracle shewed it |
to me & my skryer; Also the fyer was marvelous greate |
& bright, & tourned into gold, as before. And sodainly casting |
my eye asyde, there was a greate blacke cloude, which |
gathered into a sharpe pointe, into the west, & spreade |
very brode into the top towardes the East, being marve- |
louslye inclosed with fyer, having 6 sundry pointes as |
followeth

[60v]

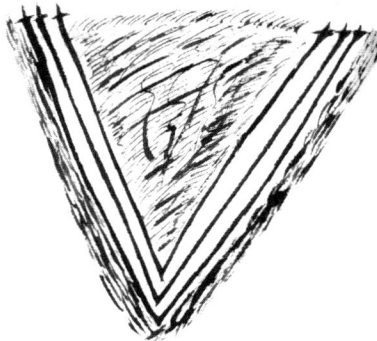

26 In marg: 14 Martii. | 1567
27 In marg: A fier.

of blacke, hauing under ech bundle on the south syde a ^{longe} |
streyke of gold, very bright, wch were inclosed wth greate fyers. |
and after the litle streike, there ap~ered about them 2 great |
bundles of golden streikes, wch stoode about ech of the golden |
strikes, but the bundle þ^t stoode uppermost, was not soe bright |
as he þ^t stoode belowe. There was a greate blacke cloud |
betwene these 2 bundles, & about the topp of this m~velous |
thinge there was a greate quatitye of greene, as before |
ap~ereth apereth. And betwene of the 6 blacke clowdes as |
before there was a greate number of fyer betwix eche |
of the~ as before you see. Also there apered on the south |
syde of yt uppon the nethermost bundle of gold, a square |
golden hyll wth 4 corners, wth 5 Angles standing about yt, | ²⁸
at ech corner one, whose names were Mathewe, Marke, Luke, |
John, being barefoted wth bookes in there handes. Ther being |
a grate tre of bloud in the middle of the golden hyll, Also |
there passed by us 2 dogges runnying on the grounde, which | ²⁹
were spirites coming from the south towarde the north; |
the first of the~ was white, red and blacke, & went lering |
away apace wch had noe tayle. Then followed the other |
dog wch was all blacke, wth a long tayle. And when he |
was right against me & my skryer, he loked first on the |
miracle before drawen, & then on me, & then on it againe; |
and soe passed awaye.

Visions.

[61r]

These dogs had little leges and greate brode feete like |
unto horses. All w^c thinges ap~th to us wth in one howeres |
space. And when I went from the place, all thinges vani- |
shed awaye. |

---

28 In marg: ut s.
29 In marg: 2 Doggs.

The Angles saide unto H.G. that he should feare nothing. |
And þᵗ he had a good seraunte of Solomon, whose counsall |³⁰
he should followe; for he would advise hym for the beste. |
And that he should rede whe~ Solomon appointed hym; for he wo- |³¹
uld doe nothing to his hindrance. And that they would apeare |
to him in the element whe~ he would: And that they would teach |
him all arts, and howe to make Bookes.³²

Nota.

I, and my Skrier, sawe the 15 daye of March, Anno 1567 be- |³³
twene 9 and 10 in the morning as followeth. |
Fyrst a {illeg.} ᵍˡʸᵐˢᵉˢ white which passed very sodaynly away |
before us on the grounde. Then there apeared in the ground |
a graye cony, wᶜʰ stoode still & loked uppon us. Also a far of |³⁴
these was trowling on the grounde 2 greate blacke winges |³⁵
ioyned togetther, without any body, hard by the grounde; which sodainly |
went into the grounde to their sightes. |
Also there did apeare a greate number of little thinges, like |
little mights of christall, wᶜʰ daunsed, & tarryed a good while, |³⁶
nere & rounde about us, sauing on the left syde. |
Also there came 2 little birds from the north to the south, |
flying had before, & ˡⁱᵍʰᵗᵉᵈ {illeg.} on the south side of us, wᶜʰ was |
on the left hande. And these 2 byrds did fly again fro~ |
the south to ᵗᵒʷᵃʳᵈᵉ the north. Then there came another byrd from þᵉ |
south side of us, & flew towarde the north {illeg.} & came |
backe agayne to wardes us, & flewe towardes the north againe, |
& then circled on the south side of us.

30 In marg: Salomo~ servaunt | to H.G.

31 'Rede' is used here in the sense of following a rule, or direction – although both variants 'rede' and 'reade,' referring to the act of reading aloud, are also found in the MS.

32 Harvey: (Ars notoria inspirta.)

33 In marg: 15 martij 1567

34 In marg: grey cony.

35 In marg: winges.

36 In marg: lyttle cristalls.

Nota.

Also on the said 15 daye after none, betwix 1 and 2 after none |
I saw a greate blacke dog, wth a white long spot on his nose, & the | ³⁷
like on his tayle, having small legges, & greate horse feete which |
was neither flesh, bloud, nor bone. |

And at the same tyme, thr~ flewe 3 byrds from the weste to the east, | ³⁸
whereof one of these was white, which had very long tayles, Also after them |
4 more byds which had long neckes, & long tayles.
Also 4 other blacke byrdes coming cut of the west to ^toward the East, |
hauing long neckes & long tayles, w^th ^greater {illeg.} feete, all big as there
    bodys. |
Also thr~ came 2 other byrdes fro~ the west to ^toward the East,, with greate |
winges, & long tayles, wch came on {illeg.} ^owr right side, ^the having noe
    heades. |
All the rest ~~wch we sawe~~ commying ^that ~~to~~ we sawe at this tyme, came |
on the left syde. |
Also there came a larke from the Easte toward the west, w^c flew | ³⁹
very {illeg.} hye, & came somwhat neare us, before o^r faces on the |
left hand of us, somtyme as yt were swyming in the aire. And |
somtyme much fluttering, being continually inclosed wth fyer. |
And after {illeg.} he had thus flyed a pretye while, he came dow~e |
to the grounde, before our faces m~uelous swiftly, seming les & les |
And soe piched into the grounde, out of our sightes, being verye |
little and rounde at his falling. |
And as I came homeward, ^ther I sawe a greate brended dog, | ⁴⁰
commyng toward me, And then I turned my horse and my |
<u>skryer turned his horse also</u>, And galoped ^towards {illeg.} hym, And |
when I mett him, he would needs ^have pressed uppo~ me And my skryer |
And then I said to him, O thou wicked & rebellious spirit |
I charge the to stand: And for all that he would needs have |

[61v]

37 In marg: Dogs.
38 In marg: Byrdes.
39 In marg: a lark on fyer.
40 In marg: Dog.

come uppo~ me. And then I sayd O thou wicked & rebellious |
spirite, <u>God confounde</u> the. Speaching w^c wordes I drewe |
out <u>my dagger & cast towarde</u> hym; and then he ran away | [41]
& sodainly vanished out ~~out~~ of my sight. I knew not howe. |
All these dogs, byrds & white glymses, wth the cony and |
winges were spirites; as I after proved by the spirit of |
Solomon.

Nota.

H.G. with his skryer did see the 17 of Marche, ante meridian | [42]
intwe 10 et 12. 2 blacke byrds flying from the south to the |
north, wthout heads; which were <u>2 Angeles</u> called <u>Ancor</u> and | [43]
<u>Amulor</u> which shewed many <u>good bookes for them.</u> After þ^t they |
did heare sundry unp~fitt soundes & the sound of bells & |
many other instruments; And at the last there ap~red these |
2 Angeles to H.G. sight; & his skryer should not se them; |
<u>Toby</u> & <u>Gabriell</u> in the likeness of <u>2 larkes</u>, wch said after | [44]
they were commanded by H.G. as followeth.

Visions

Nota. Anno Domini 1567.

Also the 17 of Marche somewhat before 4 of the clock at after |
noone there ap~ed 2 <u>marvelous greate Ravens</u> standing on the | [45]
grounde. And H.G. being willed by Solomon to speake to them | [46]
then one <u>of the~ came</u> flying uppo~ hym, & soe flew towardes the |
southweste; and be whilst H.G.and his skryer did before hym, |
the other flewe awaye; but wth much calling they went into the east, |
& divided them selves in 3 crowes & came, & fell downe by |

41 In marg: cast hys dagger | at hym.
42 In marg: 17 Martij.
43 In marg: Ancor | Amulor | Angels.
44 In marg: Angels { Toby | Gabriell | like 2 larkes.
45 In marg: Ravens.
46 In marg: Solomon.

them & being soe co~maunded did staye & speake these wordes: |
that they did first apere like Ravens, and afterwards devided |
them selves in to 3 crowes because they might not knowe them. |
And said further that they had certaine bookes, & other thinges which we
     will | [47]
not name in keping which H.G. must have; & also have us in |
rule, wᶜʰ they are lothe to do, And H.G. is apointed to mr us, |
wᶜ we had none agreable while; & the more so eyre we are for yt; | [48]
& these were there words. |
Also there ap~ed half an hower before 5 a white man in the aire, |
in the north west hauing 4 fingers in the right hande & a |
thomb, but he had but 3 fingers in his left hand and a thomb; |
his garments were of white lynnen cloth, very large. |
And at the same tyme, there ap~red towards the west of hym |
in the ayre a dog, also a greate square hill of gold. |
And about 5 of the clock the same daye, at after noone |
as they were coming homewardes, there went the spirit of |
Jobe along the way as they rod, before their horses a good p~t þe | [49]
waye. And the~ H.G. speake to hym who answered þᵗ he was |
apoynted to serue hym, & to make many secret bookes for hym; |
And did of hym selfe goe into a christall stone, that H.G. had | [50]
in his pockitt; being apointed for to doe by the Angles.

Nota.

That as H.G. was cursing, depriving & condemning of the 4 |
kyngs, & bleth for these disobediences, Aᵒ d~ 1567, 22 Martij in the | [51]
2 et 3 ᵖᵒˢᵗ meridie, there came of hymselfe the Evangelist Luke | [52]
into a christall stone, þᵗ lay on the bourd and willed mr to |
leave using the names of god, to hurt wicked & rebellious spirits; |

47 In marg: bookes in | kepinge.
48 In marg: H.G. there | Master; and they | had none a | great whyle.
49 In marg: Jobe ma-| keth the | bookes.
50 In marg: Job of his | owne wyll | into a | christall | stone.
51 In marg: 22 Martij | 1567
52 In marg: Luke the Evangliste | into a christall | stone.

offering <u>hym selfe to doe all things</u> for me, *&* to <u>teach me</u>, howe to | ⁵³
have al things <u>done by the Aungels</u>, wthout such cursing, *&* couniering |
by the <u>word *&* names of god</u>, p~missing me that he would come to me | ⁵⁴

[62v]   whersoever I would have hym. And I having the spirit of | ⁵⁵
k Solomon, *&* the spirite of Jobe before. They both fell on |
there knees to Luke whe~ they sawe hym. And the wicked in-|
ferior <u>bleath</u> ran continually away, from one place to another | ⁵⁶
rownde about the stone as fast as might be.

              Nota.
On the 6 day of Aprill, A⁰ 1567 my boy went to So- | ⁵⁷
lomons howse in the morning, *&* came home to me againe |
aboute 9 of the clocke in the forenone, And brought me fro~ |
there a booke writted by Saint Luke the Euaungelist.

His principal Authors:⁵⁸ {   Salomon.
                           Job.
                           <u>S. Luke</u>.
                           Bacon.
                           Agrippa. }

S. Luke's Gospel: Petite et dabitur vobis:
quaerite et invenietis pulsate et aperietur vobis.
Si ille perseveraverit pulsans; et si non dabit illi,
quod amicus ejus sit; propter inprobitatem tamen ejus,
surget, et dabit illi.

---

    53 In marg: Luke hys | Aungells.
    54 Lucas ins~tar omnium Magorum.
    55 In marg: Solomo~ and Jobe | fell on there | knees before | Luke
    56 In marg: Bleath played the | vyce.
    57 In marg: 6th Apryl. | A booke fro~ Salo-|mon's howse wrytten | by St. Luke | (draw-
ing of house or book?)
    58 This text and that which follows is in the hand of Gabriel Harvey.

S. John's Gospel: Amen, amen dico vobis:
si quid petieritis, Patrem in nomine meo,
dabit vobis. Petite, et accipietis: ut
gaudium vestrum sit plenum

These two Gospels, with the seven Psalms,
the Litany, & De Profundis; commonly
read of these Salomonical Artists,
in their greatest experiments.

Experiments of Azasel, Ancor, Anycor & Analos

FROM ILLINOIS PRE-1650 MS. 0102

Go to the grave of a dead body that you know the name of, and call him thrice by his proper name at the head of the dead body. And saye thrice. N., and after say thus: *I conjure thee Azazel, that art Lord of dead men's bodies, that* [69] *thou go into the court, and ask leave that he may come to me this night, and tell me truly of that treasure that is hidden in the earth in such a place, N., or what other place it is hidden in, and how I may come thence or have it by any manner of wise or else speak or show where it is become and who has it in keeping, and how I may come thereby; for this is true without any peril.* And when thou hast said that, then take of the earth of the grave of the dead body at the head, and bind it in a clean cloth of linen, and then lay it under thy right ear when thou list to sleep. And in the night he shall come to thee and tell thee the truth, or else it shall be shown thee in dreaming what thou desirest to ask of him.[1]

Ista inuocati debit dixi novies absque interpellatione dierum post primatione luna cressentis.[2]

Now it is to go to the grave, and stand at the foot and write above on the grave this name: *Tetragrammaton* +, with a hazel wand. Then go a stride backwards and there, as you stand, write this name: + *Iesus*. And go backward another stride, and with the same hazel wand smite 3 times on the grave and say this: N. N. N. or any other name whatsoever it be.

I conjure thee, I require thee, and I charge thee by the Christendom that thou hast tak- [70] *en, and by the sacrament that thou hast received, and by the obedience that thou owest to God the Father, the Son and the Holy Ghost, that thou take leave of thy Lord Azazell, and master, and come to me this night in the hour of N. of the clock, meekly. And I shall do for thee to thy help, and answer me of all things that I shall ask of thee. I conjure thee, N., spirit per verbum caro scatum*[3] *est et per sanguinem Iesu Christi qui virgo conceptit et peperit in nomine Iesu omne Iesu flectatur celestium terrestium et infernorum. Quia dominus Ieus Christus est in gloria dei patris vivi per deum et per*

---

1 Compare with the experiment from Case MS. 5017, which terminates at this point.
2 This invocation to be said nine days without interruption after the new moon.
3 This should read 'per verbum caro factum,' e.g. through the Word made flesh.

sanguinem conceptum et virgine pro nobis redimentis. Fiat, fiat, fiat. Amen.

Then go home into a clean chamber, and make thy bed in the middle of a circle about, and then sleep and he shall come and call you. And then say what thou wilt. And if he come not, go again the next night and do the same as you did before. And then go and sit thee upon thy bed and there call the spirit Azazell to bring him with these words:

[71] *Thou follow and come, thou N., by the baptism of Christ. I require thee and charge thee by the sacrament that thou hast received, and by the manhood of Christ, that was dead and rose again, and appeared openly through the might and power of God, [&] after was borne up into heaven, both body and soul openly. And by the virtue of her assumption, arise, arise thou and come openly. As Lazarus was dead four days and rose openly, and appeared through the great power of God's miracles, arise thou through that might. I charge thee by the might of God, and by all thee that have been dead and risen again openly by the power of God, I charge thee that thou come. I conjure and require thee by the holy precious blood of Jesus Christ, and by his blessed mother Mary that was verily conceived and childed, being a maid pure and clean without sin. Enoch and Eli shall be dead in Jerusalem and shall rise again openly, through the might of God. Through that might and power [that] thou, N., hath by thy Christian name, I require and charge thee that thou arise. Upon pain of all pain, arise and appear openly here. And for the word to whom thou owest obedience. And all other creatures, heavenly, and earthly, and hellish. And by the obedience that thou owest to thy Lord God in*
[72] *trinity, I call thee that thou appear here before me, amen, and answer to me, amen.*

This done say: *Quicunque vulte; spiritus istius experimenti.* When any sprit appears, charge him to do thy commandment as follows:

O thou spirit which cometh here, I conjure thee by the virtue of God of Heaven, and by the virtue of the Holy Trinity, et per dignitatem et virtutem beate Marya virginis et per vertutem verborum et nominum die. By whose virtue thou art obedient to me, and by the virtue that I have made thee to come, that thou say to me whatsoever I ask of thee, or whatsoever I purpose to ask of thee. That thou answer me truly, without any craft or disobedience. By him that reigns, God of the world of worlds, amen.

Lycencia spiritus:

I conjure thee (or you) spirit, by the virtue of our Lord Jesus Christ who was put upon the cross, that you return to your proper place, and by the virtue of the high God that you annoy me not, nor hurt me, nor scare me, nor any manner of creature, but that you return to your proper place; and when I shall call you again, to answer me quickly with obedience and be ready for me. Recede, recede, recede in pace.

Finis per me no bodie.

To have a true answer of gold or silver or treasure [87]
in the earth, or to have the carrier [4]

Go to the grave of a man or woman within three days after the burying, and be sure to know the name, and then say as follows:[5]

O thou Azazell, as thou art the keeper of dead men's bones, and keepest here the bones of this man, N., I command thee, and also charge thee, and I conjure thee, by the virtue of almighty God, the Father, the Son and the Holy Ghost, and by all that ever God made in heaven and in earth, and by his might and power, and by the sacrament of the altar and by his substance, and by his resurrection, and by his ascension, that thou [88] come to me, (naming the place and also the time and hour),[6] and at the entering into the place to give three knocks so that they may be perfectly heard, and that thou come quietly and peaceably, and without making any noise, and without doing any hurt to me or to any other creature of God, and that thou appear in the likeness and form of a child of six years of age.[7] By the virtue of Jesus Christ, the which shall come to judge the quick and the dead and the worlds by fire. Amen.

4 GDI88/25/1/3 prefaces this ritual with the words: 'Bleathe – should a young beginner begin withall, he aught to call Azasellis the most noblest art whose character follows:', beneath which the same sigil on the first page of the *Excellent Booke* is repeated three times.

5 GDI88/25/1/3 asks that the conjuration is repeated four times.

6 GDI88/25/1/3: 'come to me, M.P., at the hour of five.'

7 GDI88/25/1/3: 'seven years old.'

And when he comes, say:

I charge thee, Azazell, by the virtue of the Father, the Son and the Holy Ghost, and by the blessed virgin Mary, and by all that ever God made in heaven and in earth, and by the blessed Trinity, three persons in one God in unity, and by the dreadful day of doom, that thou do not lie, but show to me the truth of such things as I shall ask and require of thee, by the sufference of almighty God.

[89]   And then say:[8] *I charge thee, Azazell, by virtue of the Father, the Son and the Holy Ghost, by the Holy Trinity, and by the sacrament of the altar, and by the five principal wounds of our Lord Jesus Christ, and by the cross that Christ suffered on, and by the nails that went through his hands and feet, and by the blood that he bled upon the cross, that thou go and fetch me some goods that do no man good, or else that thou bring me a carrier that has no Lord but God, and that he be neither of the highest, nor of the lowest order. I charge thee by the virtue of God.*

Then he will say that it is great peril, and that he cannot do it. Then ask him why, and he will say that he has not humanity. Then say:

I charge thee, Azazell, by the virtue of God the Son and Holy Ghost, and by all that our God made in heaven and earth, and by the holy sacrament of the altar in the form of bread and wine, and by the five wounds of our Lord Jesus Christ, and by the cross that he died on, and by the precious blood that he bled thereon, and by Saint John Baptist, and by Saint John Evangelist, and by all the holy company of heaven, that thou, Aza-zell, do bring to me some spirit that will be obedient unto me at all times, and that

[90]   *thou bring the name of that spirit with thee. Also I charge thee by the virtue of God, and by the virtue of the blessed virgin Mary, and by all the fellowship in heaven, that thou, Azazell, come again* (and you must name the hour), *and sign thee with the sign of the cross, and bring me my humanity again, and if thou do not, I condemn thee, Azazel, by the power of God into everlasting pain in hellfire, there to be bound with chains and bonds until the day of doom. Fiat, fiat, fiat. Amen.*

---

8 GD188/25/1/3: 'Then ask him what thou will and he will show the truth, then may you command him to provide or for to bring forth treasure, or else a carrier as thus:'

Then blow your humanity against him, and that done, you shall abide and betake your body and soul to Almighty God, saying: *In manus tuas domine*, and other prayers on your knees, on your feet, or standing, or sitting. For he will keep his honour. And you must have a plate of lead four-square and clean plumbed and ruled. And when he comes again, say: *Benedicte*, and he will say: *Domine*. And then you shall see the spirit kneeling before you.[9] Then ask the name of the spirit, and Azazell will tell you. Then charge him thus:

I charge thee by God almighty, the Father, the Son, and the Holy Ghost, three persons and one God, and Holy Trinity, and by the blessed sacrament of the altar, and by the [91] *virtue of his substance, and by his power and providence which he had when the world was made, and by the wisdom whereby he made both heaven and earth, and the four elements of the world, and by all Angels, Archangels, Thrones, Dominations, Principles, Potestates, Vertues, Cherubim, and Seraphin, and by all the Prophets, Patriarchs, Apostles, Masters, Confessors, and by all holy Saints, and chiefly by the power of all the holy names of God. Elye + Sabaoth + Adonay + Emanuell + Tetragrammaton + Messias + Sother + Usion + Alpha + et Ω + Athanatus + thou shalt fulfil my desire, and request of all times whensoever I shall command thee to do any thing or things for me. Look that it be speedily done at all times, whensoever I shall pledge to command thee. Also I charge thee by the virtue of God, and by his blessed blood, bled upon the cross, that thou write thy name, by which thou being called thou wilt soonest appear and obey openly, on this plate of lead, that all men lettered may read it, and that thou do give it to me again.*

When thou hast done this, then cast him the plate. Then when thou hast it again, ask thy humanity again, and then charge him thus:

The discharge

I charge thee, N., by the virtue of God, and by the blessed sacrament of the altar in [92] *form of blood and wine, and by the cross that he died on, and by the blood that he bled on the cross, and by the dreadful day of doom, that thou go to the place again where thou wast before, until the time that I call you again. And also I charge thee by the*

---

9 GD188/25/1/3 mentions spirits, plural.

dreadful phantom that shall be at the day of doom that thou do not hurt me bodily,
nor ghostly, nor any other creature of God, nor anything that helps a creature, as thou
hope to be saved and not condemned at the day of doom, either in thy going or in thy
coming.[10]

Then say the discharge:[11]

Azazell: [Go] to the place or grave where thou wast before, as God has ordained thee to
be in, without any hurt to me or any other creature of God. By the virtue of God, and
by the dreadful day of doom. Fiat, fiat, fiat. Go in peace, and peace be between thee
and me. In the name of the Father and of the Son, and of the Holy Ghost. Amen.

Finis.[12]

A Call of Ancor; Anycor; Analos[13]

First say three Pater Nosters, three Aves, and one Creed, and these Psalms:
[93]   *Miserere Mei Deus, Misereatur Nostri, Laudate Dominum.* [Then say:]

O Lord God, king of glory, send down – I beseech thee – from the throne of thy right
hand, three good Angels – Ancor, Anycor, Analos – in the sight of this crystal stone,
who shall declare unto me the very truth of all things which I shall ask or demand
of them. O Lord Jesus Christ, I beseech thy goodness, send unto me these three good
Angels to appear unto me in this crystal stone, by our Lord Jesus Christ, who was con-
ceived by the Holy Ghost and born of the virgin Mary, [who] suffered under Pontius

10 GD188/25/1/3 adds 'As thou hopest to be saved at the day of judgement per virtute
dei omnipotentis virtutis in secula seculorum, amen.'
11 In GD188/25/1/3, the discharge is addressed to a hitherto unmentioned spirit called
Althenothe. One might speculate that this is possibly the name of the spirit delivered to
'M.P.', the scribe of the manuscript. The same manuscript also adds 'Then bless thee saying: In nomine patris et filii &c. Then he will go away and when thou wilt doe any thing,
call him by his privy name & he will come shortly then show thou what he shall do. That
done license him as before said &c.'
12 GD188/25/1/3 closes with a drawing of the lead plate – a square with four ruled
lines across it, providing enough room for five names to be inscribed upon it.
13 Compare with the Latin version of the experiment in Folger MS. v.b.26, pp.225–6.

Pilate, was crucified, dead and buried, and even as thou art true god and man, send
me three good Angels to appear in the light of this crystal stone, that is to wit: Ancor,
Anycor, Analos. By these most holy names of God: Eloy + Tetragrammaton + Princip-
ium et Finis, help me, O you Angels, by our blessed virgin Mary, mother of our Lord
Jesus Christ, and by the nine orders of Angels, Archangels, Thrones, Dominations,
Principals, Potestates, Virtutes, Cherubim, and Seraphim, and the archangelical virtue
of Michael, Gabriel, Raphael, and Uriel, who do not cease continually to cry before the
seat of God, saying: 'Holy, Holy, Holy, Lord God of Sabaoth, who is, who was, and
who is to come, who shall judge the world by fire.' And by all the holy relics which are
in heaven and in earth, and by the milk which our Lord Jesus sucked out of the paps of
our blessed virgin Mary, his mother, when he was a child, and died in this world, and   [94]
by the purple robes which he wore, and by the oil which Mary Magdalene anointed his
feet withall and wiped them with the hairs of her head, that openly, without any delay,
you appear unto me in the sight of this crystal stone, as it were in a cloud.

And if they come not the first day, call them [on] the second. If not, call them
[on] the third, for without doubt they will come and appear. And when they
are appeared, say to the first:

O Ancor, thou Angel of God, thou art welcome in the name of the Father, and of the
Son and of the Holy Ghost, amen, and by the intention which God had in mind when
he put down Lucifer from heaven, into the pit of infernal hell, and hath chosen you for
most valiant Angels.

To the second, say:

O Anycor, thou art welcome, in the name of the Father and of the Son, and of the Holy
Ghost, amen, and by the virginity of the blessed virgin Mary, and by the virginity of
Saint John Baptist, and by his head.

To the third, say: [95]

O Analos, thou art welcome, in the name of the Father, and of the Son, and of the
Holy Ghost, amen, and by the virtue of the sacrament of the altar, which our Lord
Jesus Christ gave to his disciples: 'Take, eat; this is my body.'

Vos Angeli rogo, vos precipio, et vos exorcsiso per nominum dei que non licit homini nisi in hora noctis, et per virtutem spiritus sancti.

Then make a cross on the crystal and say:

Per reverentiam sacramenti altaris; et per reverentiam passionis dominum nostrum, Jesu Christi quod monstretis mihi sini falisitate vell fallatio requisita petenda.

Then say:

O you Angels of God, I command you and exorcise you by the principal names of God, which are not lawful for man to speak but in the hour of death, by the virtue of the sacrament of the altar, that you show unto me all things which I shall ask or demand of you.

Then say:

O you Angels of God, I conjure and charge you by the almighty power of God the Father, and by the power of Jesus Christ his Son, and by the incomprehensible wisdom of the Holy Ghost, and by the power and virtue of all the words by me before recited whereby you are commanded to appear that you show unto me truly and plainly without deceit of such things, (naming it, etc.).

The Licence follows:

O you Angels of God, depart you into the place which our Lord God hath ordained you to be in; and be you ready at all times hereafter to come unto me whensoever I shall call you. In the name of the Father, and of the Son, and of the Holy Ghost. Amen.

Finis.

[96]

Go to the grave of a deade bodie that you know the name of |
And calle him thrise by his p~per na_me, At the head of the dead |
bodie; And saye thrise. N: and after saye thus; I coniure the~ |
Azazell; that arte lorde of deade mens bodies that thou go |
into the courte; And aske leave that he maye come to me this |
nighte; And tell me trulye of that treasure; That is hidd in the | [69]
earthe in suche a place; N.; or what cther place it is hidd in; And |
howe I maye come thense or have it; By anye manner of wise |
or els speake or shew wheare it is become; And whoe |
hath it in keepinge; And howe I maye come thereby; for this is |
true w^{th}out any perill; And when thou haste saide that; |
Then take o the earth of the grave of the dead bodie at the |
heade; And binde it in a cleane clothe of lynin; And then laie |
it under thy righte eare when thou liste to sleepe; And in the |
nighte he shall come to the; And tell the the truthe or else |
it shal be showed the in dreaminge; That thou desirest to |
aske of him; |
Ista inuocati debit dixi novies absque interpellatione dierum post |
primatione luna cressentis; |
Nowe it is to goe to the grave; And stande at the foote |
and write above on the grave this name, Tetragrammaton + w^{th} |
a hazell wande; Then goe a stride backwarde; And theare as thou |
standst write this name + Iesus; And goe backwarde an other |
stride; And wth the same hazell wande smite 3 times one the |
grave and saye this; N. N. N. or anye other name what soe- |
ever it be; |
I Coniure the I require the and I Charge the by | [70]
the christendome that thou haste taken; And by the sacrament |
that thou hast received; And by the obedience that thou oweste |
to god the father the sonne and the holye ghost; that thou take |
leave of they lorde Azazell; and mr; And come to me this night in |
the houre of N. of the clocke meekelye; And I shall doe for |
the to thy helpe; And answere me of all thinges that I shall |

aske of the; I Coniure the N. spirit p~ verbum caro ſcatum est | [1]
et p~ sanguinem Iesu Christi qui virgo concep~it et pep~it in nomine |
Iesu omne Iesu flectatur celestium terrestium et infernorum; quia |
dominus Ieus Christus est in gloria dei patris vivi p~ deum et |
p~ sanguinem conceptum et virgine p~ nobis redimentis; fiat; |
fiat; fiat; Amen. |
Then goe home into a cleane chamber And make |
thy bedd in the middest of a Circle aboute; And then sleepe |
and he shall come and calle the; And then saye what thou |
wilte; And if he come not goe againe the nexte nighte, And |
doe the same as thou diddest before; And then goe and sit the |
uppon thy bedd; And there calle the spirit Azazell to bringe |
him wth these wordes: Thou follow and come thou N. by |
the baptisme of Christ; I require the and Charge the by the |
[71] sacramente that thou haste received; And by the manhode of Christ |
That was deade and rose againe; and appeared openlye |
throughoute the mighte and power of god; After was borne up into |
heaven both bodie and sowle openlye; And by the virtue of her |
assumption, arise arise thou and come openlye, As Lazarus |
was dead .4. daies and rose openlye and appeared through the |
greate power of gods miracles; Arise thou through that mighte; |
I Charge the by the mighte of god; And by all thee that have |
beene deade and risen againe openlye by the power of god; I Charge |
the that thou come; I Coniure and require the by the holye p~cious |
blood of Iesus Christ And by his blessed mother Marye that was |
verelye conceaved and childed beinge a maide pure and cleane wth |
out sinne; Enoc and Elye shal be deade in Iherusalem and shall rise |
againe openlye; Through the mighte of god; Throughe that |
mighte and power thou N. hathe by thy christen name; I require |
and Charge the that thou arise uppon paine of all paine arise |
and appeare openlye heare; And for the worde to whome thowe |
oweste obedience. And all other creatures, Heavenlye, and Erthleye, |
and Hellye; And by the obedience that thou oweste to thy Lorde |

1   This should read 'per verbum caro factum,' e.g. through the Word made flesh.

god in trenetie; I Call the that thou appeare heare before me.
Amen; and answere to me Amen; | [72]
This done saye quicunque vulte; spiritus istius experimenti; |
When anye sprit appeareth charge him to do thy |
thy commandement as followeth; |
O Thou spirit wch cometh heare I Coniure the by the |
vertue of god of heaven; And by the vertue of God of heaven |
And by the vertue of the holye trenetie; et p~ dignitatem et vir-|
tutem beate Marya virginis et p~ vertutem verborum et nomi- |
num die. By whose vertue thou art obediente to me, And by the |
vertue that I have made the to come; That thou saye to me |
whatsoever I aske of the; or what so ever I porpose to aske of the |
That thou answere me trulye wth out anye crafte or disobedience |
by him that raigneth, god by the worlde of worldes Amen; |
Lycencia Spiritus; |
I Coniure the or you spirite by the vertue of our lord Iesus |
Christ; wch was put uppon the cross; That you retourne to youre |
p[ro]per place; And by the vertue of the heigh god; That you |
noys me not; nor hurt me not; nor scare me not; nor no maner |
of creature. But that you returne to your p~per places. And when |
I shall calle you againe to answere me quickleye wth obedience and |
be redye for me; Recede; Recede; Recede; in pace |
finis per me no bodie;
To have a true answere of Goulde or Silver or treasure in the | [87]
earth; or to have the Carier; Goe to the grave of a man or woman w^thin |
3 daies after the burienge; And be suer to know the name; And |
then saye as followeth;
O Thou Azazell, as thou arte the keeper to dead mens |
bones, And keepest heare the bones of this man; N. I Com- |
mande the And also Charge the and I coniure the by the |
vertue of almightie god; The father the sonne and the holye |
ghoste. And by all that ever god made in heaven and in earth |
And by his mighte and power; And by the sacramente of the |
Aulter and by his substance; And by his resurrection. And | [88]
by his ascention; That thou come to me; Naminge the place |

and also the time and hower. And at the enteringe into |
the place to give 3 knockes so that they maye be p~fectly heard |
And that thou come quietlye and peaceablye; W^thout anye |
noyse makeinge; And w^thout any hurte doinge to me or to |
any other creature of god; And that thou appeare in the |
likenes and forme of a childe of .6. years of age; By the |
vertue of Iesus Christ the wch shall come to judge the quicke |
and the deade and the worlds by fier. Amen.
And when he cometh saye |
I Charge the Azazell by the vertue of the father the |
sonne and the holye ghoste; And by the blessed virgin Marye |
And by all that ever god made in heaven and in earth; And |
by the blessed Trenetie; .3. p~sons in one god in unities; And |
by the dreadfull daye of doome; That thou do not lye butt |
shewe to me the truth of suche thinges as I shall aske; And |
require to the; By the sufference of almighte god; |
And then saye; |
I Charge the Azazell by vertue of the father the sonne |

and the holye ghoste; By the holye Trenetie; And by the sacrament |
of the Aulter; And by the .5. principall woundes of our lorde ~
Iesus Christ. And by the cross that Christ suffered on And by the |
nayles that went throughe his handes and feete. And by the blood |
that he bled on the cross; That thou goe and fetche me some |
goods that doeth noe man good; Or els that thou bringe me a |
Carrier that hath noe lorde but god; And that he be nayther of |
the highest nor of the lowest order; I Charge the by |
the vertue of god; |
Then he will saye it is great perill; And that he he can |
not do it; Then aske him whye; and he will saye he hath not huma- |
nitie; Then saye; |
I Charge the Azazell by the vertue of god the sonne and holye |
ghoste; And by all that our god made in heaven and earth; And |
by the holye sacrament of the Aulter in forme of bread and wine |
And by the .5. woundes of our lorde Iesus Christ; And by the |
cross that he dyed on; And by the precious blood that he bled there |

on; And by Sn^t Iohn Baptist; and by Sn^t Iohn Euangelist; And by |
all the holye companye of heaven; That thou Azazell do bring |
to me som spirit that wil be obedient unto me at all times; And that |
thou bringe the name of that spirit wth the; Also I charge the |
by the vertue of god; And by the vertue of the blessed virgin |
Marye; and by all the feloshippe in heaven; That thou Azazell |
come againe, And thou muste name the ower; And signe |
the wth the signe of the Crosse; and bringe me my humanitie |
againe; And if thou do not I do condemne the Azazel by the |
power of god into everlastinge paine in hell fier there to be |
bounde wth chaines and bondes until the daye of doome; |
fiat; fiat; fiat; Amen. |
Then blowe thy humanitye againste him, And that |
doone thou shalte abide; And betake thy bodye and soule |
to Almightye god; |
Sayinge, in manus tuas domine, And other prayers |
one thy knees; one thy feete; or stantinge; or sittinge; For |
he will keepe his honour; And thou muste have a plate |
of leade .4^{or}. square and cleane plummed; And ruled; |
And when comethe againe, saye Benedicte. And |
he will saye domine; And then thou shalte see the spirit |
kneelinge before the; Then aske the name of the spirit |
and Azazell will tell the. Then charge him thus; |
I Charge the by god almightye the father the |
sonne and the holye ghoste; .3. p~sones and one god; And |
holye trenitie; And by the blessed sacrament of the Aull- |
ter, And by the vertue of his substance; And by his power |
and p~vidence wch he hadd when the worlde was made; And |
by the wisdom whereby he made both heaven and earth; And |
the .4^{or}.; Elements of the worlde; And by all Angelles; Archan- |
gelles; Thrones; Dominations; Principles; Potestates; Vertutes; |
Cherubim; and Seraphin; and by all the p~phetes; Patriarches; Ap- |
postles; Masters; Confessores; and by all holye Sn^{te}; And chefelye by |
the power of all the holye names of god. Elye + Sabaoth + Adonay |
+ Emanuell + Tetragrammaton + Messias + Sother + Vsion + Alpha |

[90]

[91]

+ et Ω + Athanatus + thou shalte fulfill my desire; And requeste |
of all times when soever; I shall commande the to do any thinge |
or thinges for me. Looke that it be spedelye done at all times; |
when soever I shall pledge to commande the. |
Also I Charge the by the vertue of god; And by his blessed |
blood bledd uppon the crosse; That thou write thy name by w^ch |
thou beinge called thou wilte soonest appeare; And obeye openlye |
in this plate of leade; That all men lettered may reede it; And |
that thou doe give it to me againe; When thou haste done then |
caste him the plate; Then when thou haste it againe; Aske |
thy humanytie againe; And then charge him thus; The discharge. |
I Charge the N. by the vertue of god; And by the |

[92] blessed sacramente of the Aulter in forme of blood and wine |
And by the crosse that he died on; And by the blood that he |
bledd one the crosse; And by the dreadfull daye of doome; |
That thou goe to the place againe where thou waste before |
untill the time that I calle you againe; And also I charge the |
by the dreadfull fentome that shal be at the daye of doome; |
That thou doe not hurte me bodilye nor ghostlye nor any other |
creature of god; Nor anye thinge that helpeth a creature |
As thou hopethe to be saved and not condemned at the daye |
of doome; Nether in thy goinge nor in thy cominge.
Then saye the discharge;
Azazell; to the place or grave wheare thou wast before |
as god hath ordayned the to be in; W^thout anye hurte of me |
or anye other creature of god; By the vertue of god; And |
by the dreadfull daye of doome; fiat; fiat; fiat; go in peace |
And peace be betewene the and me; In the name of the |
father; And of the sonne; And of the holye ghoste. Amen. Finis. |

A Calle of Ancor; Anycor; Analos

Firste saye 3 pater nosters; .3. auies and one creed; And these |
psalmes. miserere mei deus; misareator nostri; Laudate dominum |

O Lord god kinge of glorye sende downe I beseche the from |
the throne of thy righte hande; .3. good Angelles; Ancor. Anycor |
Analos; in this sighte of this Chrystall Stone; wch shall declare unto |
me the verye truthe of all thinges wch I shall aske or demande of |
them. O Lorde Iesus Christe I beseche thy goodnes sende unto |
me these .3. good Angelles; to appeare unto me in this Christall |
Stoone by our lorde Iesus Christ; W^{ch} was conceaved by the holye |
ghost and borne of the virgin Marye suffered under Ponce Pilate. |
was crucified deade and buried; And even as thou art true god |
and man sende me .3. good Angelles to appeare in the lighte of |
this Christall Stone; That is to witt Ancor; Anycor; Analos; by |
these moste holye names of god; Eloy + Tetragrammaton + Principium |
et finis; Helpe me o ye Angelles; by our blessed virgin Marye mo- |
ther of our lorde Iesus Christ And by the .9. auders of Angelles; |
Archangelles; Thrones; Dominations; Principals; Potestates; Virtutes; |
Cherubim and Seraphim; and the Archangelicall virtu of Michaell; |
Gabriell; Raphaell; and Vriell; wch do not cease continuallye to crie be- |
fore the seate of god sayinge; Holye; Holye; Holye; lorde god of Saba- |
oth wch is; wch was; and wch is to come; W^{ch} shall judge the worlde |
by fyer; And by all the holye reliques wch is in heavene and in earthe; |
And by the milke wch our Lorde Iesus suced out of the papes of our |
blessed virgin Marye; his mother when he was a childe; And died |
in this worlde; And by the purple robes wch he wore; And by the |
oyle wch Marye Magdalin anoynted his feete wthall and wipped |
them wth the hears of her heade; That openlye wthout anye |
delaye you appeare unto me in the sighte of this Christall stone |
as it were in a cloude. |
And if they come not the first daye calle them the ;2; if not calle |
them the ;3; for wthout doubte they will come and appeare |
And when they are appeared; saye to the firste; |

[93]

[94]

O Ancor; thou Angell of god thou arte welcome in the |
name of the father and of the sonne and of the holye ghoste |
Amen; And by the intention wch god hadd in minde when he |
putt downe Lucifer; from heaven into the pitte of infernall |
hell; And hath chosen you for moste valiate Angelles; |
To the seconde saye; |
O Anycor; thou arte welcome; in the name of the father |
and of the sonne and of the holye ghoste Amen;and by the |
virgenitie of the blessed virgin Marye; and by the virginitie of |
Sn^t Iohn Baptiste and by his heade; |

[95]   To the thirde saye; |
O Analos; thou arte welcome; in the name of the father and |
of the sonne; and of the holye ghoste; Amen; And by the vertue of |
the sacramente of the Aulter; wch our lorde Iesus Christ gave |
to his disciples; Take eate this is my bodye; |
Vos Angeli rogo; vos p~cipio; et vos exorcsiso p~ nominum dei que non |
licit homini nisi in hora noctis; et p~ virtutem spiritus sancti; |
Then make a Crosse one the Christall and saye; |
P~ revirentiam sacramenti Altaris; et p~ reverentiam passionis |
dominum nostrum; Iesu Christi quod monstretis mihi sini falisitate vell |
fallatio requisita petenda; Then saye |
O You Angelles of god I Commande you and exorcise you by |
the principall names of god; W^{ch} are not lawfull for man to speake |
but in the hower of death; By the vertue of the [sacr]amente of the |
Aulter; that you shewe unto me all things wch I shall aske or de- |
maunde of you; Then saye; |
O Ye Angelles of god; I Coniure and Charge you by the all- |
mightie power of god the father; And by the power of Iesus |
Christ his sonne; And by the incomprehensiblie wisdome of the |
holye ghoste; And by the power and vertue of all the wordes by |

[96]   me before recited whearby you are commanded to appeare |
That you shewe unto me trulye and playnlye wthout deceipte |
of suche thinges; Naming it et c; |

The Lycence followethe; |
O Ye Angelles of god dep~te you into the place wch our |
lorde god hath ordeyned you to be in; And be you redye at |
all times heare after to come unto me; When soever I shall |
calle you; In the name of the father; And of the sonne; And |
of the holy ghoste; Amen. Finis.

An Experiment of Bleth

FROM SLOANE 3824

Of the spirit Bleth, who is mostly called upon and appears in a glass of water.

Have a glass made of pure white metal, pretty thick, made in the form of a urinal, and make a cover thereto of virgin wax or parchment with the characters made thereon as hereafter follows. Then fill the glass a little above half full of water, and set it upon the table of practice, or other convenient place, where it may stand very sure and steady from shaking or jogging. Let it stand on your left hand and set the cover thereof by it on your right hand &c. Let the table or place on which the glass and its cover stand be covered with a linen cloth very white, and so when all things are decently set in order, invocate as follows:

> I adjure & call upon, command and constrain thee, O thou spirit which art called
> Bleth: in & through the names of the Father & of the Son & of the Holy Ghost,
> three persons in trinity, & one God in unity, & by this incomprehensible name,
> of the most high and omnipotent creator of Heaven & Earth, Tetragrammaton,
> Jehova, I powerfully and earnestly urge and constrain thee, O thou spirit Bleth,
> and I call upon & command thee to appear visibly & affably unto me in this glass
> of water set here before me, as a fit and appointed receptacle to entertain you. And
> I do again adjure, call upon, bind, command and constrain thee, O thou spirit
> Bleth, by the virtue and might of those great & powerful names, by which wise Sol-
> omon bound spirits, and shut them up: Elbrach, Ebanher, Goth, Joth, Agla, Othie,
> Venoch, Nabrat,[1] to appear & show thyself fairly & fully and plainly visible unto
> me, in that glass of water here before me, which I have set to receive you in and to
> resolve & openly & manifestly to show me the truth, verity & certainty of all such
> matters & things as I shall demand & request of you, without any fraud, guile,
> dissimulation, or other crafty or deceitful illusion whatsoever, wherefore I now call
> upon & constrain thee hereby, O thou spirit Bleth, in and through these high &
> potent names of our Lord & Saviour Jesus Christ, Messias, Sother, Emanuel, Alpha
> & Omega, to move, appear & show thyself plainly unto me, & fulfil my demands,

1 This formula of Solomon, consisting of the words Elbrach, Ebanher and so on, seems to be a well-worn magical rubric. Two instances are found in Folger MS. v.b.26: 43, 44; and in Scot's Discoverie of Witchcraft (1584): 227. It later appears in a badly corrupted version in the Grand Grimoire (in the Citatio Praedictorum Spiritum).

desires & requests in all things according to your office wherein you may, or can, without any further tarrying or delay, but immediately prepare you & come away and do for me as for the servant of the highest:

Repeat this conjuration often, and when the water stirs a little & a smoke seems to be seen in the glass, then does the spirit enter: for this is the fore-showing sign of his appearance. And when this is perspicuously discerned, then lightly cover the glass with the cover, & bind it all about so surely that nothing may go out &c: Then ask what you will, & he will either resolve it *viva voce*, or it will be seen written on his breast.

[f115v]   The spirit Sonoryan may be invoked & called upon, as any of the foregoing spirits Vassago, Agares or Bleth, being exemplary alike, only changing the name in his invocation. Some use oil in the glass instead of water, for so did Cardinal Richelieu, with whom this spirit Sonoryan was very familiar, frequent & conversant withall &c.

This character is to be made on the cover of the glass.[2]

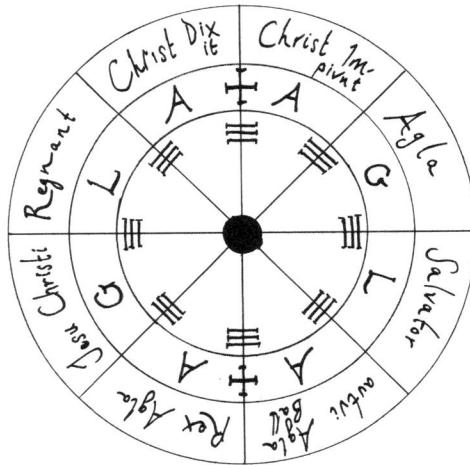

2 The words on the seal are: Rex Agla, Jesu Christi, Regnant, Christ Dixit, Christ Impi-unt (?), Agla, Salvator, Autui, Agla, Ball.

Of the Spirit Bleth, who is mostly called
upon and appeareth in a glass of water

Have a glass made of pure white mettle pretty thick, made in the form of |
a Urinall, and make a Cover thereto of Virgin Wax or parchment with the
  Charact~ |
made there on as hereafter followeth, then fill the glass a little above half full
  of |
water, and seat it upon the table of practice, or other Convenient place,
  where |
it may stand very sure and steady, from shaking or jogging & let it stand on |
yor left hand and set the cover thereof by it on your right hand &c: Let the
  table |
or place on wch the Glass and its Cover standeth be Coverd with a Linnen
  Cloth |
very white: and so when all things are Decently set in Order, Invocate |
as followeth:

I adjure & call upon com~and and constrain thee ^O thou Spirit which art
  called |
Bleth: in & through the names of the Father & of the Son & of the holy Ghost, |
Three persons in trinity, & one God in Unity, & by this in comprehensible |
name, of the most High and Omnipotent Creator of Heaven & Earth, Tetra |
gram~aton, Jehova, I powerfully and Earnestley Urge and Constraine the O |
thou spirit Bleth and I call upon & com~ad the to appear Visibly & affably |
unto me in this Glass of water set here before me, as a fit and appoynted
  Receptacle |
to Entertaine you, And I doe againe adjure Call upon, bind com~and and
  Constrain the |
O though Spirit Bleth, by the Vertue and might of those Great & powerfull
  names, |
by wch Wise Solomon bound spirits, and shut them up Elbrach, Ebanher,
  Goth, Joth, |
Agla, Othie, Venoch, Nabrat, to appear & show thy selfe fairly & fully and
  plainly Visible |

unto me, In that Glass of water here before me, which I have set to Receive
yoᵘ in |

And to Resolve & openly & manifestly to show me the Truth Verity & Certan-
ty of all |

Such matters & things as I shall Demand & Request of yoᵘ, wᵗʰout any fraud
guile |

Dissimilation, or other Crafty or Deceitfull Illusion whatsoever, wherefore I
now call upon |

& Constrain the here by, O thou Spirit Bleth in and through these High &
potent |

names of our Lord & Saviour Jesus Christ, Messias, Sother, Emanuel, Alpha &
Omega |

to move appear & show thy selfe plainly unto me, & fulfil my Demands,
Desires & |

Requests in all things according to yor Office wherein yoᵘ may or Can with-
out any further |

Tarrʸing or Delay, butt immediately prepare yoᵘ & come away and doe for
me as |

for the Serva~t of the Highest: |

Repeat this Conjuration often and when the water Stirreth a Little ᵉ a smoak
seemᵉth |

to be seen In the Glass, then doth the spirit Enter, for this is the foreshowing
Signe |

of his appearance, & when this is perspiceuously Diserned, then Lightly
Cover the Glass |

with the Cover, & bind it all about So Seurely that nothing may Goe out &c: |

Then Ask what yoᵘ will, & he will either Resolve it viva voce, or it will be seen |

Written on his Brest.

The Spirit Sonoryan may be Invocated & calld upon, as Either of the fore-
    going |
Spirits Vassago, Agares or Bleth, being Exemplary alike, onley Changing the
    name |
In his Invocation, Some use Oyl in the Glass in stead of water, for so did
    Cardinal |
Richlieu who this Spirit Sonoryan was very familiar, frequent & Conversant |
w^{th}all &c.

This Character is to be made on the Cover of the Glass.

Related Experiments

FROM CASE MS. 5017

Asazel, Raphan, Oberian.[1]   [6]

By the virtue of these holy names, Jah + Theos + Agla + Ozam + Deus + Eloy + which
the sea heard and returned back and gave way, the air was fixed and set, the earth
trembled, the fire was quenched, and all powers – both celestial and terrestrial – did
quake and were troubled. And by these holy names of God On + Alpha et Omega + El
+ Elohim + Soter + Emanuel + Sabaoth + Adonay + Egge + Yaya + Yeye + things are
consecrated.

[Smudged drawing, possibly of a sword]

Solomon always used a consecrated sword in the calling of spirits. In the
Ark of God the golden ring was borne. By the holy name of God Celao + and
virtue of Noah and all that were with him preserved.

Pro reducendo res furto ablatas   [12]
    Raguel et Uriel.
Pro amore { Almazim et
           { Elicona
Aosel pro Thesauris
Aozai dat Aurum et Argentum[2]

Character of Blethe   [13][3]

1 Although these names appear at the head of the page, suggesting a title, they seem to
be unconnected to the consecration that follows.
2 Compound list of spirits from the Case MS. exemplar of *Regula Utilissima in Arte Magica*.
3 This page includes a number of sigils in the lower half, although they are uniformally
poorly executed. They include: Asophel, Robeas, Baron, Andromalcus, Blethe, Eypia,
Mosacus, Haphage.

A *true experiment for treasure hid,*
or for anything you would know.

Go to the grave of a dead body, and three times call him by his proper name. Then put your head to the grave and say I *conjure thee,* calling him by his name, *by Azazel Asiel who is Lord and has the bones of dead men in keeping in his power; that thou ask license of him to come to me this night at the hour of two: and that thou tell me the truth of any thing that I shall desire or ask of thee.*

Then take the earth of the grave at the head of the dead and put it in a clean linen cloth and bind it and lay it under your head in your cap and sleep thereon. And in the night you shall dream: and one shall come to you and say the truth of all that you can demand.

Asazel, Raphan, Oberian. |

By the virtue of theis holie names, Jah + |
Theos + Agla + Ozam + Deus + Eloy + w^{ch} |
the Sea heard and ritourned back and gave way |
the Aire was fixed and set, the earh trembled, |
the fier was quenched and all powers both |
celestiall and terestriall did quake and |
were troubled. And by theis holy names |
of God On + Alpha et Omega + El + Elohim + |
Soter + Emanuel + Sabaoth + Adoray + |
Egge + Yaya + Yeye + things are consecrated.

[Smudged drawing, possibly of a sword]

Solomon allwais usd a consecrated sword |
in the calling of Spiritts. |
In the Ark of God the golden ring was borne. |
By the holy name of God Celao + and virtue of |
Noe and all that were with him preserved.

Pro reducendo res furto ablatas | [12]
    Raguel et Uriel. |
Pro amore { Almazim et |
       { Elicona |
Aosel pro Thesauris |
Aozai dat Aurum et Argentum | [1]

Charact^r  Blethe. [13]

---

1 Compound list of spirits from the Case MS. exemplar of *Regula Utilissima in Arte Magica*.

[23] A true Experim^t for Treasure hid. |
or for any thing you would know. |
Go to the grave of a dead body, and |
3. tymes call him by his proper name |
Then put thy hed to the Grave and say |
I conjure thee calling him by his name |
by Azazel Asiel wch is Lord and hath |
the bones of dead men in keeping in his |
power; that thou ask license of him to com |
to me this night at the houre of two: |
and that thou tell me the Truth of any |
thing that I shall desire or ask of thee. |
Then take the earth of the grave at the hed |
of the dead and put it in a cleane linen cloth |
and bynd it and lay it under thy hed in thy |
cap and sleep thereon. And in the night |
thou shalt dreame: and one shall com to thee |
and say the truth of all that thou canst |
demand.

2 CONTEXTS

Sorcerous Significances

OF THE EXCELLENT BOOKE AND ITS VISIONS

The *Excellent Booke of the Arte of Magicke* is an instructive grimoire for summoning spirits – from the ruler of the dead, to the king of the spirits of the East, to the ghosts of famous magicians – complete with prayers, conjurations, and various nota of injunctions and advice for the aspiring conjuror. It is a tome of spirits whose hairy and crystal covers open to unlock the ghosts of dead magicians, trees of blood and crystal, passing headless bird spirits, and the transmutation of visionary fire to spiritual gold. The purpose of the *Excellent Booke*'s conjurations is to make powerful knowledge available to the magical practitioner, whether delivered by subordinate spirit, through received text, or express tuition. The appended *Visions* can be considered the magical journal accounting the experiments and scrying sessions performed alongside the reception and development of the *Excellent Booke* between 24th February and 6th April 1567. Combined, they are a unique record of early modern English necromancy.

The texts in question are attributed to Humphrey Gilbert (1537 – 1583), mariner, soldier and the older half-brother to Sir Walter Raleigh,[1] and John Davis (1550 – 1605), navigator, inventor of navigational tools, and a friend

---

1 Claire Fanger, 'Introduction.' *Invoking Angels: Theurgic Ideas & Practices, Thirteenth to Sixteenth Centuries*, ed. by Claire Fanger (Pennsylvania State Press: University Park, 2012): 13.

of Dr John Dee. Frank Klaassen calls Gilbert and Davis 'certainly colourful characters: enterprising, audacious, single-minded, self-promoting men whose violent and dramatic deaths – Davis at the hands of pirates off the coast of Borneo and Gilbert off the Azores in the wreck of a ship he had been advised to leave – were apt conclusions to lives of inveterate risk taking.'[2] Their magical partnership involves a conjurer and seer relationship, as in the angelical operations of Dee and Kelly, but quickly shows distinct and dynamic variations. Gilbert begins hearing the spirits too, and even keeping things from Davis; John for his part also constrains spirits with his book.

My intention here is to survey and foreground the very real necromancy and demonology of this text, give insight into how conjuration and spirits were approached by tool and technique, and highlight a few historical, philosophical and practical significances of this powerful and important text.

DEVILS & THE DEAD

The necromancy of the *Excellent Booke* can be clearly evidenced in two ways – by the identity of the chief spirit who grants authority within the grimoire – 'Assasel'; and by the spirits who offer the most knowledge, teaching, and practical conjuration assistance – angels and the shades of holy men and notorious magicians.

Assasel

'The first Spyritt' one calls 'must be the ruler of y[e] deade whose name is Assasell, and he must call him by night in the hower of (sol).'[3] Evoking various mysteries of the sun at midnight, this inversion or nigromantic corollary of service on the Lord's Day is the first of several major conjurations in the system.

The operator is instructed to charge this ruler of the dead 'in the name of his maker' to grant a subordinate spirit that will serve the operator's purposes: upon the assent of Assasel, 'you must call one into ye stone whose name is called Aosal,'[4] a spirit apparently primarily involved in divination. Following

2 Frank Klaassen, 'Ritual Invocation and Early Modern Science: The Skrying Experiments of Humphrey Gilbert,' *Invoking Angels*: 341–342.

3 Add. MS. 36674, f.47v.

4 Add. MS. 36674, f.47v.

this second conjuration, the operator is instructed to call Oriens, one of the four demonic kings, who will grant the operator a powerful magical book. But the work begins with calling on the ruler of the dead for their direct say-so and even their direct (albeit delegated) assistance in the proceedings.

Legard has pointed out that this 'king Assasel' – also referred to in the treatise as 'the Keeper of the Dead Bones'[5] – is, in his opinion, *ultimately derivative of the Jewish Azazel*. Azazel's early appearance in Leviticus is somewhat ambiguous. We are told of the two male goats to be sacrificed, the one not chosen by lot to die for Jehovah was deemed la'ăzāzêl considered as 'for absolute removal' or simply as 'for Azazel.' We are dealing, in a very real sense, with the spirit of the scapegoat; that sacrificial animal 'sent away into the wilderness to Azazel.'[6] Furthermore:

> It may be the name of the place to which the scapegoat was dispatched, or...a contraction of two Hebrew words that mean 'the goat that is sent away' or...two angels, Uza and Uzazel, to whom the goat is sent as a bribe to stop them from beguiling the Israelites at this time of possible atonement. In an ancient legend, these angels enticed humans into the illicit sex acts that are hinted at in Genesis 6:1... It is also possible that...the second goat was sent to the demonic ruler of the wilderness, Sammael, as a bribe. The Israelites were concerned that the devil Sammael would appear before God on Yom Kippur to act as a prosecutor against them by listing all of their sins.[7]

The goat is both *for* and *of* Azazel. In the Apocryphal Books of Enoch, this fallen angel of the Grigori – the Watchers who mated with human women – is supposedly responsible for teaching humans the violent and deceptive secrets of weapons and cosmetics. The demonic spirit is himself blamed fairly extensively by the Enochic God: 'The whole earth has been corrupted

5 Add. MS. 36674, f.49v.
6 The King James edition of 1611 has this as 'to let him goe for a Scape goate into the wildernesse.' Leviticus 16: 10.
7 Israel Drazin and Stanley M. Wagner (ed. & trans.), *Onkelos on the Torah: Va-yikra* (Gefen: Jerusalem, 2010): 122.

through the works that were taught by Azazel: to him ascribe *all* sin.'[8]

And so a Jewish fallen angel develops into an originator of evil who is, by the early modern period, a being approached as a ruler of the dead and of spirits. Significantly, 'similar operations involving Azazel survive in several other fifteenth- and sixteenth-century British manuscripts.'[9] We have included a few such operations in this very tome. The first demonstrates several particular forms of Azazel's power and authority: in overseeing necromancy, in empowering tools and charms, in directing the actual spirit one is attempting to work, and in ensuring disobedient spirits do what they have been commanded to do. Most broadly, you will note appeal is most often framed to Azazel specifically as they 'that arte lorde of deade mens bodies that thou go into the courte; And aske leave that he maye come to me this nighte.'[10] This conjuration is to be made at the grave 'of a dead bodie that you know the name of' when one is standing 'at the head of the dead bodie.'[11] The titles of 'ruler of the dead' and 'keeper of the bones' are not merely poetic, but seem to have direct necromantic relevance. If there were any doubts about this connection, matters are made crystal-stone clear in the operation 'to have a true answere of Goulde or Silver or treasure in the earth; or to have the Carier' (also included in the book you hold in your hands now), in which Azazel is specifically petitioned 'as thou arte the keeper to dead mens bones, And keepest heare the bones of this man; N.'[12]

Following the call to the Ruler of the Dead, the operator is instructed to 'take o the earth of the grave of the dead bodie at the heade; And binde it in a cleane clothe of lynin; And then laie it under thy righte eare when thou liste to sleepe' for dream incubation purposes.[13] Not only is Azazel appealed to in the literal conjuration of the shades of the dead, but also to oversee and empower assemblages made on their behalf and in order to work more

---

8 1 Enoch 2:8. Emphasis added.

9 Frank Klaassen, 344; 362 n.17 cites the following magical working books: Oxford, Bodleian Library, Ballard 66, ff.33–39 (s.xvii); London, British Library, Sloane 3884, ff. 47–56 (s.xvi); and Bodleian, Rawlinson D. 252 (s.xv.), ff.66v–68r.

10 Illinois Pre-1650 MS. 0102, f.68–69.

11 Illinois Pre-1650 MS. 0102, f.68.

12 Illinois Pre-1650 MS. 0102, f.87.

13 Illinois Pre-1650 MS. 0102, f.69.

closely with them. Nor is this the only instance of such a working. In the experiment of Case MS. 5017, the same procedures are followed, with the slight alteration, that the linen cloth of grave dirt be put 'under thy hed *in thy cap* and sleep thereon.'[14] Clearly such small variations and practical notae, not to mention the appearance of the same basic operation in different manuscripts, suggests this operation was performed by a variety of practitioners.

Once dream contact has been established, the operator must return to the grave, and conjure the shade themself. Now that Azazel has been petitioned to grant favour, the ghost is also conjured 'that thou take leave of they lorde Azazell…and come to me.' So authority is courted directly over the entire necromantic venture, specifically to empower assembled materia and magical links, and in addition then used to direct subordinate spirits.

Finally, in the 'Experiment of Azazell,' once the necromancer has conjured the shade directly, they must return home and make their bed in a magic circle. In theory the ghost should again visit in dream. However, if the ghost proves recalcitrant, 'and if he come not goe againe the nexte nighte, And doe the same as thou diddest before; And then goe and sit the uppon thy bedd; And there calle the spirit Azazell to bringe him.' Again, the second operation specifies that Azazel not only grants spirits, but will even tell you the name of the spirit they have brought forth to serve you.[15]

In this particular working, 'as in many conjurations of the period, the spirit is called and asked to show the way to treasure, or else deliver it from the earth.'[16] This must occur at the grave of one newly dead, and one must know their name. Legard considers that it is 'likely that the experiments of Assasel and the four kings may also have been in common circulation amongst the magically inclined of the period,' and I am inclined to heartily agree. I would add that instances of four cardinal kings in early modern sources often seem to have some connection to magic, lore or notae associated with Saint Cyprian of Antioch, and vice versa.[17]

14 Case MS. 5017, f.23.

15 Illinois Pre-1650 MS. 0102, f.90.

16 Legard: citing National Archive of Scotland GD188/25/1/3:115–120.

17 I have explored these connections further in my essay '"In the Manner of Saint Cyprian": A Cyprianic Black Magic of Early Modern English Grimoires.' *Cypriana: Old World*, ed. by A. Cummins, J. Hathaway Diaz, & J. Zahrt (Rubedo Press, 2016): 83–116.

The newer grimoires of the *Bibliotheque Bleue* period – featuring demonic spirits of the *Ars Goetia* – are sometimes criticised as sensationalist demonology for basing their conjuration authority on appeals to the three chiefs (Lucifer, Belzebeth and either Astaroth or Satan). This is a nonsense. Jake Stratton-Kent's last instalment of his *Encyclopaedia Goetica* series *The Testament of Cyprian the Mage* has shown working under the three chiefs as a practice extends back to at least the first century. Placing a powerful demonic ruler at the top of a spirit hierarchy has great precedent.

Behind this popular early modern mythic figure – this keeper of the dead bones, ruler of the dead, this bestower of treasures and granter of familiars, this inverted crux of demonic and necromantic authority – lurks a chthonic Promethean teacher of sinful secrets, a seducer, an accuser, a patron to powerful ways of war and sex. Such is 'the spyritt Assasel, which arte a lyvinge and lovinge spyritt.'[18]

Dead Magicians

The second, indeed incontrovertible, argument for the genuine necromancy of the *Excellent Booke* is made by pointing to the centrality of the shades of famous sorcerers. In short, dead magicians – along with angels and biblical characters – directly instruct the pair (via the seventeen year-old Davis) how to conjure.

The *Visions* record that, on 24th February 1567, 'at the last there appeared Assasell, Solomon, Bacon, Adam, Job, and they said to the boy's hearing who they were.' To briefly overview that rogue's gallery, we have King Solomon – renowned for his wisdom and his skills of conjuration, for binding demonic spirits into the brazen vessel, and as the attributed author of one of the earliest examples of the grimoire format that became so popular in the early modern period, his *Testament*. Solomon seems to be Gilbert's chief spirit instructor; referred to as a 'servant' throughout.

We also have Roger Bacon, a thirteenth century Franciscan natural philosopher and alchemist, who was supposedly the author of an infamous book of necromancy. Sixteenth century grimoires and the manuscript spell

18 Add. MS. 36674, f.49r.

books of working magicians frequently contain appeals to him as a magician predecessor as well as various 'Baconian' methods of nigromancy.

The appearance of Job gives us a notable scriptural personage, whose chapter features a rather unique perspective on the Devil. Job was frequently cited in critical English demonological discourses concerning witchcraft, held up as an example of dutifully bearing bad fortune as God's will, rather than immediately and violently seeking a scapegoat or witch.[19]

And finally there is Adam: not only First Man but, in many traditions, the First Magician. Adam who named the animals, who existed in (various forms of) perfect prelapsarian grace, who spoke the original natural language of Creation and could thus understand God's perfect knowledge and order the cosmos to his will. Adam was also thought to have been given an important magical text upon exiting the Garden – the *Sepher Raziel*: a tome of considerable interest and utility to English magicians of the early modern period, especially those of the seventeenth century.[20]

The following day, these spirits were joined by Cornelius Agrippa, author of the encyclopaedic *Three Books of Occult Philosophy*. Agrippa had been developing a sinister reputation since his *Three Books* begun circulating in manuscript, demonologist Jean Bodin calling him 'the great doctor of the Diabolical Art.'[21] Agrippa's appearance is thus a natural conclusion for a host of ancestral figures all in some way associated with sinister occult power, usually expressly associated with powerful (and in some way sinful) books.

Examination of the further significances of these ghosts can be found in my final essay in this collection. For now, what is most important to understand is that it is by the *literal* wisdom of Solomon that the scryer and oper-

19 Calvin for instance employed Job in a long series of sermons on such matters. Susan E. Schreiner, 'Exegesis and Double Justice in Calvin's Sermons on Job.' *Church History* 58 (1989): 322–38. See also Philip C. Almond, *England's First Demonologist* (I.B. Taurus: New York, 2014): 51–52, 54.

20 Chiefly Simon Forman, and from him Richard Napier and Elias Ashmole. See Kassell, *Medicine and Magic*: 221; MS. Ashm. 1491, 1303–9; Ashm. 1790, f. 116; Sloane 3822, f. 24. Forman even recorded conversations he held with the angel Raziel. MS. Ashm 1491, 1303–9; Ashm 802, ii, ff.3v, 14r–v; Ashm 1790, f. 116. These sometimes yielded very practical medical advice, such as the proper planetary virtues and uses of mistletoe. MS. Ashm 1491, 1278.

21 Jean Bodin, *De la démonomanie des sorciers* (Jacques du Puys: Paris, 1580), f. 51r.

ator are commanded to rule the spirits, including Solomon's ghost himself, with an iron hand:

> And Solomon said that H. G: & Jo. should rule him; and also Job said to Jo.'s hearing: 'Trust no spirit visible or invisible, but the spirit of dead men. For they love man more then the others do.'[22]

Here is our explanation for why one would summon ghosts. Here is our justification for the dark arts of necromancy. Here too is a perspective on spirits that contextualises the pair's suspicious and violent conjuration style. At the foot of this page, the later editorial hand of Gabriel Harvey adds: 'Negromantia. The black art.' As if to make doubly clear the express involvement of the spirits of the dead, and to distinguish these practices from *simply illicit* 'black magic' he adds 'Sciomantia' – that is, divination by the shades of the dead.

ADVICE & INJUNCTIONS

On the 25th February, the operators are told by Adam they must 'goe cleane in apparell; & be good to the poore, & leave swearing; and goe in a black cote & cloke, And never tell none [that] thou sauest us; And then nothing thou shalt lacke.'[23] This advice forms the first instructions of the Excellent Booke following a prayer 'to be said when and before you deal with any spirit' which had been 'revealed by King Solomon, Anno Domini 1567 on the 20 February circa 9 – 10.'[24] Bacon's shade in particular is emphatic that 'Jo[hn]. yor skryer, especially in ap[pare]l & cloke of black clothe continually; & your selfe [i.e. H.G.] also except when you ride.'[25] I want to concentrate on this last feature, as it seems to have received special emphasis; necromancers' sartorial proclivities are not merely stylish: they may to some degree be necessary for their operations.

22 Add. MS. 36674, f.59r.
23 Add. MS. 36674, f.59v.
24 Add. MS. 36674, f.47r.
25 Add. MS. 36674, f.60r.

Black Clothes

Black garments hold Saturnine virtues, and standard astrological texts describe black cloth and those who dyed it as under the influence of this planet. In *Picatrix*, such dark garments are especially related to doctors,[26] recalling most immediately that physicians dealt in the inevitability of death. I have elsewhere considered the occult (and especially Saturnine) significances of taking black vestments:

> Black is literally the colour of *melancholy* ('the black bile') and associated with the Dark Arts of black magic. Such dark receptive heaviness, the very Platonic qualities of Earth,[27] would sympathetically *pull* spirits to it. This receptivity made dark earthy people more susceptible to possession by spirits: 'black choler, which is so obstinate, and terrible a thing, that the violence of it is said by physicians, and natural philosophers, besides madness, which it doth induce, also to entice evil spirits to seize upon men's bodies,'[28] indeed, 'so great also they say the power of melancholy is of, that by its force, Celestiall spirits also are sometimes drawn into men's bodies.' The link between Earth and chthonic spirits was further reinforced by wordplay rendering Goetia as 'Geocie,' and described as 'being familiar with unclean Spirits.'[29]

The black garb of an academic doctor might also bring to mind the supposedly sombre cogitations of melancholy *genius* (a term itself denoting both depth of thought and a spirit), a pervasive intellectual, medical and artistic trend in early modern England.[30] Certainly Robert Burton and Marsilio Ficino both wrote at length about the melancholies of schol-

26 *Picatrix: Atratus*, III.7, 159.

27 'to the Earth [were attributed] darkness, thickness, and quietness.' Agrippa, *Three Books*: 7.

28 Agrippa, *Three Books*: 133.

29 Heinrich Cornelius Agrippa, *The Vanity of Arts and Sciences* (London, 1676): 115.

30 See Winfried Schleiner, *Melancholy, Genius, and Utopia in the Renaissance* (Wiesbaden, 1991); Douglas Trevor, *The Poetics of Melancholy in Early Modern England* (Cambridge, 2004); Angus Gowland, *The Worlds of Renaissance Melancholy: Robert Burton in Context* (Cambridge, 2006). See also N.L. Brann, *The Debate over the Origin of Genius during the Italian Renaissance: The Theories of Supernatural Frenzy and Natural Melancholy in Accord and in Conflict on the Threshold of the Scientific Revolution* (Leiden: Brill, 2002).

ars,[31] and Hamlet too connects scholarship and spirit conversation.[32] We should however also bear in mind that 'in popular discourse before the twentieth century the title was not restricted to those with a university training,' but was also conferred upon 'those who were skilled with herbs and magic.'[33] A doctor – physicist, physician and philosopher – might be a magician almost by default. Certainly to dress in black was to attract shades by the gravity of the grave.[34]

If this practice of garbing in black has indeed some link to older methods of consorting with specifically Saturnine spirits – often *shades* of the dead themselves – by resembling them, might we perhaps consider other practices whereby the magical operator attempts to frame *themselves* in similitude and sympathy with astrological spirits they conjure?

Secrecy

The command to 'never tell none [that] thou sauest us' is also I believe significant in light of common conjuration instructions to keep secret one's magical practices, especially for those operations involving demonic 'unclean spirits' – also known generally as 'Inferiors' – and the shades of the dead.

Reginald Scot, in his *Discoverie of Witchcraft* – which is now described as 'the first grimoire printed in the English language'[35] – notes a ritual to con-

31 See, for example, Robert Burton, *Anatomy of Melancholy* (London, 1623). 1.2.3.15 'Love of Learning, or overmuch study. With a Digression on the misery of Scholars, and why the Muses are Melancholy'; Marsilio Ficino, *Three Books on Life*, trans. Carol Kaske & John R. Clark (Tempe, 1998), 1.11–X:111–137.

32 William Shakespeare, *The tragicall historie of Hamlet* (London, 1603), I.I. f. 2. Indeed, Horatio is even said to have attended Wittenstein, a university so infamous for demonology its namesake 'letters' linger as a folk euphemism for black magic across Europe.

33 Davies, *Popular Magic*: 74.

34 Alexander Cummins, 'The Azured Vault: Astrological Magic in Seventeenth-century England.' *The Celestial Art*, Austin Coppock and Daniel Schulke (eds.) (Three Hands Press, 2018): 221–222.

35 'what amounted to the first grimoire printed in the English language,' which while published with the intention 'to prove the worthlessness of its contents...unwittingly ended up democratizing ritual magic rather than undermining it.' Owen Davies, *Grimoires: A History of Magic Books* (Oxford, 2009): 70. See also S.F. Davies, 'The Reception of

jure the spirit of a dead person (preferably a suicide) that one should 'let no persons see thy doings,' or you 'can do nothing to any purpose.'[36] Furthermore, the 'Tried and True *Experimentum* for Love' of 'a herbal and medical miscellany of the fifteenth century,'[37] which involves sacrificing doves at a midnight crossroads or 'a place where thieves are hung' to one of the very spirits of the *Ars Goetia* popularised in *Discoverie*, features the instruction 'do not speak to anyone, neither going nor returning.'[38] The second injunction of the 'Instructions of Cyprian,' which grace the beginning of the working book attributed to Arthur Gauntlet, is that the magician 'must be secret And betray not the secrets of his Art but to his fellows and to them of his counsel.'[39]

Secrecy is also a consistent theme in Gilbert and Davis' dealings with spirits. In an entry in *Visions* he notes that particular spirits appearing as various corvids promise him 'they had certain books, and other things which we will not name in keeping which H.G. must have.'[40] Earlier, it is noted 'there apeared two Angles to H.G.'s sight, and his skryer should not see them: Toby and Gabriel in the likeness of two larks.'[41] Bonds of secrecy divided even conjuror from seer.

It has been pointed out that secrecy is a common theme in books of magic in general, from Albert the Great's *Mirror of Astronomy* to *Picatrix* and beyond.[42] Alchemists warn text should not fall into the 'wrong hands,' and various authors on the occult employ deliberate obscurantisms wherein they use 'enigmatic phrases, invent secret words and alphabets, mix together different languages, abbreviate heavily, and so forth.'[43] Kieckhefer presents two main purposes for such secrecy: 'the subjective need to maintain an aura of mystery, and the alleged objective need to keep the secrets out of the hands

Reginald Scot's Discovery of Witchcraft: Witchcraft, Magic, and Radical Religion.' *Journal of the History of Ideas* 74, 3 (2013): 381–401, 393.

36 Scot, Discoverie: 244.

37 'Liber de Angelis, Annulis, Karecteribus & Ymaginibus Planetarum.' Fanger, Conjuring Spirits: 33.

38 Fanger, Conjuring Spirits: 61, 63.

39 Gauntlet: 39; Sloane MS. 3851, f.2.

40 62r.

41 61r.

42 Kieckhefer, Magic in the Middle Ages: 140.

43 Kieckhefer, Magic in the Middle Ages: 140.

of bunglers who will give magic a bad name by their very failure.'[44] Roger Bacon is specifically mentioned as further propagating the idea that just as study of the occult meant attempting to understand the hidden operations of the cosmos, so too should such knowledge and its organisation and transmission mirror the nature of its content and remain in some way *occulted*.

Secrecy — as also advised by the shades of Agrippa et al — I am arguing is not merely a form of self-preservation when attempting to practice illicit or illegal magic, or a set of trade secrets protected for their value to livelihoods and the respectability of magic itself, but is actually a sorcerous advantage or even necessity for the efficacy of certain chthonic works.

Ethics

In terms of the wider ethical behaviour of the necromancer, Klaassen points out that injunctions of purity are 'commonly found in the early folios of ritual magic works.'[45] The order 'to be good to the poor' is even repeated in the diabolic pact working with Lucifuge Rofocale of the *Grand Grimoire*. Yet Klaassen also considers the lack of sexual taboos to be a significant change from such older practices, suggesting 'sexual purity appears to have become less crucial in sixteenth-century operations, perhaps under the influence of Protestantism, but also potentially due to a declericalisation of ritual magic.'[46] Necromancy appears to have acknowledged shifting religious and ethical sensibilities, and 'democratised' along with other forms of magic. Whatever the reasons, it is clear neither Catholicism nor the celibate had exclusive rights to the dead.

---

44 Kieckhefer, *Magic in the Middle Ages*: 141.

45 Klaassen: 343. He goes onto specify: 'The *Practica nigromanciae* attributed to Roger Bacon specifies clean clothing among the rules [citing London Society of Antiquaries, 39, fols. 15v–17v], and the *Liber iuratus* gives a strong emphasis to keeping good company [citing *Liber iuratus Honorii: A Critical Edition of the Latin Version of the Sworn Book of Honorius*, ed. Gosta Hedegard (Stockholm: Almqvist & Wiksell, 2002), 1.20–29, 61]. Almsgiving is an instruction found in the *Ars notoria*'s *Opus operum* and in John of Morigny's work. Medieval ritual texts uniformly emphasize good behavior and moral purity, something assured by seeking confession prior to operation [citing, for instance, Oxford, Bodleian Library, Rawlinson D. 252, f.49v].' 343–344, 361 n. 9, 10.

46 Klaassen: 359.

Furthermore, the taboos and ethics of this grimoire are considered by the magicians using it to be based not in the authority of older books of magic, but from the lips of the magician-heroes and saints and angels and spirits themselves. They considered these regulations imperatives – or at the very least, ratified – by the results gleaned from ritual congress with spirits, rather than a scholasticism or mimicry beholden to older magical systems or grimoires.

On the very first day of the scrying records, Solomon tells the operator and the scryer that they 'should rule' a spirit who has appeared.[47] Solomon's tuition appears to be the result of requesting Assasel to grant the operator 'one of the beste spyritts of a deade man, that ever was in the worlde, to teach me all manner of Artes appertayninge to learninge and hid knowl-ede.'[48] It is also significant that our cast of dead holy men and magicians tell the operators 'when Solomon biddeth you to call us, we will obey.'[49] Thus, not only is the (actual rather than literary or figurative) ghost of Solomon their teacher of magic, but also instrumental in the conjuring of other ghosts. Furthermore, the magical operator seems not simply advised but potentially bidden by a superior spirit to call other ghosts. Klaassen points out that the deliberate workings with Assasel and Oriens were 'supplement-ed by the *unsolicited* appearances of Saint Luke.'[50] This would appear to have important resonances for modern spirit-based practices, particularly those prosecuted under the tutelage or patronage of a senior sorcerer spirit.

STONES & TOMES

Of central importance to the style of conjuration instructed in the Visions and Excellent Booke is the shewstone. All spirits, from Assasel through the demonic regents down to minor inferiors, are called into the stone.

It is made clear a spirit can be present in the stone without being seen, though the instructions state that one should always ensure a spirit can be seen before attempting to set it a task. The sign of the spirit is, at the very least, 'a thing shadow[y].' The Excellent Booke teaches 'The Art how to call any

47 Add. MS. 36674, f.59r.
48 Add. MS. 36674, f.50r.
49 Add. MS. 36674, f.59v.
50 Klaassen, 'Ritual Invocation': 342. Emphasis added.

spirit out of one crystal stone where he is invisible into another crystal, to make him appear visible to all men's sights.'[51] Not only is this a possible projection onto a 'big screen' crystal, it shows that, though the shewstone is often referred to in the singular, it is clear that more than one was employed.

Various phenomena occur and proper procedures must be observed during conjuration with a shewstone. The text entreats that, upon conjuring Oriens for example, 'when he is come commaunde him straightly to appeare to yor sighte, or else that he wyll make the stone to leape 3 tymes from the place where the stone lyeth, and yf he wyll not, commaund him straightly as followeth...' and that furthermore 'when he hath by your compulsio[n] appeared say that you see A thinge shadowe in the stone, wch is in the wall, And therefore appare to mee and speeke or wrighte for I wyll not beleve, that here is any thinge to my syghte, except thou speake or wryte, and appeare to my syghte, and speake to my hearinge: or else I wyll accurse the[e]...'[52]

Note that we are told the stone is 'in the wall.' Given that the calls, prayers, charges and constraints to the demonic regents (Oriens, Amaymon, Paimon and Egyn) are directed towards each 'quarter of the world and turning your face accordingly'[53] this also might suggest multiple stones. As well as being mentioned as mounted on the wall, the operator is also instructed to place the crystal on 'the board' at key moments in the recitation of the calls – again, a procedure in keeping with Dee and Kelly's later angelical operations. Note also that Oriens is allowed to write as well as speak – an essential feature of using the stone to 'deliver books' and their understanding.

Likewise, some angels enter willingly to manifest to visible appearance: the stone could be home to holy and trustworthy spirits and visions. Indeed, the *Excellent Booke* offers two designs to engrave on one's stones – one 'for Aungelles, for Inferiors and other Spyritts,' and 'another christall, to call Aungells, or spyrittes into: But yf you do call bothe, then must ye never call any spyrittes into that stone you call Aunngels into. And of bothe it is beste for you, to kepe this laste next before you for the Aungells.'[54]

51 Add. MS. 36674, f.54r.
52 Add. MS. 36674, f.48r.
53 Add. MS. 36674, f.51r.
54 Add. MS. 36674, f.56v.

Shewstones were utilised by early modern magicians to call spirits and have visions – most famously, of course, by Dee and Kelly. Lilly describes the 'berril' of Mr. Gilbert Wakering thus: 'it was of the largeness of a good big orange, set in silver, with a cross on the top, and another on the handle; and round about engraved the names of these angels, Raphael, Gabriel, Uriel.'[55] Archangelic divine names frequently appear upon shewstones or their fixtures. John Aubrey describes another crystal stone, also calling it a 'Berill':

> a perfect Sphere, the Diameter of it I guess to be something more than an Inch: It is set in a Ring, or Circle of Silver resembling the Meridian of a Globe: The stem of it is about Ten Inches high, all gilt. At the Four quarters of it are the Names of Four Angels, viz. Vriel, Raphael, Michael, Gabriel. On the top is a Cross Patee.[56]

Significantly, the berril is explicitly linked to prophecy, to seeing the future and to apocalypticism: 'Berill…is one of the Twelve Stones mentioned in the Revelation.'[57] As I shall attempt to show, this element of apocalypse – after all, an unveiling – is also deeply significant for the kinds of workings that Gilbert and Davis describe as 'imparted unto me for secrets of much importance.'[58]

The stone of the *Excellent Booke* is specified as a little different from the crystal ball of the berril: 'your stone must be flat on both sides, and clean, and without cracks or stains, and as large as may be gotten, and of a good thickness.'[59] It should also be engraved directly, rather than bearing decorated fittings. But the stone also shares an operational feature with the more typical spherical crystals, as Aubrey confirms of berills:

> The Prophets had their Seers, viz. Young Youths who were to behold those Visions, of whom Mr. Abraham Cowly writes, thus,

55 Lilly, History: 232.
56 Aubrey, Miscellanies: 131.
57 Aubrey, Miscellanies: 128.
58 Add. MS. 36674, f.58r.
59 Add. MS. 36674, f.56r.

With hasty wings, time present they outfly,
And tread the doubtful Maze of Destiny;
There walk and sport among the years to come,
And with quick Eye pierce every Causes Womb.[60]

In the case of Gilbert and Davis, the 'Causes Womb' they wished to pierce was the amniotic chamber of their own nascent sorcerous aptitudes. Gilbert and Davis saw themselves doing magic through this magical lens – from these visions they learned how to do magic: to focus attention on a spirit who would be a helpful servant in the magicians' quest for knowledge and power. For instance, examine their first recorded vision:

> There appeared a long blue cloud, like a streak from the east to the west, on the which H.G. went, having a gilt sword in his hand, & Jo. Davis going after him with a book covered with a skyn, the hairy side outward. Himself [H.G.] being apparelled in a black robe and cape cloak, with a payer of black silk netherstocks gartered with black, gathered above the knee; having a velvet cap, & a black feather. And very many, like men, running away before him, kneeling and falling down, holding up their hands to him. And he followed them very cruelly, and struck one of them, that had a crown on his head, with the sword in his hand, most royal to behold. And he struck the king so cruelly that he fell down on his knees to him, holding up his hand.[61]

Initially, they see the pair of them in fine black clothing, before they have been told by Adam and company that this is necessary to the work. The 'many, like men' are identified as spirits, and the striking of them is taken as instruction – nay, 'appointment' – to treat the spirits aggressively in order to ensure their obedience. The visions of themselves acting in the spirit-world are interpreted as commands and justification for conducting magical operations, just as the words of their ancestor-heroes. From such scrying, lessons were learned and secrets were unveiled.

60 Aubrey, *Miscellanies*: 128.
61 Add. MS. 36674, f.59r.

Book Delivery

It is somewhat of an understatement to say that books play an important role in the *Excellent Booke* and its *Visions*. In the first vision, although Gilbert's violence cows the spirits it is only when Davis 'opened his book, holding it abroad' that the spirits 'said to the boy's hearing "What lack you that you show such cruelty unto us? Shut your book, and you shall have what you will desire."'[62] This is the first of many examples of dominating spirits by opening and holding up a book. It is the book that seems to ultimately command the spirits – the striking and cursing is unpleasant, but it is the book which compels.

This first book is recorded to be 'written with black, white, yellow, blue, green and red.' As further evidence for the case that the pair were using these visions to inform their practice, the very first entry in the *Excellent Booke* is a list of inks and the command 'these colour inks must be had.'[63] These are the same colours, with a few exceptions: black is omitted (presumably due to its ubiquity); 'white' becomes 'silver'; and 'notable gold' is added. Special ink is a feature of most Solomonic grimoires; mostly derived from the blood of animals or (in the cases of the more infernal tomes) the operator. *Sepher Raziel*, mentioned briefly previously, actually includes some of the most detailed instructions for making inks. The main instances of seven colours of ink being specified I've found are in instructions for framing planetary pentacles; as in the *Key of Solomon* grimoires – especially in the Rabbi Solomon Family, such as Wellcome MS. 4670. Yet there are no pentacles specifically listed in the *Excellent Booke*. I would suggest this demonstrates a point at which the immediacy of spirit contact and experience combined with book-learning and traditionalism in the operations of Gilbert and Davis: potentially, a new use for an established component.

Along with the taboos and advice already mentioned, it is insisted 'The master must also have one or two good books to call by; as after you shall here find.'[64] Such a 'book of calls' is expressly mentioned as needed for cursing and compelling recalcitrant spirits, especially ensuring Oriens gives you

62 Add. MS. 36674, f.59r.
63 Add. MS. 36674, f.47r.
64 Add. MS. 36674, f.47v.

'the best book.'[65] And so the visions inform the instructions, and a book is used to get more books to unveil deeper secrets and unlock further power.

And how are these books acquired? One way was through the aforementioned Oriens:

> comaund him to give you the beste booke, that ever was, *Seinge thou art the kynge of the spyritts of the Easte* I *charge the[e] doe it,* and when he hath brought you A booke in the stone to yo[r] sighte, then charge him to delyver yt to you, or appointe him some place where he shall lay it, and let yt bee doon w[ith] speede.[66]

Legard considers this text-granting function the primary role of Oriens in the *Excellent Booke.*[67] This function extends expressly into tuition: the grimoire instructs that upon receiving your text, 'yf you can not read it, then come to him [Oriens] againe and saye *what haste thou given mee? I knowe not whether yt bee good or yll. Therefore* I *charge the[e] out of hande, to showe me the readgine and understandinge of yt.*'[68] Oriens delivers not merely the text, but the 'understandinge' of it.

Another means of receiving texts appears to be a particular visionary procedure. It is derived from another vision on the 24th February, after the pair had received their authority from Solomon, this time as the sun set:

> Jo. saw a great wood, having a great house in the midst of it with a little house by it most strongly built, having an front door, with nine key holes. There being written on the door these characters following [characters] And in this house he saw a chamber richly hanged with gold, in which chamber there was a tree of crystal which was written upon very well, having many branches, with a door on him, as it were with seven keyholes, which had the chinks written on it. Within the which there were many books, whereof one had a crystal cover, another with the

---

65 Add. MS. 36674, f.48r
66 Add. MS. 36674, f.48r.
67 Legard: citing Folger MS. v.b.26(a): 188.
68 Add. MS. 36674, f.48r.

hairy side of a skin out-ward; with diverse other goodly books. This tree spread, & grew as the next leaf followeth.[69]

Books with hairy or crystal covers reappear throughout the *Visions*, and are clearly significant. We are not dealing with a single channelled text, but a systematic procedure – complete with visionary location, seals, keys, and chambers – for accessing many texts.

The following day the two return to 'the wood & house,' and this time it is made clear that this is 'where Solomon dwelt.'[70] We have a patron of this body of knowledge – indeed, one of the central patrons of European magic. By 6th April 1567, the procedure is so familiar, Gilbert simply records 'my boy went to Solomon's house in the morning, and came back home to me again about nine of the clock in the forenoon, and brought me from there a book written by Saint Luke the Evangelist.'[71] We should have absolutely no doubt as to what they are doing here – traversing a visionary landscape, arriving at a familiar place of power presided over by a powerful spirit who has previously granted his patronage, using seals, unlocking portals, accessing a repository of secret knowledge and power, and – in contrast to other temporary peak experiences of gnosis or nebulous cosmic oneness – bringing it back as a text.

The lack of distinction between physical and astral realms in the travel between them – like the lack of distinction between the vision of a spirit in a shewstone and its conjured presence – is mirrored in the manner by which these tomes from the very house of Solomon are brought back. The books are pulled, in some sense, from spirit vision to tangible manifestation.

TORTURE TACTICS

The majority of the *Excellent Booke* is taken up with calls: opening prayers, calling the spirit into the stone, threatening secondary calls if the spirit is not immediately obedient, maledictions and curses if they remain obstinate or absent, bonds to constrain and licenses to depart. But the most important technique and approach of the *Excellent Booke* is threat and spirit torture.

69 Add. MS. 36674, f.59r–v.
70 Add. MS. 36674, f.59v.
71 Add. MS. 36674, f.62v.

The texts give us not only methods of torture, but explicate why one would need to do so. In short, spirits, especially the 'wicked' sort, have no desire to grant the operator anything. Spirits themselves tell the pair that they were 'loathe' to be ruled over, and deliberately made it difficult for a magician to do so by changing shape and even number.[72] Thus, 'you by Art must doe, or else you shall never have nothing done for you.'[73] Force must be used.

Luckily, Gilbert and Davis had sanctioned authority to do just that. Time and again, Solomon authorises them to command spirits. Later Job similarly relates he has been 'appointed to serve him [H.G.], & to make many secret books for him.'[74] They are sanctioned by the Evangelists Mark, Matthew, Luke, and John who appear as angels with books of gold, and even Adam admits 'when Solomon bids you to call us, we will obey.'[75] The angels themselves promised: 'thou shalt have servants that shall teach thee...and our help shall be to it.'[76] At another point it was assured:

> The Angels said unto H.G. that he should fear nothing. And that he had a good servant of Solomon, whose counsel he should follow, for he would advise him for the best. And that he should read when Solomon appointed him, for he would do nothing to his hindrance. And that they would appear to him in the element when he would, and that they would teach him all arts, and how to make books.[77]

Gilbert seems especially proud of one set of techniques in which the operator attempts to back foot the conjured spirit by claiming it is lying even when it is not. Chief among these are a set of what might be termed 'distrust games': 'you must allway hide thinges to make them fynde yt; And make the[m] do thinges for you that you doe knowe allready to be true.'[78] The text recommends a test of honesty as simple as hiding a ring and asking the

---

72 Add. MS. 36674, f.62r
73 Add. MS. 36674, f.48r.
74 Add. MS. 36674, f.62r.
75 Add. MS. 36674, f.59v.
76 Add. MS. 36674, f.60r.
77 Add. MS. 36674, f.61r.
78 Add. MS. 36674, f.48v.

spirit to find it. However, crucially the operator 'must never seeme to beleve them, howe trulye soever they saye.'[79] The conjuror is encouraged to accuse the spirit of lying even if they both know they did not, and to use this false sleight in demanding satisfaction and in straightforward intimidation.

The *Excellent Booke* gives frequent advice on how to torture spirits who do not cooperate with the conjuror. One interesting detail to emerge from studying these techniques of discipline and punishment shows spirits being understood and manipulated according to elemental identities:

> [I]f ye be of the fire: then punish him with stinking water, either of man or woman, and put stinking things into it; and then putt the stone into it. and straightly command him to come forth out of the stone into the water that you did putt him in, and there to tarry, until you do command him to come into the stone again. And if he be of the water then take brimstone and burn it, and command him first to go into some stone for the purpose, and then put him into the burning brimstone; and that is for the punishment of them (of fire and water), reading a curse over them. And if he be of the air then you must command him to go forth of the stone into some vile stinking mud, and to tarry in it, until you do command him to go into the stone again. And if he be of the Earth then you must curse him in God's name. And then that will serve them sufficiently.[80]

Significantly, even one of the classic spirit tortures of the grimoires is given an explicitly elemental gloss: 'Note, that there is noe plauge so greate, as to burne a spyrittt's name, and *characte*: most espetially, that is, yf the spyritt be of the Ayer.'[81] Necromancers and diabolists worked with elementals. More broadly, the practice of commanding a spirit to go forth from a stone once constrained within it – especially to be affected by external conditions – raises interesting questions concerning the intersections of scrying and enchanting in conjuring. Interestingly, considering the usual approach to spirits, the *Excellent Booke* notes, 'You must never keepe any inclosed above

79 Add. MS. 36674, f.49r.
80 Add. MS. 36674, f.48v–49r.
81 Add. MS. 36674, f.47r.

24. howeres.'[82] This similarly serves thinking about seating spirits in spell objects and other magical tools: a dedicated spirit seat requiring continual reconsecratory actions.

Sometimes a show of strength was necessary before even beginning to command a spirit. In the operation to transfer a spirit from one stone to another to make them visible, after initial prayers for the action's success, 'then you must putt a little brimstone into the fire, and hold the stone [in which] the spirit appear invisible over it, in the smoke thereof, and a little to touch two or three times the flame thereof with the stone, and then say as follows:

> O thou spirit N., who art in this crystal stone. If thou do not appear presently to my sight thou seethe thy punishments, and worse than this. Therefore, delude not with me, for I will use Art with thee.[83]

Certain recent trends in modern conjuration have sought to emphasise respectful relations with spirits over the pomp and brimstone of such antagonistic actions. These 'spirit-friendly' models stress building relationships with one's working spirits over repeated operations, and adopt practices of feeding, housing and consulting reminiscent of those involving witches' familiars and sorcerer's imps. The perspective offered by the *Excellent Booke* at the very least suggests this approach has potential to jump the gun in presupposing an inclination on the part of the spirit to explore a pact or working relationship. Introductions are rather more like bird catching than hiring a mercenary. In this context, certain shows of force, displaying capacity and ability to inflict potential violence against the spirit-realm, are demonstrations of competence as well as dominance. Maledictions, threats of earning God's displeasure, threats of physically injuring the spirit through various elemental tortures, Gilbert's distrust games and other techniques seem necessary tools in the conjuration and employment of certain spirits, which require cajoling, strong-arming, outwitting and occasionally outright bullying. Even the operator's book – the repository of liturgy, ossuary of spirit offices and seals, and the calls of conjuration themselves – takes on the

82 Add. MS. 36674, f.48r.
83 Add. MS. 36674, f.54r.

air and authority of the exorcist's holy symbol, cowing spirits to its coercive virtues and bending their wills to submit to that of the magicians.

An emphasis on a results model that defines success only in terms of the continued appearance or manifestation of these sorts of spirits, without binding or constraining them in some way to actually perform the work they are tasked with, is in serious danger of trying to domesticate birds of prey without gauntlets. With such an approach, the spirit merely flying away never to return is arguably a best case scenario.

Nevertheless, it should interest the twenty-first century karcist to learn that certain elements of the basis of Gilbert's approach are eventually rebuked, by the angelic Evangelist St Luke himself, no less, who:

> willed me to leave using the names of God to hurt wicked & rebellious spirits, offering himself to do all things for me, & to teach me, how to have all things done by the Angels, without such cursing, & conjuring by the word & names of God, promising me that he would come to me wherever I would have him.[84]

This is especially interesting as it presents us a third manner of conjuring wicked or unclean spirits from Agrippa's twofold taxonomy of 'Geocie or Conjuring, curs'd for being familiar with unclean Spirits':

> For some of them make it their business to adjure and compel Evil Spirits to appearance, by the Efficacy and Power of sacred Names; because seeing that every Creature doth fear and reverence the Name of its Creator, no wonder if Conjurors, and other Infidels, Pagans, Jews, Saracens, or prophane Persons, do think to force the Devils Obedience by the Terrour of his Creators Name.
>
> Others, more to be detested than they, and worthy the utmost punishment of Fire, submitting themselves to the Devils, sacrifice to them, and Worship them, become guilty of the vilest subjection and Idolatry that may be.[85]

84 Add. MS. 36674, f.62r–v.
85 Agrippa, Vanity: 116.

To have an angelic authority keeping these spirits in line now seems a middle way. Previously, Gilbert's 'deprivations' involved reeling off a litany of how 'God the Father curse thee, God the Son curse thee, God the Holy Ghost curse thee, with their power deprive thee for thy disobeying of these holy words. All Angels and Archangels curse thee and condemn thee and, for thy disobeying of thy office, deprive thee. Lord I beseech thee that this rebellious spirit N., may be deprived for his disobeying. All saints curse thee' etc.[86]

VOICES & VISIONS

It might help us to understand the emphasis on constraint and bonds in these conjurations by looking at how spirits appeared in the Visions: mostly as elusive animal forms streaking through the air from one place to another; nebulous apparitions of vague colour and shape; and animals with strange heraldic features. These were not generally concrete, discrete, entities easily apprehended.

The vast majority of spirits in the Visions appear as birds:

> there came two little birds from the north to the south, flying had (sic) before, and lighted on the south side of us, which was on the left hand. And these two birds did fly again from the south toward the north. Then there came another bird from the south side of us, and it flew toward the north and came back again towards us, and flew towards the north again, and then circled on the south side of us.[87]

There is a sense of moving through a landscape of spirits, frighting these creatures away. The most common descriptor to follow any mention of spirit sighting is the direction it came from, usually followed by the direction it was heading. These clearly have utility in calling the spirits, and I doubt it is solely the four kings that responded to specific ritual directionality.

Even beyond spirits appearing as birds, flight is a commonality: 'three dragons flying in the air. One green; the other red, the third blue. Their tongues were like spears and [they] had long tails.' After these are dealt with

86 Add. MS. 36674, f.55v.
87 Add. MS. 36674, f.61r.

(by the showing of the book), 'then appeared two fowls that were black running in the air.'[88] We even encounter 'in the air a dog,'[89] and 'a great number of little things, like little mites of crystal, which danced, & tarried a good while, near & round about us.'[90] Often spirits, and even visions of Gilbert and Davis themselves, appear from clouds: 'A blue cloud, like a man with one leg, holding up the other.'[91]

Often, spirits have some kind of chimerical or otherwise monstrous feature: 'birds from the west toward the east, with great wings, and long tails, which came on our right side, these having no heads'[92] or 'four other black birds coming out of the west toward the east, having long necks and long tails, with greater feet, all as big as [their] bodies.'[93] Strange feet are not an unusual feature of spirits across the world, and likewise, the pair encounter several dogs with 'little legs and great broad feet like unto horses.'[94] Indeed after birds, dogs are probably the most common animal form.

Perhaps my favourite sighting – in the sense of being so unnerving – is that of 'trawling on the ground two great black wings joined together, without any body, hard by the ground.'[95] It is joined by a 'grey con[e]y,' that is, an heraldic rabbit, both then disappear into the ground.

It is worth briefly contextualising the very particular appearances of spirits in the Excellent Booke and Visions in light of contemporary grimoires. Chronologically these spirit encounters precede the spirit lists of both the Book of the Offices of Spirits (published recently as the Book of Oberon) and Scot's Discoverie which informed the Ars Goetia of various Lesser Keys of Solomon. It is recorded that at a certain point 'sundry imperfect sounds and the sound of bells and many other instruments'[96] are heard – a feature in common with

88 Add. MS. 36674, f.59v.
89 Add. MS. 36674, f.62r.
90 Add. MS. 36674, f.61r.
91 Add. MS. 36674, f.59r.
92 Add. MS. 36674, f.61v.
93 Add. MS. 36674, f.61v.
94 Add. MS. 36674, f.61r.
95 Add. MS. 36674, f.61r.
96 Add. MS. 36674, f.61v.

the other goetic grimoires[97] and especially said to herald the appearance of the four kings, who feature most prominently in the *Excellent Booke*.

There are many bird spirits in both lists. However it seems significant to point out that there are spirits in the *Visions* who deliberately change shape:

> Also the 17th of March, somewhat before four of the clock at afternoon there appeared two marvellous great ravens standing on the ground. And H.G. being willed by Solomon to speak to them then one of them came flying upon him, and so flew towards the southwest. And whilst H.G. and his skryer did before him, the other flew away. But with much calling they went into the east, & divided them selves in three crows and came, and fell down by them, and being so commanded did stay and speake these wordes: That they did first appear like ravens, and afterwards divided themselves in to three crowes because they might not know them.[98]

Spirits, after all, are tricksy, and loathe to be pinned down and thus commanded. My broader point is that the spirits of the *Visions* — essentially appearing in animal form, albeit with somewhat monstrous features (headlessness, weird feet, etc.) — precede both the more quotidian animal appearances of the *Offices of Spirits* (in which spirits appear as swans, geese, hedgehogs, and bears) who nonetheless have particular functions and offices, and the more expressly chimeric spirits of the *Ars Goetia* such as Zagam (who, by the seventeenth century, as Zagan, 'cometh abroad like a Bull, with Griffins wings; but…taketh humane shape').

I contend that this 'chimerification' has something to do with a wider epistemological shift occurring in early modern Europe in which sight and vision themselves are troubled, problematised, and increasingly questioned,[99] which combines with a theological move away from the Devil as a physical person and towards a more subtle agent of temptation. This is not to attempt to explain away encounters with the spirit world and its denizens

97   For example see the entries for Paimon, Beleth and Amdusias in the *Ars Goetia*.

98   Add. MS. 36674, f.62r. These very spirits in fact identify themselves by significant names historically associated with scrying itself. For more on this, see my final chapter in this collection.

99   For more on this, see Stuart Clark, *Vanities of the Eye* (Oxford University Press, 2007).

using purely sociological or anthropological blinds for an underlying materialist denial of the reality of such spirits. Rather, it is to draw parallels in the light reflected from a glimmering shewstone between how spirits were being perceived and how perception itself was being understood. After all, staring into the dark mirror we meet our own gaze. These two historical turns meet at the midnight crossroads of the heretical imaginal, where the imagination itself (most closely associated with vision) is held in suspicion as a portal for bedevilled perception.

The older British fairy and familiar lore of unbidden encounters with a black cat or dog that suckles at the blooded witch's teat are superseded as the chief agents of black magic – at least in the popular imagination – by daemonically nebulous spirits who manifest in phenomenological instantiations of circle and stone; fantastic hybrids of lion-faced apparitions, giant ravens, three-headed humanoids holding snakes and weapons and so forth.

However, this is not to suggest a ceremonial formalism to these goetic workings themselves. The *Excellent Booke* has but few specific astrological timings, and no consecrations. Indeed, it is at pains to point out the shewstone can be prepared at any time. It also merely insists on 'great plenty of sweet powders, and perfumes' rather than giving specific correspondences.

The concentration on instructions and taboos for proper conduct, rather than sacred periods or ingredients of conjuration, suggests more a way of living in relation to spirits, seeking to apprehend and contemplate one's spiritual purpose and engagements.

CONCLUSIONS

So what can be concluded about the significances of these workings? Firstly, they are primarily aimed towards knowledge: chiefly, knowledge of occult machinations and personal destiny. The initial preparatory prayer claims 'knowledge is all my desire,' and entreats 'O Lord send me some of his good hidden work, that has not been revealed to any man.'[100]

Indeed, Klaassen's brief treatment (the only extant specific academic treatment of these texts) can be summarised as partly considering these treatises evidence of an early modern text-based magical practice with one

---

100 Add. MS. 36674, f.47r.

foot firmly in the 'old dirty' medieval ritual magic, and with the other foot at least stepping toward (if not actually in) the experimental process episte-mology of the emerging scientific movement. The idea is to generate new knowledge, exploring both divine and infernal means for unveiling the truths of Nature.

Secondly, it is worth foregrounding that, if this talk of four book-bear-ing angels standing at the corners of a golden hill, of sevenfold locks and seals, of dragons in the sky, of trees of blood, puts us in mind of the Book of Revelation, this is no accident. There is a simmering apocalypticism to these experiments, knowledge and gnosis is begged of the Almighty against a very real millenarianism. To give the preparatory prayer more attention, such entreating for knowledge comes specifically in this context: 'Then for that cause I desire thee O God to send it to me, that in these our last days it may be known.' Once more, these experiments, which precede Dee and Kelly, show attempts to understand Nature before all is consumed. Without wanting to overstate the importance of these texts, it is also clear that such an apocalyptic perspective is relevant to our own times, in which we face very real ecological collapse.

Desire for knowledge and the haemorrhaging hourglass imperative of apocalypse commingle in a two-handed bid for the right hand of insight and the left hand of control. Throughout the Booke and its Visions, Gilbert and Davis appear to level up, to wrest more understanding and authority. Indeed, after Solomon's pledge of support comes Job, and after Job comes St Luke:

> And I having the spirit of King Solomon, and the spirit of Job before, they both fell on their knees to Luke when they saw him. And the wicked inferior Bleath ran continually away, from one place to another round about the stone as fast as might be.[101]

It is clear from the reactions of the spirits themselves that this is a spiritual elevation. Indeed, Gilbert is eventually promised by the angels standing over the tree of blood:

---

101 Add. MS. 36674, f.62v.

Thou art blessed of God surely, for thou hast a servant that will make thee a saint. And I trust by our help, you shall come to this tree, and we will do all that ever we can, for thee.[102]

I want to emphasise once more the unequivocal judgment that spirits of dead men are more trustworthy than other spirits. This runs directly contrary to Swiss pastor Ludwig Lavater's dismissal of ghosts (itself based on a Protestant rejection of Purgatory) as delusions, tricks of the light or demonic spirits in disguise. The *Excellent Booke* describes a necromancy not founded upon spookiness for spookiness' sake: but because the dead have a great love and care for the living.

It is also worth restating that the tutelary spirits who offer this empowerment are some of the forefathers of the art of magick itself. Some forms of spirit tutelage are an accepted part of early modern ritual magic – angelic conversation, after all, was conducted by international court magi and local practicing astrologer-physicians alike[103] – but Add. MS. 36674 demonstrates that ghosts, saints and underworld spirits were also consulted. In fact, far more than consulted about particular answers to troubling questions ('What is Rudolf II up to?', 'Is this patient mad, or bewitched, or both?'), they were called to teach sorcery itself. It appears in the *Excellent Booke* and the *Visions* – running alongside the more studied early modern practices concerning Adamic keys, planetary angels, and benevolent archangels – we have evidence of a practiced ancestral chthonic pedagogy of spirit tuition and initiation presided over by the lord of the dead and the demonic kings of the spirits.

102 Add. MS. 36674, f.60r.
103 I refer here of course in the former to John Dee (1527 – c.1608) and in the latter to magician, clergyman, and astrologer-physician Richard Napier (1559 – 1634), who reportedly frequently conducted medical consultations with the Archangel Raphael for his patients, and who seems to have been regarded as an expert in various magical and medical impairments of mental and emotional faculties. Michael MacDonald's *Mystical Bedlam: Madness, Anxiety, and Healing in Seventeenth Century England* (Cambridge University Press, 1981) is an excellent overview of his practice, and his patient case notes have been made available by the team directed by Lauren Kassell as a fully searchable database: see Casebooks Project, http://www.magicandmedicine.hps.cam.ac.uk/, last accessed 2014-8-21.

Finally, I hope that in examining these experiments and their results, we begin to consider discrete definitions that seek to separate conjuration and scrying as thoroughly troubled. The vision and the presence of spirits elide. Scrying and conjuration dreamily cohere in the stone's yolk. They produce an ontological feedback in the hallucinatory and often dream-like Visions, where distinctions between the magicians themselves and their phantasmagorical appearances are elided as they move through ecologies of spirit, prophecy, and revelation; reality bends and shudders to birth textual manifestations of the imaginal, visionary spiritual revelation.

Even the texts themselves – the Excellent Booke (instructions that are more a reflexive set of nota and advice than a full system of magic, as in the Heptameron) and the Visions (scrying records that are less a spirit list or journal of angelic conversations than a set of astral travelogues) – blend and overlap, interpenetrating each other, demonstrating once more an admixture of conjuration and divination.

Which is to say, to see oneself performing magic or reading a book from the library of Solomon in the stone was to know how to do magic, is to engage in a self-fulfilling prophecy of empowerment. Time becomes a magic circle. Delineations between seership and sorcery, between vision and appearance of a spirit, and between acting and knowing dissipate as clouds moving across a crystal. The world is unveiled. The fire is made gold. Scrying and conjuring, prophecy and empowerment, knowledge and action, affect and effect – all are one in the books delivered from the stone.

By stone and by call

MEDIEVAL & EARLY MODERN SCRYING

Scrying may be described as the practice of 'seeing visions in a smooth surface or clear deep, or both.'[1] Hardly a new invention of the early modern period, Deborah Harkness has demonstrated that 'the practice of looking into a shiny or reflective object to aid in prophecy had a long history extending back to the Greeks.'[2] Richard Kieckhefer offers a set of subdivisions of 'specific forms such as *catoptromancy* (divination by means of a mirror), *crystallomancy* (by a crystal), *cyclicomancy* or *lecanomancy* (by a cup or basin filled with liquid), *hydromancy* (by water in a natural body), *onychomancy* (by an anointed nail),' also clarifying that *catoptromancy* is 'sometimes also used as the generic term.'[3]

It seems that scrying was a particularly widespread practice, for 'if frequency of reference in magical works of the period is any guide, the use of

1 Christopher Lionel Whitby, 'John Dee's Actions With Spirits: 22 December 1581 to 23 May 1583', (PhD Thesis: University of Birmingham, 1982): 75 n. 24. See also Theodore Besterman, *Crystalgazing: A Study in the History, Distribution, Theory and Practice of Scrying* (W. Rider & Son: London, 1924): 2.

2 Deborah Harkness, *John Dee's Conversations with Angels: Cabala, Alchemy, and the End of Nature* (Cambridge University Press, 1999): 17.

3 Richard Kieckhefer, *Forbidden Rites: A Necromancer's Manual of the Fifteenth Century* (Penn State University Press, 1998): 97 n. 6.

200

mirrors (catoptromancy) and of crystals (crystallomancy) were the most popular methods of divination in the sixteenth century.'[4] When considering the early modern popularity of scrying – in terms of folk magic and common conceptions, as well as more abstract occult philosophy – we must address the mythic precedents, functions and roles afforded to objects associated with scrying. The legend, often associated with Virgil, 'of a far-seeing mirror by which a ruler could guard his realm'[5] has bearing on the magical significance of mirrors and mantic vision. Likewise, Christopher Whitby attributes the popularity of the magic mirror-and-crystal to equally popular stories concerning Roger Bacon's 'glass prospective.'[6] This object is recounted in The Famous History of Fryer Bacon (1627):

> of that excellent nature, that any man might behold any thing that he desired to see, within the compass of fifty miles round about him: With this glasse he had pleasured divers kinds of people: for fathers did oftentimes desire to see (thereby) how their children did, and children how their parents did; one friend how another did, and one enemy (sometimes) how his enemy did: so that from far they would come to see this wonderfull glasse.[7]

This practice had utility beyond enabling monarchs to gather information and reign; such as the more quotidian and interpersonal divinatory services in the interests of familial bonds of kinship and care. In keeping with other so-called 'low magic' practices of popular cunning-craft, 'the most common uses of crystallomancy were for the discovery of buried treasure and the recovery of stolen goods.'[8] This was an apparently standard practice in late medieval and early modern Europe, even in the face of Church vilification.[9]

---

4 Christopher Whitby, 'John Dee and Renaissance Scrying.' Bulletin of the Society for Renaissance Studies 3.2 (1985): 28.

5 Kieckhefer, FR, 97–8 n. 10.

6 Whitby, 'Renaissance Scrying.' 28 and n. 10.

7 Whitby, 'Thesis.' 77 n 29: The Famous History of Fryer Bacon, Early English Prose Romances III (London 1858), 1L4.7.

8 Whitby, 'Renaissance Scrying.' 29.

9 Harkness, 117. See also Keith Thomas, Religion and the Decline of Magic (New York:

Scrying was not limited to the practical seership of village sorcerers and local cunning-folk. By the early modern period, both magicians and natural philosophers (when we can distinguish the two) theorising on various occult principles of cosmology – especially those engaged in communication with spirits – tended to use crystal stones and certainly we have plenty of evidence of scrying crystal use.[10] But scryers employed various shining reflective surfaces, 'even the polished fingernail of a child or virgin was more popular than a crystal showstone like Dee's.'[11]

There are both historical and practical reasons for this. The practice of fingernail divination 'dates back to the Babylonians, it is mentioned in the Talmud and it appears in Rashi's commentary' as well as appearing in the instructions of the fifteenth century grimoire manuscripts (such as *Bononiensis Univers. 3632*) and the Codex Gaster 315, a Spanish Hebrew manuscript dated to between the sixteenth and seventeenth centuries.[12] Moreover, it must have been easier and almost certainly cheaper than sourcing a crystal ball. Twelfth century diplomat and bishop John of Salisbury relates in his *Policraticus* an account from his childhood that:

> The priest anointed the boys' fingernails, or used a polished basin, to provide a reflecting surface in which figures might be seen. He then recited incantations, which led the fellow pupil to see 'misty figures', although John himself saw nothing.[13]

In Leicester in 1440, Abbot William Sadyngstone was accused of sorcery by his two Augustinian canons: 'when no one confessed to stealing certain

Charles Scribner's Sons, 1971): 215; Benjamin Goldberg, *The Mirror and Man* (Charlottesville: University of Virginia Press, 1985): 12 – 13.

10 British Library MSS Add. 36674 f.27r and 33r; Sloane 3849, ff.1 – 27; Sloane 2544, f.59v; Sloane 3846, ff. 61v, 64v, 148 – 151, 157 – 161; Sloane 3851, ff.39 – 40, 50, 52, 92 – 109, 115; Sloane 3884, f.57v – 61.

11 Harkness, 118; citing Add. 36674 f.27r and 33r.

12 Ioannis Marathakis (trans. & ed.), *The Magical Treatise of Solomon or Hygromanteia* (Golden Hoard Press: Singapore, 2011), 113, 18; see also Samuel Daiches, *Babylonian Oil Magic in the Talmud and in the Later Jewish Literature* (London, 1913), 28 – 30.

13 Kieckhefer, FR, 97 n. 4.

funds, he had allegedly rec_ted inca_tations, applied ointment to the thumb-nail of a boy called Maurice, asking this medium what he saw there revealed, and learned that the culprit was one of the canons, Brother Thomas Asty.'[14]

Legal Records

Tracing the record left in legislation provides wider context for scrying and its popularity. Kieckhefer notes 'synodal legislation as early as the fifth century condemned *specularii* who engaged in these practices, and the condemnation was often repeated,' highlighting how 'the *Fasciculus morum* condemns those *phitonici* and *specularii* who gaze into mirrors, bowls, pol-ished fingernails, and so forth, and claim that marvellous things are thus revealed to them.'[15] The English courts' severity damned scrying through both secular and ecclesiastical law, and the years of 1467, 1534, and 1549 saw court proceedings against it.[16] Offenders faced death and the forfeiture of their goods. Whitby notes that 'while it is difficult to gauge the distribution of the practice, it is perhaps a significant pointer that the statute against conjuration and witchcraft of 1541–1542 expressly prohibits it.'[17] Specifically, this act forbids:

> sondry persones unlawfully haue deuised and practised inuocacions and coniuracions of spirites pretendynge by suche meanes to vnderstande and gette knowledge for theyr owne lucre, in what place treasure of gold and syluer shoulde or moughte be founde or had in the earth or other secrete places.[18]

---

14 'The other monks reported the incident to the bishop, who condemned the abbot for sorcery.' Kieckhefer, FR, 100 n. 20.

15 Kieckhefer, FR, 97 n. 7.

16 György E Szönyi, 'Paracelsus, Scrying, and the Lingua Adamica: Contexts for John Dee's Angel Magic.' Stephen Clucas (ed.), *John Dee: Interdisciplinary Studies in English Re-naissance Thought* (Springer: Dordrecht, 2006): 214 n. 42.

17 Whitby, 'Renaissance Scrying.' 30.

18 *The Second Volume Conteinyng those statutes whiche haue ben made in the Tyme of the Most Victorious Reigne of Kynge Henrie the Eight* (London, 1543), Anno XXXIII, Ch. vii, sigs. B5v–B6r.

Whitby admits 'although crystals are not specifically mentioned, it is clear that the act is intended for the suppression of scrying.'[19] I would also suggest the express mention of spirit conjuration marks an important component of scrying. Of course, given 'scrying was mostly used for finding lost or stolen property, the possibility of financial gain meant that the law was often disregarded,' and Szönyi even goes as far to say that 'although such practices were strictly private, almost all astrologers and alchemists can be suspected of having exercised them.' He cites the journal of astrologer, physician, and magician Simon Forman: specifically that, by 1588, Forman started recording his efforts 'to practise necromancy and to call angells and spirits.'[20]

Scryers

So who were these scryers? They have been described as 'the skilled laborers who made such an inquiry into the mysteries of nature possible,' who 'traveled about in early modern England, making a living through their reputation for visions and trying to maintain a balance between the economic necessity of adopting a public persona as a practicing seer and an interest in maintaining secrecy for purposes of self-preservation.'[21] This emphasis on itinerancy and secrecy should not however obscure the numbers of known magical practitioners widely reputed to use 'the sight' for a variety of purposes who where sought out by clients.

In the notes of Dr John Dee, imploring God for a scryer, we see some of their overall significance:

> at length hearing of one (A Master of Arts, a preacher of thy word admitted) accownted as a good Seer, and skryer of Spirituall apparitions, in Christalline receptacles, or in open ayre, by his practice, procured: and trusting to frame him, by my ernest & faithfull prayers vnto the (my God) to some my help in my foresaid Studies: tyll, thow (o hevenly father) woldest by thy unserchable providence, send me somme apter man or means thereto.[22]

19 Whitby, 'Renaissance Scrying': 30.
20 Szönyi, 'Paracelsus, Scrying, and the Lingua Adamica.': 214 n. 43.
21 Harkness: 17, 16; citing Thomas, *Religion*: 215, 230.
22 Sloane MS. 3188, f. 7a–b.

One particular technique that appears to have persisted is the use of children or youths as seers. Speaking of the divinatory experiments of the Munich manual of spirit conjuration, Kieckhefer notes 'cooperation of a medium, usually a young boy, is vital; it is he alone who actually sees the spirits that are conjured.'[23] Early modern commentators knew this was a longstanding practice, citing as precedent 'the Prophets had their Seers, viz. Young Youths who were to behold those Visions.'[24]

Techniques such as onychomancy were apparently commonly used in these operations, as 'Johannes Hartlieb tells how a *zaubermaister* stands behind a child and recites *secret words* into his ear in the practice of hydromancy. In *pyromancy* as well… Anoint the hand of an innocent girl or boy, so that it *shines brightly*, then he speaks secret words into the child's ear, thus making a vow and forming *a pact*.'[25] This requirement of shining brightly emphasises the necessity of light in scrying, a feature demonstrating the relevance of pyromancy to our study as well as the reflective surfaces of liquids used in hydromancy. Scrying oils can also be seen to offer a practical optical effect of glistening, as well as magical consecratory ritual functions. The 'secret words' mentioned highlight the importance of particular verbal components in successful scrying. In this case, the words seem to be *nomina magica* calling particular spirits with whom a pact is formed. These verbal components might be rendered in written form, further emphasising the contractual (and, potentially, binding) aspects of this practice. This would certainly help contextualise 'another form of pyromancy [which] involves engraving many characters and figures around a steel mirror, then whispering secret words into the ear of boy as prelude to interrogation.'[26]

Harkness' relation of a difficult period in the angelic conversations of John Dee foregrounds an important and apparently rather traditional reason for the use of young scryers:

During the breakdown of his relationship with Kelly, Dee tried to use his son, Arthur (b. 1580), as a scryer Arthur was first drawn into the angel

23 Kieckhefer, FR: 103.
24 John Aubrey, *Miscellanies* (London, 1696): 128.
25 Kieckhefer, FR: 98.
26 Kieckhefer, FR: 98.

conversations on 15 April 1587, after Kelly's repeated assertions that he no longer wished to scry for Dee.[27] Arthur's youth and virginity – two attributes traditionally prized in scryers – did not yield satisfactory results, however.[28] Despite an initial success when Arthur perceived two crowned men in the stone, Dee was frustrated by the lack of information his son was able to receive from the angels through the showstone. The rich sight and sounds Dee was accustomed to from Kelly's scrying were replaced by straightforward images – 'squares, lines, pricks' and a few letters.[29] Three days after they began, Arthur and John Dee admitted defeat. No further suggestion was ever made regarding Arthur's scrying, nor is Arthur known to have commented on it in his later life.[30]

The magical virtues of youth and virginity are related in some sense here. Indeed, Aubrey notes explicitly that the youth of a seer is predicated on this belief: 'they say it must be a pure Virgin.'[31] Kieckhefer remarks 'the use of young and putatively innocent boys in divination must be seen as part of a broader clerical fascination with the ideal of *innocent* boyhood,'[32] which can thus firmly relate the seer's youth to concepts of virginity and chastity in grimoire instructions for the construction of tools, gathering and utility of materia, and preparations and taboos for the operator.

Let us now focus on a few historical examples, beginning with the confession made by William Byg on 22nd August 1467, 'regarded as typical of the practice':[33]

[Byg] used a boy of less than twelve years of age as the scryer and after making the boy say 'the Pater Noster, Ave and Credo,' he would make the

27 Harkness: 23; Meric Casaubon, *True and Faithful Relation of What passed for many Yeers Between Dr John Dee.. and Some Spirits* (London, 1659): *3–*8.
28 Thomas, *Religion*: 230.
29 TFR: *7.
30 Harkness: 23.
31 Aubrey, *Miscellanies*: 131.
32 Kieckhefer, FR: 103. Emphasis added.
33 Whitby, 'Renaissance Scrying': 29; cites J. Raine, 'Divination in the Fifteenth Century by Aid of a Magical Crystal.' *The Archaeological Journal* XIII (1856): 372–374.

boy say 'Lord Jesus Christ, send to us three angels from thy right hand
to tell or show us the truth of all that we shall ask.' Sometimes the boy
would see the stolen goods and sometimes the thieves; sometimes the boy
would see one angel and sometimes two. If angels appeared, they would
be requested to reveal the information necessary to recover the goods or
apprehend the thieves, which they would do by showing a vision rather
than by speaking. Byg himself never saw anything in the stone and there
were occasions when the boy scryer also saw nothing.[34]

Pious 'high' and practical 'low' magic are united, as angelic godly spirits are
appealed to in order to locate property and criminals. The specific practice
of invoking three angels is also found – as we shall see – in many other
instances of calls and conjurations designed for working scrying crystals
throughout the early modern period.

The Good Doctor Dee

The most famous, and certainly most studied, practitioner to carry out scrying experiments is undoubtedly John Dee. Through his scryers, Dee received
visions, messages, magical systems and the instructions on their use, as well
as confirmation of his prophetic status within an apocalyptic worldview.

Scrying was employed by the good doctor in order to acquire the highest
knowledge and understanding of the cosmos. Dee had sought other means
of learning this language of nature, writing:

> I have sought [...] to fynde or get some ynckling, glyms, or beame of such
> the foresaid radicall truthes: But after all my foresaid endevor I could
> fynde no other way, to such true wisdom atteyning, but by thy Extraor-
> dinary Gift.[35]

Szönyi estimates that 'Dee seems to have become interested in divination
in 1569 and started scrying in 1579 [...] The first well-documented instance
of scrying with the help of a medium, Barnabas Saul, took place on 22nd

---

34 Whitby, 'Renaissance Scrying.': 29. Whitby notes 'Byg escaped with a public sham-
ing.' Whitby 'Renaissance Scrying.': 30.
35 Sloane MS. 3188, f.6v.

December 1581.'[36] Of course Dee's most (in)famous set of magical operations were conducted with the scryer Edward Kelly, between March 1582 and (at least) May 1587. Much has been written on these angelic conversations, and while they are undoubtedly fascinating, they are also broadly beyond the purview of this current study. There are however a few features worth picking out as relevant for comparison to the workings of the *Excellent Booke* and early modern scrying more broadly.

While Dee and Kelly's work delineates their apocalyptic cabala of nature, it seems Dee's experiments became even more explicitly concerned with the end of days – and his role in them – after his partnership with Kelly ended and his work continued with another scryer, Bartholomew Hickman:

> Dee's relationship with Hickman was governed by Dee's belief that the summer of 1591 marked the beginning of a period of waiting and conversing with angels that was to last nine years and several months, and would culminate in a marvellous revelation or reward.[37] When the nine years and three months milestone was reached, Dee lamented that the period of waiting had been 'co[n]futed as vayne.' On 29 September 1600 Dee had manifested his disappointment by burning the angel diaries that he had kept during those nine long years. Despite this sobering incident, Dee and Hickman remained in close contact until the end of Dee's life, as is evident from the few angel conversations which Dee recorded in his aging and almost illegible hand and which still survive.[38]

We should be wary of equating Dee's total body of work to the magical revelations and empowerments he operated and received with Kelly. While millenarianism and apocalypse are more background concepts in the *Excellent Booke*, they are nonetheless present. The records of Gilbert and Davis' work certainly demonstrate matters of spiritual authority and empowerment as central to their magical work.

36 Szönyi, 'Paracelsus, Scrying, and the *Lingua Adamica*': 214 n 46. Whitby argues Barnabas Saul started scrying for Dee in 1579, a position Harkness seems to share. Harkness: 19; Whitby, Thesis: 50.

37 Harkness: 24; Bodleian Library, Ashmole MS. 488, entries for September 1600.

38 Harkness: 24.

In contrast with the *Excellent Booke*, however – specifically, the instructions for secrecy – Dee not only kept excellent private records of his 'Actions with Spirits' but 'was willing to show them to those he felt ought to know some of the great truths that he believed were being revealed to him.'[39] There are a number of high-profile examples of such sharing of his scrying results. On 15th September 1584 Dee showed his accounts to one Dr Curtius, an emissary of the emperor Rudolph II; furthermore on 27th May 1585, King Stephen of Poland was actually present during one of Dee's 'Actions.'[40]

In terms of the importance of a shewstone itself, it has been remarked that 'for Dee, the focus of his angel conversations was not his library, alchemical laboratory, study, or oratory, but his showstone,' and Harkness specifically outlines 'at least three showstones in the angel conversations: a "great Chrystaline Globe," a "stone in the frame" and a stone Dee believed had been brought by the angels and left in his oratory window at Mortlake. The last was the most powerful, and only Dee was allowed to touch it.'[41] Dee certainly kept and used several crystals or 'shew-stones' and is said to have possessed a mirror of black obsidian.[42]

Dee's relatively fastidious note-keeping of his actions also gives us useful data on ritual timing for using a shewstone, especially as this relates once more to the importance of light.[43] Specifically, 'the vast majority of angel conversations took place after sunrise and before sunset,' and in an especially pertinent piece of angelic communication we learn 'in the earliest surviving conversation, the angel Anael instructed Dee to communicate with the angels on 'the brightest day, When the Sonne shyneth: in the morning, fasting, begynne to pray. *In the Sonne Set the stone*.'[44] This seems to suggest placing the showstone to catch the light of the sun, producing optical effects conducive to visionary activity.

39 Whitby, 'Renaissance Scrying': 31.

40 TFR: 239–240, 404–406.

41 Harkness: 29; Whitby, Thesis, I: 137–141 and II: 217–18.

42 Whitby, 'Renaissance Scrying': 28. Whitby notes 'The authenticity of the mirror is not proved': 35.

43 'Dee adhered to these instructions as best he could, as may be seen in his notations of the time of each conversation, as well as the date.' Harkness: 119

44 Harkness: 119; Dee, Thesis, II: 15. Emphasis added.

Dee: *High versus Low Magic*

There is an infrequent historiographical question posed in analyses of Dee's scrying and his use of a shewstone, concerning both philosophical and practical dimensions of such magical operations. As Whitby puts it, 'the man who in 1570 could write that through the contemplation of number a gnosis leading to unity with the Creator could be achieved was eleven years later indulging in a kind of magic that belongs to the tradition of the charlatan and the vagrant: using a medium to see visions in a crystal ball.'[45] Indeed, the same question – that of how and why an expert would engage in a practice that seemed to combine 'high' with 'low' magic – is likewise expressed elsewhere: 'what becomes perplexing for the cultural historian is that Dee, having been acquainted with the most complex magical theories and techniques, finally ended up practising the crudest divination, that is *crystallomantia*, and, having pursued it till the last days of his life, lost no faith in it at all.'[46] The inquiry can be more bluntly stated: how could such a supposedly clever man do something so apparently (at least to modern thinking) stupid?

Firstly, as we have started to observe in discussion of the role and reception of the work of Roger Bacon, medieval and early modern studies of optics were far from some abstracted academic precursor to theoretical physics. Rather, they informed a panoply of occult experiments and metaphysical meditations. Dee's work on optics was backed by careful manuscript collection and analysis, and is attested in his own work in this field. We should obviously be wary of imposing modern juxtaposing distinctions of magic and science; but equal care should be taken to ensure we do not implicitly read such a distinction onto a 'proto-science vs. folklore' account of scrying and the occult dimensions of scrying. Eschewing the complicated ceremonies of ritual magic in favour of ardent prayer, 'Dee's use of the showstone represented the most traditionally occult aspect of his angel conversations.'[47] And while the actual equipment might be magically low-brow, the theory behind it was decidedly academic. Dee's sources for his approach – using a shewstone to receive universal knowledge and exalted understanding – were

---

45 Whitby, 'Renaissance Scrying': 26.
46 Szönyi, 'Paracelsus, Scrying, and the *Lingua Adamica*': 213
47 Harkness: 30; Goldberg: 3–162.

Ficino, Agrippa and Paracelsus, plus a variety of medieval manuscripts.[48] The use of stones, glasses and crystals by con-men and mountebanks did not discredit their potential for a pious magus such as Dee.

Moreover, when we consider how folk and learned magic interacted in early modern praxis, we could do worse than listen to angelical advice: 'the angels frequently inform Dee that "*omnia vnum est*" (all is one) and he saw nothing to be disdained in practicing an art usually associated with more mundane matters such as the recovery of stolen goods.'[49]

The Crystal's Philosophical Place in Wider Magic

There are of course deeper technical questions to be posed here: was this blurring or combining of popular and elite practices unique to Dee's magic, or demonstrative of a wider turn? Perhaps even more chiefly, how was scrying thought to work in the early modern period?

D.P. Walker, in the course of considering the 'natural' magic of the Renaissance, has posited that demonic magic is 'easily discoverable' in Ficino's writings – positing that at the end of the sixteenth century demonic and intellectual elements of magical theory and practice were being combined and elided.[50] Although Dee's earlier work (especially his *Propaedeumata Aphoristica*) might be considered 'an intellectual kind of magic,' one could also characterise 'his involvement with scrying [as] partly a result of a collapse of the borders between the different branches of magic.'[51] One historian's collapsing borders is another magician's canopy of interconnecting branches.

It is perhaps at this point worth briefly reminding ourselves of what ritual magical activity in the early modern period actually involved. Clucas points out that 'the practice of Pseudo-Solomonic magic' – generally reliant on grimoires attributed to the wise king – 'involved the burning of suffu-

---

48 György E. Szönyi, 'John Dee as Cultural, Scientific, Apocalyptic Go-Between.' Andreas Höfele and Werner von Koppenfels (eds.), *Renaissance Go-Betweens: Cultural Exchange in Early Modern Europe* (Walter de Gruyter: New York, 2005): 98.

49 Whitby, 'Renaissance Scrying': 34.

50 Specifically, demonic and intellectual 'strands of the tradition come together again in the planetary oratory of Paolini and the magic practiced by Campanella.' D. Walker, *Spiritual and Demonic Magic* (Penn State University Press: University Park, 2000): 75.

51 Whitby, 'Renaissance Scrying': 27.

migations, the pronunciation of the orations, prayers and magical names of God and his angels, and the contemplation, or "inspection" of the talismans or "figures," and sometimes the use of "stones," "glasses," or "crystals."'[52] When crystal stones were used, the manuscripts often mentioned ritualistic preparations such as fumigations or anointing, which Dee did not include in the descriptions of his practices.[53] These are further suggestive of Dee's perception of his pious occult endeavours: he was not a simple conjurer reliant on the virtues of sorcerous tricks and words in smoke, but a learned and holy man seeking communion with the Most High and its messengers.

But how might the very instrument of charlatanry, the crystal ball, offer the ennobling theological veracity of revelation that Dee sought? To answer this question we must ultimately consider the place of theoretical optics in Neoplatonic thought. But we can begin by looking to an infamous patron of the art of scrying: for 'catoptromancy has a medieval tradition extending back to the elusive magus Artephius (or Artesius), who recommended the fabrication of *instruments that could unite and concentrate celestial rays* and who mentioned the "mirror of Almuchesi" for purposes of divination.'[54]

The Sword of Artephius

Beyond a legendary status as a powerful magician of the past, most of our specific information about this figure comes from 'a remark of William of Auvergne, who mentions a certain Artesius known for his ability to conjure up visions by placing a glossy sword over a water-basin so that the glittering of the two caused the viewer to see strange sights.'[55] As our initial panoply

52 Stephen Clucas, 'John Dee's Angelic Conversations and the *Ars Notoria*: Renaissance Magic and Medieval Theurgy.' Clucas (ed.), *John Dee: Interdisciplinary Studies in English Renaissance Thought* (Springer: Dordrecht, 2006): 243 n. 141: 'See, for example, *Ars notoria*, British Library, Sloane MS. 313, fourteenth-fifteenth century, ff.2v – 4v, and *Liber sacer*, BL, Royal MS. 17.A.XLII, ff.9v *et seq.*, which describes 'the makinge off the seale off the true and lyuinge god.'
53 Harkness: 118: Add. MS. 36674, f.33r.
54 Jan R. Veenstra, 'The Holy Almandal: Angels and the Intellectual Aims of Magic.' Jan N. Bremmer and Jan R. Veenstra (eds.), *Metamorphosis of Magic from Late Antiquity to the Early Modern Period* (Peeters: Leuven, 2002), 214; citing Delatte, *La catoptromancie*: 18 – 20. Cf. also Pico della Mirandola, *De rerum praenotione*, 11.5. Emphasis added.
55 Szönyi, 'Paracelsus, Scrying, and the *Lingua Adamica*': 210 n 14: citing NP: 168.

of terms for different divinatory practices highlighted, we should be wary of expecting scrying to always involve a crystal or mirror. Yet what we do observe once more is the importance of 'glittering,' of catching light and reflecting it back at the seer.

William of Auvergue included divination by inspection of sword-blades as well as mirrors and human nails in his list of execrable practices.[56] The Parson of Chaucer's tale demonstrates scrying a sword as a familiar and comparable divinatory practice when he remarks, 'Let us go now to thilke horrible swering of adiuracioun and coniuracioun, as doon thise false enchauntours or nigromanciens in bacins ful of water, or in a bright swerd, in a cercle, or in a fyr, or in a shulder-boon of a sheep.'[57] In Robert of Brunne's criticism of the practice we observe both a connection between divination and sorcery, and the common thief-detection utility of such apparently diabolical ways of knowing: 'If you ever had to do with nigromancy, or made sacrifice to the devil through witchcraft, or paid any man to raise the devil in order to disclose anything stolen ("done away"), you have sinned. If you have made any child look in sword or basin, in thumb[nail] or in crystal – all *that* men call witchcraft.'[58] Further developments of this connection between seeking knowledge and trafficking with demons is explicated in 1287 by Bishop Peter Quival of Exeter when he recommends 'let the penitent confess if he has broken the First Commandment by rendering unto demons or other creatures the worship due to God alone: to wit, by performing sleights, that is, by recourse to conjurations, as is wont to be done for theft, in a sword or a basin, or in names written and enclosed in clay and put in holy water.'[59]

56 William noted specifically that 'from this pest of curiosity proceeded that accursed and execrable work called *Liber sacratus*.' Lynn Thorndike, *A History of Magic and Experimental Science* (Columbia University Press: New York, 1923), Vol. 2, 287; citing *De legibus*, ca24: 68 in ed. of 1591.

57 Geoffrey Chaucer, 'The Parson's Tale,' 37, in Walter William Skeat (ed.), *The Complete Works of Geoffrey Chaucer* (Clarendon Press: Oxford, 1900), Vol. 4: 607.

58 Robert of Brunne, 'Handlyng Synne,' vv. 339–354, ed. Furnivall (Roxburghe Club), 1862: 12–13; cited in George Lyman Kittredge, *Witchcraft in Old and New England* (Russell & Russell: New York, 1929): 192 and 508 n. 47.

59 Kittridge, *Witchcraft in Old and New England*: 193 and 509 n. 53; citing *Modus Exigendi Confessiones*, Synod of Exeter, Wilkins, *Concilia*, II, 162.

As we can see, such sword divination was also reportedly employed in the kind of scrying operations involving a young seer, in which 'the child may be made to gaze at a polished sword'; indeed Kieckhefer notes Hartlieb knew of 'one great prince who used an old executioner's sword for this purpose – or a crystal.'[60] The relation between these objects – their glinting – is also attested in an early modern collection of charms and rituals. In the 'Perfect Experiment of a Glass or Mirror' contained in the so-called Foreman text, attributed to Paul Foreman, the operator is instructed to 'make the glass of pure steel,' and moreover 'let it be polished clean and *bright as a sword*.'[61] There is a commonality of materials employed in the 'glass' and the sword; moreover, the sword is a touchstone of brightness, and possibly cleanliness too.

Jan R. Veenstra highlights a twelfth century explanation of Artephius' theory which relies on 'regarding the sun as a mirror that reflects the *images of all things*, so that capturing the sun's rays in shining objects may produce a *reflection of present realities* and perhaps reveal the secrets of nature.'[62] This idea of light – especially the sun's light – mirroring and being mirrored had deep philosophical implications. Indeed, Kieckhefer reasons 'the notion of perceiving hidden and future realities in a mirror receives its ultimate extension in the Neoplatonic notion of the *divine mind itself as a mirror* in which particularities can be *foreseen*, so that it can be said of a saint with the gift of prophecy that "in the mirror of divinity *everything to be was present* to him."'[63] Magical philosophy and activity seem to move from tracing an occult optics of natural celestial rays to a more sacred theological approach to scrying.

---

60 Kieckhefer, FR: 98.

61 Paul Foreman, *The Cambridge Book of Magic: A Tudor necromancer's manual*, ed. Francis Young (Texts in Early Modern Magic: Cambridge, 2015): 33. Emphasis added.

62 Veenstra, 'The Holy Almandel': 214; citing Delatte, *La catoptromancie*: 21, refers to a marginal note in Berlin, MS. 956, fol. 21v. Emphasis added.

63 Kieckhefer, FR: 98 n. 11. Emphasis added.

Optics and Alchemy

Dee had notes on a work known as the *Ars Sintrillia* by Artephius, who had 'always been regarded by the alchemists as one of the masters.'[64] An understanding of alchemy considerably assists in an occult philosophical understanding of optics, especially bearing in mind both utilise what Urszula Szulakowska refers to as pragmatic and theurgic theories.[65] That is, alchemy can be considered both as 'practical procedures with chemical matter' and 'spiritual transformation, that is, ascent from base existence to supernatural understanding'; so 'similarly to alchemy, in which the two orientations overlapped, medieval optics was also a mixture of mystical concepts and practical observations.'[66]

Optics and Magic

Dee's library catalogues attest to his interest in medieval optics, indeed, Dee seems to suggest magic and optics — and specifically their talismanic application — lie at the heart of natural philosophy.

> APHORISM LII
> If you were skilled in 'catoptrics' you would be able, by art, to imprint the rays of any star much more strongly upon any matter subjected to it than nature itself does. This, indeed, was by far the largest part of the natural philosophy of the ancient wise men. And this secret is not of much less dignity than the very august astronomy of the philosophers.[67]

In examining Dee's notes in more detail we should consider that mention of Artephius is directly followed by a listing for 'opticall science,' a descriptor of a discipline combining physics and crystallomancy, and from this Szönyi goes on to argue that Dee 'saw no fundamental division between natural philosophy and spiritualism.'[68] While Artephius might seem a somewhat

---

64 Szönyi, 'Paracelsus, Scrying, and the *Lingua Adamica*': 209 n. 11.

65 Urszula Szulakowska, *The Alchemy of Light: Geometry and Optics in Late Renaissance Alchemical Illustration* (Leiden, 2000): 29.

66 Szönyi, 'Go-Between': 98.

67 Szulakowska, *The Alchemy of Light*: 38.

68 Szönyi, 'Paracelsus, Scrying, and the *Lingua Adamica*': 210.

mysterious semi-legendary forefather, the work of Roger Bacon in the Middle Ages was far more concrete though perhaps no less mythologised. Medieval optics at its most basic covered radiation and the reflection of light, and Bacon was a 'key figure' in this discipline: especially in the reception of mathematical approaches to optics (known as *perspectiva*) such as those of Ibn al-Haytham's De *aspectibus*, and in reconciling such notions 'with those of Aristotle, Augustine, Grosseteste, and other authorities.'[69] Bacon also appears to have exerted a profound influence on Dee, 'and it was partly this influence which raised his ambitions to catch the power of the stars by help of mirrors, interpreting this activity as a scientific version of ancient talismanic magic.'[70] Again, a nascent scientific methodology and intended magical utilities appear to inform and develop one another in a cohesive scrying praxis.

It is Harkness' view that 'Dee's angel conversations employed the physics and metaphysics of light to lend the *authority* of natural philosophy and theology to traditional scrying practices and distance his use of the show-stone from common forms of divination,' citing that 'the light metaphysics of Grosseteste and Roger Bacon informed Dee's earliest published works, the *Monas Hieroglyphica* and the *Propaedeumata Aphoristica*, as well as the later "Mathematical Preface" and angel conversations.'[71] Yet if an appeal to righteous authority was the prime intention, it seems Dee could have picked his sources from thinkers with less diabolical reputations. Despite Bacon's status as a clergyman and natural philosopher, by the early modern period he was also expressly considered a necromancer. Indeed, he was called the author of that infamous treatise, De *Nigromancia*, which (perhaps not co-incidentally) can be found in English bound into the collection that is Add. MS. 36674. It seems likely that Dee was aware of the more sinister aspects, in popular perception, of Bacon and his works. It is possible that Dee dismissed these as ignorant rumours. Yet if the main purpose of employing Bacon's work was authority or even credibility, it seems a public relations decision gone wrong; one that might even presage Dee's own eventual defamation as a black magician or, worse, a dupe consorting with devils. Rather, I think the operational *utility* (rather than authority) of Bacon's work – in combining

69 David C. Lindberg, *Theories of Vision from Al-Kindi to Kepler* (Chicago, 1976): 104.

70 Szönyi, 'Paracelsus, Scrying, and the *Lingua Adamica*': 210.

71 Harkness: 118; see also Harkness, Ch. 2. Emphasis added.

(proto-)scientific and magical procedures to approach light, affect, and astral virtue – should be seen as a primary motivator for its employment by Dee and other scryers.

The other great influence on early modern optics and its occult philosophy was, of course, derived from Arabic sources. Veenstra considers 'the most dominant theory by far as the one disseminated by al-Kindi's *De Radiis Stellarum*, on the rays of the stars penetrating the earth and determining all processes of life and movement,' arguing that 'it is mainly through this theory that optics, i.e. the mathematical study of rays, came to play such an important role in magic and astrology.'[72] More specifically, Dee believed that optics could teach one to 'imprint the rays of any star more strongly upon any matter subjected to it,'[73] and utilised reflective mirrors and lenses, as natural catchers of light, to achieve this. Understanding astral rays meant tracing the influences and inertias of the forces acting upon events and agents, and being able to marshal and wield the means to make such impressions according to one's own designs operationalised this occult knowledge into magical activity.

We should consider both Dee's work and the general milieu of early modern scrying as drawing on many sources, and that 'what makes [Dee's] esoteric experiments fascinating is the ease of syncretism with which he freely exploited quite distinct traditions, from medieval Baconian magic through Old Testament traditions to some semi-scientific, semi-popular practices of dubious origin.'[74] We shall examine in more detail some particular appeals to scriptural precedent and magical technology below, along with a number of other influences. For now though, we should – as focused operators – return our attention to the stone itself.

The operation of transforming theoretical principles into the apprehension of affect can be seen in the use of the stone not merely as a passive receiving tool, but as a practical locus of profound 'actions' with spirits. Clearly, 'the showstone was the focal point of the conversations; it ordered the physical space and drew on the options so central to Dee's natural phi-

72 Veenstra, 'The Holy Almandel': 214.

73 Nicholas H. Clulee, *John Dee's Natural Philosophy: Between Science and Religion* (Routledge: London 1988): 66–67.

74 Szönyi, 'Paracelsus, Scrying, and the Lingua Adamica': 213.

losophy'; moreover, 'understanding the properties of the showstone was, in Dee's mind, his supreme achievement, because its use produced tangible results in the form of new information and angelic communication.'[75]

Locus of Divinity

Considering Dee's angel conversations, Harkness insists 'the showstone clearly served as *a locus for divinity*, a sacred space capable of representing the world in microcosm.'[76] This notion of the microcosm appears to explicate Dee's comment that within the stone 'the whole world in manner did seme to appear, heven, and erth, etc.'[77] Not only did the whole world appear, but scryer and operator were specifically shown their own private sphere – the very study in which the operations were conducted. Dee records of a session 'Saturday Cracoviæ, 7 Maii, Mane, hora 6,' in 1584:

> there appeared the like furniture of Table with a white Cloth, a Candle-stick, and Taper on it, with a Desk and Cushions (which I had caused to be made with red crosses on them :) also E.K. himself and I appeared in the same Stone. In effect, all things we had before us... that shew of our furniture, and our selves...[78]

As in Gilbert and Davis' *Visions*, the seer and magician often perceived themselves in the stone. In the case of the *Visions*, they even saw themselves

75 Harkness: 117. This also highlights a particular historiographical debate about wheth-er Dee's angel conversations can and should be seen in relation to natural philosophy, which itself seems tied up in a discussion of whether the doctor thought he was 'doing magic.' Harkness holds that 'he could relate his showstone and its use to the existence and behaviour of visible and, more important, *invisible* rays. If, as Nicholas Clulee has persuasively argued, "Dee's natural philosophy was based on a theory of astral radia-tion," then his use of the showstone can be seen as the culmination of his natural philos-ophy, and quite possibly his "archemastrie."' She goes on in the footnote: 'I have used the assertions of this early article to contradict Clulee's later belief that the angel conversa-tions were influenced by Dee's natural philosophy but "cannot be considered as science or natural philosophy in its own right." Clulee, 203.' Harkness: 117 n. 69.

76 Harkness: 31. Emphasis added.

77 Whitby, Thesis, II:48.

78 TFR: 115.

performing ritual actions and observing their interactions with the ecologies of spirits revealed thereby.

When considering this theme of the sacred dimensions of scrying, it is important to note that Dee's 'angels made explicit references to the safe, sacred nature of the showstone, wherein "No *unclean* thing shall prevayle."'[79] The revelations imparted by such scrying properly backed by divine assistance were supremely trustworthy, for 'this stone could contain only true, holy angels.'[80] Harkness goes on to explicitly compare this assurance with the instructions at the end of the *Excellent Booke* on not calling inferiors with your angel stone. Yet the inference of the potential for more demonic entities to influence (other) scrying efforts should be understood as the darker, more suspicious underside of the merging of conceptions of demonic and spiritual magics. The question remained: how exactly did such divination work, and how holy were the spirits ministering this process?

We land therefore at a key place of tension in early modern magic and arguably of the Renaissance humanist project as a whole — what was naturally magical and thus designed and by extension permitted by God, and what was powered by demonic (and therefore inherently corrupting and harmful) knowledge and action? Kieckhefer emphasises that the fifteenth century interpretation offered by Pedro Garcia 'was perhaps more influential' in considering 'whether the divination of hidden affairs and the accomplishment of wondrous works can be done through the power of nature', or if it truly is simply 'brought about by the aid of demons':

> the first manner is by gazing at luminous bodies and instruments. The principle here is that the *acies* of the human mind in one who gazes on such instruments reflects back upon itself, for the luminosity of the instrument prevents direction or concentration of the mind on exterior things, and repels it, and turns it back upon itself, so that it is forced to gaze upon itself.
>
> Thus, according to the philosophy of Plato, if it is purged and cleansed of defilements, which come from the body and cling to the soul, they see

79 Whitby, Thesis II: 247 (Dee's emphasis).
80 Harkness: 31.

as in a clear and clean mirror, and when they inquire about all hidden things, or some portion of them, or some particular hidden thing, it is no surprise that the soul, turned back into itself, should see such hidden things, for according to Plato the human soul is created fully inscribed with the forms of all knowable things, in respect of its intellectual power [...] Thus it is, according to the opinion of these magicians, that these luminous bodies function, and particularly mirrors. When the soul of the gazer is turned back on itself, it absorbs the attention and fixes the *acies* of the intellect in its inward turning, and the more inwardly it is fixed, the more fully and clearly it turns upon itself and knows and divines hidden things – and the more it is filled within by God, so that the beholding is turned into the soul, which can be so turned in to itself and as it were recollected within itself, that the recollection becomes rapture or a state near to rapture, or ecstacy or a condition near to ecstasy. [...] According to the philosophy of the Platonists, this is one manner of saving the divinations of hidden matters through [demonstration] of purely natural causes without any aid of demons, explicit or secret.[81]

While there are many fascinating intricacies to draw out from this source concerning occult philosophy, optics, philosophy of mind, vision and epistemology, it is expedient at this point to emphasise that 'Dee was certainly not alone among his contemporaries, either in his belief in the properties of the shewstone, or in taking Pseudo-Solomonic theurgy as a model for his magical practices.'[82] Let us examine some of these contemporaries.

Scrying in Early Modern Magic

In a letter (dating somewhere between 1534–40) from the abbot of Abingdon to Thomas Cromwell, the abbot requested a sentence for an arrested priest who had also 'certeyn bokes of conjuracions, in the which ys conteyned many conclusions of that worke; as fyndyng out of tresure hydde,

81 Kieckhefer, FR: 98–99 n. 15; citing Petrus Garsia, In determinationes magistrales contra conclusiones apologales Ioannis Pici Mirandulani Concordis Comitis praemium (Eucharius Silber: Rome, 1489), sig. Kiv v through Kv r; Lynn Thorndike, History of Magic and Experimental Science 4 (Columbia University Press: New York, 1934): 497–507.
82 Clucas, 'John Dee's Angelic Conversations and the Ars Notoria': 257 n. 259.

consecratyng of ryngs with stones in theym, and consecrating of a cristal stone wheryn a childe shall looke, and se many thyngs.'[83]

In the manuscript attributed to 'Dr Caius' (also contained within the Additional MS. 36674 collection) are found extracts of Agrippa, Abano's *Elementa Magica* and 'various conjurations, one of which is for use with a crystal.'[84] Here we see again the importance of using sacred words in the proper employment of a scrying tool. By the seventeenth century, the necessity of such calls was enshrined in the study of 'Berills or Crystall' made by John Aubrey in his wonderfully fortean *Miscellanies*, explaining 'there are certain Formulas of Prayer to be used before they make the inspection, which they term a Call.'[85] The call was a feature of an 'animistic philosophy' in which 'the scryer's visions are naturally held to be the work of spirits, or in many cases to be the spirits themselves disporting themselves before his eyes.'[86] Such 'calls' are sacralising entreaties to the divine to grant their scrying endeavours success. Dr Caius' crystal call ran:

> In the name of the father + and of the son, and of the holye ghost + amen, I pray the heavenlye father, as thou art the maker of heavne and the earthe, and of all thinges then conteined, and not onlye hast made them, but allso doist worke besides ther creation wonderfullye in them; asweell in angels thye celestiall spirites, as also in men, foule, fishe, and beste, as in other sensibell thinges, as in wodes, trese, water, stones, gresse, and herbes, bye the whiche ther operation, we are moved to prayse thye holye name: and to saye, holye god and heavnelye father, make me now to perceive and understande, thye mervilous workes, in this clere and puer cristall.[87]

In terms of Dee's contemporaries, Aubrey's discussion of such calls for scry-

83 Whitby, 'Renaissance Scrying': 30; cites *Original Letters Illustrative of English History*, ed. Sir Henry Ellis, 3rd series, 4 vols (London, 1846), III: 41–42, letter CCLXVIII.

84 Whitby, 'Renaissance Scrying': 31; Add. MS 36674, f. 40a–b.

85 Aubrey, *Miscellanies*, 129.

86 Northcote W. Thomas, *Crystal Gazing: Its History and Practice, with a Discussion of the Evidence for Telepathic Scrying* (London, 1905): 82.

87 Whitby, Thesis, 86–7 n. 47: Additional MS. 36674, ff. 40a–40b.

ing also reports that 'in a Manuscript of Dr. Forman of Lambeth (which Mr. Elias Ashmole had) is a Discourse of this, and the Prayer. Also there is the Call which Dr. Nepier did use.'[88] As mentioned earlier, in 1588 Forman accounts he 'began practicing necromancy and to call aungells and spirits.'[89] Specifically, Forman is said to have been experimenting with a 'new method…of magic'; a method which Gabriel Harvey (the seventeenth century commentator on Add. MS. 36674) not only described as 'inspired by the *ars Notoria*,' but which apparently involved the use of a '*speculum omniscium*,' an 'all-seeing mirror.'[90] Harkness notes that the section of Add. MS. 36674 assembled from the notes of Dr Caius 'for example, included instructions for engraving crystals to facilitate the appearance of spirits and angels.'[91] Indeed, our copy of the *Excellent Booke* itself was once claimed to be written in Forman's hand, an identification which the British Library catalogue confirms as 'certified by Mr Macray of the Bodleian, July 1868.'

Beyond Forman's operations at the beginning of the century, 'the practice of scrying continued well into the seventeenth century.'[92] We should also not forget scrying could be used for that old dependable trade of the diviner: foretelling love-lives. Lilly paints a brief picture of the practices of a Staffordshire astrologer-magician, William Hodges, who also practiced 'surgery and physick': 'he resolved questions astrologically; nativities he meddled not with; in things of other nature, which required more curiosity, he repaired to the crystal: his angels were Raphael, Gabriel, and Uriel.'[93] This offers a glimpse of how different divinations were utilised in an individual's practice, as well as highlighting the specific angels one might call for assistance. While

88 John Aubrey, *Miscellanies*: 129.

89 *The Autobiography and Personal Diary of Dr Simon Forman*, ed. James Orchard Halliwell (London, 1849): 19.

90 Virginia F. Stern, *Gabriel Harvey: His Life, Marginalia and Library* (Oxford: Clarendon Press, 1979), 242; citing Add. MS. 36674 f.47.

91 Harkness: 118: Add. MS. 36674, f.36v.

92 Whitby, 'Renaissance Scrying': 32.

93 William Lilly, *History of his Life and Times* (London, 1715): 116. Lilly mentions that Hodges was occasionally inaccurate in his divination (especially over matters relating to royalist causes), chastising that 'his life answered not in holiness and sanctity to what it should, having to deal with those holy angels.' The main (perhaps sole) evidence of this lack of sanctity mentioned is Hodges' propensity to swear.

John Scott (another physician friend of Lilly's) was staying with Hodges and assisting him 'to dress his patients, let blood, &c,' Scott asked Hodges for a familiar magical service. Lilly related the story in his autobiography:

> Being to return to London, [Scott] desired Hodges to shew him the person and feature of the woman he should marry. Hodges carries him into a field not far from his house, pulls out his crystal, bids Scott set his foot to his, and, after a while, wishes him to inspect the crystal, and observe what he saw there. 'I see,' saith Scott, 'a ruddy complexioned wench in a red waistcoat, drawing a can of beer.' 'She must be your wife,' said Hodges. 'You are mistaken, Sir,' said Scott. 'I am, so soon as I come to London, to marry a tall gentlewoman in the Old Bailey.' 'You must marry the red waistcoat,' said Hodges. Scott leaves the country, comes up to London, finds his gentlewoman married: two years after going into Dover, in his return, he refreshed himself at an inn in Canterbury, and as he came into the hall, or first room thereof, he mistook the room, and went into the buttery, where he espied a maid, described by Hodges, as before said, drawing a can of beer, &c. He then more narrowly viewing her person and habit, found her, in all parts, to be the same Hodges had described; after which he became a suitor unto her, and was married unto her; which woman I have often seen. This Scott related unto me several times, being a very honest person, and made great conscience of what he spoke.[94]

While we cannot be sure if Hodges specifically requested the visionary guidance of an angel in this nuptial divination – the 'after a while' between beginning the operation and the vision is particularly curious – we can see the use of a 'shew-stone' as not only a medium for the conjuration of angels but the more direct means by which a client themselves might see their answer appear before them. Significantly, this vision included not merely physical appearance of a future spouse, but also her 'person' and 'habit.' Not only did the showing of the stone offer the visionary experience to the client, it also potentially secured the practitioner from prosecution: after all, it was not *they* who had claimed to see the vision.

94 Lilly, *History*: 117–8.

It also seems especially significant that such a service is offered in 'a field not far from his house': yet we are left unsure if the provision of operating outdoors was an actual necessity, or merely a convenience, or perhaps of no real overall significance to the scrying. Given that Hodges 'carries' Scott to the field, I would estimate at least the second of these possibilities seems most likely. We have already observed how stones were to be set and consulted to catch sunlight. Hodges and Scott examine the stone outside, heavily implying the operation occurred during the daytime. At the very least, this account shows us that scrying was not merely the endeavour of courtly magi with studies, oratories, dusty libraries and expensive laboratories. It could be conducted literally in the field.

In discussing Dee and his contemporaries, we should examine the reception of Dee's works and his wider reputation, both of which reveal a particular influence on magical practices of the late seventeenth century. Most people encountered the juicy details of Dee's 'actions with spirits' through the character assassination of Meric Casaubon's *A True and Faithful Relation*, which popularised the notion of Dee as gullible mark and accidental necromancer. However, very like the adoption and use of Scot's *Discoverie of Witchcraft* by cunning-folk, 'despite Casaubon's fervent desire that people would abstain from attempting to contact "false lying Spirits," *A True and Faithful Relation* seems only to have encouraged such activities.'[95] Indeed, we have concrete records of such attempts.

> A set of manuscript diaries now in the British Library records the activities of a group that gathered between 24 July 1671 and 18 December 1688 to converse with angels through a crystal. The dates of the last conversations suggest that the group initially became involved with the angels after reading Casaubon and discovering that there was some ambiguity in Dee's mind as to whether the much prophesied year of cosmic restitution was actually 1588 or 1688. Like Dee, the group employed a scryer 'E. R[orbon],' and two other regular participants are mentioned: "R.O." who occupied Dee's role in the conversations, and another referred to at times as 'E.C.' and occasionally as 'Brother Collings.' The angels that the

95 Harkness: 222; citing Casaubon, TFR, 'Preface' sig. Dv.

group conversed with were identical to Dee's, and the angels Madimi and Guluah frequently appeared – two of Dee's most idiosyncratic angels. Although these later conversations superficially resemble Dee's, however, the practitioners were not deeply engaged with natural philosophy but were primarily concerned with their financial security, and there was a great deal of interest in the recovery of buried riches.[96]

These operations seem to have been conducted very much in the style of Dee, or at least an impression of what Dee's style was thought to be. Not only were they engaging (or at least attempting engagement) with the same angelic entities, they were working towards and developing out a previous and explicitly millenarian conception of 'cosmic restitution.' These operations appear to have meant more to the group than simply using Dee's systems; the operators seem to have considered themselves carrying on Dee's actual work, in all its apocalyptic significance. On the other hand, Harkness claims the specific results the group attempted to realise – finding buried treasure – seem at odds with the good doctor's mission, despite Dee's own treasure hunting endeavours.[97]

When considering the records left behind of scrying experiments, we would do well to reiterate a point made by Szönyi:

the sixteenth- and seventeenth-century manuscript literature abounds in secret diaries, notes and copies of grimoires, revealing the widespread magical practices of the day. Journals of actual divination are nevertheless more of a rarity: interested amateurs did not get much beyond collecting and copying magical materials, prayers, incantations, and books of rituals which, at least theoretically, were intended to equip the reader for contacting the spirit world.[98]

96 Harkness: 221–22; citing Sloane MSS. 3624–3628, *passim*.
97 For instance, 'Meredith Llyod told Aubrey of the conjuring of Dr. John Dee and associates at a pool in Brecknockshire: "They found a wedge of gold," but "a mighty storme and tempest was raysed in harvest time, the countrey people had not knowen the like."' Kittredge: 158 n. 56.
98 Szönyi, 'Paracelsus, Scrying, and the *Lingua Adamica*': 214 n. 44.

The ownership of magical texts does not prove a magical practitioner of course. Antiquarian collecting tendencies, purely literary and historical interest, and the phenomenon of armchair occultists appear to be motivations present both then and now. A journal of actual magical experiments conducted, with their results recorded, is somewhat of a rare treasure. While a charm recipe or details of a ritual might be coldly abstracted – Agrippa's historicisations commonly utilised distancing conceits of prefixes such as 'it is said' – divination is usually in some way both particular and personal. Someone must utter the prophecy, after all; someone must see the vision in the stone.

We should therefore note a further context for the lack of specific records of particular divinatory experiments: that of necessary secrecy. Specifics on the practices of spirit-trafficking magicians are occasionally obscured, often by the magicians themselves. As MacDonald notes, 'aware of Dee's misfortunes, Napier was careful to leave few traces of his secret arts in his main body of papers and did not imitate him by broadcasting his success.'[99] Dee did indeed suffer accusations of sorcery, diabolism, and necromancy throughout his career for his conjuring activities.[100]

Biblical Precedents

It was not merely the usefulness of the method or the tantalising knowledge that it offered which persuaded magicians to ignore the legal and theological proscriptions against scrying; many early modern practitioners genuinely seem to have believed in the biblical precedence and justification for it, perhaps none more so than Dee. Their case is not without evidence. Two verses from Genesis 44 attest that Joseph, as well as interpreting dreams, used a silver cup for divining as well as drinking.

In his preparatory prayers, made preceding his first angelic operation,

---

99 Michael MacDonald, *Mystical Bedlam: Madness, Anxiety, and Healing in Seventeenth-Century England* (Cambridge University Press: Cambridge, 1981): 18.
100 For introductions to the life of Dee, and the accusations he faced, see Peter J. French, *John Dee: The World of an Elizabethan Magus* (London, 1987). For more on Dee's magic, see György Endre Szőnyi, *John Dee's Occultism: Magical Exaltation Through Powerful Signs* (University of New York Press: Albany, 2004).

Dee mentions 'the Shew-stone, which the high priests did vse,'[101] which Whitby explains as referring to 'the stones of the breastplate described in Exodus 28 which the high priests of Israel are supposed to have used for divinatory purposes.'[102] It seems Dee related his shewstone in some way to 'the Urim and Thumim of the high priests of Israel in which they sought the light of God to resolve doubts and questions.'[103] Certainly, the golden breastplate was said to have borne twelve stones for the tribes of Israel,[104] and Szönyi extrapolates that 'the shining breastplate could also be used for purposes of divination (helping the gazing prophet to fall into a trance) and it is in this sense that medieval lapidaries refer to it.'[105] This was also a common belief of the early modern period, with John Aubrey mentioning Dr Spencer of Cambridge's discourse 'That the Priest had his Visions in the Stone of the Breast-plate.'[106]

The medieval lapidary works of Ephodius and Epiphanius are known to have been studied, referenced and annotated by Dee.[107] In particular, he 'drew attention to Epiphanius's remarks about "Adamanta,"' a stone 'in which diverse signs are given for responding to God,' and to the Jewish

101 MS. Sloane 3188, f. 7a.

102 Whitby, 'Renaissance Scrying': 27; citing M. Gaster 'Jewish Divination', *Encyclopaedia of Religion and Ethics*, 12 vols (Edinburgh, 1908–1921): 806–814.

103 Veenstra, 'The Holy Almandel': 214–15; citing Clulee, *John Dee's Natural Philosophy*, 207. On the Urim and Thumim, see also Florentino Garcia Martinez, 'Magic in the Dead Sea Scrolls.' *Metamorphosis of Magic*: 13–34.

104 Specifically, 'thou shalt set in it settings of stones; euen foure rowes of stones: the first row shalbe a Sardius, a Topaz, and a Carbuncle: this shall be the first row. And the second row shall be an Emeraude, a Saphir, and a Diamond. And the third row a Lygure, an Agate, and an Amethist. And the fourth row, a Berill, and an Onix, and a Iasper: they shalbe set in gold in their inclosings. And the stones shall bee with the names of the children of Israel, twelue, according to their names, like the engrauings of a signet: euery one with his name shall they bee according to the twelue tribes.' Exodus 28: 17–21.

105 Szönyi, 'Paracelsus, Scrying, and the *Lingua Adamica*': 213 n. 36.

106 Aubrey, *Miscellanies*: 128.

107 'Dee noted some of its connotations in a presentation copy of selected angel conversations, *De heptarchia mystica*. In this volume he noted the work of Ephodius and Epipanius on precious stones, as well as an unspecified "book received at Trebona."… Dee did own Epiphanius' work on the breastplate of Aaron, contained in a 1565 collection of works on stones and gems.' Harkness: 31 n. 85.

belief that the original laws given to Moses on Mount Sinai 'were expressed in sapphires.'[108] Considerations upon the exact manner of this expression once more unite visionary scrying with prophecy and sacred language. Certainly these are deep themes in Dee's work, and we should perhaps frame his interest in Adamanta – the stone of Adam – as part of his focus upon the spiritual power and authority of prelapsarian Man. Indeed it seems in hunting for the Adamical or angelical tongue, he found only the method of learning it; for 'Dee, on the basis of his readings on Enoch, associated the learning of Jared's son with the use of a "shew-stone," a crystal ball that could be used as the connecting device in communicating with angels.'[109] As we shall see below, the use of a stone, crystal or glass to speak to angels was not by any means unusual by the sixteenth century.

As perhaps the last puzzle-piece in this complex of occult theological epistemology, Aubrey also makes explicit the apocalyptic meanings afforded these stones, at least by the seventeenth century: 'a Berill [another common early modern term for a shewstone] is a kind of Crystal that hath a weak Tincture of Red; it is one of the Twelve Stones mentioned in the Revelation.'[110] While these twelve jewels do not necessarily exactly reproduce the twelve of Aaron's breastplate, the allusion is deliberate and the inference clear: visionary stones are (by scriptural example no less) godly, revelatory, eschatologically significant and could be employed for their occult potency.

Paracelsus

While many magicians were drawing both legitimising justifications and practical inspiration from respectable biblical sources, they were also pursuing exploratory innovation through new theories and practices. Perhaps most groundbreaking and publicly challenging to established scholarly authorities were the ideas of sixteenth century alchemist and physician Philippus Aureolus Theophrastus Bombastus Von Hohenheim.

Paracelsus speaks of the *ars beryllistica* 'which aims at gaining visions from diamonds, mirrors and other glossy materials, such as black coal':

---

108 Harkness: 31; citing Dee, *De heptarchia mystica*: 64.
109 Szönyi, 'Go-Between': 96.
110 Aubrey, *Miscellanies*: 128.

VISIONS. This species sees in crystals, mirrors, polished surfaces, and the like, things that are hidden, secret, present or future, which are present just as though they appeared in bodily presence.[111]

Likewise, Paracelsus' notions of divine knowledge or wisdom were read in an encouraging light:

He who inherits God's wisdom walks on water without wetting his feet; for in the true art inherited from God, man is like an angel... God is powerful and He wills it that His power be revealed to men and to angels in the wisdom of the arts. He wills it that the world and the earth be like Heaven.[112]

There is, in this last line, also an expressly apocalyptic millenarian bent to this transformational wisdom. In inheriting God's wisdom, humanity is elevated to the likeness of angels.

Spirits and Crystals

We have conducted this historical and historiographical survey thus far without touching on the summoning of spirits. Most scholarly works on scrying have presented Whitby's neat distinction between catoptromancy and crystallomancy: 'invocations for crystals always summon angels or spirits to give desired information, whereas accounts of catoptromancy do not always contain the appearance of such creatures. Mirrors usually present visions of the future or of some far distant place.'[113] Both the flatness and cleanness of the stone required in the Excellent Booke — a neat instance of 'glass' (mirror) and 'stone' not necessarily being easily distinguished — and the combination of spirit conjuration and visions of distant and possible future places present in the records of the Visions trouble this distinction. The Excellent Booke is not even the only treatise in its collected volume that instructs in scrying. Additional MS. 36674 also features a working 'to have a

111 Szönyi, 'Paracelsus, Scrying, and the Lingua Adamica': 213 n. 37.
112 Paracelsus, De fundamento scientiarum sapientiaeque, quoted in Paracelsus, Selected Writings, ed. Jolande [Shékács] Jacobi (Princeton University Press: Princeton, 1951): 163.
113 Whitby, 'Renaissance Scrying': 28

spirit in a glasse to tell all things.'[114] The ſtone could both contain an invoked spirit and reveal scenes of engagement between operators and spirits.

Equally, distinctions between conjuration and divination become blurred in the everyday cunning-craft of 'evocatory scrying.' We see this admixture of remote viewing and consultation with spirits in the observation that 'this practice of divination was mostly used by village sorcerers in order to find lost property or to call on the dead for advice.'[115] The remark about the prevalence of detecting lost or stolen goods certainly seems especially accurate.[116] Kieckhefer accounts several cases between the early fourteenth and late fifteenth centuries in which persons were accused and investigated for 'invoking spirits to appear in fingernails, mirrors, stones, rings, and so forth, to reveal the future or the location of lost objects,' concluding that in 'London repeatedly in the later fifteenth century, victims of theft were said to have solicited the services of alleged necromancers ("negremaunsers" or "nigromansiers").'[117] Nor was this a practice limited to the capital. In Coventry during the mid-1480s one John Haddon, having been the victim of a theft of £40, consulted necromancers to find the perpetrators.[118] Such examples of nigromancer-as-thieftaker in the historical record start to appear all too common when one begins to look for them.[119] If this expressly necromantic dimension seems anomalous, we should bear in mind the older medieval meaning of 'necromancer' was a broader one, and could more generally be used to refer to those who trafficked with *any* spirits – whether shades of dead people, angels, demons, fairies, or less obviously classifiable spirits.[120] Thus, scrying

114 Add. MS. 36674 f.66a.

115 Szönyi, 'Go-Between': 98; citing Martino Delrio, *Disquisitionum magicarum libri sex* (Lyons, 1608): 283; Jules Boulenger, *Opusculorum systema* (Lyons, 1621), 2: 199–200. See also Whitby, 'Renaissance Scrying': 25–36.

116 'Judging from the cases reported in the judicial records and chronicles – and judging also from the experiments contained in the Rowlinson necromantic manuscript – divination of this sort seems to have been used mostly to recover lost or stolen goods.' Kieckhefer, FR: 100.

117 Kieckhefer, FR: 100 n. 17 and 21

118 These consultants were alleged to have made this identification 'usyng the craftes of Sorcery, Wychcraftes, and Nygromancy.' Kittridge: 188.

119 See Kittridge, especially chapter XI 'Mirrors and Thieves.'

120 For more on this 'dual sense of nigromancia' see Charles Burnett, *Magic and Div-*

was 'caught between the extremes of natural and demonic magic'[121] not only in theoretical philosophising, but also practical operation.

The exact function of the stone within these operations can be unclear. Whitby reports that several theorists have made 'claims that the spirit "inhabits" the crystal,' although he admits he finds it 'hard to say how literally one is to take that description.'[122] Study of English angelic scrying operations, revealing what Veenstra considers 'the only novelty that the English Almandals offer when compared to their medieval ancestors,' is especially helpful when attempting to understand evocatory scrying:

> The medieval texts explain that the angels appear above the almandal, without giving further details, but apparently we may infer that they are apparitions hovering over the altar. The English Almandals, however, are more precise in their descriptions: the angels are said to become visible in a 'crystal stone', meaning a show-stone used in scrying. This is clearly an innovation in the text since it is absent from the German Almandals. Such a change may indicate a shift in interest from word (or name) to image, especially images seen in show-stones, but this would show disregard for the great interest in word-magic and natural language theories that were dominant in the early modern era. It is more likely that the additional element of scrying resulted from ideas on the visualisation of angels. Probably these ideas derived from optics, or at least from the complementary views of physics and metaphysics on reflection and illumination.[123]

As we have (albeit briefly) explored, crystal stones clearly did not have to supersede an interest in the magic of language, whether in the search for an angelical tongue or use of *voces magicæ* or divine names, yet express mentions of such equipment are certainly worthy of further study. Lilly's 'account of Sarah [Skelhorn]'s activities is interesting in that angels also appeared out-

---

ination in the Middle Ages (Aldershot: Variorum, 1996) and Claire Fanger, 'Libri Nigromantici: The Good, the Bad and the Ambiguous in John of Morigny's Flowers of Heavenly Teaching.' Magic, Ritual, and Witchcraft 7, 2, (2012): 164–189.

121 Veenstra, 'The Holy Almandel': 214.
122 Whitby, 'Renaissance Scrying': 29.
123 Veenstra, 'The Holy Almandel': 212–13.

side of the crystal as they are also recorded as appearing on a few occasions during Dee's experiments.'[124] Further troubling the neat distinction between scrying as divination and conjuration, the magical workbook which Elias Ashmole judged to be 'in the hand of one Mr Arthur Gauntlet, who professed Phisick and lived about Graies Inn Lane'[125] (Sloane MS. 3851) contains 'a number of invocations for making angels appear in crystals *and* mirrors.'[126] Arriving at this nexus of magical techniques and intentions, it seems clear that the relationship between scrying and spirits requires analysis. So who were these spirits, and how were they involved in scrying?

Calls

One component of scrying utilising spirit calling in order to effect visionary activity can be evinced from Lilly's brief account of 'Ellen Evans, daughter of my tutor Evans,' whose 'call unto the crystal' was this: 'O Micol, O tu Micol, *regina pigmeorum veni, &c.*'[127] Micol is identified as the 'Queen of the Fairies,' demonstrating the variety of entities one might contact in the course of using a shewstone. It is unclear if Evans Junior was actually calling Micol into the stone, merely appealing to the Queen's authority, or both. The calling of a senior fairy into a stone is certainly evidenced however in the operation found in both Scot's *Discoverie of Witchcraft* and in Gauntlet's workbook.[128]

Aubrey demonstrates an understanding of the consecratory and preparatory use of these incantations when he explains 'there are certain Formulas of Prayer to be used before they make the inspection, which they term a Call.'[129] In another, far more complete set of instructions demonstrating the connections between spirits and scrying equipment, we see that the engraving as well as the writing of spirits' names was operatively useful, even necessary. The Foreman text (Cambridge University Library MS Additional

---

124 Whitby, 'Renaissance Scrying': 33; TFR: 1.

125 Sloane MS. 3851 f.2b.

126 Whitby, 'Renaissance Scrying': 32; Sloane 3851 f.40b. Emphasis added.

127 Lilly, History: 239.

128 Reginald Scot, *Discoverie of Witchcraft* (London, 1584: 1665), 244–247; *The Grimoire of Arthur Gauntlet*, ed. David Rankine (Avalonia: London, 2011): 237.

129 Aubrey, *Miscellanies*: 129.

3544), dated to 1536–1539,[130] contains several scrying experiments. One such experiment, 'The working with a crystal stone,' is especially illuminative:

> Take a chrystall stone or a berall stone that is bryghteste & the bygnes of a thombe [i.e. thumb], & washe hem wth cleane water & wype hem cleane wth a cleane clothe then anoynte hem wth oyle of olive & call the moste treweste spryte in the name of Onely & that name wryte yn the stone wth the said oyle then put the stone into the hand of a chyld that ys wthin ten years of ayge then hold the name of Onely agaynste the sonne then knele downe vppo[n] yor knyes holdi[n]g vp yor hand towards heavyn & say thys prayer & co[n]iuracon...[131]

Once more, there is a slight uncertainty if the 'spryte' called into the stone is Onely or merely if spiritual authority to perform the operation is called upon 'in the name of Onely.' The first incantation given contains 'six names' (Egipia, Bonahan, Iahandesiu[m], Alredesyn, Kaysyn, Obenym) and the conjuration itself is 'by the name of Chymon, and by the name of Alpha and Omega' and actually addressed to 'ye sprytts of the easte...the weste...the southe...[and] the northe.'[132] Young identifies Onely as 'a variant name of the spirit Honely who is called into a crystal to detect theft in the Munich Hand-book.'[133] This fifteenth century experiment also features writing the name in oil, while another experiment ('for obtaining information about a theft by gazing into a fingernail') on the following folio of Clm. 849 features a set of very similar names to those given in the Foreman incantation.[134]

Familiarly, anointing with oil is important; this time however the oil seems primarily used to write a powerful name. A 'fayre crystall stone' left behind by two sorcerers in a field near London in 1590 – interrupted during their 'witchcrafte or conjuringe' – bore the name 'Sathan' written on it, per-

---

130   *The Cambridge Book of Magic*: xvi.
131   *Cambridge Book of Magic*: 26–27.
132   *Cambridge Book of Magic*: 27–29.
133   *Cambridge Book of Magic*: 125 n. 16; citing Kieckhefer, FR: 244–5
134   Including 'Egippia, Benoham, Beanke...Reranressym, Alredessym.' Clm. 849, ff. 44v–45v.

haps pointing to an appeal to demonic hierarchy with such crystal-writing.[135] Magical oil is certainly attested in *De Nigromancia*, and a long testament to its scriptural significances is instructed to be incanted as a consecration.[136] It is worth noting this operation is specifically for the manufacture and empowerment of an 'ointment, wherewith you shall anoint your eyes; & all spirits will appear unto you such that you may see them when you please.'[137] Such visionary substances have a long and illustrious tradition in European magical practice, and recipes and instructions for their sorcerous production are found in a variety of early modern occult texts.[138]

The use of oil and mention of the size of a thumb should more directly call to mind fingernail divination. Following a brief description of the rite, the experiment for Onely is suddenly discussed as 'wroughte yn the nayle of a chylde his thombe'[139] and this switch occurs before the prescribed prayer and conjuration is actually given. I believe the inspiration from the Munich manuscript's two separate experiments explains this apparent jump to discussing onychomancy. We also see the prevalence of the use of a child seer, and of holding the stone to the sun. Weather conditions are especially important, for 'this maye not be donne but when the sonne shenethe.'[140] It is also worth noting that this operation also depends upon certain ritual taboos, the operator should 'note thou be in cleane lyfe.'

This clean living is further emphasised by Onely's appearance in a further series of scrying experiments later in the Foreman text. Not only does 'a certain *angel* called Onely…like to appear in a beryl stone or a crystal or in a urinal[141] half-filled with *holy water*,' but he specifically 'shows himself to

135 Kittredge: 94, n. 136.

136 DN IV, C4: 60 – 65.

137 DN, IV C4: 60.

138 See for instance *The Grimoire of Arthur Gauntlet*: 289, 290; *The Complete Grimoire of Honorious*, ed. David Rankine & Paul Harry Barron (London: Avalonia, 2013): 141.

139 *Cambridge Book of Magic*: 27.

140 *Cambridge Book of Magic*: 27.

141 As Young points out, a 'urinal' was both a chamber pot and a glass vial used for uroscopic analysis. It was also 'used in alchemy to mean a glass phial or vial shaped like the medical instrument.' Young, *Cambridge Book of Magic*: 125 n. 30; citing A. Oizumi (ed.), *A Complete Concordance to the Works of Geoffrey Chaucer*, 2nd edition (Hildesheim: Olms-Weidmann, 2003) vol. 13: 1348; L. Abraham, *A Dictionary of Alchemical Imagery*

virgins, between seven and twelve years old, and not to men unless his mind has been *sanctified* to the highest contemplation of God.'[142] The 'angel' Onely was asked, 'by the virtue of Our Lord Jesus Christ, and by all the names of God which I will recite, that without delay, wherever you may be, you would come to me and appear in this stone certifying and showing the truth of this matter concerning which I shall ask you.'[143] Once more, purity and sanctification is a measure and means of veracity, ensuring the truth of the things seen and questions answered in the stone. It is said that, once the correct sacred incantations are made, 'at once shall come one dressed in white, and he will appear to others covered in hair.'[144] It is tempting to attribute this whiteness to a sacred purity, piety, and trustworthiness. Certainly conversely, a connection between hairiness and evil (made by a spirit no less) can be seen in Uriel's remarks during Dee's actions recording in TFR 'for, now, the World hath hoary hairs, and beginneth to be sick.'[145] The spirit's hirsute appearance in others' perceptions nevertheless also seems to implicitly suggest a certain, perhaps fundamental, subjectivity in spirit-sighting.

The writing of magical names upon one's scrying equipment is also attested by Aubrey and Lilly, who both mention inscriptions of archangelic names on the frames into which crystals are set. The stone 'is set in a Ring, or Circle of Silver resembling the Meridian of a Globe...at the Four quarters of it are the Names of Four Angels, viz. Vriel, Raphael, Michael, Gabriel.'[146] Lilly reports a very similar crystal given to Sir Robert Holborn by Gilbert Wakering, 'it was of the largeness of a good big orange, set in silver, with a cross on the top, and another on the handle; and round about engraved the names of these angels, Raphael, Gabriel, Uriel.'[147] Specifically, Holborn had been able to have 'conference with Uriel and Raphael' until he lost the ability to contact them. Lilly implies this was through a lack of observation of taboos,

---

(Cambridge: Cambridge University Press, 1998): 207.

142 *Cambridge Book of Magic*: 47. Emphasis added.

143 *Cambridge Book of Magic*: 48.

144 *Cambridge Book of Magic*: 48.

145 TFR: 238.

146 Aubrey, *Miscellanies*: 131. Aubrey also mentions a 'cross patee' atop the design, also indicated in the accompanying illustration on 130.

147 Lilly, *History*: 231 n. 18.

for 'neatness and cleanliness in apparel, a strict diet, and upright life, fervent prayers unto God, conduce much to the assistance of those who are curious these ways.'[148] The likeness of the described (indeed, pictured) scrying tool to a monstrance should not escape us. It makes sense that divinely-sanctioned visions would have required sacred, or at least sacred-looking, tools.

Angels

The most common late medieval and early modern operations calling spirits using a stone – or at least certainly the most likely to be recorded – are angelic. Dee's angel conversations, and especially efforts to discredit them and him as the demonic work of a gullible dupe, highlight the notion that 'although the crystal showstone facilitated communication with angels, it was not sufficient to ensure it.'[149] In spite, or perhaps because of this, measures were expressly taken to attempt to prevent wicked spirits arriving or, even worse, masquerading as angels. The call of 'Speculatrix' Sarah Skelhorn, praised as having 'a perfect sight, and indeed the best eyes for that purpose I ever yet did see,' began with an appeal to ensure 'good angels, only and only' would be present in and through her crystal.[150] While the appearance of holy divine messengers was not assured, many scryers appear to have believed it could be ensured through additional preparations and ritual.

One of these forms of ensuring proper and pious spirit contact was a reliance on various forms of spiritual cleanliness. In Gauntlet's grimoire an operation for 'how you shall work to have sight and conference with one Good Angel' is interrupted by the recording of three psalms, including the famous 51st Psalm, which entreats God Almighty to 'purge me with Hyssop and I shall be clean Thou shalt wash me and I shall be whiter than snow.'[151] The operation, following a short prayer, the Lord's Prayer and the Creed, also begins: 'I call upon and Invocate thee O Omnipotent God which art King of all things Eternal Governor of all the world uncorrupt unspotted undefiled

---

148 Lilly, History: 232.

149 Harkness: 119.

150 Lilly, History: 228. One has to wonder about his phrasing and the spirit Onely, an orthography frequently used for the word 'only.'

151 Gauntlet: 128.

Invisible wonderful most faultless irreprehensible Almighty ruler.'[152] Proper consecrations of operator and operation, dedicated to and conducted under the auspices of the purity of the Most High, would not only successfully contact a spirit; they would contact the right spirit.

The Three Angels of the Stone

As briefly mentioned above, there appears one particular feature of angelic scrying across the medieval and early modern period: that of summoning not simply one angel, but three. The fifteenth century commonplace book of Robert Reynys specifies an operation, designed for scrying in a boy's fingernail, in which the conjurer is to ask for 'Lord Jesus Christ, king of glory, send us three angels to tell us the truth and not falsehood in all matters about which we shall inquire.'[153] A specific injunction delivered against falsehood should of course be understood as a preventative measure against wicked or deceiving spirits.

Similarly, the Gauntlet workbook contains an experiment 'to call three good Angels into a Crystal Stone or Looking Glass to thine own sight' entreating 'O holy Lord God give unto me thy unworthy servant to see Three of thy good Angels in this Crystal Stone (or Glass)': when the angels appear one is further instructed to remind them to tell 'nothing but the truth as you will answer it at the day of doom before your God and mine.'[154] The manuscript also contains an alternative operation, 'How to call Three Heavenly Angels into A Crystal Stone or Looking Glass to the visible sight of A Child,'[155] and procedures to follow 'if you mistrust them to be false Angels,'[156] 'How you shall make your demands to the Three Angels And first for a Friend,'[157] 'for [discovering] Theft to the Three Angels,' 'for Treasure hidden,' 'for Cattle that are stolen or Strayed away,' 'for Sickness,'[158] and even a conjuration 'for a

---

152 *Gauntlet*: 127.

153 *The Commonplace Book of Robert Reynes of Acle: An Edition of Tanner MS. 407*, ed. Cameron Louis (New York: Garland, 1980): f.169.

154 *Gauntlet*: 113.

155 *Gauntlet*: 114.

156 *Gauntlet*: 116.

157 *Gauntlet*: 117.

158 *Gauntlet*: 118.

Spirit of Prophecy' and a variety of sorcerous cures to follow after 'The Three Angels being Invocated.'[159] In these last cases, the calling of the three angels is not merely a scrying technique for receiving visions, but established as an opening rite, perhaps even an appeal to the angels' spiritual authority. It is a modular component for magical operations composed of several actions, designed to effect specific changes in the world external to the operator.

An earlier working book, the Foreman text, appears to offer the actual names of these angels. In the operation mentioned earlier, once the 'angel' Onely has been called and given license to depart, the operator is to ask the Almighty 'to deign to send your three holy angels from your right hand, that is, Ancor, Anacor, [and] Anelos…so that this boy, enlightened by the Holy Spirit, may be able clearly and perfectly to see; and that they tell us the truth without deceit concerning all the things about which we shall ask them.'[160] Nor do these names exist solely for abstract theological speculation. Gauntlet's sort of practical applications, for finding stolen goods, are also present in the operation detailed in Sloane MS. 3849: 'Let the childe name them by these names sainge *antor, anasor, anelor*[,] shew mee the persons and the apparel of them that hath such a man's mony to this child…'[161] This manuscript also instructs 'let the child sit with his face toward the sune lookinge in the christal and ever ask him what hee seeth as you reade.'[162]

These 'names' and their variations – even when simply given as a 'barbarous' formula of *voces magicæ* – have a long pedigree throughout various grimoires. *Liber Juratus*' Oration 17, for instance, contains 'Hancor, hanacor, hamylos iehorna, theodonos' – marking these words as at least a fourteenth century formula.[163] As Joseph H. Peterson has pointed out, 'the Orations found in *Liber Juratus* parallel (and are probably derived from) those found in the *Ars Notoria*.'[164] It is in the Notary Art's Oration of the Physical Art (for 'if you would have the perfect knowledge of any Disease, whether the same

159 *Gauntlet*: 121–6.
160 *Cambridge Book of Magic*: 49.
161 Sloane MS. 3849, f.4b.
162 Sloane MS. 3849, f.4b.
163 Royal MS. 17Axlii, f.37v.
164 Joseph H. Peterson, *Liber Juratus, or the Sworne Booke of Honorius*, ed. Sarah Kane French (2008).

tend to death or life: if the sick party lie languishing, stand before him, & say this Oration three times with great reverence') that we find 'Ancor, Anacor, Anylos Zohorna, Theodonos.'[165] In trying to find earlier instances, we should note the twelfth century Arabic manual of astrological magic *Picatrix* mentions 'the angel Ancora, who dwells in the fourth heaven.'[166] Although this current study employs editions of these texts published after the Foreman text had already been compiled, these three tomes were extremely popular and obviously (at least sections of them) would have been available to magicians from the sixteenth century onwards.

As for their appearance in other 'mainstream occult sources,'[167] these words are clearly most often involved in some form of consecration, such as for sanctifying either ritual garments or silken cloth used to wrap and store other magical tools. One *Key of Solomon* manuscript features such somewhat similar-sounding consecrations, one for vestments ('Amor, Amator, Amides, Ideodaniach, Paucor, Playor, Anitor')[168] and one for the silk cloth ('Ancor, Anachor, Anilos, Theodomos').[169] The second of these also features the word 'agnefeton,' and Peterson goes on to detail an apparent branch of various *Keys of Solomon* — which can to an extent be marked by this 'Amides' derivation — that feature apparent appeals to St Agnes.[170] There appears, at the very least, to be an operationalisation of a typo linking 'Ange(l)s' and Agnes, not an unusual feature of medieval and early modern grimoire transmission, reception, and utility. The sense of appealing to Agnes, both expressly understood as a lamb and a virgin, is obvious when considering consecra-

165 Robert Turner (trans.), *Ars Notoria* (London, 1656): 24.

166 John Michael Greer and Christopher Warnock (ed.), *Picatrix: Liber Viridis*: 264. The editors footnote that, 'in the Arabic text, this angel is named Antur.' My thanks to Joseph Clinton Ragan for bringing this to my attention.

167 Joseph H. Peterson, *John Dee's Five Books of Mystery: Original Sourcebook of Enochian Magic* (Weiser: York Beach, 2003): 26.

168 British Library MS. Additional 10862, f.116v.

169 Add 10862, f.64v.

170 'ancor, amacor, amade. Theodonia, Pancorpsagor, Anotor, parles merites des Saint Anges [sic],' Sloane MS. 3091, f. 84v; 'Ancor, Amacor, Amade, Theodonia, Pancor = psagor, Anitor, par les merites des Saints Anges', Harley MS. 3981, f.112v; 'Ancor, Amacor, Amade, Theodonia, Pancor, Psagor, Anitor, parles merites, des Saints Ange', Kings MS. 288 f. 111v. See Peterson, *John Dee's Five Books*, 26 – 27 n. 73.

tions of textiles as well as general ritual purity for trafficking with spirits in a shewstone.

The popular grimoire of planetary spirit conjuration, the *Heptameron*, features the formulae or angel names 'Ancor, Amacor, Amides, Theodonias, Anitor,' 'to be said, when the Vesture is put on,' and the possible appeal to Agnes has been resolved to 'by the merits of your holy Angel, O Lord.'[171] The later *Lemegeton*'s identical garment consecration clearly derives from the *Heptameron*'s.

A host of sixteenth century texts use this incantation or variations thereupon. Sloane MS. 3847 – an early (perhaps earliest) *Clavicula Salomonis*, dated 1572 – features a consecration of 'virginne paper,'[172] and the *Book of Magic* catalogued as Folger Shakespeare MS. V.b.26 features 'Ancor, Amacor, Amides, Theodonias, Anitor, per merita Angelorum.'[173] The compilation of various texts that make up Additional MS. 36674 itself also contains several uses of this complex of words. A *Key of Solomon* (specifically, Book 2, chapter 19) contains mention of 'Amor, Ananator, Anilis, Theodomos.'[174]

Perhaps most (in)famously, the 'angels Ancor, Annasor, Anelos, Ansex and Amilos are to be found invoked in a scrying experiment' of Dee.[175] Indeed, the first scrying experiment of Dee and Kelly features 'Anchor, Anachor and Anilos.'[176] We should bear in mind the lack of standardisation of spelling before engaging in too much micro-typology of distinct angelic entities. Whitby speculates about a number of variations in these names ('Amacor could well be Dee's Anachor') as well as some origins of these variations ('either by Kelly misreading Abano, or by Abano mistaking his sources') before ultimately judging that 'while a definitive source for the names cannot be traced, they do seem to have a certain traditional flavour.'[177] Most significantly for our present focus, Gilbert and Davis unequivocally demonstrate not

171   *Fourth Book of Occult Philosophy*, trans. Robert Turner (London, 1665): 76.
172   Sloane 3847 ff.60r–v.
173   The '*oratio dicenda quando Induitur vestis*,' Folger V.b.26, 225.
174   Additional MS. 36674, f.82v. See also f.15v.
175   Whitby, Thesis: 211; citing Sloane MS. 3848 f.3b.
176   Joseph H. Peterson, *John Dee's Five Books of Mystery: Original Sourcebooks of Enochian Magic* (Weiser: York Beach, 2003): 26.
177   Whitby, Thesis: 211.

just that these words were indeed understood as spirits' names, but even how the spirits appeared: 'H.G. with his skryer did see the 17th of March, ante meridian ["17 Martii"] between ten and twelve. Two black birds flying from the south to the north, without heads, which were two Angels called Ancor and Amulor who showed many good books for them.'[178]

In light of both the comments above concerning English Almandals and the appearance of the spirits as headless birds to Gilbert and Davis, it seems significant that the three angels are asked in the Foreman operation to come 'to this place or into the crystal,'[179] suggesting that spirit sightings could be located around and not merely within the stone. This is perhaps a feature of earlier sixteenth century conjurations and that, by a century later in Gauntlet's book, it was more common to have the angels appear actually in the stone. Certainly this tradition of calling (these) three angels for scrying has been suggested to stretch back to at least the fifteenth century. Whitby judges that:

> From the authoritative manner of the instructions [of Gauntlet, not to mention the copybook nature of the workingbook] it is likely that this is a copy of some compendium of scrying, perhaps circulated in manuscript. The invocation to 'call three Heavenly Angells into a Christall Stone or looking Glasse to the visible sight of a Child' bears many similarities to William Byg's confessed method and suggests that Byg may have followed a standard work on the subject.[180]

Naming Names

Tracing the appearances and permutations of this formula of angelic names leads us to question who were the other spirits (specifically, *named*) involving in scrying.

Whitby tells us 'in 1549 Sir Thomas Smith examined a certain William Wycherly upon accusations of conjuring spirits... At first he used a solomonic circle to call up a spirit called Bare.'[181] Given the common orthographic

---

178 Add. MS. 36674, f.61v.
179 *Cambridge Book of Magic* 49.
180 Whitby, 'Renaissance Scrying': 32. Sloane 3851 f.40b.
181 Whitby, 'Renaissance Scrying': 30

that could render Baron as Barō, as well as contemporary permutational transmission and reception of the names of spirits, I believe it is reasonable to link this spirit with 'Baron,' who appears in both the Folger Book of Magic and a century later in the working copybook of Arthur Gauntlet whom David Rankine judges to have 'derived from Folger Vb.26(1), as may be seen in both the text…and the sequence of characters.'[182]

Also present at Wycherly's conjuration were 'one Robert Bayly the scryer of the crystalle stone, syr John Anderson the *magister operator*, syr John Hickley, and Thomas Gosling,' who collectively raised up 'a terrible wynde and tempest', rather than the 'orientalle or septentrialle visible spirit Baro.'[183] Thereafter the band seem to give up use of the circle, reverting to the simple use of a crystal to 'invocate the spirit called Scariot.'[184] Wycherly claimed success in recovering stolen goods this way 'about a hundred times.' Moreover it seems important to note that 'Wycherly attempted to invoke particular spirits rather than just any supernatural creature.'[185] The accused didn't simply name the names of spirits, but also another four people involved in one magical operation and 'he also implicated another four scryers in addition to those mentioned above…if the deposition is true it is clear that belief in its efficacy [i.e. evocatory scrying] was not confined to the common people.'[186]

While it is tempting to understand the name Scariot as a derivation of Judas Iscariot, it should be noted that Sloane 3848 offers 'an experyment approved and unknowne of Ascaryell to see most excellent and certainlye in a christall stone what secretts thou wilt.'[187]

> First take a christall stonne or a glasse, the greater the better so that it be fayre and cleare, without any ragges cracks or holes broken within and thou must have a thonge of harts skinn, to wrappe thy stonne in so that thy stonne may be well seene in the middest of the bindinge, and ever

---

182 *Gauntlet*: 20.
183 Kittredge: 158.
184 Kittredge: 189.
185 Whitby, 'Renaissance Scrying': 31.
186 Whitby, 'Renaissance Scrying': 31.
187 Whitby, 'Renaissance Scrying': 31–2; Sloane 3848, f.148. The complete ritual follows until f.151a.

when thou dost wrappe the stonne about with the thonge say thus In *nominie sanctæ trinitatis et dietatis nanc gemmam tecondo:*

Then holde the christall stonne which is so dight in thy right hande against the .o. [Sun] which must be done in the heate of the [Sun] at noone when the [Sun] is in the highest and hottest and soe call him [Ascaryell] in such likenes as thou wilt by the conjuration followinge and he will come and shew thee what thou wilt in all countryes of all thinges whatsoever thou wilt aske him and thou shalt commaund him to bringe his fellowes with him.[188]

This operation was combined with an incantory element 'the special conjuration' which was utilised at this point of commanding the spirit.

Unclean Spirits

Angels or angelic spirits were not the only intelligences to work with, as demons and other 'unclean spirits' could also called by these techniques.[189] Pushing our dates back even earlier, in 1323 near Paris, it is reported that a conjuration of the spirit Berith was attempted in order to recover stolen money, and involved a cat skin circle.[190]

The abbot of the Cistercian monastery at Cercanceau (Seine-et-Marne) had lost much treasure. He consulted a sorcerer (*sortilegus*), who engaged that by his arts it should be restored and the names of the robbers and their fautors should be disclosed. The wizard buried a black cat in a chest with food for three days at a crossroads, with an arrangement of hollow reeds to give the creature air. The food was bread soaked in chrism, holy oil, and holy water. After three days the cat was to be skinned and its skin was to be cut into strips to form a magic circle. Then the magician, entering the circle, was to call up the demon Berith, who would give the information desired.[191]

188 Whitby, Thesis: 88−9 n. 51: Sloane MS. 3848, f.148. The complete ritual continues until fol. l5la. See also Thomas, Crystal Gazing: 84, 85.
189 Kieckhefer: 97 n. 5.
190 Kieckhefer: 100 n. 18.
191 Kittredge: 202, n. 112, 113.

The actual operation was prevented from occurring after passing shepherds heard the cat mewing underground and, with the approval of a local judge, dug the box up and rescued the poor cat. The carpenter who made the box informed on the sorcerer, who was burned, and his assistant, who died in prison.

The name Berith is often connected to the biblical Baalberith of Judges 8:33.[192] This spirit certainly seems widely-travelled by the sixteenth century, turning up in the catalogues of Weyer, the *Livre des Esperitz*, and in the *Book of the Offices of Spirits* as under the Regent of the South, Amaymon. Scot's entry on Berith in his *Discoverie of Witchcraft* asserts the spirit is worked under different names by 'Jewes' and 'Nigromancers.'[193] At least these nigromantic associations would seem to be supported by the affair in 1323.

Expressly devilish entities could certainly be trafficked with using a crystal or stone. Conjurations of Vassago and Agares – two of the *Ars Goetia's dramatis personæ* – found in a seventeenth century collection of magical operations include some very particular descriptions of such scrying apparatus.[194] Significant to the role of the four kings in the *Excellent Booke*, this conjuration of Agares expressly calls 'Thou Spirit Agares the first Captain under the King of the East,' demonstrating once more the use and function of appeals to these cardinal authorities.[195] In this case more specifically, a relationship between the spirit Bael (Agares' predecessor in their rogues' gallery catalogue, a king who holds the first entry in most spirit-lists) and Oriens are further evidenced.[196] Even outside of the specific *Ars Goetia* sequence, Agares

192 'And it came to pass, as soon as Gideon was dead, that the children of Israel turned again, and went a whoring after Baalim, and made Baalberith their god.'

193 Scot, *Discoverie of Witchcraft*: 233.

194 'If [the magician] useth a Crystal Stone, It ought to be about the bigness of a goose Egg, it matter not whether It be round or oval and to be Set on a frame, which may be done by a jeweler, with a Ring of flat wire, or narrow plate about it, at the bottom whereof Let it be fastened, a Stem of indifferent Length, as the handle of a beer bowl, with a ponderous or heavy pedestal or foot to It, that it may stand firm & steady, & then hath [the operator] a Complete Recepticle.' There follow instructions and suggestions for a glass scrying crystal. *The Book of Treasure Spirits*, ed. by David Rankine (Avalonia: London, 2009): 150–151.

195 *The Book of Treasure Spirits*: 145; again, in the contract, 147.

196 For more on Oriens, and Bael, see Jake Stratton-Kent, *The Testament of Cyprian the*

is still understood in terms of this relationship with the King of the East.

Consorting with such unclean spirits had tangible goals, and fairly expressly diabolic tones:

> Divinatory conjuration could, of course, be used for other purposes as well, such as finding buried treasure. A group of men were tried in Norfolk in 1465 for using necromancy to discover such a trove. Allegedly they invoked and made sacrifice to accursed spirits. When a *spiritus aerialis* appeared, at Bunwell, they promised it the body of a Christian man in exchange for its leading them to treasure; the spirit revealed in a crystal the location of a hill filled with treasure, whereupon the adventurers baptized a rooster with a Christian name and sacrificed it to the spirit.[197]

Both this operation, and the Baro conjuration earlier, ultimately concern one of those most practical matters: money. They also show more of how appeals of folk like John Haddon to necromancers to return lost or stolen items or monies may well have been conducted. These necromancers seem not only to have been conjuring the vision of the sought-after objects, but an agent who might be sent to retrieve them or otherwise seek to impel the thieves to return the goods. If other thief-compelling formulae are to be believed, these impulsions were probably not pleasant for the accused thief. The boundaries of divination and sorcery, of knowing and acting, can be seen to once more blur. Certainly in the battlefield for the magicians' souls, raging across each glimmering scrying surface, the lines drawn distinguishing natural or intellectual magic from the attentions and ministrations of demons blurred significantly. Such once more are the particularities of a broader sea-change in the status of magic and natural philosophy out of the Renaissance.

Mage (Scarlet Imprint: Dover, 2014): 52–92, and *passim*.
197 Kieckhefer: 102 n. 27.

Prophecy, Millenarianism and Personal Destiny

When comparisons involving Dee's angelic operations are made by historians and practitioners alike, there is a certain exceptionalism that can be detected in their treatment. It seems commonplace within these studies to affirm that 'Dee's use of crystallomancy is significantly different to what may be seen as the inherited tradition.'[198] This difference is more explicitly articulated in terms of complexity, and intellectual worth, as much as historical coverage and significance; as when Harkness considers that 'although many occult practices, including divination, relied on stones or mirrors, Dee's utilization of the showstone was more optically sophisticated.'[199] Dr Dee is considered a 'better sort.'

I suggest part of this supposed sophistication came down the nature of the matters about which spirits were consulted by magicians as much as the techniques of conjuration by which these consultations occurred. In short, there seems a tendency of the Enochian angels to be epic: to conspire to deliver (supposedly) cosmologically significant gnosis in an expressly eschatological and millenarian light – rather than be content to work more everyday and practical operations. Indeed, when consulted on precisely such a matter, 'concerning treasure supposedly left behind by the Danes, the angels demand that earth from eleven specified places be collected, but when requested what is to happen next, they prevaricate and then quietly drop the matter in favour of new material concerning the created universe.'[200]

Answers concerning the grand cosmic scale of the whole of Creation, such as those received by Dee and Kelly, also may have inspired a more exceptional use of shewstones. While using a crystal to discern aspects of one's destiny was not unusual in divinations – such as that familiar form of love divination performed for Scot by William Hodges – Dee's use to confirm his own magical career as some kind of a divinely-appointed quest is rather less usual. It is fair to agree such 'prophecy, [and, perhaps more importantly] Dee's faith in it and its consequences upon the course of Dee's life and its continual postponement [...] make Dee's use of crystallomancy far exceed the limits

---

198 Whitby, 'Renaissance Scrying': 33.
199 Harkness: 117; Thomas, Religion: 215; Goldberg, The Mirror and Man: 12–13.
200 Whitby, 'Renaissance Scrying': 33; Sloane 3188 f.86a.

of common practice.'[201] Gilbert also used a shewstone to unveil his personal destiny and elevate his spiritual authority.

Kelly's spiritual intel gleaned from the angelic operations has been characterised as 'largely concerned with orders of spirits and intelligences who govern various parts of the Creation and with the prophecy of a new age in Europe in which Dee and Kelly are to play an important role, having been elected by God to perform certain rites that will herald in this penultimate era in world history.'[202] These duties cast Dee as ever more the prophet:

> URIEL: "The Lord hath chosen you to be Witnesses, through his mercy and sufferance...in the offices and diginites of the Prophets...wherein you do exceed the Temples of the earth; wherein you are become separated from the world...'[203]

The world was conceived and experienced as undergoing profound transformative crises, and within these shifting circumstances of fate and faith 'Dee's prophetic role went hand-in-hand with his increased powers to see and judge the decay of the Book of Nature.'[204] These sharpened faculties of awareness, understanding, and judgement were themselves partly secured by the revelation and use of the natural Adamical language, being the only way to ensure perfect knowledge upon this fallen earth.[205] While Davis and Gilbert's scrying was less expressly revelatory of cosmological apocalypse,

---

201 Whitby, 'Renaissance Scrying': 33.

202 Whitby, 'Renaissance Scrying': 33.

203 TFR: 233.

204 Harkness: 146; citing TFR: 400.

205 We may certainly see the pre-tremors of later important philosophical reform in this approach, for 'central to the Baconian project of recovering edenic wisdom was a concomitant interest in the recovery of the Adamic language, or *lingua humana*, that gave expression to Adam's perfect understanding of the natural world,' as 'the intellectual perfections Bacon describes both result in the ability to use language precisely and, paradoxically, are derived from the very linguistic precision that they produce'; indeed, thusly, 'the words and wisdom of Eden are inextricably linked.' Zachary McLeod Hutchins, *Inventing Eden: Primitivism, Millennialism, and the Making of New England* (Oxford University Press: Oxford, 2014): 135, and chapter 5 ('Translating Paradise: Hebrew, Herbert, Milton, Fox, and the Pursuit of Linguistic Purity'), *passim*.

it was still set against a background of the Last Days and certainly involved discovery and assumption of a divinely appointed power and role – at least for H.G.

It is in the light of this self-belief in his own prophetic role and responsibility that we should consider some of Dee's more impertinent diplomatic interactions with foreign courts and rulers – indeed, 'the angels encouraged him to verbalise and publicise his insights outside the tight circle of the colloquia, and scolded him when they thought he should have made "a more ample declaration" of their remarks.'[206] While the angels encouraged Dee to make some of their messages all too public, like the experiments of Gilbert and Davis, secrets were also kept between Dee and his scryer. The angels both promised Kelly he would be 'a great Seer: Such an one as shall judge the circle of things in nature,' but also warned him that certain 'heavenly understanding, and spiritual knowledge shall be sealed up from thee in this world.'[207]

It is worth noting that Dee's point was not merely to see the angels, but speak to them *about* and *in* the language of Adam:

> I have read in thy bokes *&* records, how Enoch enjoyed thy favour and *conversation*, with Moses thou wast familiar: and also that to Abraham, Isaac, and Jacob, Josua, Gedeon, Esdras, Daniel, Tobias, and sundry other, thy good Angels were sent, by thy disposition to instruct them, informe them, help them, yea in worldly and domesticall affaires, yea, and sometimes to satisfy theyr desires, doutes *&* questions of thy Secrets. And furdermore considering the Shew stone which the high priests did use, by thy owne ordering.[208]

For a start, this appeal to scriptural precedent seems partly an effort by Dee to frame his work within a perceived pious tradition of Christian mysticism. This framing should not be seen as merely attempting to make Christian excuses for nigromantic practices, but rather stemming from sincere self-perception. Dee genuinely 'believed himself heir to the prophetic biblical

---

206 Harkness: 146; citing TFR: 400.
207 TFR: 61.
208 Sloane MS. 3188, f.6v. Emphasis added.

tradition of Enoch, Elias, Esdras, and John the Divine.'[209] Dee especially was interested in Enoch, whose eyes were opened by the Lord that he 'might see and judge the earth, which was unknown unto his Parents, by reason of their fall'; who had 'the use of the earth' and was 'full of the spirit of wisdom.'[210] Enoch, who exchanged words with the Almighty.

We can thus see angelic information about Enoch would be especially useful and significant to a magus looking for the perfect knowledge that itself could perfect nature. Merely successfully conversing with certain spirits about certain matters – provided one observed the proper protocols and spoke in the proper language that allowed it – also seems to have been thought to impart a form of spiritual elevation. To speak with the tongue of Eden somewhat inherently redeemed the mortal speaker as it evoked the state of humanity in its prelapsarian voice, and it certainly afforded the ability to ask more potent questions to more attentive and powerful spirit-teachers.

It is then doubly significant to point out that Dee and Kelly are chided for not completely learning and employing this cosmologically potent tongue.

Spirit Tuition in Magic

In closing this essay on scrying, shewstones, and spirits, I would like to consider the means and results of courting and employing the advice and instruction of spirits:

A stone as sacred and significant as Dee's required a proper setting, so he used a special table and wax seals to further delineate the sacred space surrounding his showstone. Though the showstone was not dependent upon its environment to function properly, it was nonetheless a holy object to be revered and set apart from the mundane world. Because the stone was so crucial to Dee's angel conversations, the diaries record specific information about the furnishings, personal items, and books that complemented it. During each angel conversation Dee placed the show-

209 Harkness: 146–47. 'Each prophet had served as a "divine scribe" obediently recording the information received from God and the angels in books of wisdom.'
210 TFR: 174.

stone on a large wax seal, which was itself resting on a 'Holy Table.' Together, these items provided a larger sacred space with increased religious and occult connotations. Dee's use of a wax seal, for example, was *related to medieval and early modern Solomonic magical practices involving the use of sigils and talismans*, and his 'Holy Table' served as an altar adorned with figures and inscriptions. *The designs for these objects did not come from standard occult references but from the angels themselves.*[211]

Wax seals are not merely 'related' to medieval and early modern magic beyond and encompassing a 'Solomonic' tradition: they are utterly a component of it, evidenced in the encyclopedic occult philosophy of Agrippa, and in practical instructions from grimoires and working books.[212] Such Enochian technologies highlight a combination of grimoire-based research and spirit-led revelations in Dee and Kelly's angelical operations. This combinatory approach, this ability to innovate and be responsive to individuated tuition from spirits as well as base one's practices in the worked traditions of one's forebears, should be held up as an inspiration to modern practitioners at least as much as the actual system(s) channelled by the doctor and his seer.

A somewhat more practical form of tutelage came in the form of intercessory actions by certain patron spirits: as attested by Girolamo Cardano, for example, who recounted 'the conjuration of a young scryer who sees angels in a crystal by the help of Saint Helena.'[213] This role, of a saintly authority by whose protection and support a magician can work their spirit-craft, cannot help but remind us of the eventual role of St Luke in the operations of the *Excellent Booke* and its *Visions*.

However, the most obviously important tutelary spirits for Gilbert and Davis appear to have been the veritable astral college of dead magicians that turned up to offer them advice on how to perform their magical operations. It is to these spirits that we now turn the flickering living lamps of our investigations.

211 Harkness: 33. Emphasis added.
212 For medieval sigils and talismans, see Richard Kieckhefer, *Magic in the Middle Ages* (Cambridge University Press: New York, 1990): 75–80.
213 Szönyi, 'Paracelsus, Scrying, and the *Lingua Adamica*': 214 n. 40.

Tutelary shades

The epistemological application of conjuration – summoning spirits specifically to deliver knowledge and understanding – is a consistent feature of the *Excellent Booke*, whether demanding Oriens, the king of the East, deliver a tome and its teachings, sending Davis to bring some of the 'many books' back from the crystal tree in the house of Solomon, or returning time and again to the golden hill and the angelic book-bearing patronage of Saint Luke, the illumination of various forms of supernaturally facilitated knowledge is consistently sought. This is, it should be stressed, a somewhat different form of divination than we may expect: Assasel is very clear that the spirits called 'were not for to tell things, past, present, and to come.'[1] This is no mere fortune-telling; but rather the explication and elevation of the magical prowess and (even, perhaps, the destiny) of the operators.

Frank Klaassen makes the case for this epistemological significance in terms of emergent scientific endeavours – they are after all *experiments* to discover the nature of nature.[2] This kind of ritual empiricism might be seen to stand somewhat in contrast to the reliance upon the texts and judgments of

1 Add. MS. 36674, f.60r.
2 Frank Klaassen, 'Ritual Invocation and Early Modern Science: The Skrying Experiments of Humphrey Gilbert.' Claire Fanger (ed.), *Invoking Angels: Theurgic Ideas and Practices, Thirteenth to Sixteenth Centuries* (Pennsylvania State University Press, 2012): 341–366.

the past that has characterised Aristotelian scholasticism. This new approach gets its information from live spirits, not dead writers. Yet this contrast is complicated by the necromancy of the *Excellent Booke* and its *Visions*, in which such dignitaries of magical thought and practice are *encountered as spirits*.

Of the cast of characters that appear in the *Visions* – from angels to evangelists to biblical personages – four key figures stand out. They are each, in their own ways, luminaries in the history and practice of European magic: the 'Omniscii.'[3] It is they – Solomon, Adam, Roger Bacon and Heinrich Cornelius Agrippa – that offer instruction in the art of magic, specifically those magical operations themselves focused upon receiving texts, knowledge, and understanding. Harvey's annotation of the text makes it clear this is certainly a form of 'sciomantia': divination by the shades of the dead.

Necromancy as 'Negromantia…the black art'[4] has attracted a wealth of decriers and diatribes throughout its European history. Many of these condemnations of necromantic practices are rooted in the objections of biblical writers.[5] As previously mentioned, the post-Reformation works of Lavater challenged not only the morality of consulting the dead, but its actual foundational eschatology. With purgatory abolished, the only spirits one could hope to contact were demons disguised as the dead, making the necromancer doubly foolish and doubly sinful. It is against such deep-rooted mediation of the Church between the living and the dead, as well as the shifting contemporary notions of the reality of spirits, that the *Excellent Booke's Visions* attest the value, function, and sensibility of learning magic from dead magicians. Certainly the worldview espoused by its nota and tutelary spirits do not question that many spirits are entirely untrustworthy, or at least unwilling to assist the conjurer of their own free will, and must be bound and forced to do one's bidding. Indeed, it is this very suspicion that is used to actually recommend such necromancy: 'Trust no spirit visible or invisible, but the spirit of dead men. For they love man more then the others do.'[6]

3 Add. MS. 36674, 59r marginalia.
4 Add. MS. 36674, 59r marginalia.
5 See, for instance, Hugo Enrique Mendez, 'Condemnations of Necromancy in the Hebrew Bible: An Investigation of Rationale' (Unpublished MA thesis: University of Georgia, 2006).
6 Add. MS. 36674, 59r.

King Solomon casts a looming and significant shadow over Western grimoire magic and spirit-work. His legends and their subsequent reception
leave no doubt that he was 'regarded as the wisest man in the history of
the world,'[7] and indeed 'few have a richer and more varied documentation
than that which glorifies the wisdom of Solomon.'[8] Like other scholars of
Solomon's spectre before me, I should note that 'with the facts behind the
tradition I am not concerned. The reputation which the great king actually
deserves may be left to students of the Old Testament.'[9] In this exploration of
necromantic patronage, we are interested in how the spirit appears throughout historical magic posthumously.

In examination of the influence of this sorcerer-king, we may note that
'Solomon has had a double reception history, part literary and part legendary, based on the characterisation of 1 K[in]gs and linked to the theme of
his wisdom and that of the construction of the Temple.'[10] In shadowing the
afterlife of Solomon we follow him through biblical and apocryphal sources, through the commentary and interpretation of a wealth of Midrashim,
and a host of sources testifying to the various roles and rites of magicians
themselves. Tomes such as the 'Wisdom of Solomon as well as Jewish Antiquities
of Josephus introduce within the body of the text an image of King Solomon
that adds traits that are not present in their biblical sources and suppose an
incorporation of ideas related to the so-called "popular" Hermeticism.'[11] Citing the work of Gideon Bohak on 'outsider accounts' and 'insider evidence,'

7 Lynn Thorndike, A History of Magic and Experimental Science, Vol. 2 (New York: Macmillan Co, 1923): 279.

8 Indeed, McCown even claims 'It may well serve as an example of the manner in which
the human mind works in certain fields.' McCown, 'The Christian Tradition as to the
Magical Wisdom of Solomon.' Journal of the Palestine Oriental Society 2, (1922): 1.

9 McCown, 'Magical Wisdom': 1.

10 Pablo A. Torijano, 'Solomon and Magic. Joseph Verheyden (ed.), The Figure of Solomon
in Jewish, Christian and Islamic Tradition: King, Sage and Architect, (Brill: Leiden, 2012): 107.

11 Torijano characterises this popular Hermeticism as 'concerned principally with
astrology, and later on with medicine, alchemy and magic, whereas "learned" Hermeticism was interested in theology and philosophy.' Pablo Torijano, 'Solomon The Esoteric
King: From King to Magus' (Thesis: New York University, 1999): 118; A.J. Festugière, La
révélation d'Hermès Trismégiste, 3 vols. (Les Belles Lettres: Paris, 1986) 1.187–200.

Torijano aptly draws this knife edge of analysis 'between the representation of magicians and references to them by people who are not themselves involved in magic and the picture which emerges from the texts and artefacts manufactured and utilised by the magicians themselves.'[12]

Some of the first outsider references are Pseudo-Philo's *Biblical Antiquities* of the first century CE and references in the New Testament.[13] Both stress Solomon's identity, and even power or authority, as founded upon his being the son of David. In 1 Samuel 16:14–23, the story of David employing his musical ability to keep a demon from tormenting Saul is extended to now include a 'psalm of exorcistic content'; moreover, 'David warns the evil spirit about his future descendent who will conquer it,' and Torijano judges 'this is quite likely an earlier echo of a tradition about Solomon the exorcist.'[14] It seems pertinent to examine this traditional exorcism association first.

The Exorcist-King

Torijano considers the first 'insider source' on Solomonic exorcism traditions to be 'a small scroll, 11QPs11, that contains what seems to be an exorcist's handbook,' dated to around 50–70 BCE.[15] It further emphasised the use of Solomon's name as 'part of an apotropaic formula': a formula that also seems to expressly identify him as 'son of David,' by this point apparently a distinct part of Jewish exorcism practices.

Josephus, in his *Jewish Antiquities*, commends the king for the wisdom granted him by God 'of the art used against demons (τὴν κατὰ των δαιμόνων τέχνην) for the benefit and healing (εις ωφέλειαν και θεραπείαν) of men.'[16] The author of the *Antiquities* is also keen to point out that the great exorcist Solomon bequeathed instructions in this very art, meaning, 'among other things, that in Josephus' time, a magical text existed which taught how to exorcise

---

12 Torijano, 'Solomon and Magic': 108; cf. Bohak, (2008): 70.

13 NT refs can be grouped into two: firstly, Mark 10:46–52, paralleled in Matt. 20:20–34; 9:27–31 and Luke 18:35–43. Secondly, Matt. 12:22–30.42–45 and Matt. 15:22.

14 Torijano, 'Solomon and Magic': 109; Jacobson (1966), 1.82, 187–188, 2.1173–1180.

15 Torijano, 'Solomon and Magic': 111.

16 *Antiquitates Judaicae* (8.45). See Martin Friis, 'Josephus' Antiquities 1–11 and Greco-Roman Historiography' (PhD Thesis; University of Copenhagen, 2015): 77.

daemons in the name of Solomon.'[17] We should be under no misapprehension: Solomon's 'development into a magical character of great power…began when his fame as an exorcist was already established.'[18] Indeed, McCown calls this 'the cornerstone of the Jewish foundation upon which the Christian tradition regarding Solomon rests.'[19]

More specifically, Josephus also relates how Eleazar exorcised a demon from a man 'in the presence of Vespasian and his court' by 'holding under the nostrils of the demoniac his ring, which had under the seal one of the roots indicated by Solomon' as well as by 'mentioning Solomon and repeating the incantations which he composed' – and thus 'the power and wisdom of Solomon are clearly established.'[20] McCown notes this demonstrates a 'living, popular tradition' of Solomonic exorcism by the first century CE. Johnston summarises this expansion from wise exorcist to fully-fledged magician:

> The basis of Solomon's reputation as a controller of demons (and later, a worker of all sorts of magic) goes back to 1 Kings 4:29–34 (5.9–14 in Hebrew), which describes him as being extremely wise, as having composed 3000 proverbs and 1005 songs (translated as ôidai in the Septuagint), and as knowing a great deal about plants and animals. Over the centuries, these statements were interpreted to mean that he wrote incantations (epôidai) and knew of magical uses of plants and animals… The Dead Sea Scrolls contain a fragmentary recension of Psalm 91, known to the Rabbis as an exorcistic text, which mentions Solomon's name just before the term 'demons,'[21] and the Targum Sheni to Esther describes him as ruling over not only animals but also devils and spirits of the

17 Valerie Flint, 'The Demonisation of Magic and Sorcery in Late Antiquity: Christian Redefinitions of Pagan Religions.' Bengt Ankarloo and Stuart Clark (eds.), Witchcraft and Magic in Europe: Ancient Greece and Rome (University of Pennsylvannia Press: Philadephia, 1999): 117.

18 Torijano, 'Solomon and Magic': 118.

19 McCown, 'Magical Wisdom': 3.

20 McCown, 'Magical Wisdom': 3; cf. Antiquitates viii 2, 5 (45-49).

21 11Q11 cf. Garcia Martinez and Tigchelaar, The Dead Sea Scrolls (Leiden, 2000), Vol. 2, 1200–1205.

night. Thus, by the first century AD, Solomon's reputation as a controller of demons seems to have been well on its way towards becoming a central part of his legend, if it were not so already.[22]

But where might we find an early crux of the wise king and the conjuration he would so heavily be associated with by the time of the *Excellent Booke* and its *Visions?*

The Testament of Solomon

Solomon lends his patronage to one of the early instances of the kind of text that would come to be known as a grimoire. *The Testament of Solomon* has been described as a 'curious document written in Greek, but based on a Jewish text' and according to one expert 'probably composed in the early third century AD.'[23] To give an idea of the plurality of academic judgments on its exact date, we find 'proposals clustering in the first five centuries of the Common Era'; and it has been said that 'most scholars accept that some of the traditions underlying the *Testament*, most importantly the tradition that Solomon could exorcise demons, go back at least as far as the first century BC.'[24] Such themes emerge from particular contexts of course. Peter Busch concludes that *Testament* is 'to be situated at the background of fourth century hagiographies and takes its distance from hagiographic tales of ascetic desert-monks performing exorcisms in favour of professional exorcists,' even going so far as to highlight 'it may be interpreted as a marketing document of the Sanctuary of the Holy Sepulchre in Jerusalem.'[25]

Certainly the *Testament* has plenty to enthral an audience, being called by

22 Sarah Iles Johnston, 'The *Testament of Solomon* from Late Antiquity to the Renaissance.' Jan N. Bremmer & Jan R. Veenstra (ed.), *Metamorphosis of Magic from Late Antiquity to the Early Modern Period* (Peeters: Leuven, 2002): 39.

23 Flint: 116.

24 Johnston, 'Testament': 37; citing Duling, 'The Testament' (1983): 940–943; McCown, *The Testament*: 105–106.

25 Peter Busch, 'The *Testament of Solomon* in its Cultural Setting.' Joseph Verheyden (ed.), *The Figure of Solomon in Jewish, Christian and Islamic Tradition. King, Sage and Architect* (Brill: Leiden, 2012): 194.

one scholar an 'amazing' mixture of 'folktales and a magician's *vade mecum*':[26]

> The *Testament of Solomon* may be safely dated in the fourth century of
> our era. The author is a Christian exorcist who attempts to work up the
> demonological and magico-medical knowledge of his syncretic envi-
> ronment into a practical *vade mecum*. His materials go back ultimately
> to Babylonia, Persia, Egypt, Palestine and the Greek world. The thread
> upon which these materials are strung is the story of Solomon's use of the
> demons in building the Temple. The book closes with an account of the
> great king's ignominious fall.[27]

These strung materials are brought together from a variety of sources. History's scissors confound purists, and the *Testament* is truly a 'document like to
so many other religious documents from the late antique Mediterranean: it
is a well mixed *bricolage* to which we can hardly assign an ethnic or religious
background in any useful sense.'[28] Nevertheless, we might still responsibly
trace the various origins and vectors of these components. Flint summarises
McCown's opinion, that 'its magical formulae and recipes relate it to the
execration tablets, the amulets and the Greek Magical Papyri,' with the 'chief
ideas of this document' being 'daemonology, astrology, angelology, magic
and medicine.'[29] Indeed, this link to the Papyri demonstrates something
more than syncretic theorisation to Flint, as we may note when he adjudges:

> The *Testament of Solomon* deserves most careful study, because, in a sense,
> it adds a dimension to the PGM. It shows the magician who calls himself
> King Solomon in action and gives us a good idea of his spiritual world
> which is rather complex. This magician was not a simple charlatan, trav-
> elling through the cities of the Near East: He was a scholar, a missionary
> and a kind of mystic, more like an Egyptian occultist.[30]

26 Flint: 116; cf. McCown (Leipzig, 1922): 1.
27 C.C. McCown, 'Solomon and the Shulamite.' *Journal of the Palestine Oriental Society* 1
(1920–1921): 116.
28 Johnston, 'Testament': 39.
29 Flint: 116.
30 Flint: 116.

Work on Solomon's *Testament* continues of course, and the turn of the archaeologist's spade is ready to excise supposition and best-guesswork. What can definitely be said, especially when considering the spirit of Solomon, is that the *Testament* 'had a significant and extremely long-lived effect on both the ways in which magic actually was practiced in the centuries after its composition and on the way in which magic was *imagined* to be performed.'[31]

It is pertinent to briefly examine this influence, at least in terms of what the text actually testifies of Solomon the magician. He is said, *inter alia*, to have 'mastered and controlled all spirits of the air, on the earth, and under the earth' (ToS1). When he prays for authority over the demon plaguing a boy, Michael brings him a ring, which bears a seal on an engraved stone (ToS5). Upon finding the spirit Ornias unwilling to be subject to him, Solomon calls Uriel (ToS11), whereupon Uriel commands Ornias to cut stones, but also sends him to collect Beelzeboul (ToS12). Our magician-hero praises God for making him wise and with the power of demons subject to him (ToS14). By the end, Solomon has the formula down: he questions a demon (Tephras) on their restraining angel (Azael), summons said angel, sets a seal on the demon, and orders it to work on the Temple (ToS33).

The Wisdom of a Magician

Solomon's initiatory empowerment comes in the form of the divine knowledge or wisdom he was granted. Consulting the *Wisdom of Solomon*, likely composed in the first century BCE in Greek in Alexandria, we find a speech from Solomon himself attesting this knowledge and wisdom:

> God…gave me true knowledge of things, as they are; an understanding of the structure of the world and the way in which elements work, the beginning and the end of eras and what lays in-between…the cycles of the years and the constellations…the thoughts of men…the powers of spirits…the virtues of roots…I learned it all, secret or manifest.[32]

31 Johnston: 48.
32 Flint: 116.

As Flint notes, 'clearly, Solomon is pictured as the greatest scientist, but also as the greatest occultist, of his time: he has studied astrology, plant magic, daemonology, divination but also *ta physika*, "natural science."'[33] Torijano concurs, adding that the magical text known as 'the *Hydromancy* seems to be at the origin of this new development in characterizing Solomon as a magician.'[34] Combined with another tome, the *Magical Treatise of Solomon*, such associations of book and king marked Solomon's patronage of distinctly more natural and less demonic magics: astrological sorcery, plant lore, and suchlike.

Significantly, the knowledge granted is (sprung from God's) *perfect knowledge* — it 'is "infallible" because it is divinely given and it encloses the whole universe ("the things that are"), its constitution ("the structure of the world") and the working of its ultimate components ("the activity of the elements").'[35] Torijano also points to the significance of time and chronological matters in this Solomonic knowledge. It is not simply concerned with the 'eras' of human history, but 'the times measured by the cycles of the planets,' specifically phrased in *Wisdom* 7:19 as 'the cycles of the year and the positions of the stars.'[36] We are concerned here then with potent astrological sorcery. Moreover,

> The knowledge of time and its division is directly linked with the theory of cosmic sympathy, since on many occasions that power also depends on the exact hour, day and month or on the planet that rules in that moment. Thus, Solomon is depicted not as a[n] astronomer or even an astrologer, but as one who knows the relation between time and prayer.[37]

Here are some of the old roots connecting Solomon and astrological knowledge and power, and a simultaneously pious and sorcerous utility of such power. Such links are made consciously and, apparently, unconsciously. For instance, it is likely an inspired combination of two central mythic elements

33 Flint: 116–117.
34 Torijano, 'Solomon and Magic': 121.
35 Torijano, 'Esoteric King': 122.
36 Torijano, 'Esoteric King': 123.
37 Torijano, 'Esoteric King': 123.

of Solomon's character – his wisdom from God and his wealth from his mines – that Gervase of Tilbury (c.1152–c.1220) 'told how Solomon himself was the first to perceive the magical virtues of gems.'[38]

Thus we may delineate a staged development of the figure of Solomon from exorcist to magician, with Solomon the astrologer as an intermediary phase. Crucially, perfect Solomonic 'knowledge is used and portrayed in an active manner, so that it makes possible dominion over supernatural realities and with it change of the present world.'[39] So active is this knowledge and wisdom, in fact, that its very mythic historicity formed a sort of appeal: in an 'Experiment of Sybilla' in one sixteenth century collection of magical operations, a spirit is conjured by 'Christ's blood,' 'John the Baptist's head' and 'the wisdom of Solomon.'[40] The concept of the wisdom itself, and the deployment of it referenced in rites of conjuration, has grown from inspiration or influence to an active and affective authority that may actually impart a potency to the works of the operator.

By the time we reach the medieval age, the Ars Notoria – the text proffering the means to acquire divine wisdom of our own – draws its authority from King Solomon. As Klaassen details, 'it elaborates upon the account in 2 Chronicles 1:9 – 12 and 2 Kings 3:5 – 14, where God appears to Solomon in the night. Among other things Solomon has asked for, he is granted *sapienta, scientia et intelligencia*... Similarly, in Luke 21:15 Christ promises to endow certain Christians with the gift of wisdom... In a similar way, the Ars notoria seeks the acquisition of knowledge and/or other special gifts, such as rhetorical skills, through a program of prayers, rituals, and meditations that employ the inspection of complex figures inscribed with prayers.'[41] Thorndike reports that 'in the first half of the thirteenth century William of Auvergne, bishop of Paris, in his treatise on laws declares that there is no divinity in the angles of Solomon's pentagon, that the rings of Solomon and the seals of

---

38 Kieckhefer, *Magic in the Middle Ages* (Cambridge University Press: New York, 1990): 105.

39 Torijano, 'Esoteric King': 251.

40 Paul Foreman, *The Cambridge Book of Magic: A Tudor necromancer's manual*, ed. Francis Young (Texts in Early Modern Magic: Cambridge, 2015): 9.

41 Frank Klaassen, *The Transformations of Magic: Illicit Learned Magic in the Later Middle Ages and Renaissance* (Pennsylvania State Press: University Park, 2013): 89.

Solomon and the nine candles (*candariae*) are a form of idolatry, and involve execrable consecrations and detestable invocations and images.'[42] Yet 'by the fifteenth century CE Solomon has become the magician *par excellence* among Christian practitioners; his influence had become so great that the *Clavicula* was translated into Spanish, French, and English.'[43] The persistence of Solomon's tools is also apparent. Appeals such as those made 'by the ring and seal of Solomon, and by the nine celestial lights'[44] combine the ring of binding, the seal of protection, and what looks to be some kind of astrological sorcery.

Signs and Seals, Keys and Characters

Many books concerned with the king's importance in occult matters concentrate on his role in Freemasonry, with varying degrees of conspiratorial speculation. To reiterate my goal however, we shall be concentrating upon the figure of Solomon in ritual magic, particularly the conjuration of spirits and in European grimoire traditions. The broadest and most obvious influence of Solomon on the grimoires can be evidenced from his name and patronage to the *Key of Solomon*, 'the most famous of Grimoires, or handbooks of magic.'[45] More specifically, our magician-king is explicitly invoked at the end of a prayer to consecrate pentacles; for the Almighty 'gavest to Solomon, King David's son, wisdom and knowledge above all other men, and didst vouchsafe to reveal these present pentacles unto him.'[46] Beyond the (in)famous 'Pentacles of Solomon' themselves, which arguably form a further subgenre or component within the Solomonic grimoire traditions, we encounter several other seals, signs or characters associated directly with our king. In the Foreman text, published recently by Dr Francis Young, several 'Seals of Solomon' are utilised in the Construction of the Circle,[47] an operation

42 Lynn Thorndike, A History of Magic and Experimental Science, vol. 2 (New York: Macmillan Co, 1923): 279–280.

43 Torijano, 'Solomon and Magic': 122; cf. Butler (1949: 1979): 47–153.

44 Daniel Harms, James R. Clark, Joseph H. Peterson. The Book of Oberon: A Sourcebook of Elizabethan Magic (Llewellyn: Woodbury, 2015): 307.

45 Joseph H. Peterson, 'The Key of Knowledge' http://www.esotericarchives.com/solomon/ad36674.htm, last accessed 06/04/17.

46 'Key of Knowledge', Add. MS. 36674, 9r.

47 Cambridge Book of Magic: 5.

which also ends by detailing that the use of four elemental colours in the crown of your fellows (and the operator?) 'was Salomons doinge & also saynt Cypryan.'[48] An appeal to Solomon immediately before orders are issued is also found in a working with a crystal stone – 'by all the signs, characters and seals that ever Solomon and Virgil or other man made'[49] – and in the 'Revenge of Troy' working – 'I conjure you by the rods with which Christ was cruelly beaten, and by the rod of Moses and the crown of Solomon.'[50] This notion of commanding spirits by the totality of Solomon's magic is also found in the Folger Book of Magic, where the operator works 'by the virtue of all the words and names of God, seals, signs, and characters of Solomon, and by Jesus Christ'[51] Such is the status of Solomon, interpolated between the Almighty and the saviour. Also interesting to note the apparent distinction between these different markings which is repeated later in an appeal to 'all holy characters, signs, and seals that King Solomon used.'[52]

These seals were primarily for protection, but they were not the only means of Solomonic protection. In an 'Experiment to Call the Spirit Mosacus' from the Foreman text, there is a whole prayer entitled 'the protection of Solomon' (*protectio Salomonis*).[53] This experiment also includes 'the third invocation of Solomon' (*inuocat[i]o Salomonis tertia*) which conjures the spirit 'by these names + Maoth + Naoth + by which Solomon contrained you' (*per que[m] Salomon constringebat*).[54] Significantly, this is also the final appeal before the actual command to the spirit to appear is issued.[55] The binding of the spirit is similarly performed 'by whose virtue and sapience Solomon (which was the most expertest) yoked and tamed you, and by his authority he may command you, which liveth and reigneth, one God, without end.'[56]

---

48 *Cambridge Book of Magic*: 7.
49 *Cambridge Book of Magic*: 29.
50 *Cambridge Book of Magic*: 85.
51 *Book of Oberon*: 311.
52 *Book of Oberon*: 329.
53 *Cambridge Book of Magic*: 11.
54 *Cambridge Book of Magic*: 16–17.
55 Specifically, the command is to appear without delay in the form of a three year-old boy 'having a red head and a white face.' *Cambridge Book of Magic*: 17.
56 *Cambridge Book of Magic*: 21.

The Foreman text also provides 'The Most Secret Sign of Solomon,' which promises that it will ensure the favour of kings and the love of women as well as protection from various dangers ranging from war to evil spirits.[57]

'Brasen Pans' and Glass Vials

A conjuration of obedience ends 'by which Solomon the king did bind up the Devil, and spirits in brasen pans, so do I bind thee to my obedience.'[58] Indeed, Solomon specifically 'did bind the devils and spirits and shut them up in the brasen pans *for disobedience*.'[59] Given the *Excellent Booke's* early emphasis on binding and intimidating spirits, this aspect of Solomon's reputation and power seems especially significant.

In a sixteenth century text attributed to our wise king – and 'there are many treatises with similar titles, but this does not agree with the *Clavicula* edited by S. L. M. Mathers (London, 1889), nor with the treatise known as *Lemegeton*'[60] – we find a resort-conjuration, to be used if the spirit will not appear. The operator conjures *inter alia* 'by the Angelic potestates of heaven, and by the great providence of Almighty God, and by the seal of Kinge Solomon, which he received of that Almighty.'[61]

Elsewhere, in an operation to conjure the spirit Baron: 'by the virtue of the most holy and dreadful names of God, all which are graven in this scepter[62] pentacle, representing the strong pentacles of Solomon containing in it the foresaid dreadful names of God + El + Eochye + Elan + helt + Agla + Yonthachy + Theanothe + Nalta + by the which he subdued and included all spirits in a vessel of brass or glass.'[63] The 'glass' has clear relevance to scrying and shewstones. The idea that Solomon bound not simply seventy-two, but *all* spirits is further evidence of his great power. It also perhaps hints at an

---

57 *Cambridge Book of Magic*: 93–95.

58 *Book of Oberon*: 125.

59 *Book of Oberon*: 127. Emphasis added.

60 Catalogue entry for British Library Additional MS. 37764.

61 'Key of Knowledge' Add. MS 36674, 7v.

62 Elsewhere: 'by that most excellent name which is carved on the top of my sceptre, which name is + Tetragrammaton +' *Book of Oberon*: 443. For more on scepters in conjuration, see *De Nigromancia*.

63 *Book of Oberon*: 349–350.

influence from the Jewish and Arabic traditions of Solomon, rather than strictly Christian ones: although the ideas of 'Solomon's rulership over the jinn, his use of them in building his temple, and his sealing the rebellious in bottles' was 'common property in both the East and the West.'[64]

Another experiment to summon the spirit Mosacus (this time from Folger Vb.26's Book of Magic) lists the precise words 'by which Solomon constrained you, that wherever you might be to come at once and without delay, in the form of a handsome boy seven years old, showing yourself to me having white colour and red hair.'[65] Elsewhere, a generic invocation – for 'the spirit N.' – deploys 'these words, Nyoth, Naoth, that Solomon bound spirits in vessels of glass.'[66] Another stakes its efficacy 'by that same power that God gave to King Solomon, when he bound all spirits into a vial of glass. So I bind all thieves that hither come...'[67] Likewise, Solomon is said to have bound spirits identified as fairies in a vessel: and of course this is mentioned in an operation which requires a vessel.[68] The first counsellor of Oberyon (the king of fairies), Caveryon – presumably a fairy himself – is 'exorcise[d] ... by all celestial, terrestrial, and infernal powers, and by King Solomon who bound you.'[69] As in the instructions of the Excellent Booke, these binding commands are significant in ensuring the spirit appears properly. Thus the spirit is instructed 'by the nine heavenly candles which was revealed unto Solomon, that thou appear in this stone.'[70]

It should be noted, in light of the daemonical hierarchy of the Excellent Booke, that the wise king and his potent exorcisms are occasionally men-

---

64 McCown, 'Magical Wisdom': 5; cf. 'Quran, Sura 38:35ff., SBE IX (II) 179 (cf. Sale, ad loc.), 27:7, SBE IX (II) 101. Nights 566f., ed. Lane-Poole III 110f., ed. Burton VI 84f.'

65 Book of Oberon: 448.

66 Book of Oberon: 463.

67 Book of Oberon: 497.

68 Book of Oberon: 362.

69 Book of Oberon: 468.

70 Book of Oberon: 98. Arthur Waite refers to the medieval treatise De novum candariis (in characteristic half-helpful manner) in discussion of necromantic manuscripts: 'The treatise De Novem Candariis Salomonis, containing curious figures and sigils, deserves particular mention, as this again seems unknown to students. Its attribution notwithstanding, it is the work of a Catholic writer.' Arthur Edward Waite, The Book of Ceremonial Magic (William Rider & Son: London, 1911): 23.

tioned alongside direct appeals to various senior chiefs of Hell. In an experiment 'to make a thief to come again with that which he hath stolen', Solomon is appealed to along with various spiritual authorities, some of which are less than (traditionally) holy: 'by Satan, who you must obey, and by all the elements and all their powers, or by the four plagues of the world, and by Lucifer, the power of hell, and by all herbs, trees, precious stones, by the bonds of Solomon, and by all celestial, terrestrial, and infernal beings.'[71] This distinction between Lucifer, Emperor of spirits, and Satan is important. It is certainly significant for discussions pertaining to the conjuration structures and system processes of our *Excellent Booke* that Solomon is also named as a specific restitutionalist intercessor in dealing with Satan in his role as devilish overseer of the Four Regents.

Satan 'is wont to ask of the master conjurer that he should with Solomon pray the Creator, that he may come to his Throne again, but that he that is master shall say that he fell not of his own will, and for that cause he abideth in the air, and is not cast into hell.'[72] More specifically pertinent to working with the four demonic kings at the angles of the world, it is advised that one should 'look that thou have the ring of Solomon' amongst other religious garments – specifically, that one should 'hold thou thy ring upon thy face' – when working with Amaymon, in this case called the king of the south.[73] Similarly, when working with Egyn, regent of the North, 'so soon as he appeareth, show him the Seal of Solomon, and his ring, and forthwith he will fall down to the earth and worship the master, and the master shall take and thank him therefore.'[74] More generally, the pentacle of Solomon is used in calling spirits from the 'four parts of the world,' and – given the significance of the Four Regents – this would appear to shed further light upon the fact that Solomon's pentacle and Solomon's seals are listed amongst the 'necessaries for this art of Necromancy.'[75]

---

71 Book of Oberon: 181.
72 Book of Oberon: 192.
73 Book of Oberon: 193.
74 Book of Oberon: 195.
75 Book of Oberon: 290.

Lineage

Magical lineage forms the very core and crux of this chapter. It is Solomon who first appears to H.G. in dream to presage the reception of the Book, its nota and Visions; and he is the first and arguably most important of the host of tutelary shades that appear before the operator and his seer. It is for this reason we come to King Solomon lastly. His name and patronage of the Solomonic tradition of magic means that he is central to Western occultism, exorcism and conjuration. Moreover, the appearance of the king's ghost in H.G.'s dreams and Davis' visions is the clearest and most direct example of the sponsorship and tutelage of this active necromantic lineage in process. But there are certainly plenty of earlier hints that this form of Solomonic magic includes appeal to other sorcerers.

Thus it is we find our magician-hero mentioned in appeal to a lineage of wisdom: 'Moses, David, Solomon, Hermes, Cyprian, Lombard, Bacon They and divers and others say best in philosophy in magic and also in necromancy etc.'[76] Also their works directly appealed to, as when 'I conjure thee spirit or spirits, what kind so ever ye be, of fire, water, earth, or air, malignant or infernal, by all the conjurations, invocations, vincles, and licenses that ever Cyprian, Solomon, Alexander, Aristotle, Bacon, Bungi, Lumbarte, Wale Cornelius or any other spake or wrote, and by the dread that thou spirit or you spirits have in thine or your lord, and by the virtue of the four kings of the air and their four princes under them.'[77] Here, not only a specific lineage is invoked, but a totality of all magical speech ever pronounced to work spirits seems to be cited. Furthermore, they are listed alongside the authority figures of the spirits themselves – spirit-lords who command by dread as much as sympathy. These lords are specified as both the particular senior of the spirit or spirits conjured, and the four general authorities of 'the air' (most likely a reference to the Four Regents) which, if referring to cardinal directions, themselves represent a totality of all directions and thus their omnipresence. Likewise, 'Solomon, Saint Cyprian, and all professors of this high science called secret of secrets' are called to 'curse and maledict' recalcitrant

76 Book of Oberon: 135.
77 Book of Oberon: 317.

spirits.[78] Elsewhere, an invocation is completed with an appeal 'by the power and virtue of wise Solomon, Cyprian, and Roger Bacon, who had power to command, bind, and enclose you and all spirits, etc.'[79]

A possible distinction is made between the exact roles of Solomon and Cyprian in another set of appeals: 'by Saint Cyprian, who subjugated you with his command, and also by the most wise Solomon, whose orders forced you to obey.'[80] It should be noted, however, that this potential distinction is complicated by instructions to spirits 'to fulfil my desires truly, as you obediently subjugated yourself to the true and wise and most skilled Solomon.'[81] Distinguishing separate functionalities of subjugation and enforced obedience to commands, and their specific contexts and meanings in early modern conjuration, puts us squarely in the same analysis from which assessment of constraint, binding, *ligatio*, and other such terminology proceeds.

In a particularly lengthy and involved operation to create an oil by which to see spirits, the objective is to make a particular spirit 'as familiar with me as you were with King Solomon, that mighty prince, and as you were with King Arthur, that valiant prince and as you opened and showed to King Solomon the hidden natures, properties, and virtues of metals, precious stones, trees, and herbs, and the secrets of all sciences underneath heaven, even so I command, require, and adjure you…to do the like to me at all times…'[82] The appeal is explicitly to the precedent of the spirits' historical actions and arrangements with previous magicians in a modality of capacity – the spirit is demonstrably able to do these things, as they have done them before, and thus is asked to repeat its performance – yet there also seems an implicit assumption of the mantle of Solomon (and Arthur),[83] that the pact is not an identical copy, but perhaps the very same agreement extended to the present operator.

78 Book of Oberon: 313.

79 Book of Oberon: 467.

80 Book of Oberon: 438–439.

81 Book of Oberon: 442.

82 Book of Oberon: 360–361.

83 For more on Arthur (and the dead and hell), see Jean-Claude Schmitt, *Ghosts in the Middle Ages: The Living and the Dead in Medieval Society* (University of Chicago Press: Chicago, 1998): 116–121.

Our magus-king also confirms a certain variety of Adamic magic, for 'Solomon sayeth that there be seven Semoferas' – those magical names and/or signs 'which God gave to Adam in paradise.'[84] Furthermore as regards our present study, the third Semoferas is said to be for and from 'when he (Adam) spoke with demons and with dead men, which to every of his questions, sufficiently answered.'[85] Exactly who the dead men in the Garden of Eden were remains a slightly mystifying matter.

We can close with Klaassen's concise understatement on the crossroads of tradition and innovation staked at the appearance and influence of Solomon's shade:

> The spirit of Solomon also dictated a new prayer to be used at the beginning of the operations. They not only employed this prayer but included it on the first page of the manual. While the careful record keeping that makes it possible for us to see this process might be a sixteenth-century innovation, the process of innovation itself and the mythology that supported it were far from new.[86]

ADAM

Adam is not simply an ancestor, he is the very first ancestor; the original image of the Creator. He has long been considered a patron – indeed, inventor – of many arts and sciences. More significantly for this examination of magical mythic lineage, Adam is not only the first human, but the First Magician. Our first forefather plays a subtle but significant role in the medieval and early modern lore of grimoires, and the wider practice of such contemporary magic. His name is, aptly, first in Reginald Scot's list of authors attributed to wicked books of conjuration, and Scot is clear such attributions are made in order 'to adde credit to that arte.'[87]

---

84 Book of Oberon: 162.

85 Book of Oberon: 163.

86 Klaassen, Transformations: 170.

87 '...further, to adde credit to that arte, these conjurors carrie about at this daie, bookes intituled under the names of Adam, Abel, Tobie , & Enoch.' Reginald Scot, Discoverie of Witchcraft (London, 1584: 1665): 451.

Naming

Adam's act of naming the beastly denizens of the earth makes him an obvious authority to which one might appeal for binding spirits by certain names: whether the spirits' or the sacred sobriquets of the divine.

The sacred names of God said to have been used by Adam were considered both holy and magically potent in their own right, as we shall see when we address the Adamic 'Semaforas' below. Moreover however, such divine names are specifically considered in the light of Adam (and by extension Adamic authority) as being capable of being used to perform god-like feats because he himself is God-like. In one *vinculum* from a sixteenth century collection of magic, the spirit is informed: 'if you be disobedient and rebel, I charge, conjure, and command thee in the nam[es] and by the name + Adonay + Aloe + Alion + Sabaoth + Saday + which is the Lord God on high and king omnipotent of Israel, which said, "Let us make man *according to our likeness and let him bear rule* over the works of our hands," and by the nam[e] [+] y + et v + which Adam heard and spake.'[88] Adam's status as (first) image of the Almighty Creator makes him a powerful figure for appeal by historiola.

Superhumanity

Adam was thought of as a perfect being, not only human but in some ways beyond (postlapsarian) humanity. What was lost in the Fall was not merely innocence, but some apparently superhuman abilities. It was vital to Christian theology and moral philosophy that God had made Adam *perfect*. One immediate consequence of this was his perfect health: 'Adam's body in his innocent estate, was naturally incorruptible *ex hypothesi*; that is, so long as hee stood in holinesse, there was such a harmony amongst the qualities of his body, that they could breed no distemperature, or bring death to him.'[89]

More than a dependable immune system or a slightly more theologically shaky notion of his immortality (at least before the incident with the fruit), Samuel Pordage held that Adam was 'incapable of destruction.'[90] Indeed, it was fairly intuitively obvious that if being cast from Eden included now be-

---

88 Book of Oberon: 98. Emphasis added.

89 John Weemse, *The Portraiture of the Image of God in Man* (London, 1627): 32.

90 Samuel Pordage, *Mundorum Explicatio* (London, 1661): 59.

ing subject to Death, prior to the Fall Adam surely must have been immortal. Some even held that this immortality, even when removed as a consequence of their transgression in the Garden, still afforded Adam an exceedingly long life: 'Adam after his fall lived 930. yeares...what made this? nothing but the reliques of that naturall immortalitie, which was in man before the fall.'[91]

Martin Luther considered the First Man to possess incredible strength and even 'telescopic vision.'[92] Indeed, Joseph Glanvill judged him such a superman he had a kind of 'X-ray vision,' and thus was capable of seeing distant stars and microscopic biological activity: 'Adam needed no Spectacles. The acuteness of his natural Opticks...shewed him much of the Coelestial magnificence and bravery without a Galileo's tube... It may be he saw the motion of the bloud and spirits through the transparent skin, as we do the workings of those little industrious Animals through a hive of glasse.'[93] The notion that perfect sight will create (or itself is predicated on) perfect knowledge presents an illustrative example of the influence and application of an Aristotelian hierarchy of the senses, which privileged vision with seniority. This is deeply significant for the wider project of the *Excellent Booke* and indeed our study of it: the occult philosophy of optics underlies the very use of the shewstone, sight being especially able to pierce and explore the empyrean realms of spirits and the divinity of nature.

The importance of optics also highlights how perspectives on Adam's perfection and subsequent Fall impacted technological and epistemological perspectives.

Postlapsarian humanity required learned magic and its artifice and artisanship – its lens-grinding and mathematics – to return ourselves to the level of knowledge Adam (originally) possessed. Contrary to any notion of being simpler, 'earthier,' or any kind of innocent in the Garden – of the oldest human magic being some noble savagery – pre-modern lapsarian theology necessitated a perspective on their epistemology as an anamnesis: a loss of the forgetfulness that was caused by our Fall. Once more we must consider not only notions of human perfection, but of perfect knowledge itself.

91 Weemse: 35.
92 William Hazlitt (trans.), *The Table Talk of Martin Luther* (London, 1848): 57.
93 Joseph Glanvill, *The Vanity of Dogmatising* (London, 1661): 5–6.

Perfect Knowledge

Adam's most miraculous and most important power was his perfect knowledge of the world and everything in it. This was the 'ultimate source of his dominion over nature,'[94] and was thus expressed most neatly by his naming of the animals paraded before him.

For some, such as Glanvill, this perfect knowledge was a natural result of such keen powers of sensory perception. But for most others Adam's knowledge was not simply the product of perception and cognition, of (in other words) empirical experiment, but more fundamentally also in some way imbued by God directly. This 'infused' knowledge 'farre surpassed the knowledge of all the Prophets, for his Body and Soule being *hypostatically* united to the God-head, he must have a more perfect *knowledge* than any other man could have infused in him.'[95] Adam emerged already containing or having absorbed perfect knowledge from the divine Creator. This infusion of knowledge was also conceived in a more aerial manner. The notion of *inspiration* – conceived etymologically as the 'breath of spirit,' after all – neatly parallels Adam's bodily creation. One gardening encyclopaedia expressed a typical consideration that God had 'inspired him with the knowledge of all natural things.'[96]

The utility of this infusion and inspiration of perfect knowledge should of course fascinate us in light of scrying, divination and other forms of magical knowledge-at-a-distance. Certainly we can detect strong undertones of occult potency and practice in, say, Giovanni Loredano's exposition that Adam possessed 'an infused knowledge that enabled him to understand all sciences; knowing perfectly the nature of all Plants, Stones, Herbs, and animalls; and understanding the virtue, and properties of the heavens, elements, and stars; perceiving himself finally to have the scepter of dominion over all creatures…'[97] Crucially, this divinely-imbued knowledge survived the Fall.

94 Philip C. Almond, *Adam and Eve in Seventeenth-century Thought* (Cambridge University Press: Cambridge, 1999): 45.

95 Weems: 82.

96 John Parkinson, *Paradisi in Sole* (London, 1629), Epistle to the Reader.

97 Giovanno Loredano, *The Life of Adam. Written in Italian by Giovanni Francesco Loredano, a Venetian noble-man. And renderd into English by J.S.* (London, 1659): 10.

Patronages

This knowledge of the stars, considered by Loredano, highlights a tradition of considering Adam the first astrologer.[98] This was particularly important as it furthered his perfect knowledge to include perfect *foreknowledge*. Foreknowledge, or at least the accurate understanding of prophecy, was also a basis upon which some thinkers claimed Adam as first Christian. Despite being born before the Anointed One, a combination of God's prophecy (specifically in Genesis 3:15) and the First Man's perfect prognostication allowed him to know of the coming of the Son of God. Our First Man and Woman are referred to on their Feast day (24th December) as Saint Adam and Saint Eve — the only time in the liturgical year they are so called. Owing to Adam's salvation by faith alone, again thanks to God's insider information and our First Man's perfect knowledge, he was also commonly regarded as the first Protestant.[99] Claiming Adam's membership of one's lineage, of tracing your sodality's perspective all the way back to him, is a longstanding tradition.

Along with a patronage of astrology, Adam was also considered the first alchemist. Epistemological perspectives on the infusion of knowledge mentioned earlier take on additional layers of significance in light of this patronage over naturally divine transmutation. This should in part be understood as a development of that core notion that he knew the occult virtues 'in all Hearbes, Plants, and Stones.'[100] Opinions such as those of John Parkinson demonstrate an extension of this expertise in natural materials into the realms of both food and medicine.[101] Robert Bostocke gave an especially Paracelsian spin on Adam as the original chemical physician.[102] Overall, it was considered that Adam's perfect knowledge must, by definition, extend to the supernatural realms, but opinions were less unanimous about how much of God's unknowability that included. Such tensions — between what is human knowledge and what should be kept from us as purely divine knowledge — are clearly reflections upon the central transgression of Eve and Adam: tasting of the fruit that grants such divine knowledge.

---

98 Christopher Heydon, *A Defence of Judiciall Astrologie* (Cambridge, 1603): 305.

99 For more on Adam's Protestantism see Almond, *Adam and Eve*: 47–48.

100 Thomas Milles, *A Treasurie of Aunicent and Moderne Times* (London, 1613-19): I. 22.

101 John Parkinson, *Paradisi in Sole* (London, 1629), Epistle to the Reader.

102 Robert Bostocke, *Aunicent Phisicke* (London, 1585), sigs. C8v, H7v.

Gardening Eden

Herbalism is a key part of many magical traditions, and the figures of the wizard and witch alike are afforded considerable expertise in the vegetal kingdom. Gerard cites Apuleius' report of the use of mullein in 'incantations and witchcrafts' by man (Odysseus), god (Hermes) and sorceress/demi-goddess (Circe) alike.[103] But the Edenic context of the birth of gardening, of the perfection of its practice in the state of (as discussed above, informed) innocence when Nature and humanity co-existed in peaceful communion, should be understood in light of Adam as 'the first Botanist.'[104] In his 'recapitulation of the mystical-spiritual Adamic State,'[105] William Coles held forth that:

> To make thee truly sensible of that happinesse which Mankind lost by the Fall of Adam, is to render thee an exact Botanick, by the knowledge of so incomparable a Science as the Art of Simpling, to *re-instate thee into another Eden*, or, A Garden of Paradise: For if we rightly consider the Addresses of this Divine Contemplation of Herbs and Plants, with what alluring Steps and Paces the Study of them directs Us to an admiration of *the Supream Wisdome*, we cannot but even from these inferiour things arrive somewhat near unto a heavenly Contentment...[106]

As Almond summarises, 'to garden was to place oneself, metaphorically at least, in that state of grace which Adam enjoyed before the Fall.'[107] The theological context was almost unavoidable, as 'for the sixteenth and seventeenth centuries, the vegetable creation was the meeting ground of Nature and Grace. Plants and poems witnessed to the presence of God in the Garden of Eden, of the Risen Lord in the Garden of Resurrection, and of the redeemed creation in the Garden of Eternity.'[108] From Gethsemane to Golgotha (and

103 John Gerard, *Herball, or, Generall Historie of Plantes* (London, 1597): 776.

104 William Westmacott, *Theolobotonologia* (London, 1694), Preface.

105 Charlotte F. Otten, *Environ'd with Eternity: God, Poems, and Plants in Sixteenth and Seventeenth Century England* (Coronado Press: Lawrence, 1985): 31.

106 William Coles, *Adam in Eden* (London, 1657), 'To the Reader.' Emphasis added.

107 Almond, *Adam and Eve*: 100.

108 Otten, *Environ'd with Eternity*: xvii.

beyond), our First Ancestor's holy duties were best observed in communion and husbandry with the natural world; in naming, pruning, harvesting, and attending. Adam's primary tools are – in hundreds of examples throughout his historical depiction and mythical invocation– the secateurs and the spade.[109]

Adam's Book of Raziel

> The *Liber Razielis* was revealed to Adam by the angel Raziel, and Solomon wrote the *Almandal* and *Clavicula*…The *Clavicula, Almandal,* and *Liber Razielis* claim to be founded upon divine revelation, a quite common element in the mythology of ritual magic texts…If not exactly redemptive in the sense of the crucifixion, the *Liber Razielis* presents itself as a kind of consolation or aid for Adam in his fallen state.[110]

Such is Klaassen's summary of the mythic status of the book delivered by Raziel to Adam. This summary should be understood in a context which acknowledges that 'various esoteric and magical treatises attributed to Raziel and based on the practical use of divine and angelic names circulated among Jews in the late Middle Ages.'[111] Joshua Trachtenberg estimated the earliest editions of the actual *Sepher Raziel* were probably 'compiled in the 13th century.'[112] It has been claimed the Book of Raziel is 'is of composite character, and there is no criterion for the age of the component parts.'[113] Nevertheless there are certainly means of approaching its material and its patron.

The mythic Book owned by Adam includes some features pertinent to examination in light of scrying practices. For instance, 'some say that book was

---

109 Almond, *Adam and Eve*: 101; Otten, *Environ'd with Eternity*: 56.

110 Klaassen, *Transformations*: 120.

111 Sophie Page, 'Uplifting Souls: The *Liber de essentia spirituum* and the *Liber Razielis,*' Claire Fanger (ed.), *Invoking Angels* (Pennsylvania State University: University Park, 2012): 81 n. 10.

112 Joshua Trachtenberg, *Jewish Magic and Superstition* (Behrman House: New York, 1939): 315.

113 Steve Savedow (ed.), *Sepher Reziel Hemelech: The Book of the Angel Rezial* (Weiser: York Beach, 2000): 10.

written on parchment, while others say it was engraved on a sapphire. How was that sapphire read? Adam held it up to his eyes, and the flame burning inside the sapphire took the form of letters, so Adam could read them there.'[114] The visionary dimensions of this legendary 'text' extend further still:

> While most accounts of this heavenly book assume that the book had already been written and that Adam heard it for the first time when the angel Raziel read it to him, the Maharal proposes an alternate scenario in which Adam had all future events revealed to him in a vision, and later they were recorded in a book. That the angel leaves the book for Adam to read later indicates that books are so important in Jewish tradition that even the first man could read.[115]

Being closer to God and to a divine state of both innocence and wisdom, it seems more accurate to say rather that *especially* the First Man was literate. Moreover, the text is explicitly understood to have been passed down from Adam. Those early modern magical practitioners working with the *Sepher Raziel* from this cultural context could consider that they were not merely appealing to Adam as First Magician in some abstract sense — they were working from a direct transmission of his established lineage's techniques and text. Indeed, it is pertinent to our reflections on lineage in terms of the assembled tutelary shades of the *Excellent Booke* that we note Solomon himself was considered an eventual owner and worker of Adam's book.[116] Furthermore, it was held that the prophet Enoch, who had relearned the Adamic tongue and thus recovered something of the perfect prelapsarian knowledge of the Garden, had also 'consulted the wondrous "Book of Raziel" that had

---

114 Howard Schwartz, *Tree of Souls: The Mythology of Judaism* (Oxford University Press: Oxford, 2004): 253.

115 Schwartz, *Tree of Souls*: 254.

116 To offer but one modern iteration of this notion: 'Tradition says that Raziel befriended Adam when he was ejected from Eden giving him the gift of a book containing wisdom for his use. This book was given, via Noah to Abraham, then Jacob to Levi, whose descendant Moses passed it on to the seventy elders of Israel until it came in to the hands of Solomon the Wise, who learned from it the secrets of the Universe.' Z'ev ben Shimon Halevi, *Adam and the Kabbalistic Tree* (Weiser: York Beach, 1974): 321.

originally been given to Adam.'[117] It can (and, I contend should) thus offer additional context when considering sources of the Angelical language received by Dr Dee and Kelly.

The Seven Semaforas

Arguably the 'most Adamic' of the Sepher Raziel material is the collection of the seven so-called 'Semaforas,' which are contained in the 'seaventh booke that treateth of names and of the vertues of them.'[118] Sophie Page points out that 'two different versions of the seventh book circulated: the *Liber magice*, which focused on image magic, and the *Liber virtutis*, an abridged version of the first appended work, the *Liber Semaforas* (Semhemaforas, Semiphoras, Seminafora, Semforas), which was concerned with names of power.'[119] Versions appear in various manuscripts, including the Folger Book of Magic.

These Semaforas are said to be contained in 'the booke which is cleped Raziel which the creator sent to Adam by the angell Raziel when upon the brink of the floud of paradice weeping thilke creator he prayed and of him forgivenes of his sinnes he besought…in which bookes that is three Orisons…The first the Prophets clepeth Semiforas which the creator gave to Adam in Paradice[,] the second booke is which the creator gave to Adam in paradice in the hower of necessity or need.'[120] The Semaforas are said to be sacred names, each first pronounced at a particularly significant moment in the Garden:

> The first is when Adam spoke with the creator in paradice. The second is when he spake with the angels.
> The third is when he spake with the divels.
> The 4th is when he spake with men and with fowels & fishes and beasts and reptiles and wilde beasts.

---

117 David Goldstein, *Jewish Folklore and Legend* (Hamlyn: London, 1980): 30.
118 MS Sloane 3826, 53v, in Stephen Skinner & Donald Karr (ed), *Sepher Raziel: A Sixteenth Century English Grimoire* (Golden Hoard Press: Singapore, 2010): 133.
119 Page, 'Uplifting Souls': 82 and nn. 17, 18. Page also points out that at least the 'Alfonsine *Liber Razielis* is structured in the form of seven books said to have been *brought together by Solomon.*' Ibid., emphasis added.
120 MS Sloane 3826, 49v; in Skinner & Karr (eds.), *Sepher Raziel*: 125.

The fifth when he spake with seeds and herbes and trees and all growing things.

The 6th when he spake with wyndes and with the 4 elemts.

The 7th when he spake with the sunne and the moone and the starres.

And by the 7 vertues of Semaforas whatever he would do he did, and what ever he would destroy he destroyed. And this Semaforu Adam had when the Creator enspired grace into him.[121]

Each of these Semaforas are thus linked back to a perfected prelapsarian first instantiation: in intoning them one was thought to be speaking as Adam did, working one's magic as the First Magician did. The book is both record of Adam's previous deeds, and our key to redeeming our knowledge of and magical effect upon the natural world. The Semaforas form something of a natural Edenic magical syllabus or *curriculum vitae*, outlining the specific magical acts – magical speech acts, at that – which our Ancestor performed. They are all worthy of further study, but of particular relevance to the spirit-work of the *Excellent Booke* is the extrapolation of the third Semaforas – not simply for conversing with 'divels' but marking 'when he spake with devils and with dead men and of them counsel he enquired, and they sufficiently to him answered.'[122] The version of the Semaforas in the Folger Book of Magic is not shy about specifying these names or their use: 'viz., Adona, Sabaoth, Adonay, Cados, Addona Amora. These thou shalt name when thou wilt gather together winds, devils, or spirits.'[123]

This seeking of counsel from spirits and shades, of turning to these beings in our hour of need, should certainly be considered from the perspective of the sundered Edenic connection. As Page muses:

The gift of the book occurs at a time when man has just lost his closest and purest terrestrial contact with the divine. Many late medieval ritual magic texts sought to recover this contact, sometimes combining this goal with an expression of yearning for the prelapsarian state of purity,

---

121 MS Sloane 3826, 54r; in Skinner & Karr (eds.), *Sepher Raziel*: 133.
122 MS Sloane 3826, 54v; in Skinner & Karr (eds.), *Sepher Raziel*: 134.
123 *Book of Oberon*: 163.

knowledge, and experience of the presence of God…The *Liber Razielis* is a revelation of the lost prelapsarian wisdom, which enables man to acquire knowledge of all corporeal and spiritual causes.[124]

Trees of Knowledge

Aquinas characterised Adam's direct knowledge of the divine as an *infusio*. Hence Aquinas distinguished 'two kinds of knowledge of God': 'by means of an internal inspiration due to the irradiation of divine wisdom,' and 'by which he knew God as we do, through sensible creatures.'[125] Ultimately, of course, the story of Adam's Fall also involves the acquiring of an all-too-earthly kind of knowledge: the tasting of the forbidden. It is here at this ardent root and reaching of desire we find the figures of Adam and Eve invoked in the countless *experimenta* for love, scribbled in the working books of cunning-folk and the receipt-filled books of secrets. The manuscript attributed to Arthur Gauntlet contains no less than eighteen love spells involving apples alone.[126] This is the most common identification of the fruit of the Tree of the Knowledge of Good and Evil: Almond suggests this is 'no doubt due to the connection of the apple with love and lovesickness in the Song of Solomon (2.5, 7.8),' as well as pointing out the Hebrew *tappuach* was rendered *malum* in the Vulgate and thus associated with evil.[127] As the alchemist Jean-Baptiste van Helmont remarked, 'there was in the Apple, the Concupiscence of the Flesh, an incentive of Lust, a be-drunkening of Luxury for a Beast-like Generation in the Flesh of Sin.'[128]

One of Gauntlet's operations called expressly on the First Mother and Father, the spirits that tempted them, and the ultimate lord of those spirits, the dead and the vicissitudes of the unheavenly earth: Lucifer.[129] Considering

---

124 Sophie Page, 'Uplifting Souls': 87.

125 For more on this, see Alastair Minnis, *From Eden to Eternity: Creations of Paradise in the Later Middle Ages* (University of Pennsylvania Press: Philadelphia, 2016): 57 n. 126 and 127.

126 *The Grimoire of Arthur Gauntlet*, ed. David Rankine (Avalonia: London, 2011):305–308.

127 Almond, *Adam and Eve*: 192–193.

128 Jean-Baptiste van Helmont, *Oriatrike* (London, 1662): 657.

129 'Write in an Apple before it fall from the tree these 3 words with the blood (['blank space suggesting the type of blood was to be filled in later, or possibly that it was the person's blood']) Lucifer Sathanas Rusal And say Conjuro to porno per omnes damones

this tension present in such an amorous sorcery, between the love of God and Lucifer, focused around the fruit of a tree, it is worth reflecting on a further medieval tradition of trees and knowledge:

> Eden was a tree garden, and the mystical trees of good and evil which grew in it never lost their appeal for the Medievals; indeed it increased throughout the period. The New Testament constantly uses trees as symbols, the greatest of them being the Tree of the Cross itself. Because of its role in the Redemption, it was depicted as the opposite of the Tree of Sins. As the Tree of the Cross became a more and more popular theme from the twelfth to the fourteenth century, so did the theme of the two opposing trees of good and evil. Whole systems of vices and virtues were worked out on these symbolic trees. The shade of the Tree of Good was generally represented in the Middle Ages as Sapientia – the true wisdom of Solomon, Ecclesiastes, the Book of Wisdom, and the shade of the Tree of Evil as scientia - the false wisdom of the world. This was in accordance with the Augustinian dichotomy between Charity and Cupidity, which was the basis of the whole iconographical scheme of the opposing trees.[130]

I contend it worthy to reflect upon these concrescent conceptions of epistemological dendrology and Aquinas' twofold Adamic gnosis precisely when we consider the trees of crystal and of blood in the *Visions*. It is tempting to impose one of these dualities – of the glittering source of pure structure, pure heavenly *a priori*, and the sanguine outpouring of embodied empiricism – while also observing a shift occurring, in which the latter is no longer expressly evil so much as simply carnal. Certainly the lack of taboos concerning chastity or sexual conduct in the *Excellent Booke's* notae has already been observed as a notable (Protestant) departure from the typical injunctions and purifications necessitated in medieval ritual magic.[131] It is tempting to see

qui tentaverint Adam et Evam in Paradisa ut quecunque mulier dete gustanerit in amore meo andeat.' [I conjure thee furthermore by all the demons who tempted Adam and Eve in Paradise so that whichever way through you the woman will taste love for me and desire me.] *Grimoire of Arthur Gauntlet*: 307.

130 Teresa McLean, *Medieval English Gardens* (Dover: New York, 1980): 125.

131 Klaassen, 'Ritual Invocation': 343–344.

in such a changing approach to knowledge of the physical world Klaassen's early modern humanist epistemological turn, framing occult experiments to gain knowledge through spirits in terms of Renaissance exploration into the material Book of Nature. To Klaassen, Gilbert and Davis were wielding 'old dirty' medieval ritual magic in experimental ways in order to not only tell but to make their future.

Combining saintly, angelic and biblical figures with the tutelary spectres of deceased Magi, the wider cast of the Excellent Booke's dramatis personae might well represent an admixture of access to (or even exemplars of) these forms of knowledge. Indeed, dead magicians especially can be thought to combine them: their experiences gathered in life running together with some evidently underlying occult metaphysic exemplified in their very ghostly existence, contact and communion.

The visions of the trees of crystal and blood are never far from the appearance of miraculous books – books that command spirits, books of gold held by barefoot evangelists – that reveal secrets, that allow the tutelary shades of forefatherly Magi to impart their old wisdom and direct the revelation of new knowledge.

ROGER BACON

Roger Bacon was a thirteenth-century natural philosopher, alchemist and a Franciscan friar. Biographer George Molland notes that 'from early traditions it seems that he came from the south-west of England, perhaps near Ilchester in Somerset.'[132] Although his work in life was concerned with natural philosophy as well as natural magic – apparently specialising in the study of optics – after his death, he began to be afforded an increasingly powerful, more diabolic reputation as a delver into mysteries best left undelved.

Notable points of Bacon's early career include pioneering the teaching of Aristotle's natural philosophy in Paris around 1245, before undergoing what Molland calls 'his new orientation' – a twenty year period of intensive study from which Bacon's endeavours 'may loosely be described as more "scientifi-

---

132 George Molland, 'Bacon, Roger (c.1214 – 1292?),' Oxford Dictionary of National Biography first published 2004, http://www.oxforddnb.com/view/article/1008?docPos=1. Last accessed 12/09/2017.

cally" and technologically oriented.'[133] Certainly by the early modern period, Bacon had a reputation as not only a learned man, but a great inventor. Naude's *History of Magic* characterises him in typical fashion:

> Rober [sic] Bacon had in like manner made one, since that, being a great Mathematician, as may be seen both by the Treatises and instruments of his invention he sent to Pope Clement the fourth and his two Books, printed within these fifteen years, of Perspective and Glasses, it is not unlikely he did many extraordinary things by the help of that Science; whereof the cause being not known to the vulgar, (which was much more rough-hewn, and barbarous than it is now) it could do no lesse then attribute them to Magick.[134]

Pope Clement IV was indeed a driving force behind the production of Bacon's first major work, the *Opus Maius*. Bacon had become acquainted with Clement back when he was Guy Foulquois, a former lawyer and soldier, and papal ambassador to England. Foulquois had 'shown interest in Bacon's schemes and asked for his writings, a request that was repeated as a command after his elevation.'[135]

Roger Bacon seems to have been a name especially associated with glasses, mirrors, and stones with which to scry. It has been noted by historian György Szönyi that Bacon was devoted to the study of light, of the optics of reflection and radiation.[136] Chapter 6 of the *Opus Maius* — sandwiched between the chapter dedicated to 'mathematics (including astronomy and astrology)' and

---

133 Molland, ODNB.

134 Gabriel Naudé, *The history of magick by way of apology, for all the wise men who have unjustly been reputed magicians, from the Creation, to the present age* (London, 1657): 231–32.

135 Molland, ODNB.

136 György E Szönyi, 'Paracelsus, Scrying, and the Lingua Adamica: Contexts for John Dee's Angel Magic.' Stephen Clucas (ed.), *John Dee: Interdisciplinary Studies in English Renaissance Thought* (Springer: Dordrecht, 2006): 210 n. 16; recommending David C. Lindberg, *Theories of Vision from Al-Kindi to Kepler* (Chicago, 1976), and Urszula Szulakowska *The Alchemy of Light: Geometry and Optics in Late Renaissance Alchemical Illustration* (Leiden, 2000).

the one on 'experimental science' – concerned optics specifically.[137]

The connection to the papacy overshadowed Bacon's reputation amongst Protestants after the Reformation. At least one early modern text suggested this was particularly significant for Bacon's posthumous reputation as a practitioner of black magic, and was written as 'an Apology... the usher to his other Workes, which may happily breath a more free Air hereafter, when once the World sees how clear he was, from loving Negromancy'; claiming 'Twas the Popes smoak which made the eyes of that Age so sore, as they could not discern...'[138]

After completing his *Opus Maius* at Pope Clement IV's specific request-cum-demand, Bacon was apparently plagued by those anxieties typical of authors – that the book was too long and unwieldy, that he may have left important material out, and that it might be lost on route to Rome. So he began work on an *Opus Minus* to both précis and addend the previous tome. Molland seems to consider that the very same anxieties about the second book also prompted the third work (called, perhaps unsurprisingly, the *Opus Tertium*), which 'may never have been properly revised to Bacon's satisfaction, and was quite probably never sent to the pope, who died in 1268 without leaving any known record of how he reacted to Bacon's ideas.'[139]

It was not only his links to the head of the Vatican that may have contributed to Bacon's later reputation for working with more sinister magics. According to one account (written a century after the fact) a head of the Franciscan order 'condemned and disapproved the teaching of Brother Roger Bacon, Englishman, Doctor of Sacred Theology, as containing certain suspect novelties, on account of which the said Roger was condemned to be imprisoned.'[140] Some accounts claim this master-general of the friars was Girolamo

137 'Part 1 treated the causes of human ignorance; part 2, the relation of the other sciences to theology; part 3, grammar and the power of languages; part 4, mathematics (including astronomy and astrology); part 5, optics (*perspectiva*); part 6, 'experimental science'; part 7, moral philosophy.' Molland, ODNB.

138 *Frier Bacon his discovery of the miracles of art, nature, and magick faithfully translated out of Dr. Dees own copy by T.M. and never before in English* (London, 1659): iii.

139 Molland also notes 'The editorial state of these three works, as of many others in the corpus, is unsatisfactory, but is steadily improving.' Molland, ODNB.

140 Roger Bacon, 'Chronica XXIV generalium.' T. Crowley, *Roger Bacon: The Problem of*

da Ascoli, others Raimondo Gaufredi. Still other accounts suggest Bacon was merely placed under various internal clerical restrictions, probably connected to the condemnations of 219 heretical propositions issued by the bishop of Paris in 1277. Through the historical murk and brackish rumour we can discern that Bacon's work was thought to place him in conflict with the order's orthodoxy, likely around proscriptions against work concerning the natural magic and philosophy of astrology and alchemy.

Writings on alchemy attributed to Bacon circulated thoroughly posthumously: 'some alchemical works (quite probably all spurious) were published in 1603 at Frankfurt under the title *Sanioris medicinae…de arte chymiae scripta*, and in the same place in 1614 Johann Combach brought out two volumes containing genuine mathematical and optical writings, largely drawn from the *Opus maius*.'[141] Works *about* Bacon certainly contained alchemical material. The ninth chapter of the *Miracles*, for instance, is titled 'Of the Manner to make the Philosophers Egge,' promising to teach 'the dissolving the Philosophers Egge, and finding out the parts thereof; a work which will give beginning to other enterprises.'[142]

Bacon himself is supposedly printed in *The Mirror of Alchimy* – a compilation of various alchemical treatises and instructions, which Allison Kavey calls out as a 'pseudo-Bacon text'[143] – in the titular piece and in the later 'excellent discourse of the admirable force and efficacie of Art and Nature.'[144] Bacon's textual legacy should be contextualised in terms of both his great renown as an alchemist and the relative lack of authentic (or at least authenticated) writings by the friar. Such conditions led to a large quantity of (pseudo-)Baconian texts attributed spuriously, erroneously or deliberately falsely.[145] The blanks between a well-known name and their poorly-known

---

the Soul in his *Philosophical Commentaries* (Éditions de l'Institut superieur de philosophie: Louvain, 1950).

141 Molland, ODNB.

142 *Miracles*, 41. Chapters X and XI also deal with alchemy.

143 Allison Kavey, *Books of Secrets: Natural Philosophy in England, 1550 – 1600* (University of Illinois Press: Chicago, 2007): 39.

144 *The Mirror of Alchimy* (London, 1597): 54.

145 'in alchemical circles he was sufficiently renowned to have attracted a wealth of pseudepigrapha to his name', but given that 'Bacon's undoubtedly genuine writings on

works were filled in by the projections of what common and uncommon knowledge expected of an author infamous for (but, crucially, not terribly accurately quoted on) both tenebrous and dazzling mysteries. Here again, the posthumous processes whereby a nigromancer is inversely canonised can be observed, as a susurrus of suspicion and ghoulish fascination thickens in whispers of ill deeds and forbidden knowledge.

The public perception, at least by the early modern period, was that Bacon was a magician of some sort. In decrying ignorant misapprehensions of various historical agents, Naude also highlights Bacon's attributed occult expertise: 'however it be, we may adde this cause to the precedent, as one of the principall that hath caused learned men to be thought Magicians, and upon account whereof the curiosity of Albertus magnus, *the naturall Magick of Bacon*, the judiciary Astrology of Chicus, the Mathematicks of Sylvester, and heresy of Alchindus, and certaine superstitious observations, have been reputed Geotick and diabolicall Magick.'[146] Bacon's actual endeavours into natural philosophy and natural magic are configured as some grit-speck of truth around which formed the nebulous pearl of his nigromantic reputation. It also foregrounds a tradition of calling learned folk magic of the shadier, grubbier and more illicit variety *geotick* or goetic. Naude is of course eager to point out 'yet Johannes Picus, the miracle and astonishment of his age, sayes expressely in his Apologie, that he knew but three men that had made the best advantages of naturall and lawfull Magick, Alchindus, Roger Bacon, and William Bishop of Paris.'[147] Bacon is seated, most aptly, between a clergyman and an alchemist.

Bacon's name can also commonly be found in lists of (in)famous occult theorists in a rather different light. Agrippa includes Bacon in the list of authors attributed and led astray by 'all those books of darkness': 'now in these dayes there are carryed about books with feigned titles, under the names of Adam, Abel, Enoch, Abraham, Solomon, also Paul, Honorius, Cyprianus, Albertus, Thomas Hierome, and of a certain man of Yorke, whose toies Alphousus King of Castile, Robert an English man, Bacon, and Apponus,

alchemy are small in volume… it is hard to feel secure in accepting any of the later ascriptions.' Molland, ODNB.
146 Naude, History: 52. Emphasis added.
147 Naude, History: 168.

and many other men of a deplored wit have foolishly followed.'[148] Several of these men are amongst the shades who turn up for Gilbert and Davis.

Naude goes on to account that 'this hath given some occasion to imagine, that many great men have not been charg'd with Magick, but merely...the books unjustly father'd upon them':

> we find in certain Catalogues, who furnish us with their titles in such
> a manner, that we cannot judge, unless by some other circumstances,
> what the Authours drift and designe was in the composition of them,
> whether to illustrate or confute, plead for or against, mantain or con-
> demn the subject they treat of, and busie themselves about. Whence it
> came to passe, that many finding by these Catalogues, that Alexander
> Aphrodisaeus had written of Magicall Arts, Aquinas of judiciary As-
> trologie, and Roger Bacon of Necromancie, have presently entered into
> imaginations contrary to what they should, beleeving that they contain'd
> nothing else, but the precepts and direction we are to follow, to be perfect
> in the practice of all those Divinations, and consequently, that there was
> much reason, why the Authors should be accounted Magicians.[149]

The ignorant public was supposedly not simply judging books by their covers, but authors by their titles. With this explanation, the tide of more (conspicuously) educated popular perception of Bacon rolls to admit he may have *written on* necromancy without allowing (indeed, in order to expressly deny) that he *practiced* necromancy. Nevertheless, to write on demonology was to amass and pronounce dangerous transformational knowledge. For-bidden and foreboding texts, containing sealed spirits, were understood by their virtues of contagion: who could know what might escape their pages if opened.

148 Agrippa, *Three Books*: 573.
149 Naude, *History*: 44.

On Necromancy

So it was opined that Bacon wrote *something* on necromancy. His reputation in matters of optics and scrying would have perhaps assisted the spread of this notion: those who gazed in stones saw shades and spirits, and an expert in the former could be expected to know of the latter. The case of De Nigro-mancia (also known as the *Thesaurus Spirituum*) doubles down on its associations with legendary magicians of ill-repute, being considered a book by Bacon but also somehow of Saint Cyprian. So a legend of illicit knowledge and power builds upon earlier disreputable rumour, in a circle of infamy. Molland levely states 'there seem no grounds for regarding him as the author of such works as the De *nigromantia* attributed to him, and apart from some stories retailed by a late fourteenth-century Franciscan chronicler, it is not until the sixteenth century that a full account of his supposed doings appears – in an anonymous romance, The Famous Historie of Fryer Bacon, which formed the basis of Robert Greene's play, The Honorable Historie of Frier Bacon, and Frier Bungay.'[150]

Curiously, for all the rumour, we do have a specific necromantic technique attributed to Bacon:

> For whe[n] the spirite is once come before the circle, he forthe with demaundeth the exsorciste a sacrifice, whiche moste commenlye is a pece of waxe co~secrated, or hallowed after their owne order (For they haue certayn bokes, called bokes of consecration) or els it is a chicke[n], a lapwing, or some liuinge creatur, whiche when he hath receyued: then doeth he fulfill the mynd of the exsorcist, for oneles he hath it, he will neither doe, neither speake any thinge. Of this testefieth bacon in his boke of Necromancie.[151]

When considered against Agrippa's twofold categorisation of necromancers, it situates Bacon's legacy at the high and low *crux* of discourses concerning licit and illicit magic. Trafficking with spirits – the base medieval definition

---

150 Molland, ODNB.

151 Francis Coxe, A short treatise declaringe the detestable wickednesse, of magicall sciences as necromancie. coniurations of spirites, curiouse astrologie and such lyke (1561): f.24.

of necromancy, or nigromancy – could be performed by dominating and threatening spirits with the awesome and terrific names of their Creator, but it could also be done through allegiances and collaborations with these entities. The surest sign of such 'worship' was, of course, the making of sacrifices.[152] Allegations of such a sacrificial component in Baconian necromancy by pious writers demonstrate of course a further denigration of his magic and power.

Moreover, this assessment contextualises 'demands of sacrifice' in the long texts of spirit lists associated with the goetic magicians. Indeed, Agrippa specifically calls these kinds of techniques the endeavours of 'Geotick' practitioners. Writing 'Of Conjuring and Necromancy,' he offers a definition of 'Geocie' as 'being familiar with unclean Spirits,' specifying it as the practices of 'those that Invoke the Souls of dead Bodies, who Inchant Children, and cause them to give the Answer of the Oracle; and as we read of Socrates, carry about with them certain Pocket-Daemons; and who, as they say, nourish little Spirits in Glasses, by which they pretend to Foretel and Prophesie.'[153] Such 'glasses' firmly cohere at least an alleged tradition of scrying, familiars, and the dead around the same term used to describe various books of spirit conjuration. The glass was considered container, spirit house or trap, as well as the porthole out upon the ocean of the world of spirits. This tradition is comprehended through the citation of Socrates, and thus considered as being both ancient Greek and an extant Renaissance practice.

Bacon has associations with another even more influential Greek philosopher, Aristotle, or rather 'the important pseudo-Aristotelian work, *Secretum*

152 'All these proceed in a twofold manner. For some of them make it their business to adjure and compel Evil Spirits to appearance, by *the Efficacy and Power of sacred Names*; because seeing that every Creature doth fear and reverence the Name of its Creator, no wonder if Conjurors, and other Infidels Pagans, Jews, Saracens, or prophane Persons, do think to force the Devils Obedience by the Terrour of his Creators Name. Others, more to be detested than they, and worthy the utmost punishment of Fire, submitting themselves to the Devils, *sacrifice to them, and Worship them*, become guilty of the vilest subjection and Idolatry that may be; to which Crimes though the former are not quite so obnoxious, yet they expose themselves to manifest dangers. For the Devils are always watchful to intrap Men in the Errors they heedlesly run into.' Heinrich Agrippa, *Vanity of the Arts and Sciences* (London, 1676): 116.
153 Agrippa, *Vanity of the Arts and Sciences*: 115–116.

secretorum, which he believed to be by Aristotle himself,' which 'takes the form of a long letter on kingship addressed to Aristotle's erstwhile pupil Alexander the Great, and has as a strong theme the extreme usefulness of philosophy, of various sciences (including those that would now be called pseudo-sciences), and of medicine.'[154] It is Steven J. Williams' considered opinion that 'Bacon invested a great deal of time and care on his...edition of the Latin *Secretum* that is superior to most extant manuscripts'; indeed, 'the signs of Bacon's diligence are many.'[155] Williams judges that Bacon considered the *Secretum* 'possibly Aristotle's greatest production': offering not only useful information, but also hitherto unavailable secrets.

Baconian Renewal

The revisions of the *Secretum* are somewhat metonymic of Bacon's wider project and calling. Subscribing to a version of the doctrine of *prisca theologia*, Bacon held that the holy and sacred truths of the highest philosophy had been issued by God to The Ancients (those perennial homogenised thinkers of some past Golden Age), but that this knowledge had become steadily more corrupted. Rather than simply lamenting for a past utopia however, Bacon significantly concluded that various great reform projects had been necessary throughout history to set the flow of knowledge down the ages

154 Indeed, 'this theme was especially important to Bacon in his new orientation' towards empirical experimentation away from traditional scholasticism, 'and from at least 1267 he cites the work with great frequency.' Molland, ODNB.

155 Specifically, Williams lists: 'correcting his base text with four supplementary copies of the *Secretum*, he penned in numerous alternative readings; not satisfied with these four copies, he consulted yet others. He made a number of discrete changes in the text, inserting snippets of material here and there, emending passages he believed were factually wrong. He rationalized the *Secretum*'s organization from ten books of widely disparate length into a more evenly balanced four-book format. He wrote extensive explanatory notes to the text. He made a detailed table of contents whose shortened titles also appear at the head of the book's chapters. He added a chart and a diagram at the end of the medical section for determining the influence of the planets on human activity. And he prepared a prefatory treatise complete with six illustrations meant to aid the reader's comprehension of the astronomical and astrological references in the *Secretum*.' Steven J. Williams, 'Roger Bacon and his edition of the Pseudo-Aristotelian *Secretum Secretorum*,' *Speculum* 69, 1 (1994): 63.

back on its proper course. He held three legendary reformers of knowledge in particular regard – Solomon, Aristotle and Avicenna – even suggesting they had received some kind of divine revelation or illumination. Furthermore, 'it seems fairly clear that Bacon saw himself as the potential provider' of a fourth Christian renewal of knowledge. This assumption (in either sense) of a personal sacred duty is a practice in which early modern magical practitioners involved in scrying operations – specifically, both Dee and Gilbert – also seem to have indulged.

Bacon saw optics as one of the forms of knowledge he was destined to reform. Certainly 'Bacon's account of optics was indeed more systematic than that of other special sciences, and this was especially because he was able to draw heavily on the recently translated work of the great Arabic scientist Ibn al-Haytham, who flourished in Egypt in the early eleventh century, and became known in the West as Alhazen.'[156] Nor was this interest purely theoretical or merely academic. Following the work of Alhazen and also Petrus Peregrinus, Bacon 'had several concave mirrors made for his own use.'[157]

Early modern works dedicated to understanding Bacon's optics, such as the *Miracles*, suggested practical uses for such theory and experimentation. Lenses could produce telescopes and reading glasses: 'glasses so cast, that things at hand may appear at distance, and things at distance, as hard at hand: yea so farre may the designe be driven, as the least letters may be read, and things reckoned at an incredible distance, yea starres shine in what place you please.'[158] Similarly, once it was understood, 'by the framing of Glasses, bodies of the largest bulk, may in appearance be contracted to a minute volumne, things little in themselves show great, while others tall and lofty appear low and creeping, things creeping and low, high and mighty, things private and hidden to be clear and manifest,' it was far more comprehensible that they might be used in the discovery of that which was hidden, or occult.

As regards the theme of invisible forces, optics did not merely consider light but the movement of light through the medium of various airs and winds. For instance, notions of sundogs and moondogs, phenomena in

---

156 'Bacon seems to have been the first Latin writer to have assimilated his work with any thoroughness.' Molland, ODNB.
157 Molland, ODNB.
158 Bacon, *Miracles*: 20.

which these luminary bodies appear to be duplicated in the sky, expanded this Baconian conception of optical illusions based on 'vapours':

> As Pliny in the 2d Book, Nat. Hist. chap. 30 saith, That Nature so dispo-seth of vapours, as two Sunnes, and two Moons; yea sometimes three Sunnes shine together in the Air. And by the same Reason one thing may in appearance be *multiplied to an infinity*, in regard that after any creature hath exceeded his own virtue (as Aristotle cap. de vacuo.) no certain bounds is to be assigned it.[159]

Furthermore, the field-like qualities of a vaporous medium could be utilised in more directly affective transmission of virtue: 'glasses may be framed to *send forth Species*, and poisonous infectious influences, whither a man pleaseth.'[160] Once more, the natural magic and philosophy of optics had a contagious mechanism to consider. Citing one of his admired Aristotle's siege warfare applications of this principle[161] demonstrates how 'Bacon apparently thought that the required change of air could be brought about by mirrors deflecting the celestial virtues'[162] for 'by a change of the air that contains celestial virtues, men's customs are changed.'[163] The astral magic implications of this technique should not be overlooked.

Multiplication and action-at-a-distance through a medium were not two different applications of optics; they were integral components of an overarching vision of natural magic. Mirrors might be employed to produce useful illusions, especially in duplication, as when 'Glasses and Perspectives may be framed, to make one thing appear many, one man an Army, the Sun and Moon to be as many as we please.'[164] Such feats of multiplication played

---

159 Bacon, *Miracles*: 19.

160 Bacon, *Miracles*: 21.

161 'And this invention Aristotle shewed Alexander, by which he erecting the poison of a Basilisk upon the Wall of a City, which held out against his Army, conveyed the very poison into the City it self.' *Miracles*: 21.

162 Molland, ODNB.

163 *The Opus Majus of Roger Bacon*, ed. John Henry Bridges (Clarendon Press: Oxford, 1897–1900): 1.393.

164 Bacon, *Miracles*: 19.

an extremely important role in Bacon's metaphysics and cosmology, and the natural philosophy of action-at-a-distance magics:

> Optics not only reinforced Bacon's faith in mathematics: it also suggest-
> ed a generalization. Bacon's universe was a very active one, and he was
> extremely interested in how action was transferred from one body to
> another, especially when they were not in contact. A clear example was
> the transmission of lighting and heating action from the sun to things
> below, and Bacon proposed that other forms of action at a distance were
> of the same kind, whereby substances and qualities radiated species or
> likenesses of themselves in all directions, which were 'multiplied' through
> the medium in stages, with first one part of the medium being altered,
> which then altered another adjacent to it, and so on.[165]

The principle of reflection, of central importance in occult and hermetic arts could itself be considered a form of contagion.

The centrality of scrying stones to pre-modern magic offers vital context for Bacon's afterlife journey from natural philosopher of optics to reputed necromancer, even a patron of dark arts and their forbidden tomes, and demonstrates the results of links (whether in 'high' occult philosophy or popular folk conception) between crystal-gazing as knowledge-at-a-distance and the conjuration of spirits. Such an apparent concrescence of such suppos-edly disparate faculties, of divination and conjuration, has been dubbed 'evocatory scrying' when encountered in the spells of the PGM.[166]

Conjuration consists (inter alia) of both calling and ensuring the presence of a spirit or spirits. It requires some form of awareness of the conjured entity as well as incantations, gestures, or other types of ritual summoning. The Excellent Booke seems clear on this detail: do not set a spirit a task until one has bound it, and one cannot bind it until one can observe it.[167] Sight or some other visionary phenomenon is the pre-eminent means of perceiving or verifying spirit-sign.

165 Molland, ODNB.
166 Skinner, *Techniques of Graeco-Egyptian Magic* (Golden Hoard Press: Singapore, 2014): 246–267.
167 Add. MS. 36674, ff.47v, 48r, 48v.

We might recall how proper use of a 'Berill' often included reciting the proper call. That many of these activating calls seem tailored and specific to a certain stone illuminates the notion of enshrining particular spirits in or from the stone whom ensure successful scrying. One calls a spirit into the stone, or perhaps awakens it from within the berill; it is this spirit which brings forth visions of other spirits. Once more, conjuration and divination find interrelation, perhaps most simply expressed as the *how* and the *what* of a scrying operation.

The successful perception and employment of spirits in scrying is used for knowledge: whether seeing from afar (that is, receiving information such as 'Where is my lost property?' or 'What are the courts of Europe up to?'), working on expressly tutelary relationships with spirits (improving one's understanding and ability of how to perform magic), or comprehending one's own destiny in relation to a revealed enspirited magical cosmos (what we might term spiritual elevation). In this case, some form of empowerment accompanies *mere* divining: understanding and ability seemingly bootstrapping each other. I would propose that a fundamental why of scrying presupposes the inclusion of an *initiatory* function for operators.

As the katabasis of Bacon's shade demonstrates, wandering with a close enough association with 'glass recepticles' will eventually lend one the status of magician. Here we find a centrality of the power of illumination, and the amplification of mirrors, in the practice of the dark arts.

HEINRICH CORNELIUS AGRIPPA

And so we come to our final ghostly tutor, our final magician's shade who dispensed advice to the receivers and operators of the *Excellent Booke*. Of these spectres, Heinrich Cornelius Agrippa von Nettesheim is the most contemporaneous to Humphrey Gilbert and John Davis, the youngest dead man of the *Visions*. As such, he is the one about whom we can be most sure of biographic details. Born in Cologne, Agrippa attended the university there, studying various forms of occult philosophy (such as alchemy, Christian cabala, and angelology) and demonstrating a precocious talent for languages. He began teaching at the University of Dole in 1509, and a year later sent the abbot Johannes Trithemius – himself known as an occult philosopher and cryptographer as well as a senior clergyman – a draft of the work he is now best known for: the *Three Books of Occult Philosophy*, an encyclopaedic summary of early modern magical theory. Certainly the 'later printed version became by far the most famous and influential esoteric document of the Renaissance.' By the end of his life, Agrippa was 'one of the most influential magical thinkers of the Renaissance'[168] and was 'for the next two centuries continually cited (positively or negatively) along with Paracelsus as a founding thinker of the magical schools of thought.'[169] Indeed, his name became a very byword for scholarly intellect, occult expertise and magical power: in Christopher Marlowe's *Doctor Faustus*, the eponymous (anti-)hero pledges to become 'as cunning as Agrippa was, / Whose shadows made all Europe honour him.'[170]

Heinrich Cornelius Agrippa von Nettesheim is undoubtedly the greatest shade to preside over the histories of European magic. Frank Klaassen in fact presents the necromantic experiments of Gilbert and Davis – summoning the ghosts of magicians to deliver magical texts and instruction – as particularly instructive in highlighting the importance of Agrippa's afterlife in the thought and praxis of his descendants:

> in the late 1560s Humphrey Gilbert employed the demon Azazel to call up the ghosts of a select group of magicians: Adam, Job, Solomon, Roger Bacon, and Cornelius Agrippa. A mere three decades after his death, Agrippa had attained a position next to the greatest reputed magicians of the ancient and Christian eras. If the calling up of Agrippa's ghost is a little surprising, the estimation in which Gilbert held Agrippa is not. Among the second generation of Renaissance writers on magic, his is unquestionably the most influential and colorful. His great work on magic, *De Occulta Philosophia*, became an instant classic in the library of occult learning. The work won him a place on the indices of Venice, Milan and Rome in 1554, as well as in the processes of the Holy Office at Fruili. More telling, however, is the shadow he cast in the library of magic. Within

168 Frank L. Borchardt, 'Magus as Renaissance Man.' *The Sixteenth Century Journal* 21, 1 (Spring, 1990): 65; cf. Charles G. Nauert, Jr., 'Agrippa and the Crisis of Renaissance Thought.' *Illinois Studies in the Social Sciences* 55 (University of Illinois Press, 1965): 229.
169 Christopher I. Lehrich, *Language of the Demons and Angels: Cornelius Agrippa's Occult Philosophy* (Brill: Boston, 2003): 1–2.
170 Christopher Marlowe, *Doctor Faustus* (London, 1604), I. i. 118.

twenty years of Agrippa's death, his restless ghost was already present in the form of pseudonymous works printed under Agrippa's name. His notoriety and influence in the world of sixteenth-century occultism are also well attested in manuscripts of magic…no other Renaissance occult writer was quoted, extracted, or cross-referenced with such frequency. Agrippa's project is therefore central to our understanding of magic…[171]

Agrippa's ghost rather sinks into his works, into his books written and allegedly written. He becomes a different sort of intermediary shade – an archivist of sources and summations, case-studies and curiosities, evidences and wonder. He becomes, in his quotations and citations, an interlocutor of the judgments of the dead. The books made him famous, and his fame made the books powerful. Becoming as it did the go-to tome for occult philosophers, the shade of Agrippa charted a new crossroad, a new staging-house for pilgrims seeking further studies, at a junction of Graeco-Roman and Christo-Cabalistic magical synthesis.

Controversy

Agrippa did not shy away from controversial positions and disputes during his life, leading to several (usually anonymous) accusations of heresy. In 1518, for instance, he became involved in defending Jacques Lefèvre d'Etaples' hagiographic refutation that the three Marys were all daughters of Saint Anne; for which he was anonymously accused of being a heretic. Christopher Lehrich notes that Agrippa 'immediately wrote a *Defensio* in an angry, sarcastic style which would be typical of his later refutations, rebuttals, and apologies.'[172] Understandably, this style would embroil him in further trouble.

Having landed in some difficulty for his controversial writings, he wrote a work intended to clarify matters and bring his contemporaries and peers back on-side. Unfortunately, 'Cornelius himself, in his solemn recantation in his books, *De Vanitate Scientiarum*' was 'not believed by all men, to have been

---

171 Frank Klaassen, *The Transformations of Magic: Illicit Learned Magic in the Later Middle Ages* (Penn State Press, 2013): 198–199.

172 Lehrich, *The Language of Demons and Angels*: 27; cf. *Defensio propositionum praenarratarum contra quendam Dominicastrum earundem impugnatorem, qui sanctissimam deiparae virginis matrem Annam conatur ostendere polygamam*; 'see Van der Poel, 88–91 et passim on this work.'

so sincere, as it should have been.'[173] Indeed, *De Vanitate* itself was denounced on eighteen points by the Louvain Faculty of Theology in a secret document presented to the Imperial Privy Council. The treatise was also 'publicly condemned by the Sorbonne Faculty on March 2, 1531.'[174] Such denunciations directly led to a further academic and political fall from favour. In 1531 Agrippa was imprisoned for his debts.

In Agrippa's last years, the historical record seems to go dark: 'no correspondence survives, and his final years are unknown.'[175] It is perhaps partly this darkness, along with a lifetime of being controversial in the light, that allows rumours to grow; that allows a brilliant mind to be considered a twisted heretic. Whatever the exact formula of gossip, slander, jealousy, professional discourtesy *et al*, 'after his death, stories of Agrippa's traffic with demons circulated, leading to his incorporation into the Faust legends and his reputation for black magic.'[176]

The Unattended Grimoire

One story, a particularly grim version of the classic unattended grimoire trope, is relayed by Martin Del Rio:

> This happened to Cornelius Agrippa at Louvain. He had a boarder, who was too curious, and Agrippa having once gone somewhere, had given the keys of his museum to the wife whom he afterwards divorced, forbidding her to allow any one to enter. That thoughtless youth did not omit, in season and out of season, to entreat the woman to give him the means of entering, until he gained his prayer. Having entered the museum, he fell upon a book of conjurations – read it. Hark! there is knocking at the door; he is disturbed; but he goes on with his reading; some one knocks again; and the unmannerly youth answering nothing to this, a demon enters, asks why is he called? What is it commanded him to do? Fear stifles the youth's voice, the demon his mouth, and so he pays the price of

---

173 Meric Casaubon, A Treatise Proving Spirits, Witches, and Supernatural Operations (London, 1672): 34.

174 Lehrich, The Language of Demons and Angels: 29.

175 Lehrich, The Language of Demons and Angels: 30.

176 Lehrich, The Language of Demons and Angels: 30.

his unholy curiosity. In the meantime the chief magician returns home, sees the devils dancing over him, uses the accustomed arts, they come when called, explain how the thing happened; he orders the homicide spirit to enter the corpse, and to walk now and then in the market-place (where other students were accustomed frequently to meet), at length to quit the body. He walks three or four times, then falls; the demon that had stirred the dead limbs taking flight. It was long thought that this youth had been seized with sudden death, but signs of suffocation first begot suspicion, afterwards time divulged all.[177]

By 1587, accounts of his nigromancy extended back to his student years:

Likewise, there was a student who unfortunately got into godless company, by the name of Heinricus Cornelius Agrippa, a fine student and Freyfechter, who came to Ingolstadt just as the Katzianers had invited the students to a fight. But although they could all have accepted, some students told the others they should stay calm. They knew someone who could master them all, him all of the others followed. Heinricus Cornelius offered them an earnest fight, and told them to defend themselves, as he alone would defeat them all. Now as they came to strikes, he brought out (cast) his black magic that could devour all swords. The furriers worried that if that happened with their fencing weapons it could even reach past their Katzbalgers, and took to the heels and left. This Henricus always had a black dog with him.[178]

---

177 Martin Del Rio, *Disquisitionum magicarum libri sex*, Lib. ii, Quaest. XXIX; quoted, cited and edited by Lehrich, *The Language of Demons and Angels*: 31: 'quoted and translated in Morley, 314 – 15, from the 1657 Cologne edition; I have correlated this with the 1608 Louvain edition and made a few trifling changes.' Lehrich, *The Language of Demons and Angels*: 31 n. 75.

178 Roger Norling, 'Heinrich Cornelius Agrippa, A Fine Student, Black Magician – and a *Freyfechter*?' http://hroarr.com/heinrich-cornelius-agrippa-a-fine-student-black-magician-and-a-freyfechter/, last accessed 24/05/2017; cf. Johann Scheible, *Das Kloster, weltlich und geistlich. Meist aus der ältern deutschen Volks-, Wunder-, Curiositäten-, und vorzugsweise komischen Literatur*, Verlag der herausgebers, 12 vol. (Stuttgart, 1846).

So it was that the demonologist Jean Bodin eventually came to call Agrippa 'the great doctor of the Diabolical Art.'[179]

Appeal to Agrippa

Thomas Ady, in his *A Candle in the Dark* (written with the intent of 'shewing the divine cause of the distractions of the whole nation of England and of the Christian world'), lamented 'Whether do not some preferre the mad imaginations of Cornelius Agrippa and others, before the Scriptures, for the defending their opinions?'[180] Similarly, another heresiographer complained, 'In this question of Witchcraft, some haue preferred the wicked folly of man, before the holy wisdom of God, & would haue vs to credit their owne practise, the knowledge also and experience of Cornelius Agrippa, Iohn Wyerus, Nero, Iulian Apostata, and such like: Their experience, to say no more, was vnsufficient, most wicked and detestable.'[181]

In a chapter 'On the Necromancy, Sorcery, and Conjurations of Priests and Friars' in an anti-Catholic publication, the anonymous author makes the rhetorical flourish, 'Avant therefore all Agrippa's, and Merlins.'[182] Nor was this an isolated comparison. The second canto of Robert Dixon's *Canidia* begins by reciting a lineage of (foolish) magicians: 'Agrippa, Merlin, Faustus, Asses / And Dunces to us Stygian Lasses.'[183]

One collection of seventeenth-century witticisms giving sardonic advice on how to demark oneself a 'quack' suggests 'your Table be never without some old musty Greek or Arabick Author, and the 4th Book of Cornelius Agrippa's Occult Philosophy, wide open, to amuse spectators; with half a dozen of Gilt Shillings, as so many Guinneys received that morning for Fees.'[184] The conspicuous display of books of alleged power (from occult philosophy to very large and impressively bound mathematics textbooks) was

---

179 Jean Bodin, *De la démonomancie des sorciers* (Jacques du Puys: Paris, 1580): f.51r.

180 Thomas Ady, *A Candle in the Dark* (London, 1655): 8.

181 Henry Holland, *A Treatise Against Witchcraft* (London, 1590): f.3.

182 *Rome's Rarities, or, The Pope's cabinet unlock'd and exposed to view* (1684): 175.

183 Robert Dixon, *Canidia, or, The witches a rhapsody* (London, 1683): 4.

184 Humphrey Crouch, *England's jests refin'd and improv'd being a choice collection of the merriest jests* (1687): 158.

certainly a documented practice by early modern cunning-folk.[185]

Agrippa's work was certainly appealed to directly in grimoire manuscripts, such as the marginalia in the Folger Book of Magic, where notes such as 'See Agrippa 570' have been pencilled in citation.[186] Whole sections of the *Three Books* are frequently copied out in magicians' working-books – from sections on incense correspondences[187] to chapters detailing the occult philosophical specifics of spirit-work.[188]

Agrippas

Agrippa's darkening reputation as an actual sorcerer as well as an occult philosopher lends his crowning accomplishment a further corona of rumour, gravity, and both dextrous and sinister virtue. The book of a magician – the mythic sorcerer's book written by them, or used by them, or even spuriously attributed to their patronage – has power. Agrippa's name became a byword not simply for scholarly acumen, especially in occult matters, but for the very oft-heretical tomes of magic which the demonologists enthusiastically categorised and vehemently proscribed. As testament to such admixture of text and spirit, books attributed to him began to be informally referred to simply as *Agrippas*. Furthermore, some of these texts acquired demonic reputations and even personalities of their own. In France these were frequently kept chained up under padlock, 'said to be a living book that hated to be consulted and hid its *characters* until it had been compelled, by beating it.'[189]

Agrippa's reputation for mastery in occult philosophy posthumously extended his patronage of magical books, as various texts dealing with such allegedly sorcerous matters began to be pseudonymously attached to him. The most famous text to illustrate this phenomenon is the *Fourth Book of Occult Philosophy*, whose authorship is still disputed by historians:

185 Owen Davies, *Popular Magic: Cunning-folk in English History* (Hambledon Continuum: London, 2007), chapter 5 (Books) and *passim*.

186 For instance, Book of Oberon: 218, 258, 259.

187 Book of Oberon: 385.

188 Sloane 3853, f.112v–114v for instance contains an abridged version of Ch. XXXIII of Book 3; see Grimoire of Arthur Gauntlet: 254.

189 Claude Lacouteux, *High Magic of Amulets and Talismans*, trans. Jon E. Graham (Inner Traditions: Rochester, 2014): 43–44.

Despite bearing an attribution to Heinrich Cornelius Agrippa, the proper authorship of the full volume (a compendium of sorts) remains uncertain. Although the real Agrippa authored an included tract on geomancy, the portion of the volume self-designated as the Fourth Book proper carries no such provenance. Other appendixes are known to be drawn from other sources altogether.[190]

Common opinion holds that even the second of the six tracts on magic that make up the Fourth Book – the eponymous treatise actually titled 'The Fourth Book of Occult Philosophy' – 'is attributed to Agrippa but is probably written by someone else.'[191] The Fourth Book also has the dubious honour of being advertised, in a thoroughly negative but nonetheless alluring light, in King James' own Daemonologie, from which the interested reader could gather that 'if he woulde knowe what are the particuler rites, & curiosities of these black arts (which is both vnnecessarie and perilous,) he will finde it in the fourth book of Cornelius Agrippa, and in VVierus, whomof I spak.'[192] This pronouncement must have done considerable work for the book's reputation and nigromantic appeal.

Jim Baker illustrates the variety of magical practitioners engaging with Agrippa's textual magical legacy, of both actual and pseudonymous works, pointing out even 'simple village and back-street Cunning-Folk' were 'often familiar with Reginald Scot, Agrippa's Three Books and the misattributed Fourth Book.'[193] As far away as the British colonies in North America, cunning folk were being indicted for possessing magical texts attributed to Agrippa. One such rap-sheet from Chester County, Pennsylvania against the Roman brothers, Robert and Phillip Jnr, listed possession of 'Hidon's Temple of Wisdom which teaches geomancy, and Scots Discovery of witchcraft, and Cor-

---

190 Frank Bruckerl, 498 n. 39; cf. Henry Cornelius Agrippa, The Fourth Book of Occult Philosophy, trans. Robert Turner and ed. Donald Tyson (Llewellyn Publications: Woodbury, 2009), 1–3.

191 Fourth Book of Occult Philosophy, ed by Donald Tyson (Llewelyn: Woodbury, 2015): 1.

192 James I, Daemonologie in forme of a dialogue (Edinburgh, 1597), 'The Preface to the Reader.'

193 Jim Baker, The Cunning Man's Handbook: The Practice of English Folk Magic 1550–1900 (Avalonia: London, 2014): 340.

nelias Agrippa's Teaching negromancy.'[194] Needless to say, there is no extant work by that exact title, but this may refer to (some version of) the Fourth Book, by far the more practically 'nigromantic' of Agrippa's works.[195] Indeed, 'the tail-end of pseudo-Agrippa's Fourth Book of Occult Philosophy matches the description provided by the Grand Inquest almost perfectly, and contains explicit directions toward a practice of necromancy.'[196]

The Three Books were employed in practical magical operations, and by a range of practitioners. As Baker remarks, 'one would think Henry Cornelius Agrippa's predominantly scholarly and theoretical Three Books of Occult Philosophy (1651) would have been of less practical value to Cunning-Folk than the Fourth Book, but a copy did turn up in the hands of a poor London Wise Woman named Ann Watts (who also had copies of the Fourth Book and Scot's Discoverie) when she was discovered sleeping rough in the Essex woods in 1687.'[197] Watts was hardly the only practitioner drawing on an 'Agrippa.'

The Three Books were held in high regard by court magician John Dee, and important enough for aristocratic occultists such as John Heydon to crib whole chapters word for word.[198] They were popular too with village wizards and wise women. Owen Davies judges that, 'despite the fact that the Three Books were largely lacking in the practical spells and talismans of use to cunning-folk, its publication must have generated a good deal of interest amongst them and other less well-educated magical practitioners at the time.'[199] It generated not just interest, but practice. What follows is but one example.

In the Three Books' treatment of planetary number squares, or kamea, it is

194 Jon Butler, 'Magic, Astrology, and the Early American Religious Heritage, 1600-1760.' The American Historical Review 84, 2 (1979): 333.

195 See, for instance, David Hackett Fischer, Albion's Seed: Four British Folkways in America (Oxford University Press: New York, 1991): 528.

196 Frank Bruckerl, 'The Quaker Cunning Folk: The Astrology, Magic, and Divination of Philip Roman and Sons in Colonial Chester County, Pennsylvania.' Pennsylvania History: A Journal of Mid-Atlantic Studies 80, no. 4 (Autumn 2013): 488.

197 Baker, Cunning Man's Handbook: 436; Almond, Reginald Scot (2011): 7; Davies, Popular Magic (2003): 126–7.

198 John Heydon, Theomagia (London, 1664), all too passim.

199 Davies, Popular Magic: 122.

outlined that if made during unfavourable conditions – such as during conflicting planetary aspects – they will provoke deleterious effects. Just as the construction of a Venus talisman at a time at which the stars are configured in aspects lending favourable virtues to that exposed talisman can encourage love, one could be built and consecrated during a deleterious aspect to produce hatred and other negative responses.[200]

From an archaeological find, we know these cursing kamea were not merely theoretical:

> We find the deployment of exactly such an early modern lead cursing amulet in Lincoln's Inn in London, bearing a lunar kamea, along with the names and seals of lunar spirits, and the legend: 'That Nothinge maye prosper Nor goe forwarde that Raufe Scrope take the in hande.'[201] Significantly, this charm contains an error in the number square also found in the 1651 'J.F.' translation of Agrippa's *Three Books*, giving us direct evidence that this tome (or at least its manuscript predecessor or offspring) was indeed being used to perform practical, not to mention less than benevolent, works of magic explicitly and expressly involving magical objects.[202]

200 'This being engraven on a Silver plate, Venus being fortunate, procureth concord, endeth strife, procureth the love of women, conduceth to conception, is good against barreness, causeth ability for generation, dissolves enchantments, and causeth peace between man, and woman, and maketh all kind of Animals and Cattle fruitful; and being put into a Dove-house, causeth an increase of Pigeons. It conduceth to the cure of all melancholy distempers, and causeth joyfulness; and being carryed about travellers makes them fortunate. But if it be formed upon Brass with an unfortunate Venus, it causeth contrary things to all that hath bin above said.' Agrippa, *Three Books*: 241.
201 W. Paley Baildon, 'Sixteenth Century Leaden Charm (obverse and reverse) found at Lincoln's Inn.' *Proceedings of the Society of Antiquarians of London*, Second Series, 18, (1901), 146, *passim*.
202 Alexander Cummins, 'Textual Evidence for the Material History of Magic.' *Physical Evidence for Ritual Acts, Sorcery and Witchcraft in Christian Britain: A Feeling for Magic*, ed. Ronald Hutton (Palgrave Macmillan: Basingstoke, 2016): 176. See also Baker, *The Cunning Man's Handbook*: 272–3. This error trail also extends to later manuscript works such as Harley MS. 6482, further emphasising the *Three Books'* influence. See Adam McLean, *A Treatise on Angel Magic* (Weiser: York Beach, 2006): 121.

Agrippan Magic

When considering the influence of Agrippa upon European magic, we should not neglect the impact of his mentor and tutor, Abbot Trithemius. While usually considered in occult discussion primarily for his angelology and/or cryptography, a more fundamental theological conviction should initially be foregrounded as marking a significant aspect of 'Agrippan' magic. As Bruce Gordon summarises: 'breathing the spirit of Christocentric devotion common across northern Europe, Trithemius saw the wisdom of the magi as nothing other than the wisdom of Christ. It was this belief that he passed to his most radical pupil, Cornelius Agrippa.'[203] This principle was certainly employed in Agrippa's meisterwork.

Donald Tyson describes the contribution of the *Three Books* as codifying 'an amalgam of Greek and Roman occultism drawn from classical sources such as Pliny the Elder, Ovid, Virgil, Apuleius, and of course Hermes Trismegistus, as well as later writers such as Ficino; and the medieval Jewish Kabbalah, derived from the writings of Reuchlin and Pico della Mirandola.' Tyson judges that Agrippa was the first occultist to bring together, to 'thoroughly blend and integrate,' these two established and complex traditions of magical theory and practice.[204] In the opinion of Frances Yates, 'the extraordinary strength of the influence of Agrippa's *De occulta philosophia* has not yet been fully realised…It was central not only to the spread of Renaissance magic but also to the reaction against it.'[205] Yates was eager to underline the direct influence of the work upon early modern magical practitioners in both their theory and practice.

Lehrich has argued Agrippa's magic itself can be considered twofold: the elevation and purification of the magus to receive celestial virtues, and the empowerment and ennoblement of the magus to command spirits.[206] Bruce Gordon goes on to suggest, in terms of specifically Agrippan conjuration,

203 Bruce Gordon, 'The Renaissance Angel.' Peter Marshall & Alexandra Walsham (eds.), *Angels in the Early Modern World* (Cambridge University Press: Cambridge, 2006): 60.
204 Agrippa, *Three Books*: xli.
205 Frances Yates, 'Renaissance Philosophers in Elizabethan England: John Dee and Giordano Bruno.' Frances Yates, *Lull & Bruno: Collected Essays, Volume 1* (London: Routledge & Kegan Paul, 1982): 221.
206 Lehrich, *Language of Demons and Angels*: 185.

'the key for Agrippa lay in language.'[207] We might consider these three features the objective, utility, and technique of this particular approach to the magician's arts.

His Black Dog

Some elements of Agrippa's posthumous career as a nigromancer were seeded by events in his life. One such 'fable that enjoyed wide commerce was that Agrippa kept a familiar demon always with him in the form of a black female dog.'[208] Certainly he seems to have loved his dog. Weirus reports 'when Agrippa and I were eating or studying together, this dog always lay between us.'[209] Later, the somewhat enthusiastic demonologist Jean Bodin would sadly interpret this rather sweet domestically collegiate scene as testament that Weirus and Agrippa were homosexual lovers who engaged in bestiality with their dog.[210] Even when not expressly and salaciously slandered so, Tyson also notes that 'From the *Elogia* of Jovius we learn that the collar of the dog was inscribed with magical characters.'[211] So it is that one report of Agrippa's death stated:

> At last, having betaken himself to Lyons, very wretched, and deprived
> of his faculties, he tried all the means that he could to live, waving, as
> dexterously as he could the end of his stick, and yet gained so little, that
> he died in a miserable inn, disgraced and abhorred before all the world,
> which detested him as an accursed and execrable magician, because he
> always carried about with him as his companion a devil in the figure of a
> dog, from whose neck, when he felt death approaching, he removed the
> collar, figured all over with magic characters, and afterwards, being in a
> half-mad state, he drove it from him with these words: 'Go, vile beast, by
> whom I am brought utterly to perdition.' And afterwards this dog, which
> had been so familiar with him, and been his assiduous companion in his
> travels, was no more seen; because, after the command Agrippa gave him,

207 Gordon, 'The Renaissance Angel': 61.
208 Agrippa, *Three Books*: xxxv.
209 Johann Weirus, *De praestigiis daemonum* (Basel, 1563): 2.5.
210 Jean Bodin, *De la démonomanie des sorciers* (Jacques du Puys: Paris, 1580): 219–220.
211 Tyson, *Three Books*: xxxv.

he began to run towards the Saône, where he leapt in, and never came out thence, for which reason it is judged that he was drowned there.[212]

This story is repeated until it becomes the definitive judgement on Agrippa's life and work. After his death, rumours of summoned hell-hounds roaming the countryside began circulating.

CONCLUSIONS

The Visions mark one of the few extant appearances of the ghosts of dead magicians in a scrying record. This is remarkable for several reasons. Scrying journals, as has been previously mentioned, are far rarer than manuscript grimoires. There are at least two reasons for this; firstly, the impulse to collect and shelve a strange tome of symbols and rites is clearly — both historically and in modern times — a far more compelling drive than actually practising magic. Secondly, scrying records stand out as *de facto* evidence of magical practice, which has usually been some shade of illegal. The magical journals that do survive show that their keepers were well aware of the need to keep them secret. Ashmole's magical journals were kept in cipher. Dee burned many of his, and others were only found in *actual secret compartments* of his furniture years after his death. The merchant and astrologer Samuel Jeake, in his own diary, denies making the very astrological elections found later in that diary. Even the rather more legitimate divination records that make up the patient case files of Simon Forman and Richard Napier refuse to record actual prognoses or treatments. Given the instructions on the operative magical significance of secrecy, discussed in our earlier chapter, it makes sense that people were careful with their personal material. Some magicians — and it is nigh impossible to judge how many — seem to have been careful enough to leave little to no trace.

Beyond the importance of the scrying record — let alone one with such visionary depth, novelty, ecology, and mechanics as the Excellent Booke's Visions — the appearance of spirits of (in)famous magicians marks one of the

---

212 M. Thevet, *Portraits et Vies des Hommes Illustres* (Paris, 1584), 2, 543; quoted in Morley: 319. Lehrich, 31 n 77: 'The story first appears in Paolo Giovio, *Elogia doctorum virorum ab avorum memoria publicatis ingenii monumentis illustrium* (Basel, 1577): 236–37; see also Bodin, *De la démonomanie des sorciers*: 20 & 219–21.

most significant early modern records of the transmission of magical authority, legitimacy, and empowerment. The apparitions of these spirits mark the
received text they patronise as significant, at least to its receivers. To Gilbert
and Davis, no less than the very patrons of the art of magic deigned to make
personal appearances and offer their tuition.

Solomon grants them direct authority to command the spirits they
encounter. Furthermore, the King of Wisdom proffers his own service:
'Solomon said that H.G and Jo. should rule him.'[213] It is difficult to overstate
the significance of this. Solomon is the first initiator of the *Excellent Booke*,
appearing in dream to deliver the new prayer that unlocks the rest of the
scrying and conjuring. It is 'Solomon's house' which contains the tree of
crystal within which many, many 'goodly books' can be found.[214] Setting
aside exactly when the majority of Western grimoire magic began being
considered Solomonic, our wise king plays a very much crucial role in the
work of Gilbert and Davis. It is Solomon who directs, counsels and acts as
intermediary; the other Magi assent that 'when Solomon bids you call us, we
will obey.'[215]

Adam, First Magician, is appropriately the first of the assembled council
to offer his instruction, speaking of how to go forth, what taboos and moral
codes to observe, and assuring success if these conditions are observed. One
might, at a stretch, be able to form an association between Adam's instruction to 'go clean in apparel' and an Edenic context, just as one could posit
various egalitarian humanist readings of the garden's classless society – for,
indeed, 'who was then the gentleman?' – from the dictate to 'be good to the
poor.' Similarly, the spectre of Bacon details the black garments they must
wear. We have examined some of the reasons 'why black' in the previous
chapter on Sorcerous Significances, but we are still left pondering if there is a
particular reason Bacon himself might be privileged with particular insight
into such a set of strictures. It is tempting to wonder if there might be some
kind of early modern association between the Friar and such vestments via
the Franciscan orders and congregations who wore black, but such a tempta-

213 Add. MS. 36674. f.59r.
214 Add. MS. 36674. f.59r–v.
215 Add. MS. 36674. f.59v.

tion must also be tempered by commitment to not rationalise the results of spirit contact. What can be said with certainty is that Bacon confirms John's first vision of their black clothing, affirming this initial scene contains operative details relevant to the performance of their magic. Their scrying does not simply grant sight of the spirits, but the future of their interactions with – indeed, authority over – such spirits.

Agrippa does not appear in the first encounter with the majority of these spirits on 24th February. He waits a day, and appears in the second vision in which the assembled shades dispense more direct advice about the proper conjuration procedures. Even without any specific instruction attributed to him, Agrippa's appearance clearly lends great authority to the proceedings.

The tutelary shades foreground features already experienced by the practitioners, performing pedagogy of emphasis as much as direct transmission of bespoke material. As Klaassen has noted, few of their instructions are especially novel or alien to the deeper traditions of 'old dirty' medieval ritual magic. Rather, these ghosts indicate the elements of an emerging practice to which the operators should pay attention. They are more concerned with the conduct of the magicians in their daily lives than the specific designs of their magical circles and the use of tools during ritual. Certainly, specific prayers and shewstone engravings are transmitted, but the incense is merely 'sweet powders and perfumes.' More time is spent detailing what 'colour inks must be had' than detailing exactly which 'good books to call by.' The impression of the wider European conjuration tradition is at once more flexible and more vocational than might be assumed from that given by the closed-system specifics of grimoires such as the *Heptameron*. In following the spirit not the letter, in being a magician not simply in one's oratory but in every waking and dreaming moment, whole books and their understanding can be wrought from the stone.

Good books to call by

SPEECH AND MATERIALITY IN THE NECROMANTIC
WORKINGS OF HUMPHREY GILBERT & JOHN DAVIS

At present, in many fields of the contemporary humanities,
we find discourses arising around sensory ethnography, affect, performa-
tivity, embodiment, cognition and so on. Recently it has been encouraging
to see evidence of such cognitive and subjective approaches being explored
by a number of leading scholars engaged in the study of ritual magic and
Western Esotericism. For example, Edward Bever has explored the relevance
of psychological and cognitive sciences to the study of historical witchcraft
accounts and other cultural magico-religious phenomena,[1] while Frank
Klaassen has written on subjective experience in the practice of medieval
ritual magic, in particular the practice of *Ars Notoria*.[2] Klaassen, following
the work of Tanya Luhrmann, also recounts an exercise in dream incubation that he participated in with his students,[3] an admission that suggests
parallels with the approach to esoteric studies that Arthur Versluis has called
'sympathetic empiricism': an insistence that scholars 'keep the door open'

1 See Edward Bever, 'Current Trends in the Application of Cognitive Science to Magic.'
Magic, Ritual, and Witchcraft 7, No. 1, Summer 2012: 3–18.
2 Frank Klaassen 'Subjective Experience and the Practice of Medieval Ritual Magic.'
Magic, Ritual, and Witchcraft 7, No. 1, Summer 2012: 19–51.
3 Ibid.: 24–26.

also to an experiential understanding of the texts and practices they study[4] – although it should be emphasised that Klaassen is approaching the pedagogical role of experience from a cognitive perspective, rather than assuming any objective spiritual reality underlying the esoteric or magical practices in question. Scholars such Sørensen[5] and Asprem[6] have further undertaken to study the complex web of magical, gnostic and heterodox thoughts and practices that comprise 'Western Esotericism' by proposing methodologies and frameworks derived from the cognitive science of religion (CSR).

With the notion of the 'open door' in mind, the intention of this chapter is to tentatively suggest a framework for exploring the phenomenology of historical necromancy. Particularly, this means entertaining possible approaches that draw upon, and complement, the interdisciplinary nature of the cognitive and subjective turns within the wider study of esotericism and ritual magic. Here we will look at the subjective implications of ritual performance and materiality in the magical records of Sir Humphrey Gilbert, an Elizabethan soldier, adventurer and conjuror, and his scryer John Davis.

TRADITION & INNOVATION
Background to Gilbert's Excellent Booke and Visions

The extant records of Gilbert and Davis' magical experiments are found in two articles of BL Add. MS. 36674, namely the *Excellent Booke of the Arte of Magicke*, beginning on folio 47, and *Certain Strange Visions*, which immediately follows it from folios 57 to 62. The *Excellent Booke* could be called a grimoire of sorts, setting out as it does the conjurations, bonds and dismissals of a number of spirits, including Aosal, Assasel and the four demonic kings of the cardinal points or winds. *Visions*, as the title might suggest, presents a record of visions experienced, primarily by Davis, both prior to and during the composition of the *Excellent Booke*.

---

4 Arthur Versluis, 'Mysticism and the Study of Esotericism: Methods in the Study of Esotericism, Part II.' *Esoterica* 5 (2003): 36.

5 Jesper Sørensen, 'Magic as a State of Mind?: Neurocognitive Theory and Magic in Early Modern Europe.' *Magic, Ritual and Witchcraft* 5, No. 1, Summer 2010: 108–112.

6 Egil Asprem, 'Reverse-engineering "esotericism": how to prepare a complex cultural concept for the cognitive science of religion.' *Religion* 46, Issue 2 (2016): 158–185.

Gilbert, half-brother to Sir Walter Raleigh, was twenty-eight at the time these works were composed and had been serving under the mentorship of Sir Henry Sidney as a captain in the ongoing Tudor conquest of Ireland. Following the rout of Irish chief Shane O'Neil's army, Gilbert returned to England in November 1566 with dispatches for the Queen. In the June of that year, he had also written a navigational treatise on the proposed North-west Passage, the exploitation of which he also hoped the Queen would finance. This plan would eventually culminate in 1576's disastrous Frobisher expedition, with which his acquaintance John Dee is often also associated. An archetypal Renaissance man, one biographer describes him as 'a dreamer, yes and a scholar; but he was [also] a man of action, who on the field of battle could be as brutal, as bloodthirsty, as any personage in history – far more so than most of them,'[7] and '[T]all, well built, with a strong but refined face – a somewhat sad face – weak, dark eyes, dark hair, a soft, short beard inclined to be curly, and a "cholericke" complexion.'[8]

Both Gilbert, and his close companion John Davis, then aged 17, came from Devonshire estates, at Greenway Court and Sandridge Barton respectively, and it seems plausible that the magical experiments of 1567 took place at one of their estates. It is evident from the records that Gilbert and Davis were seeking mastery of the spirits for both metaphysical and material ends, particularly with regard to producing 'secret books.'[9] Yet, unlike Dee and Kelly's later experiments, Gilbert's work is unapologetically grounded in the magic of the late medieval grimoires. In this regard, there are roughly contemporary texts detailing operations for the spirits mentioned by Gilbert and Davis (e.g. Bleth, Assasel, Aosal and the four kings), so it is evident that the pair were developing their work from established textual traditions.[10]

The record of Visions begins on the 24th of February at sunrise. Most of the visions are described as being revealed to John Davis, presumably in a stone, glass or other scrying surface, and – one would assume – being preceded by some form of prayer or ritual, which are unrecorded. We may

---

7 Donald Barr Chidsey, Sir Humphrey Gilbert: Elizabeth's Racketeer (London: Harper Collins. 1932): 2.

8 Barr Chidsey, Sir Humphrey: 40.

9 Add. MS. 36674, f.62r.

10 For example, Folger MS. v.b. 26(a); Add. MS. 36674, f.66r.

suspect that the operations had been occurring prior to the 24th, since elsewhere in the manuscript we find a prayer 'to be said when and before you
deal with any spirit [...] revealed by King Solomon on the 20 February circa
9 – 10 AM,'[11] and the presence of Assasel in the first recorded vision suggests
that he had already been conjured by the pair. This vision describes an encounter with the spirit Assasel and the shades of notable magicians and biblical figures (Solomon, Roger Bacon, Adam and Job). Job declares that they
should 'Trust no spirit visible or invisible, but the spirit of dead men. For
they love man more then the others do.'[12] From the outset, Gilbert's magic
is explicitly demonological and necromantic, but also involves free-flowing
traffic with both infernal spirits and beatific agents, such as biblical figures,
saints and angels.

The *Excellent Booke* was composed approximately one month into the
record that comprises *Visions*, beginning at 8:30 AM on the 22nd of March.
The corresponding entry in *Visions* does not mention this, but relates that
between two and three in the afternoon Gilbert was fiercely engaged in
attempting to constrain the demonic kings, which was interrupted by the
spirit of St Luke who declared that he would instead teach Gilbert 'to have all
things done by the Angels without such cursing, & conjuring by the word &
names of God.'[13] Following the conjurations of the Four Kings in the *Excellent
Booke* we find descriptions of scrying stones said to have been revealed by
Luke. Although Assasel, his inferior Bleth, and the four kings are all mentioned in the *Visions*, the spirit Aosal whose operations are also discussed in
the *Excellent Booke* is not, prompting a consideration of how practical the material in the *Excellent Booke* may actually be: given that the book was recorded
as being begun on the morning of the same day as Gilbert wrestled with the
four kings, and that the spirit Assasel appears in the first recorded vision in
February, it seems likely that a portion of the material had already been for-
mulated by the pair, and perhaps formed a proposed magical syllabus which
was derailed by the visions.

The materials preserved in the *Excellent Booke* and *Visions* present an
important source for the study of ritual magic: within the textual tradition

11 Add. MS. 36674, f.47r.
12 Add. MS. 36674, f.59r.
13 Add. MS. 36674, f.62r.

of grimoire magic, to which the *Excellent Booke* belongs, manuscripts are usually anonymously copied, compiled, or elaborated on in circumstances that are usually unclear. It is rare to have both ritual text and experiential record together, and more so within the tradition of 'old dirty magic': other notable examples are the work of Joan of Morigny (allied to the magical genre of *Ars Notoria*) and John Dee (in the context of angelic magic). In the grimoire tradition, both ritual text and experiential account rarely travel together: regarding the latter, we have, for example, records in the diaries of Forman and Lilly concerning the results of magical conjurations of inferior spirits, but no detailed records of the accompanying procedures. We can also discern in the *poiesis* or making of this grimoire, instances of what Asprem calls *ritual innovation*:[14] Gilbert and Davis are not only drawing from textual sources, but reinterpreting and elaborating upon them as consequence of new knowledge attained from the spirits that attended the crystal at the time of the grimoire's composition (the prayer of Solomon and the glasses of Luke, for example). The visions themselves also operate in a similar area of 'tradition' and 'innovation,' although this is representational rather than textual: incorporating cultural (e.g. biblical and 'magical') personages with more free-flowing visionary elaborations, such as the recurrent vision of a four-sided golden hill[15] and Davis' trips to the 'house of Solomon' to attain magical knowledge.[16]

LINGUISTIC MAGICITY
Ritual and the Centrality of Magical Speech

One distinct feature of Gilbert and Davis' approach to conjuring spirits and provoking visions is its relative simplicity in comparison to earlier ritual magic handbooks such as the *Thesaurus Spirituum* and *Heptameron*. Whereas these texts advocate rituals involving a large amount of paraphernalia and specifics, the only tools advocated in the *Excellent Booke* are the glass, or stone, and 'one or two good books to call by.'[17] There are some moral strictures, such as avoiding drunkenness, being cleanly appareled, honest and willing

14 Asprem, 'Reverse-engineering': 175.
15 Add. MS. 36674, ff. 59v–60v.
16 Add. MS. 36674, f. 59r; f.62v.
17 Add. MS. 36674, f.47v.

to give alms, all of which would seem practicable for a pair of would-be conjurors ensconced in their rural estates. Klaassen suggests that the tempered moral code, which, for example, omits taboos against sex, may be a product of the Protestantisation of the medieval grimoire literature, itself indebted to Catholic exorcistic practices.[18] This may also account for the relatively sparse range of magical paraphernalia, or else this might be indicative of the sources from which Gilbert and Davis drew, which would seem to be a collection of individual operations with the spirits, rather than a comprehensive manual of ritual magic such as those in the *Key of Solomon* genre. As it is, the *Excellent Booke* and *Visions* provide evidence of the subjectively successful employment of ritual magic within a significantly pared-down ritual framework.

Even in this 'bare bones' framework, however, the rituals of spirit conjuration remain one of the most dramatic, and least understood, practices of historical magic. There is a vast body of literature in this genre, but explanations for the popularity of such texts and efficacy of the rituals are often at variance. Gilbert's documents indicate that the procedures *did* work after some manner at least: spirits *were* encountered by Gilbert and Davis in some way, as is recored in the book of visions, but how might we even begin to explore the complex dynamics of such rituals and experiences?

Based on a meta-analysis of definitions of 'magic,' itself a complex and amorphous cultural concept, Stausberg and Otto suggested a catalogue of features that suggest 'patterns of magicity,'[19] rather than attempting a concrete definition of 'magic' itself. Stausberg and Otto suggest the use of subscript indices to deconstruct these patterns and the interactions between them – an approach that Asprem has further associated with Taves' 'building block approach' to preparing complex cultural concepts for the study of the cognitive science of religion.[20] Each 'block' suggests a number of verticalised, interdisciplinary approaches to a particular area of study, integrated within a larger family of concepts or practices.

To begin the work of 'unpacking' or 'reverse engineering' Gilbert's ritual into a series of blocks or indices open to verticalised study, we may draw up

18 Klaassen, 'Ritual Invocation.'

19 Bernd-Christian Otto & Michael Stausberg, 'Introduction' *Defining Magic* (eds. Otto & Stausberg) (Routledge, 2014): 8 – 12.

20 Explicated in terms of esoteric studies in Asprem, 'Reverse-engineering.'

a hypothetical shortlist from Stausberg and Otto's catalogue of features. For example, ritual conjuration is related to the coercion of supernatural agents (M_{AGE}), and as such is a non-legitimate form for dealing with the supernatural. Most vitally, this magic is characterized by the belief in the efficacy of words (M_{WOR}) and performative speech (M_{SPE}), which is itself arguably emotive – or rather, affective (M_{AFF}). Stausberg and Otto omit explicit reference to the provocation of visions and the revelation of spiritual knowledge, which is arguably a node potentially containing a number of other complex concepts, and one that overlaps with similar 'gnostic' experiences in other religious and esoteric contexts. This task of further deconstruction aside, it will be treated here with the index M_{VIS} to denote the visionary, hallucinatory experience of the scryer.

To normalise some of these concepts into a schema of representation, action and event, after Asprem's association of *representation* as esoteric concept, *action* as ritual and *event* as experience,[21] we could describe the essential dynamics of the ritual extant in the *Excellent Booke* in the following scheme:

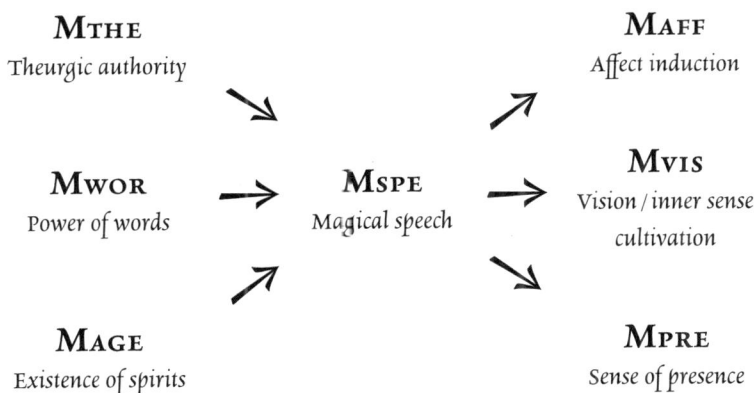

M_{THE}		M_{AFF}
Theurgic authority		Affect induction

M_{WOR} → M_{SPE} → M_{VIS}

M_{WOR}	M_{SPE}	M_{VIS}
Power of words	Magical speech	Vision / inner sense cultivation

M_{AGE}		M_{PRE}
Existence of spirits		Sense of presence

The dynamic scheme of representations, actions and events

21 Asprem, 'Reverse-engineering': 172–76.

On the left hand side of the schematic, the nodes for theurgic authority, the power of words and the existence of supernatural agents (M_{THE}, M_{WOR} & M_{AGE}) are indices that present several forms of *representation* or *metarepresentation* − that is concepts that are considered to be ontologically and epistemologically valid by the practitioners of magical arts. M_{THE} is suggestive of the representation 'God is powerful,' and that appealing to, or partaking in, divine power enables the magus to conjure, constrain and compel spiritual and demonic agents (M_{AGE}), after the model of King Solomon, Saint Cyprian and other beatific historical magi. Such authority is granted through the power of words and rhetoric (M_{WOR}).[22] This relationship between divine authority, supernatural agents and the word can be demonstrated with the following example of a commonly used formula found in Gilbert's work: 'O Lord be my help and assistance that I may, *by thy power, call him, and not by my own power*' (italics added for emphasis).[23] Sources for these notions can be historically traced to theological and philosophical discourses, notably the confluence of Neoplatonism, medieval ritual magic, Byzantine demonology (after Psellus) and Catholic exorcism rituals that typify work of the ritual magic genre. In complement to this, Asprem suggests we might investigate concepts such as minimally counterintuitive (MCI) theory to also explain the cognitive and cultural mechanisms behind the proliferation of such beliefs,[24] which may also help us explore narratives relating to the intentions of collectors and copyists of magical texts.[25]

Speech (M_{SPE}): Magical speech, or conjuration, is the chief mode of ritual *action* in Gilbert's text. Such speech, in the form of prayer, conjurations and constraints addressed to both God and the spirits is a verbal articulation of the representations expressed above. Such speech is rhetorical and perform-

22 On this subject, see also William A. Covino, 'Magic and/as Rhetoric: Outlines of a History of Phantasy.' *The Journal of Advanced Composition* 12, No. 2 (Fall 1992): 349−358.

23 Add. MS. 36674, f.49r.

24 Asprem, 'Reverse-engineering': 173−74.

25 For a summary of cultural, social and philosophical issues relating to the production of texts of 'learned magic,' see Benedek Láng, *Unlocked Books: Manuscripts of Learned Magic in the Medieval Libraries of Central Europe* (Pennsylvania State University Press, 2008): 265−74.

ative: it is uttered to *make things happen*.[26] The language of magical speech, as recorded in the texts of ritual magic, is often highly formulaic, based on appeals to the divine (e.g. God, angels, saints, holy names) in order to command supernatural agents.

Affect (M_{AFF}): Kieckhefer proposes that the general structure of ritual conjurations can be expressed by four types of statement,[27] for example:

> [**declaration:**] I conjure [**address:**] you demons [**invocation:**] by the power of the divine majesty [**instruction:**] that you should come without delay.

Certainly, many of the spoken formulae in Gilbert's work can be deconstructed after Kieckhefer, but with the subjective effects of the performance of such words in mind, we could also consider the particular *voices* found in the speeches of the *Excellent Booke*. For each of the three operations of the spirits (Assasel, Aosal and Oriens), we are generally presented with four distinct forms of magical speech: prayer, conjuration, sentence and bond. The bond marks the culmination of the ritual: it is associated with urging the spirit to remain in the stone until dismissed. The other forms of ritual speech, however, suggest the manifestation of particular affective states adjunct to their role within the ritual dynamic. Most simply, we may examine such speeches from a standpoint of 'valence,' or positive and negative affect. The 'voices' suggested in these speeches may be termed abnegative, authoritative and maledictive:

Prayer (abnegative)

Preceding the call to the spirit, each operation commences with a prayer, which emphasises the relationship between the magus and divine power through the language of religious humility. Gilbert declares that such calls should be 'said with a good heart,'[28] and a typical pronouncement begins:

26   See Covino 'Magic'; Filomena Vasconcelos, 'Occult Philosophy and the Philosophy of Language in Renaissance Europe and Elisabethan England' *Revista da Faculdade de Letras*, II Serie, vol. XXI (2004): 199–208.

27   Richard Kieckhefer, *Forbidden Rites: A Necromancer's Manual of the Fifteenth Century* (Penn State University Press: University Park, 1998): 126–153.

28   Add. MS. 36674, f.49r.

I, most wretched sinner, do desire thee to be my help that this spirit Assasel, may now come and fulfil my will. O Lord be my help and assistance that I may, by thy power, call him, and not by my own power.[29]

Conjuration (authoritative)

The tone of voice that follows the prayer is authoritative or coercive. It is addressed to the spirit itself, with appeals to divine power to compel it. Unlike the preceding prayer, Gilbert's conjurations can easily be deconstructed using Kieckhefer's typology. At variance from earlier ritual texts is the relative lack of magical words of invocation – they are not entirely absent, but they are used sparingly, perhaps indicative of Gilbert's Protestantisation and humanisation of medieval ritual magic. A typical conjuratory form follows the abovementioned prayer:

O thou spirit Assasel, which art a living and loving spirit to the commandments of God, I charge thee in the name of Jesus Christ, that thou do appear here visibly to my Skryer, here without any delay. I conjure and command thee, and by God's power constrain thee that thou do appear here, and do my commandments without any more stay.[30]

Sentence (maledictive)

Finally, if the spirit does not appear, a sentence, or curse is delivered. The voice here is maledictive, brimming with fury directed toward the obstinate spirit. Evidently, such a mode of declamation accorded with Gilbert's 'choleric' character and military background. In the diary of *Visions*, we find mention of Gilbert 'cursing, depriving & condemning of the Four Kings and Bleth for their disobediences.'[31] An exemplar of this form of speech can be found on f.49v:

O thou spirit Assasel, who hast been taken for a noble spirit and king, and [yet] I cannot find it in thee, by thy disobeying of God's word: Therefore I shall do as art wills me. O thou wicked and rebellious spirit, that rebels against God's power, I, by

29 Add. MS. 36674, f.49r.
30 Add. MS. 36674, ff.49r–v.
31 Add. MS. 36674, f.62r.

God's power, accurse thee and excommunicate thee, and deprive thee and condemn thee for thy disobedience.

The passage between abnegative, authoritative and maledictive pronouncements informs the flow of the ritual itself: the action of magical speech precipitates the affective event altering the mood and physiology of both the master and, hopefully, his scryer.

Vision (M$_{VIS}$)

The manifestation of the spirit, or the apprehension of a vision, within a 'stone' is the intended outcome of rehearsing the prayers, conjurations and sentences that comprise the ritual. The physical dimensions of Gilbert's 'stone' are not fully explained in the text, but it is evident that it is flat on both sides and 'of a good thickness' and clear.[32] This flat 'stone' was evidently moveable, being set into or on the wall[33] or otherwise placed on a pedestal[34] as part of the scrying process, or placed upon a book in order for the spirit to swear an oath.[35] The production of visions and attendant altered states of consciousness is a complex field. We do not know the dimensions of Gilbert's stone, but, set into a wall, or in a dim, candle-lit chamber, it would have taken on subtly reflective qualities. Psychological experiments with participants gazing at their own reflections in low illumination environments yield the swift onset of often radical 'facial distortions,'[36] a technique that has also been exploited by at least one contemporary Western ritual magician working in the necromantic tradition.[37] In healthy subjects such distortions are mildly dissociative, but are violently so to schizophrenics, who often experience multiple facial images in the mirror, along with a profound sense of 'otherness' associated with the distortions. This perhaps prompts a consideration of the role of personal schizotypal traits within the act of

32 Add. MS. 36674, f.56r.
33 Add. MS. 36674, f.48r.
34 Add. MS. 36674, f.55r.
35 Add. MS. 36674, f.49v.
36 For an example of mirror-gazing in a psychotherapeutic setting, see Giovanni B. Caputo, 'Archetypal-Imaging and Mirror-Gazing.' *Behavioral Sciences* 4 (2014): 1–13.
37 Carroll 'Poke' Runyon, *The Book of Solomon's Magick* (CHS Inc., Silverado: 1996).

scrying (on the assumption that the scryer in this case was more than an imaginative fraud), as well as the role of what Noll has called 'image cultivation'[38] or Luhrmann 'inner sense cultivation,'[39] the latter of which explores the gradual development of a more intuitive, inner sense of imagery, but one which, here, often phenomenologically blurs the boundaries of 'real' and 'imagined.' That this might be the case is suggested by the gradual manner in which, according to the diary of *Visions*, after three weeks of practice, Gilbert himself also begins to discern spirits both within and without the glass. It is evident that the spectrum of hallucination and pseudo-hallucination ranges from convincing exterior representations, to profound non-veridical, interior representations. There may be precedents for supposing that much of what occurs on this spectrum could be interpreted as spiritual communication. Likely drawing upon the demonic theology of Psellus, Cornelius Agrippa, the key point of orientation for Renaissance magic, describes the language of angels and spirits in ways that resonate with inner sense cultivation and 'interpretive drift,' describing it as a form of communication that slides 'into the hearer without any noise, as an image in the eye, or glass. So souls going out of the body, so Angels, so Demons speak: and what man doth with a sensible voice, they do by impressing the conception of the speech in those to whom they speak, *after a better manner* than if they should express it by an audible voice.' (Italics added for emphasis).[40]

Presence (M_{PRE})

It is evident from the text that spirits could be somehow discerned even if they were not visible to the master or his scryer. Gilbert provides several methods by which a spirit 'invisible in any stone' might be compelled to appear. Additionally, given the sense of dissociation that, for example, mirror-gazing experiments yield, it could be suggested that the psychological phenomenon of the sensed presence is an important part of the ritual dynamic. Persinger has suggested correlations between increased sensed

38 Richard Noll, 'Mental Imagery Cultivation as a Cultural Phenomenon: The Role of Visions in Shamanism.' *Current Anthropology* 26, No. 4 (Aug.–Oct., 1985): 443–461.
39 Cited in Ann Taves & Egil Asprem, 'Experience as Event: Event Cognition and the Study of (Religious) Experiences.' *Religion, Brian & Behaviour* (2015): 21–24.
40 Heinrich Cornelius Agrippa, *Three Books of Occult Philosophy* (London, 1651): III.xxiii.

presence experience and meditational practice,[41] and Cheyne with the hypnagogic and hypnopompic hallucinations associated with sleep paralysis.[42] Cheyne associates the sensed presence with low-level cognitive threat detection mechanisms, and the subsequent hallucinations as deriving from 'interpretive efforts to find, identify and elaborate source of threat.'[43] Interestingly, with regard to both visual distortions and sense of presence, the ritual magic practitioner Runyon also claims that facial distortion works for all people, but self-hypnosis techniques are necessary to further control the flow of imagery,[44] and he also cites the 'undeniable sense of alien presence' as the hallmark of a successful evocation.[45] It is such a sense of presence – of another manifest and individual entity – that may set the experience of ritual evocation apart from other forms of visionary provocation such as the beatific vision of *Liber Juratus*.

To return to the original scheme proposed for the ritual, it can be observed that the events stemming from the ritual action of speech (e.g. affect, vision and presence) are loose analogues of the representational concepts that inform them. That is to say, that affect is the manifestation of the theurgical relationship between the master and the divine: the master variously prostrates himself before God, and later invokes divine authority to compel the spirits, performing the representation of divine power and the human relation to it. If the unfolding of a vision is considered to be the language in which disembodied souls speak, it can be seen as a reflection of the 'essential' and transcendent nature of language – one that flows from soul to soul without need of speech. Finally the 'others,' the demons or supernatural agents, make themselves known by their sense of presence.

The indices contained in the dynamic schema suggest manifold approaches and research methodologies for the study of ritual magic, such as the

41   M. A. Persinger, 'Enhanced Incidence of "The Sensed Presence" in People Who Have Learned to Meditate: Support for the Right Hemispheric Intrusion Hypothesis.' *Perceptual and Motor Skills* 75, Issue 3 (1992): 1308–1310.

42   J. A. Cheyne 'The Omincus Numincus: Sensed Presence and "Other" Hallucinations.' *Journal of Consciousness Studies* 8, No. 5–7 (2001): 133–50.

43   Cheyne, 'Ominous': 144

44   Runyon, 'Magick': 13.

45   Runyon, 'Magick': 131–2.

exploration of the affect of ritual declamation on those assuming roles of 'master' and 'scryer.' Klaassen has suggested that the incantations of ritual magic function as loose 'visionary scripts,'[46] a position that makes even more sense when ritual magic is considered as a master and scryer relationship. The dynamic between the master, variously prostrating himself, commanding spirits and venting his anger at them, while the scryer sits and awaits the reception of the spirit may also suggest complex interactions between psychological states triggered by the overdrive of proposed ergotropic (arousal) and trophotropic (relaxation) systems, each of which is said to trigger the other complementary system to yield what Bever describes as a 'hybrid physiological state and state of consciousness characterised by some features of sleeping and some features of waking.'[47]

BOOKS TO CALL BY
The Materiality of Ritual and Knowledge

The material culture of ritual magic – such as the book of conjurations, the crystal stone and other paraphernalia – inhabits the same conceptual space as ritual actions: they are physical manifestations of magical representations (e.g. the power of words and prayer in book form), and they are either integral to ritual action (e.g. reading from the book), or become the focus of subsequent events (e.g. the stone playing host to the unfolding of visions).

The book in particular is an important symbol in the work of Gilbert and Davis. As we have seen, a 'good book to call by' is the chief driver of ritual action. Yet there is also the mention of a second book in the text, upon which spirits are made to swear their fidelity to the master.[48] This invokes the concept of the *Liber Spirituum*, prominently mentioned in the *Fourth Book of Occult Philosophy* attributed to Agrippa. Of interest is the method by which the spirit is made to swear on the book: the stone, into which the spirit has been conjured, is placed upon the book itself. The actions performed with the stone, and the language used to describe these, indicate to us how the stone – and the 'materiality' of the immaterial 'spirit' – were conceived of by Gilbert and Davis: they seem to believe that the conjuring of a spirit into

46 Klaassen, 'Subject Experience': 39–44.
47 Bever, 'Current Trends': 14.
48 Add. MS. 36674, f.49v.

the stone imprisons it within a physical object. Hence the bindings into the stone (e.g. 'not to depart until thou be licensed by me'[49]), and more tellingly the methods by which the obstinate spirit is punished, such as by putting the stone into the 'stinking water, either of man or woman [...] and straightly command[ing] him to come forth out of the stone into the water that you did put him in, and there to tarry, until you do command him to come into the stone again.'[50] The glass gives the spirit conjured into it a physical locus, not unlike a prison, from which only the master can release it. With further regard to the blurring of spiritual and material in this area, Gilbert suggests, following a revelation by St Luke, that there are two forms of glass: consecrated ones, suitable for calling angels, and unconsecrated ones in which to call inferior spirits.[51]

The symbolic nature of the book itself is also evidently potent to Gilbert and Davis. Within the ritual it confers the authority to call spirits upon the magus, while the Liber Spirituum further ensures that spirits are bound by contracts to the master. Yet, books also appear prominently in the visions: the first vision mentions Davis seeing himself carrying 'a book covered with a skin, the hairy side outward,' which gives him power over an assembly of spirits.[52] The second vision mentions a house, in which there is a crystal tree, with a door inside it containing both the aforementioned book and one with a crystal cover, amongst others[53] – the larger number of the recorded visions mention books or the production of books by the spirits, culminating in the final entry on the 6th of April that claims Davis 'went to Solomon's house in the morning, and came home to me again about nine of the clock in the forenoon, and brought me from there a book written by Saint Luke the Evangelist.'[54]

Like Forman, who dreamed of 'strang bockes brought me writen in Karactes,'[55] Gilbert and Davis were fixated on the materialisation of spiritual

49 Add. MS. 36674, f.49v.
50 Add. MS. 36674, f.48v–49r.
51 Add. MS. 36674, f.56v.
52 Add. MS. 36674, f.59r.
53 Add. MS. 36674, ff.59r–v.
54 Add. MS. 36674, f.62v.
55 Barbara Traister, *The Notorious Astrological Physician of London: Works and Days of Simon*

knowledge and power in book form, perhaps best summarised in the form of the prayer that precedes the *Excellent Booke*, said to have been delivered to the pair by King Solomon himself. This prayer evidently suggests an alignment of Gilbert's aims with those traditionally associated with the *Ars Notoria*, a system of medieval prayer and ritual for attaining knowledge of the liberal arts, and clearly articulates Gilbert and Davis' intentions in their necromantic rituals: 'to thy glory O God; for learning is all my desire, Lord thou knowest even as it was to thy servant Solomon. O Lord send me some of his good hidden work, that has not been revealed to any man. Then for that cause I desire thee O God to send it to me, that in these our last days it may be known.'[56]

The Realities of Necromancy: Conclusions

The work of Gilbert and Davis had received comparatively little interest until recently, with the publication of Klaassen's own paper on Gilbert and his magical experiments.[57] Yet the documents are compelling and potentially vital for the insight they give us into the processes of composing ritual magic texts and initiating visionary experiences. The circumstances surrounding the composition of the *Excellent Booke* and *Visions* can all be seen to relate to the six speculative areas of practice that Klaassen has elsewhere suggested may be vital to the successful subjective experience of magic.[58] These are summarised and contextualised below:

1. *Psychological and epistemological acclimatisation*

Klaassen suggests that practitioners of medieval magic, from which the *Excellent Booke* descends, 'learn' to make magic work, and that a shift to the more associative forms of thought associated with magical experience also trains the practitioner's nervous system to 'bring about experiences ranging from

Forman (University of Chicago Press: Chicago, 2001): 122.

56 Add. MS. 36674, f.47r.

57 Frank Klaassen, 'Ritual Invocation and Early Modern Science: The Skrying Experiments of Humphrey Gilbert.' *Invoking Angels: Theurgic Ideas and Practices, Thirteenth to Sixteenth Centuries* (Edited by Claire Fanger. Pennsylvania State University Press: University Park, 2012): 341–366.

58 Klaassen, 'Subjective Experience': 32–48.

well-being and a sense of spiritual presence, to full-blown auditory or visual hallucinations.'[59] The individual amenability to such training would depend on a wide range of cultural, social and psychological factors, but it seems that – as scryer – John Davis was able to rapidly acclimatise himself in such a way. Such an 'interpretive drift' was also evidently experienced by Gilbert himself: as the experiments progressed the magic began to 'work,' opening him to hallucinatory experiences guided by a form of magical, loosely associated thinking.

2. Re-orderings of time and space
As with religious ceremony or spiritual disciplines, the practices of ritual magic involve a conscious re-ordering of time and space. For Gilbert and Davis, sunrise and sunset became the temporal foci for their workings, and evidently this occurred in a dedicated space.

3. Social isolation
Related to the second point, Gilbert and Davis evidently practiced at a location which provided appropriate seclusion from the outside world. One can almost imagine the affective qualities of travelling to the place of working in the gloomy hour before sunrise, a sense of excitement and trepidation welling up with regard to what the spirits might have in store. After around three weeks of practice, the effect inspired by the magical atmosphere, the use of place and time, and the duration of the sessions becomes apparent, with Gilbert recording a number of uncanny experiences with spirits occurring in the afternoons following the pair's sunrise conjurations.

4. Asceticism, abstinence and sensuality
Although there are no explicit admonishments relating to sexuality in the text, a moral code is prescribed, involving the master leaving 'swearing and all drunken company,' as well as being cleanly attired, not breaking promises, and giving alms to the poor. Klaassen observes that the 'regulation of morality appears to have the short-term effect of ego-depletion, a logical and

---

59 Klaassen, 'Subjective Experience': 32.

potentially positive element in a larger program of contemplative exercises.'[60]

5. *Prayer, incantation, visualisation and intent*

We have already mentioned Klaassen's suggestion of conjurations playing the part of suggestive 'visionary scripts' as part of the master-scryer dynamic. We may also point out that the duration of each operation was likely several hours, given that sunrise was around 6AM and Gilbert often describes riding home in the afternoon following the morning sessions. One can only imagine how repetitively the ritual drama of the conjurations was rehearsed. The intent is also encoded in the language of the conjurations, but the whole structure of the operation – from the isolated location, moral strictures and re-orderings of time and space, also serve to fix the mind on the intent of the rituals and subsequently to facilitate the necessary circumstances for the drift to associative thought and subsequent re-orientation of the nervous system.

6. *Reading, contemplation, and the* Ars Notoria

Klaassen's paper concentrates more on the role of reading in the *Ars Notoria* and the mental effort connected with reading aloud the *verba ignota*, or magical words, as well as the cognitive challenge of reading rotated scripts. Given that the conjurations used by Gilbert were the product of a Protestant outlook, and use little in the way of *verba ignota*, we have concentrated here on the affective nature of reading aloud – particularly with relation to the notion of the visionary script.

The areas of practice highlighted by Klaassen are helpful with regard to further perceiving the contexts surrounding the rituals themselves, but should not be considered as an exhaustive illustration of the psychological implications of magical practice. They are illustrative examples, and perhaps could be further explored through the concept of patterns of magicity, which we have already used to propose some theoretical readings concerning the core of Gilbert's ritual procedure itself.

---

60 Klaassen, 'Subjective Experience': 39.

Throughout the work, it has been evident that the master and scryer worked together to co-produce both text and visionary experience. Reading entries in Visions, such as Gilbert's encounter with a great brended dog, which seem to occur outside the glass, we can discern the implications of associative thought and ritually-induced altered states of consciousness as they linger beyond the confines of ritual chamber. Such accounts also demonstrate the way in which these events, visions, and intuitions are explained through magical epistemology. For example, Gilbert writes:

> And then I turned my horse and my skryer turned his horse also, and galloped towards him, and when I met him, he would needs have pressed upon me and my skryer. And then I said to him, 'O thou wicked & rebellious spirit, I charge thee to stand.' And for all that he would needs have come upon me. And then I said: 'O thou wicked & rebellious spirit, God confound thee.' Speaking which words I drew out my dagger & cast toward him; and then he ran away & suddenly vanished out of my sight. I knew not how. All these dogs, birds & white glimpses, with the cony and wings were spirits, as I after proved by the spirit of Solomon.[61]

These events, on the 15th of March, mark the point in the diary in which the visions seem to escape the perimeter of the crystal and seemingly become part of Gilbert's waking reality. He writes of strange dog-like creatures with 'small legs, and great horse feet,' and birds, both headless and long-necked, whose flight paths seem somehow portentous.[62] These are all interpreted later to be spirits and angels in animal form: a sort of occult ecopoetics, suggesting Gilbert himself had succumbed to some sort of 'enchanted' perception of his environs or altered state of consciousness: the culmination of his own psychological and epistemological acclimatisation. Gilbert's appraisal of rabbits and birds as spirits also suggests parallels with Taves and Asprem's exploration of the relationship between the cognitive 'working model,' memory and emergent event narratives.[63] Furthermore, the intentional shift

61 Add. MS. 36674, f.61v.
62 Add. MS. 36674, f.61r.
63 Ann Taves & Egil Asprem, 'Experience as Event: Event Cognition and the Study of (Religious) Experiences.' Religion, Brain, & Behaviour 7, Issue 1 (2017): 43–62.

to associative epistemologies and the co-creation of such enchanted narratives is reminiscent of contemporary practices such as 'psychic questing' and 'legend tripping.'

Although many aspects of the *Excellent Booke* and *Visions* remain obscure, what is clear is that the texts help to deepen our understanding of one of the most contested areas of ritual magic, viz. the conjuration of, and encounters with, angels, spirits, ghosts and demons. Yet, we are also left with an incomplete record, particularly given the abrupt end of the *Visions* diary. It may have been the case that such visions and enchantments were, ultimately, all too subjective for Gilbert and Davis to continue their experiments: the procedures detailed in the *Excellent Booke* evidently show that the pair expected the spirits to be able to perform such feats as fetching a ring from water and laying it into the hands of the master. However, in practice, as Gilbert cursed the spirits for their obstinance, another spirit would appear with promises of another book or spirit to be conferred with. It is evident that the visions were compelling and lucid, yet it seems probable that the 'unwillingness' of spirits to act more assertively on the physical plane led to the abandonment of the work. Nevertheless, what the *Excellent Booke* and *Visions* present us with is an insight into the life-cycle of a magical text and one in which, unlike the greater body of ritual literature, we know something of the characters involved. A critical reading of Gilbert's texts and an appreciation of dynamics of ritual through the concept of patterns of magicity and the related building block-style approach perhaps indicate some ways in which Asprem's proposed interdisciplinary 'verticalised' approach might be applied to explore the historical practice of magic. Furthermore, the 'bare-bones' of Gilbert and Davis' ritual may perhaps prompt a consideration for where practice-based (e.g. performative) and experiential modes of research might also fit within such verticalised, cognitively-orientated explorations of the esoteric and extraordinary in order to further illuminate the dimensions of 'magical consciousness.' These observations are, of course, tentative, but should also not be discounted as 'mere reduction' by those invested in the practice of ritual magic: rather, they uphold to some degree the integral efficacy of ritual magic procedures, and may also help to focus practitioners on developing more effective – and affective – modes of practice.

Bibliography

PRIMARY SOURCES

Bodleian Library, MS. Ballard 66.
Bodleian, MS. Rawlinson D. 252.
British Library, MS. Additional 10862.
British Library, MS. Additional 36674.
British Library, MS. Ashmole 802.
British Library, MS. Ashmole 1491.
British Library, MS. Ashmole 1790.
British Library, MS. Sloane 3188.
British Library, MS. Sloane 3822.
British Library, MS. Sloane 3847.
British Library, MS. Sloane 3884.
Case MS. 5017.
Folger Shakespeare Library MS.v.b. 26(a).
National Archives of Scotland, record GD188/25/1/3 (photocopy of material from the Guthrie archive).

Ady, Thomas. *A Candle in the Dark*. London, 1655.
Agrippa, Heinrich Cornelius. *Three Books of Occult Philosophy*. London, 1651.
———. *The Vanity of Arts and Sciences*. London, 1676.
Ars Notoria. Trans. Robert Turner. London, 1656.
Aubrey, John. *Miscellanies*. London, 1696.

The Autobiography and Personal Diary of Dr Simon Forman. Ed. James Orchard Halliwell. London, 1849.

Bodin, Jean. *De la démonomancie des sorciers*. Jacques du Puys: Paris, 1580

Book of Oberon. Eds. Daniel Harms, James R. Clark, & Joseph H. Peterson. Llewellyn: Woodbury, 2015.

The Book of Treasure Spirits. Ed. David Rankine. Avalonia: London, 2009.

Bostocke, Robert. *Auncient Phisicke*. London, 1585.

Burton, Robert. *Anatomy of Melancholy*. London, 1623.

Casaubon, Meric. *A Treatise Proving Spirits, Witches, and Supernatural Operations*. London, 1672.

————. *True and Faithful Relation of What passed for many Yeers Between Dr John Dee...and Some Spirits*. London, 1659.

Chaucer, Geoffrey. *The Parson's Tale*, 37, in Walter William Skeat (ed.), *The Complete Works of Geoffrey Chaucer*. Clarendon Press: Oxford, 1900.

The Commonplace Book of Robert Reynes of Acle: An Edition of Tanner MS. 407. Ed. Cameron Louis. Garland: New York, 1980.

The Complete Grimoire of Honorious. Eds. David Rankine & Paul Harry Barron. London: Avalonia, 2013.

Coxe, Francis. *A short treatise declaringe the detestable wickednesse, of magicall sciences as necro-mancie. coniurations of spirites, curiouse astrologie and such lyke*. 1561.

Crouch, Humphrey. *England's jests refin'd and improv'd being a choice collection of the merriest jests*. 1687.

Dixon, Robert. *Canidia, or, The witches a rhapsody*. London, 1683.

Ficino, Marsilio. *Three Books on Life*. Trans. Carol Kaske & John R. Clark. Tempe, 1998.

Foreman, Paul. *The Cambridge Book of Magic: A Tudor necromancer's manual*. Ed. Francis Young. Texts in Early Modern Magic: Cambridge, 2015.

Fourth Book of Occult Philosophy. Trans. Robert Turner. London, 1665.

Frier Bacon his discovery of the miracles of art, nature, and magick faithfully translated out of Dr. Dees own copy by T.M. and never before in English. London, 1659.

Gerard, John. *Great Herball, or, Generall Historie of Plantes*. London, 1597.

Glanvill, Joseph. *The Vanity of Dogmatising*. London, 1661.

The Grimoire of Arthur Gauntlet. Ed. David Rankine. Avalonia: London, 2011.

Harvey, Gabriel. *Three Proper and Witty Familiar Letters*. H. Bynneman: London, 1580.

————. *Pierce's Supererogation, or A New Praise of the Old Ass, from the edition of 1593*. T. Davidson: London, 1815.

Hazlitt, William (trans.). *The Table Talk of Martin Luther*. London, 1848.

van Helmont, Jean-Baptiste. *Oriatrike*. London, 1662.

Heydon, Christopher. *A Defence of Judiciall Astrologie*. Cambridge, 1603.

Heydon, John. *Theomagia*. London, 1664.

Holland, Henry. *A Treatise Against VVitchcraft*. London, 1590.

James I. *Daemonologie in forme of a dialogue.* Edinburgh, 1597.

Lilly, William. *History of his Life and Times.* London, 1715.

Loredano, Giovanno. *The life of Adam. Written in Italian by Giovanno Francesco Loredano, a Venetian noble-man. And renderd into English by J.S.* London, 1659.

Milles, Thomas. *A Treasurie of Auncient and Moderne Times.* London, 1613 – 19.

The Mirror of Alchimy. London, 1597.

Naudé, Gabriel. *The history of magick by way of apology, for all the wise men who have unjustly been reputed magicians, from the Creation to the present age.* London, 1657.

The Opus Majus of Roger Bacon. Ed. John Henry Bridges. Clarendon Press: Oxford, 1897 – 1900.

Paracelsus. *Selected Writings.* Ed. Jolande [Székács] Jacobi. Princeton University Press: Princeton, 1951.

Parkinson, John. *Paradisi in Sole.* London, 1629.

Peterson, Joseph H. (ed.) *John Dee's Five Books of Mystery: Original Sourcebook of Enochian Magic.* Weiser: York Beach, 2003.

———. *Liber Juratus, or the Sworne Booke of Honorius.* Ed. Sarah Kane French, 2008.

———. (ed.) "The Key of Knowledge (Clavicula Salomonis)" Esoteric Archives website (accessed August 14, 2012, http://esotericarchives.com/solomon/ad36674.htm).

Picatrix: Atratus. Eds. John Michael Greer & Christopher Warnock. Adocentyn Press: 2010.

Pordage, Samuel. *Mundorum Explicatio.* London, 1661.

Rome's Rarities, or, The Pope's cabinet unlock'd and exposed to view. 1684.

Scot, Reginald. *Discoverie of Witchcraft.* London, 1584: 1665.

The Second Volume Conteinyng those Statutes whiche haue ben made in the Tyme of the Most Victorious Reigne of Kynge Henrie the Eight. London, 1543.

Shakespeare, William. *The tragicall historie of Hamlet.* London, 1603.

Weemse, John. *The Portraiture of the Image of God in Man.* London, 1627.

Weirus, Johann. *De praestigiis daemonum.* Basel, 1563.

Westmacott, William. *Theolobotonologia.* London, 1694.

SECONDARY SOURCES

Almond, Philip C. *Adam and Eve in Seventeenth-century Thought.* Cambridge University Press: Cambridge, 1999.

———. *England's First Demonologist.* I.B. Taurus: New York, 2014.

Asprem, Egil. 'Reverse-engineering 'esotericism': how to prepare a complex cultural concept for the cognitive science of religion.' *Religion* 46, 2015: 158 – 185.

Baildon, W. Paley. 'Sixteenth Century Leaden Charm (obverse and reverse) found at Lincoln's Inn.' *Proceedings of the Society of Antiquarians of London,* Second Series, 18, 1901.

Besterman, Theodore. *Crystalgazing: A Study in the History, Distribution, Theory and Practice of Scrying.* W. Rider & Son: London, 1924.

Bever, Edward. 'Current Trends in the Application of Cognitive Science to Magic.' *Magic, Ritual, and Witchcraft* 7, No. 1, Summer 2012: 3–18.

Borchardt, Frank L. 'Magus as Renaissance Man.' *The Sixteenth Century Journal* 21, 1, Spring, 1990.

Brann, N.L. *The Debate over the Origin of Genius during the Italian Renaissance: The Theories of Supernatural Frenzy and Natural Melancholy in Accord and in Conflict on the Threshold of the Scientific Revolution.* Leiden: Brill, 2002.

Bruckerl, Frank. 'The Quaker Cunning Folk: The Astrology, Magic, and Divination of Philip Roman and Sons in Colonial Chester County, Pennsylvania.' *Pennsylvania History: A Journal of Mid-Atlantic Studies* 80, No. 4, Autumn 2013.

Burnett, Charles. *Magic and Divination in the Middle Ages.* Aldershot: Variorum, 1996.

Busch, Peter. 'The Testament of Solomon in its Cultural Setting.' Joseph Verheyden (ed.), *The Figure of Solomon in Jewish, Christian and Islamic Tradition. King, Sage and Architect.* Brill: Leiden, 2012.

Butler, Jon. 'Magic, Astrology, and the Early American Religious Heritage, 1600–1760.' *The American Historical Review* 84, 2, 1979.

CAPUTO, GIOVANNI B. 'Archetypal-Image and Mirror-Gazing.' *Behavioral Sciences* 4, 2014: 1–13.

Catalogue of the Valuable and Extensive Library of Printed Books and Illuminated & Other Important Manuscripts of the Late Henry White, Esq. J.P. D.L. F.S.A. Etc. (Of 30, Queen's Gate, W.). Sotheby, Wilkinson & Hodge: London, 1902.

Cheyne, J.A. 'The Ominous Numinous: Sensed Presence and "Other" Hallucinations.' *Journal of Consciousness Studies* 8, No. 5–7, 2001: 133–150.

Chidsey, Donald Barr. *Sir Humphrey Gilbert: Elizabeth's Racketeer.* Harper Collins: London, 1932.

Clark, Stuart. *Vanities of the Eye.* Oxford University Press: Oxford, 2007.

Clucas, Stephen. 'John Dee's Angelic Conversations and the *Ars Notoria*: Renaissance Magic and Medieval Theurgy.' Stephen Clucas (ed.), *John Dee: Interdisciplinary Studies in English Renaissance Thought.* Springer: Dordrecht, 2006.

Clulee, Nicholas H. *John Dee's Natural Philosophy: Between Science and Religion.* Routledge: London, 1988.

Coles, William. *Adam in Eden.* London, 1657.

Covino, William A. 'Magic and/as Rhetoric: Outlines of a History of Phantasy.' *The Journal of Advanced Composition* 12, No. 2, Fall 1992: 349–358.

Crowley, T. *Roger Bacon: The Problem of the Soul in his Philosophical Commentaries.* Editions de l'Institut supérieur de philosophie: Louvain, 1950.

Cummins, Alexander. 'Textual Evidence for the Material History of Magic.' Ronald Hutton (ed.), *Physical Evidence for Ritual Acts, Sorcery and Witchcraft in Christian Britain: A Feeling for Magic.* Palgrave Macmillan: Basingstoke, 2016.

Daiches, Samuel. *Babylonian Oil Magic in the Talmud and in the Later Jewish Literature*. London, 1913.

Davies, Owen. *Grimoires: A History of Magic Books*. Oxford, 2009.

―――. *Popular Magic: Cunning-folk in English History*. Hambleton Continuum: London, 2007.

Davies, S.F. 'The Reception of Reginald Scot's *Discovery of Witchcraft*: Witchcraft, Magic, and Radical Religion.' *Journal of the History of Ideas* 74, 3, 2013: 381–401.

Drazin, Israel & Stanley M. Wagner (ed. & trans.), *Onkelos on the Torah: Va-yikra*. Gefen: Jerusalem, 2010.

Fanger, Claire (ed.). *Invoking Angels: Theurgic Ideas and Practices, Thirteenth to Sixteenth Centuries*. Pennsylvania State Press: University Park, 2012.

―――. 'Libri Nigromantici: The Good, the Bad and the Ambiguous in John of Morigny's *Flowers of Heavenly Teaching*.' *Magic, Ritual, and Witchcraft* 7, 2, 2012: 164–189.

Fischer, David Hackett. *Albion's Seed: Four British Folkways in America*. Oxford University Press: New York, 1991.

Flint, Valerie. 'The Demonisation of Magic and Sorcery in Late Antiquity: Christian Redefinitions of Pagan Religions.' Bengt Ankarloo and Stuart Clark (eds.), *Witchcraft and Magic in Europe: Ancient Greece and Rome*. University of Pennsylvannia Press: Philadephia, 1999.

French, Peter J. *John Dee: The World of an Elizabethan Magus*. London, 1987.

Friis, Martin. 'Josephus' *Antiquities* 1–11 and Greco-Roman Historiography.' PhD Thesis: University of Copenhagen, 2015.

Garcia Martinez, Florentino & Eibert J.C. Tigchelaar. *The Dead Sea Scrolls*. Leiden, 2000.

Goldberg, Benjamin. *The Mirror and Man*. Charlottesville: University of Virginia Press, 1985.

Goldstein, David. *Jewish Folklore and Legend*. Hamlyn: London, 1980.

Gordon, Bruce. 'The Renaissance Angel.' Peter Marshall & Alexandra Walsham (eds.), *Angels in the Early Modern World*. Cambridge University Press: Cambridge, 2006.

Gosling, William Gilbert. *The Life of Sir Humphrey Gilbert, England's First Empire Builder*. Constable & Co.: London, 1911.

Gowland, Angus. *The Worlds of Renaissance Melancholy: Robert Burton in Context*. Cambridge, 2006.

Halevi, Z'ev ben Shimon. *Adam and the Kabbalistic Tree*. Weiser: York Beach, 1974.

Harkness, Deborah. *John Dee's Conversations with Angels: Cabala, Alchemy, and the End of Nature*. Cambridge: Cambridge University Press, 1999.

Hutchins, Zachary McLeod. *Inventing Eden: Primitivism, Millennialism, and the Making of New England*. Oxford University Press: Oxford, 2014.

Kassell, Lauren. *Medicine and Magic in Elizabethan London: Simon Forman: Astrologer, Alchemist, and Physician*. Clarendon Press: Oxford, 2007.

Kavey, Allison. *Books of Secrets: Natural Philosophy in England, 1550–1600*. University of Illinois Press: Chicago, 2007.

Kieckhefer, Richard. *Forbidden Rites: A Necromancer's Manual of the Fifteenth Century*. Penn State University Press: University Park, 1998.

———. *Magic in the Middle Ages*. Cambridge University Press: Croydon, 2014.

Kittredge, G.L. *Witchcraft in Old and New England*. Russell & Russell: New York, 1929.

Klaassen, Frank. 'Subjective Experience and the Practice of Medieval Ritual Magic.' *Magic, Ritual, and Witchcraft* 7, No. 1, Summer 2012: 19–51.

———. 'Ritual Invocation and Early Modern Science: The Skrying Experiments of Humphrey Gilbert.' *Invoking Angels: Theurgic Ideas and Practices, Thirteenth to Sixteenth Centuries*. Ed.Claire Fanger: 341–366. Pennsylvania State University Press: University Park, 2012.

———. *The Transformations of Magic: Illicit Learned Magic in the Later Middle Ages and Renaissance*. Penn State University Press: University Park, 2013.

Láng, Benedek. *Unlocked Books: Manuscripts of Learned Magic in the Medieval Libraries of Central Europe*. Pennsylvania State University Press: University Park, 2008.

Lecouteux, Claude. *High Magic of Amulets and Talismans*. Trans. Jon E. Graham. Inner Traditions: Rochester, 2014.

Lehrich, Christopher I. *Language of the Demons and Angels: Cornelius Agrippa's Occult Philosophy*. Brill: Boston, 2003.

Lindberg, David C. *Theories of Vision from Al-Kindi to Kepler*. Chicago, 1976.

MacDonald, Michael. *Mystical Bedlam: Madness, Anxiety, and Healing in Seventeenth Century England*. Cambridge: Cambridge University Press, 1981.

Macdonald, Michael-Albion. *De Nigromancia*. Heptangle Books: Gilette,1988.

Marathakis, Ioannis (trans. & ed.). *The Magical Treatise of Solomon or Hygromanteia*. Golden Hoard Press: Singapore, 2011.

Markham, Clements R. *A Life of John Davis, the Navigator, 1550–1605*. G. Philip and Son: London, 1891.

Marlowe, Christopher. *Doctor Faustus*. London, 1604.

McCown, C.C. 'The Christian Tradition as to the Magical Wisdom of Solomon.' *Journal of the Palestine Oriental Society* 2, 1922.

———. 'Solomon and the Shulamite.' *Journal of the Palestine Oriental Society* 1, 1920–1921.

McLean, Adam. *A Treatise of Angel Magic*. Weiser: York Beach, 2006.

McLean, Teresa. *Medieval English Gardens*. Dover: New York, 1980.

Mendez, Hugo Enrique. 'Condemnations of Necromancy in the Hebrew Bible: An Investigation of Rationale.' Unpubished MA thesis: University of Georgia, 2006.

Minnis, Alastair. *From Eden to Eternity: Creations of Paradise in the Later Middle Ages*. University of Pennsylvania Press: Philadelphia, 2016.

Molland, George. 'Bacon , Roger (c.1214–1292?)' *Oxford Dictionary of National Biography*.

Nauert, Charles G., JR. 'Agrippa and the Crisis of Renaissance Thought.' *Illinois Studies in the Social Sciences* 55. Urbana: University of Illinois Press, 1965.

Noll, Richard. 'Mental Imagery Cultivation as a Cultural Phenomenon: The Role of Visions in Shamanism.' *Current Anthropology* 26, No. 4, 1985: 443–461.

Otten, Charlotte F. *Environ'd with Eternity: God, Poems, and Plants in Sixteenth and Seventeenth Century England.* Coronado Press: Lawrence, 1985.

Page, Sophie. 'Uplifting Souls: The Liber de essentia spirituum and the Liber Razielis.' Claire Fanger (ed.), *Invoking Angels.* Pennsylvania State University: University Park, 2012.

Popper, Nicholas. 'The English Polydaedal: How Gabriel Harvey Read Late Tudor London.' *Journal of the History of Ideas* 66, No. 3, 2005: 351–381.

Quinn, David B. *Explorers and Colonies: America, 1500–1625.* The Hambledon Press: London, 1990.

Rowlands, Alison (ed.). *Witchcraft and Masculinities in Early Modern Europe.* Palgrave Macmillan: Basingstoke, 2009.

Savedow, Steve (ed.). *Sepher Reziel Hemelech: The Book of the Angel Rezial.* Weiser: York Beach, 2000.

Schleiner, Winfried. *Melancholy, Genius, and Utopia in the Renaissance.* Wiesbaden, 1991.

Schmitt, Jean-Claude. *Ghosts in the Middle Ages: The Living and the Dead in Medieval Society.* University of Chicago Press: Chicago, 1998.

Schreiner, Susan E. 'Exegesis and Double Justice in Calvin's Sermons on Job.' *Church History* 58, 1989: 322–38.

Schwartz, Howard. *Tree of Souls: The Mythology of Judaism.* Oxford University Press: Oxford, 2004.

Shepard, Alex. *The Meanings of Manhood in Early Modern England, 1560–1640.* Oxford University Press: Oxford, 2003.

Skinner, Stephen & David Rankine (eds.). *A Collection of Magical Secrets & A Treatise of Mixed Cabalah.* Translated by Paul Harry Barron. Avalonia Books: London, 2009.

——— & Donald Karr (eds.). *Sepher Raziel: A Sixteenth Century English Grimoire.* Golden Hoard Press: Singapore, 2010.

———. *Techniques of Greco-Egyptian Magic.* Golden Hoard Press: Singapore, 2014.

Smith, G. C. Moore. *Gabriel Harvey's Marginalia.* Shakespeare Head Press: Stratford-Upon-Avon, 1913.

Steggle, Matthew. 'The Names of Gabriel Harvey: Cabbalistic, Russian, and Fencing Sources.' *Notes and Queries* 52 (2), 2005: 185–6.

Stern, Virginia F. 'The Bibliotheca of Gabriel Harvey.' *Renaissance Quarterly* 25, No. 1, Spring 1972: 1–62.

———. *Gabriel Harvey: His Life, Marginalia and Library.* Oxford: Clarendon Press, 1979.

Stratton-Kent, Jake. *The Testament of Cyprian the Mage.* Scarlet Imprint: Dover, 2014.

Strype, John. *The Life of the Learned Sir Thomas Smith, Kt.* D.C.L. Clarendon Press: Oxford, 1820.

Szőnyi, György E. 'John Dee as Cultural, Scientific, Apocalyptic Go-Between.' Andreas Höfele and Werner von Koppenfels (eds.), *Renaissance Go-Betweens: Cultural Exchange in Early Modern Europe.* Walter de Gruyter: New York, 2005.

———— *John Dee's Occultism: Magical Exaltation Through Powerful Signs.* University of New York Press: Albany, 2004.

———— 'Paracelsus, Scrying, and the Lingua Adamica: Contexts for John Dee's Angel Magic.' Stephen Clucas (ed.), *John Dee: Interdisciplinary Studies in English Renaissance Thought.* Springer: Dordrecht, 2006.

Szulakowska, Urszula. *The Alchemy of Light: Geometry and Optics in Late Renaissance Alchemical Illustration.* Leiden, 2000.

Taves, Ann & Asprem, Egil. 'Experience as Event: Event Cognition and the Study of (Religious) Experiences' *Religion, Brain, & Behaviour* 7, 2017: 43 – 62.

Thomas, Keith. *Religion and the Decline of Magic.* Weidenfeld & Nicolson: London, 1971.

Thomas, Northcote W. *Crystal Gazing: Its History and Practice, with a Discussion of the Evidence for Telepathic Scrying.* London, 1905.

Thorndike, Lynn. *A History of Magic and Experimental Science.* Columbia University Press: New York, 1923.

Timbers, Frances. *Magic and Masculinity: Ritual Magic and Gender in the Early Modern Era.* I.B. Taurus: London, 2014.

Torijano, Pablo A. 'Solomon and Magic.' Joseph Verheyden (ed.), *The Figure of Solomon in Jewish, Christian and Islamic Tradition: King, Sage and Architect.* Brill: Leiden, 2012.

———— 'Solomon The Esoteric King: From King to Magus.' Thesis: New York University, 1999.

Trachtenberg, Joshua. *Jewish Magic and Superstition.* Behrman House: New York, 1939.

Traister, Barbara Howard. *The Notorious Astrological Physician of London: Works and Days of Simon Forman.* University of Chicago Press: Chicago, 2001.

Trevor, Douglas. *The Poetics of Melancholy in Early Modern England.* Cambridge, 2004.

Turner, Robert. *Elizabethan Magic.* Element Books: Shaftesbury, 1989.

Vasconcelos, Filomena. 'Occult Philosophy and the Philosophy of Language in Renaissance Europe and Elisabethan England.' *Revista da Faculdade de Letras* II Serie, vol. XXI, 2004: 199 – 208.

Veenstra, Jan R. 'The Holy Almandal: Angels and the Intellectual Aims of Magic Appendix: The Art Almadel of Solomon (BL MS Sloane 2731).' Jan N. Bremmer and Jan R. Veenstra (eds.), *Metamorphosis of Magic from Late Antiquity to the Early Modern Period.* Peeters: Leuven, 2002.

Versluis, Arthur. 'Mysticism and the Study of Esotericism: Methods in the Study of Esotericism, Part II.' *Esoterica* 5, 2003: 28 – 40.

Waite, Arthur Edward. *The Book of Ceremonial Magic.* William Rider & Son: London, 1911.

Walker, D.P. *Spiritual and Demonic Magic*. Penn State University Press: University Park, 2000.

Whitby, Christopher l. 'John Dee and Renaissance Scrying.' *Bulletin of the Society for Renaissance Studies* 3.2, 1985.

——— 'John Dee's Actions With Spirits: 22 December 1581 to 23 May 1583.' PhD Thesis: University of Birmingham, 1982.

Williams, Steven J. 'Roger Bacon and his edition of the Pseudo-Aristotelian *Secretum Secretorum*.' *Speculum* 69, 1, 1994.

Wooley, Benjamin. *The Queen's Conjuror*. Flamingo: London, 2002.

Yates, Frances. 'Renaissance Philosophers in Elizabethan England: John Dee and Giordano Bruno.' Frances Yates, *Lull & Bruno: Collected Essays*, Volume 1. London Routledge & Kegan Paul, 1982.

Index

ACKNOWLEDGEMENTS & PERMISSIONS

Facsimile of Additional MS. 36674 ff.47r– 62v © The British Library Board.
The Tree of Crystal © Sin Eater. 'Good Books to Call By' was originally read
by Phil Legard as part of the History, Magic and Spirits panel of Exploring the
Extraordinary VII, 4th– 6th December 2015, York.